DATE			

Radio Drama

Radio Drama

Edited by
Peter Lewis

Longman
London and New York

Longman Group Limited
Longman House, Burnt Mill, Harlow, Essex, UK

*Published in the United States of America
by Longman Inc., New York*

First published 1981

British Library Cataloguing in Publication Data

Radio drama.
  1. Radio plays – History and criticism
  2. English drama – 20th century – History and criticism
  I. Lewis, Peter Elfed
  822'.02 PN1991.65 80-40577

ISBN 0-582-49052-9
ISBN 0-582-49053-7 Pbk

Printed in Singapore by Kyodo Shing Loong Printing Industries Pte Ltd

Contents

Acknowledgements

I would like to acknowledge my considerable indebtedness to Ian Rodger, devoted campaigner for the cause of radio drama and 'onlie begetter' of the Radio Literature Conference 1977, for encouraging my interest in the subject. I would like to thank the Research Fund Committee of Durham University for providing me with financial assistance during my work on this book.

We are grateful to the following for permission to reproduce copyright material:

BBC Written Archives Centre for an extract from Accession Number 7845 Val Gielgud, December 1st 1932; Accession Number 7845 R.H. Eckersley; Accession Number 37922 Val Gielgud; Accession Number 37922 Val Gielgud, September 1st 1947; Accession number 37859 Stokes and Stewart, 1949; Accession Number 7845 Filson Young and Val Gielgud, 1932; Accession Number 44987/1, 1936; Accession Number 44987/1 H.A.L. Fisher, 1936; Accession Number 7807, 1939-46; Accession Number 37922 Andrew Stewart, 1953; Accession Number 37622 Hugh Stewart; Accession Number 7838 Moray McLaren and Val Gielgud; Accession Number 7955 Listener Research and Accession Number LR/54/1062 Listener Research.

Editor's Note

I should point out that since the completion of this book the BBC has been forced to make substantial cuts in expenditure in 1980, and its Radio Drama Department has not been unaffected. After a fairly stable, even mildly expansionary, decade since the major BBC reorganisation of 1970, the Drama Department is now having to curtail some of its activities. The first victim was *Just Before Midnight*-the late-night programme devoted to fifteen-minute plays, which was dropped at once. Several other cuts and changes have since been implemented, notably the axing of the long-running daily serial *Waggoners' Walk*, the only dramatic programme on Radio 2 and the Department's most popular production in recent years in terms of the number of listeners. Another favourite of long-standing, the 'Sunday Serial' (of classic novels), which occupied a prime place on Sunday evenings, has been moved to Saturday afternoons, replacing *Saturday Afternoon Theatre*. In the current economic climate the future of radio drama in Britain remains uncertain, but there is no reason to believe that the BBC Radio Drama Department will not successfully adapt to changing circumstances as it has done in the past.

Chapter 1

Introduction

Peter Lewis

Radio drama, and indeed radio itself, has acquired the reputation of being a Cinderella subject; and although the metaphor, now nearly fifty years old (Val Gielgud, for example, used it in the first sentence of his *How to Write Broadcast Plays* in 1932), has become a cliché, it is difficult to think of a more appropriate one. None of the people one might expect to be sufficiently enthusiastic about the subject to research it and write about it – dramatic critics, literary scholars, cultural historians, sociologists of the mass media – have shown much interest in it, especially in Britain, even though BBC Radio has serious claims to provide the best radio service in the world and is the envy of many countries. It is therefore extremely ironic that scholars from Germany, which also has very high standards of broadcasting, should have not only spearheaded the academic study of British radio drama but also virtually monopolised it until very recently. One of the most distinguished of these, Professor Horst Priessnitz, is a contributor to this book and has undertaken the very difficult task of providing a succinct but comprehensive account of the principal tendencies and characteristics of British radio drama. To find an accurate measure of the status of radio today, one has only to turn to the arts pages of our quality newspapers. In the dailies, the most radio can expect is a short weekly piece to cover everything, and the output of BBC Radio alone is hardly meagre. Television does much better, as does cinema, while theatre often merits several reviews of individual productions *per day*. The same pattern can be found in the Sundays and weeklies, with stage plays and films occupying plenty of space, usually in prime positions, television doing fairly well, and radio squeezed into some nearly forgotten corner of a page. To its credit, *Plays and Players* did run a separate monthly column on radio drama for a time, but even this magazine has concentrated very largely on the stage. It is at least worth pondering the economic factors involved in this. Today in Britain we pay nothing for radio drama; we do pay something for television drama through the licensing fee; and we pay a great deal to go to the theatre. Is it true that we appreciate only what we pay for, and the more we pay, the greater our appreciation?

We undoubtedly do take radio very much for granted as part of our environment, partly because it is possible to listen or half-listen or hardly listen at all to it while doing something else. Thanks to the transistor, radio is so much with us as a purveyor of background noise – on trains, in cars, on remote beaches, at the top of Snowdon, even at home – that it seems as integral to the universe as the music of the spheres once did. Yet radio has been unfortunate in that the rivalry of its younger and more glamorous sibling, television, presented itself before radio had reached maturity. The BBC began sound broadcasting in 1922; fourteen years later television transmissions began. These were suspended during the Second World War, which is one reason why the 1940s is enshrined as part of the golden age of radio in Britain – in *Those Vintage Years of Radio* (1972), John Snagge and Michael Barsley use that title-phrase to describe the period between 1935 and 1953. However, television transmissions resumed in 1946; and with Coronation Day 1953, that major turning-point in the history of broadcasting, television achieved the dominance it has never lost. For about half of its existence, radio has consequently been outshone and overshadowed by television. During the 1950s when radio drama was poised to make its great leap forward, television stole the limelight and all the other lights too, and radio became the poor relation – at least in the world's eye.

Nevertheless the critical and scholarly neglect that radio drama has suffered from in Britain is regrettable, especially considering the range and quality of the best creative work written for the medium, not to mention the success with which so many stage plays and works of fiction have been adapted for radio. To judge from the interest shown in radio drama by academic criticism and even arts journalism, it might almost not exist, yet the output of the BBC Radio Drama Department is very considerable indeed. And even though television has turned radio drama into a minority interest, we must remember that minorities in mass-media terms are measured in tens, even hundreds, of thousands. Before television became widespread in the 1950s, audiences for radio drama were very much larger and were measured in many millions. During the 1930s and 1940s, the average person's experience of drama certainly came much more from radio than from the stage. And today, in spite of television drama, radio drama still reaches far more people than the live theatre, which really is a minority interest although it receives vastly more attention. Theorists of drama still concentrate either entirely or almost entirely on stage plays, and a book like Martin Esslin's recent *An Anatomy of Drama* (1976) is unusual in acknowledging the importance of the mass media and their mechanically reproduced drama. In the past, not surprisingly, most of the writing about radio drama has come from BBC staff members. The Radio Literature Conference, held at Collingwood College in the University of Durham in 1977 and the brainchild of Ian Rodger rather than a BBC venture, was the first of its kind. This very well-attended conference, at which several of the speakers were, significantly,

German even though the radio drama under consideration was exclusively anglophone and very largely British, succeeded in drawing attention to the radio play as an entirely proper object of academic study, but it could hardly hope to do more than bang a few drums and thump a tub or two, which it did most sonorously.

The present book, like the published *Conference Papers* (1978) and the new Cambridge University Press book *British Radio Dramatists* (edited by John Drakakis), is an attempt to open up the subject again in a way that two of the most important studies of the genre, Val Gielgud's *British Radio Drama 1922-1956* (1957) and Donald McWhinnie's *The Art of Radio* (1959) (both, incidentally, by very senior and distinguished members of the BBC Radio Drama Department), did twenty years ago. The purpose of this book is to raise some of the issues rather than to supply all the answers; and to do so about the whole range of radio drama, not just original work of 'literary' interest by distinguished writers; and to do so from several different viewpoints: the BBC producer, the radio writer, the professional reviewer, the literary critic, the cultural historian, and the sociologist of mass communication. Unlike a number of the *Conference Papers* and the essays in *British Radio Dramatists*, the focus here is not on particular writers or radio history, although the latter is not neglected, especially by Horst Priessnitz, but on particular topics, such as the art and process of production (John Tydeman), adaptation (John Drakakis and Donald Low), popular radio (David Wade), and the nature of radio as a medium for creative writing (Frances Gray and Jonathan Raban). Since sociologists interested in mass communication have been so tantalised by television since the 1950s that they have devoted themselves to it at the expense of radio, it seemed important to include a contribution from a sociological investigator of the media who is interested in radio drama (Graham Murdock). This essay, together with the factual information contained in some of the others, particularly Horst Priessnitz's, serves as a corrective to the misconceptions and false assumptions people frequently have about radio drama today (for example, that it has lost its audience and is dying), misconceptions born of ignorance of the real state of affairs. As David Wade reminds us, listening habits have changed since the advent of television, so that listening is now more a daytime than an evening activity (hence so much radio drama in the afternoons), with housebound women forming a considerable proportion of the radio audience. British commercial radio would hardly be launching into radio drama, as it is doing at the moment, if there was not a market for it and some life in the old horse yet. Furthermore, the current cult-status of Douglas Adams's *The Hitch-Hiker's Guide to the Galaxy*, which began on radio in 1978, indicates that radio is still able to generate new trend-setting and audience-catching dramatic serials capable of capturing the nation's imagination.

The terms of reference of the whole book, then, are those of the cultural historian and theorist, concerned with phenomena, rather than of the literary critic, concerned with aesthetic discrimination, and are therefore broad, inclusive and all-embracing, not narrow, exclusive and élitist. Both approaches are, of course, valid and actually complement each other. But if critics interested in the best that radio drama has to offer are not to avoid elementary errors, they need to have some grasp of the full context from which the best emerges. The history of literary criticism is full of avoidable howlers perpetrated by critics who failed to take sufficient, or indeed any, notice of the relationship between the work of art and its environment, social, political and economic as well as linguistic, aesthetic and philosophical. And one does not have to be Marxist to say that. No art is all that pure, least of all a mass-media art like radio drama. In the case of radio drama in Britain, we must always remember that for most of the entire history of broadcasting the BBC has had a monopoly, a situation that has led to accusations of its being a lackey of the Establishment, which is an easy but cheap smear. We can set up our own theatre companies and tour the land with whatever we want to perform unless it is deemed obscene. We can establish our own magazines and publishing firms to make available work we think admirable though neglected by established commercial publishers. But we cannot set up our own radio station to broadcast an alternative radio drama – not without ending up in the dock. Control of radio drama has until very recently been entirely in the hands of the BBC.

Most of the book is concerned with the British experience of radio drama, or at least takes its examples from this, but there is also coverage by Rodney Pybus and Howard Fink of the two parts of the English-speaking world in which radio drama has flourished most, though not necessarily today – Australia and North America (the latter itself containing two dissimilar experiences, the American and Canadian). These are interesting in themselves, especially as they remain so little known in Britain, but they also serve to show how varied broadcasting experience has been in different parts of the world. It is easy to forget that the British experience of radio is only one of various possibilities, not the norm. In Britain we are fond of complaining about our institutions, including the BBC, and there certainly are grounds for making fun of Auntie or the Beeb or whatever it wants to call itself and also for more serious criticism regarding its powers of censorship, but once we place the BBC in a world context we immediately recognise how fortunate we have been and still are. The Corporation deserves our gratitude for encouraging so much creative talent and for generating some of the finest radio writing the world has yet heard. And one does not have to be conservative, or Conservative, to say that.

Any approach to radio drama must begin with a recognition that it is the product of modern technology, as well as of the cultural policies of a controlling élite in public-service broadcasting, and of advertising sponsorship in commercial broadcasting. The history of the relationship between technology and the arts is both longer and more complex than we often assume, but it is manifestly true that only during the last hundred years or so has the impact of technology on the arts been immense, in some cases modifying existing art forms to a greater or lesser extent, but in other cases generating completely new ones. The arrival of the microphone combined with the facility of radio transmission brought about a revolution in mass communication, just as the subsequent development of the television camera did; and both these revolutions created new possibilities for artistic expression appropriate to the particular medium. It goes without saying that much radio, like much television, does not aspire to the condition of art, having an entirely different purpose. This is one reason why both radio and television have not been taken seriously as artistic media and have had to struggle against the stigma of being sub-art forms, if that. But what we call, whether advisedly or not, 'radio drama' and 'television drama' are art forms that, at their best, belong to their respective media and are essentially at home there, even though they may be transferred to another medium. *Under Milk Wood*, written for radio, has often been performed as a stage play, but, significantly, never all that successfully. *Vis-à-vis* radio drama, television drama has both the advantage and the disadvantage of being more recognisably like preexisting art forms, drama and film, because it exists in both visual and sound terms. This makes it easier to assimilate into our established critical systems, but also more difficult to distinguish from other forms as having an entirely separate identity. The standard television play, as opposed to the occasional work made exactly as a film would be, is more cinematic than theatre but more theatrical than cinema. It differs from theatre in numerous and obvious ways – Tom Stoppard, commenting on his television play, *Professional Foul*, said that he did not include any *coups de théâtre*, for which he is famous (the opening of *Jumpers*, for example), because on television, where anything is possible, they would have none of the impact their technical difficulty produces on stage in live performance – but, unlike film, it is rightly not recognised as a director's art, since the writer always takes the major credit, as in the case of stage plays.

Radio drama appeals not to the eye of the beholder but to the ear of the listener, and consequently departs considerably from our preconceptions about drama. We *see* or *watch* stage plays, television plays and films, but we *hear* or *listen to* radio plays. On radio, to be is to be heard; existence is sound, as is essence. Whereas in the theatre there can be plenty of silent characters, on radio a silent character has no being. The mute matchseller in Harold Pinter's *A Slight Ache* could just as easily be an hallucination as a character, and Pinter deliberately exploits this ambiguity in a way that is impossible when the play is transferred to the stage. In the theatre, a great deal can often be seen to be going on silently around the characters actually speaking, but radio, having no eyes, can provide no equivalent, except for the odd grunt or murmur to indicate that there is more there if you could only see it. The so-called blindness of radio makes it impossible for a producer to counterpoint what is seen with what is heard or to blend the visual with the aural in different ways, which a theatre director is doing all the time. Radio acting, unlike stage acting, is entirely vocal – facial expressions and physical gestures cannot be conveyed – and in its own way is extremely demanding, stretching an actor's imaginative resources to the full. The radio play does in fact remind us of how very visual a stage play is and of how much is communicated in all sorts of nonverbal ways. This in turn raises awkward questions about the exact status of a radio production of a stage play, an issue John Drakakis tackles in his essay. In doing so, he confronts the crucial theoretical implications of treating a play as a literary text, an essentially reductive process since it seeks to fix the play as some kind of timeless, unchanging essence. To approach a work for radio as a text would be equally reductive; but ignoring the small amount of radio drama that depends heavily on radiophonic effects (since the early days of broadcasting there have been advocates of 'radiophonic' as opposed to 'verbal' or 'literary' radio drama, with the producer and technicians, not the writer, as primary creators), words are of paramount importance in radio plays. Radio has long had the reputation of being a writer's medium, and it is not without significance that so many poets in different countries, from England and Germany to America and Australia, have been attracted to the medium from the early days until now – moreover, poets who have shown no inclination to write for the theatre. And if poets and prose writers with no pretensions to being playwrights have written good radio plays, some distinguished playwrights have shown little aptitude for radio in their work for the medium. More good verse drama has been written for radio than for the stage in the twentieth century, although the tendency, especially in the formative years of radio drama, for writers to feel that they had to provide an aural feast to make up for the lack of something to look at was often misguided. The radio drama of the last twenty-five years has demonstrated that words used sparely can be just as effective as indulgent rhetoric.

Before considering further the implications of this fundamental characteristic of radio as a medium for artistic expression, one point must be stressed. The scholar or critic who approaches radio from Literature or Drama is usually interested in serious and original radio writing of considerable artistic achievement. He looks to Louis MacNeice, Dylan Thomas, Henry Reed, Giles Cooper, Samuel Beckett and other distinguished literary figures, and equates radio drama with the finest work the medium, especially Radio 3 (previously the Third Programme), has to offer. With regard to a mass medium like radio, this stress on 'high culture' is of course unswervingly élitist; and although there is nothing immoral or reprehensible in this viewpoint, it can lead to falsification since it is likely to ignore that what goes under the heading of 'radio drama' is extremely varied indeed. Much radio drama is a form of popular culture, not high culture. (In this context it is as well to remember that 'theatre' and 'fiction' are also rag-bag terms, something frequently not recognised or deliberately ignored. If, as the quip has it, 'theatre' exists when the exhibitionist meets the voyeur, a sleazy strip show in a dingy Soho basement is a form of theatre no less than a performance by the Royal Shakespeare Company at Stratford, and 'fiction' comprehends pulp porn as well as Thomas Pynchon, historical romances and Alain Robbe-Grillet, science fiction and William Faulkner.) The experience and history of radio in different countries is also very varied, partly depending on whether commercial or public-service broadcasting has dominated, or indeed whether there has been peaceful coexistence and equilibrium between them. In the United States, for example, with its commercial system, television virtually killed radio drama after the Second World War since it precipitated a collapse of its sponsorship (although there have been distinct signs of a resurrection since the mid-1970s, as Howard Fink shows in his essay), whereas in Britain the BBC's long public-service monopoly in radio and its commitment to high standards and minority programmes have kept radio drama very much alive in spite of the competition from television. Yet even in countries where there have been similar patterns of broadcasting, considerable differences regarding radio drama can be found. In Britain, for example, there has been a particularly close connection between the theatre and radio drama so that radio has looked much more to the theatre both as its model and for suitable material to broadcast than is the case in some other countries. Indeed, there was a time when the Drama Department of the BBC saw its main function as broadcasting stage plays – taking the theatre to the people – and from the mid-1930s to the mid-1950s it was the Features Department, under the control of Laurence Gilliam, that was really responsible for exploring the possibilities of radio as a dramatic medium in its own right, even though much of its output was in the form of imaginative documentaries rather than radio plays. Although the link between the theatre and radio drama has not always been to the advantage of the radio play proper, Britain does have one of the finest and strongest traditions of radio drama in the world, perhaps even *the* best, but the BBC has an obligation to cater for all tastes and takes its obligation very seriously. 'Radio drama' is consequently an umbrella for many kinds of programmes, from pot-boilers to radiophonic experiments, from middlebrow realism to poetic fantasy, from lightweight entertainment to intellectual nourishment. 'Radio drama' encompasses daily serials, like *The Archers* and *Waggoners' Walk*, adaptations of stage plays from Aeschylus to Alan Ayckbourn, of short stories and novels, sometimes in serial form and sometimes as one-shots, and even of television plays, such as

Stoppard's *Professional Foul*, plays intended for the stage or television but – the usual fate – finding no takers, as well as original work written specifically for the medium and exploiting its unique qualities.

Yet it is the latter that merits an *appellation controlée* and that is most properly called '*radio* drama' (as opposed to 'radio *drama*', i.e. drama broadcast on radio, perhaps best referred to as 'radio-transmitted drama'), even though the entire corpus must be taken into account in any balanced, scholarly account of radio history, and even though some stage plays and some prose works translate very easily into radio terms. (This latter issue is particularly important today since several well-known stage playwrights began their careers as radio dramatists and, in writing for the stage, sometimes employ methods derived from radio, with the result that occasional plays intended for the theatre seem to belong much more to radio. John Arden's *Pearl*, discussed by Frances Gray in her essay, is the outstanding example.) Since radio gives pre-eminence to the word and attracts literary, as much as dramatic, writers, it seems that radio drama – here I am concentrating on the original radio play conceived for the medium – can, as Jonathan Raban contends in his essay, be as close to nondramatic literature, perhaps a good deal closer, than to orthodox drama, despite the persistence and, indeed, inevitability of the word 'play' in describing creative work for radio. Tyrone Guthrie used 'microphone play' as a label for his three experimental works written at the end of the 1920s, Dylan Thomas used 'play for voices' to describe *Under Milk Wood*, and even the German term '*Hörspiel*' indicates the dramatic although it emphasises 'hearing' and 'listening' instead of 'radio'. So although radio is unique as an artistic medium, a full realisation of a radio play being in sound alone, it may be more appropriate to look at some original creative writing for the medium as forms of '*radio* literature' – 'radio fictions', perhaps, or 'fictions of the air'. Radio does seem to be the medium in which drama and fiction come closest to meeting, and the importance that the interior monologue assumes in both radio drama and modern fiction is indicative of this. According to a number of writers, including Martin Esslin, the radio play, unlike the stage or television play, lends itself to interior monologue, which also happens to be a narrative technique frequently employed by twentieth-century novelists. Except for its length, Virginia Woolf's novel of interwoven monologues, *The Waves*, might almost have been written for radio, and in Louis MacNeice's famous adaptation it certainly suited the medium. One can also cite the relative ease with which much more conventional novels, even the most unstageable ones, can be adapted for radio. When Ian Rodger decided to call the first international conference devoted to radio drama in 1977 a Radio Literature Conference, rather than the more obvious Radio Drama Conference, he was drawing attention to this aspect of radio writing, as well as provocatively sending up signals to the academic literature establishment saying that there was an entire area of creative writing being neglected and even disdained in our schools, colleges and universities.

The characteristics of radio as an artistic medium and its affinities with literature, despite its being very much a performance art, emerge from other lines of investigation. Theoreticians of the media, in discussing the specific characteristics of radio, television and film, often seem to fly in the face of commonsense when they say that the sound track of a film can be its most visual aspect, or that television is an essentially tactile, rather than visual, medium, or that radio is more visual than aural. Literature too has been called a visual medium, partly, but only partly, because it is read on the page. Yet Structuralism has taught us that such paradoxes are sometimes much nearer the truth than commonsense would have us believe and indeed that common-sense is often devoid of sense and is a far from reliable guide. To say that radio is a visual medium when in one sense it is completely nonvisual is to bring out the way in which radio encourages the listener's imagination to visualise what he is listening to, to create for himself the visual dimension he is apparently deprived of, to construct the settings and the appearances of the characters from the clues that words and sounds provide. Radio has gradually acquired its own iconography and ways of coding information, just as cinema has. It is sometimes argued that this stimulus to the imagination, especially the visual imagination, belongs to radio alone, and if we are thinking in terms of 'drama' this is unquestionably correct. Theatre, television and film give us little or no choice about what we see and prevent our visual imaginations from functioning: our eyes have plenty to keep them occupied. But if we think about fiction instead of drama, we find something much more similar to radio in this respect. In silent reading, our eyes are obviously busy in a way they are not when we listen to radio, but they are not engaged in the way they are by the theatre, television and film. Fiction, providing no picture to look at, stimulates the visual imagination in ways similar to radio; again we create and construct pictures for ourselves from the words the writer provides. One of the defects of the literary criticism that has become the prevailing orthodoxy in the twentieth century, at least in the anglophone world, is its emphasis on the complete autonomy of the verbal icon so that the work of art is presented to us as an immutably objective artefact that we have to treat with enormous respect. What New Criticism frequently discounts in its pursuit of objectivity is the complex process of communication in which the words on the page play only a part: the necessary interaction between text and reader, the unavoidable element of the personal and the subjective, and the way in which each reader recreates the text for himself. Reading is a highly imaginative process, not a completely passive one, the words providing the stimulus to the reader's imagination, just as words heard on the radio do. The text is, therefore, a starting point rather than an end in itself. Each generation, whether it recognises it or not, reads the classics differently and finds different things in them. What makes a classic is precisely this somewhat fickle ability to constantly appear new, this chameleon changeability, rather than – and this is the traditional view – some permanently fixed and static element. One thing that the major French literary theoretician Roland Barthes has taught us is that as readers we should have a healthy disrespect for the text, otherwise we only succeed in embalming literature and in turning the classics into museum pieces.

To liken the imaginatively active process of listening to a radio play to that of reading a novel, rather than to the more passive process of watching a film or a play on stage or on television, does not mean that the processes are identical. Radio drama, as a verbal art form except in extreme cases, can obviously be subsumed under the heading of 'literature' in the widest sense (i.e. not only words on the page); but we must be wary of the temptation to mutate radio into literature in a reductive way in order to give it academic respectability. Radio can present a more fleetingly intangible world than any other art form employing words, partly because the most natural dramatic mode of the medium is, arguably, the interior monologue, with its ability to incorporate fantasies and memories; and as Frances Gray argues in her contribution to this book, the radio play is particularly at home in rendering a dream world without a consistent or solid reality. But if we continue to think of the radio play as being much closer to drama than to literature, it is partly because our modern conception of literature is so closely identified with the printed page and with the *visual* activity of *silent* reading. So conditioned to this are we by our education that we tend to forget the oral and aural origins of literature in prehistory, as well as the long tradition of literature as a primarily oral activity, something to be spoken and to be listened to. Even novelists, notably Dickens in the nineteenth century (as Donald Low reminds us in his essay) and several contemporary ones at the time of the recent poetry-reading boom, have given public 'performances' of their work, and the reading of stories and serialised novels on radio has always been, and remains, very popular. Radio has, in fact, provided the equivalent of the family reading around the fireside of pre-radio days. The most positive achievement of Dylan Thomas's sensational and sensationally successful poetry-reading tours of America at the end of his life was the reminder that poetry belonged to the voice and the ear, not only the eye, and that it inhabited the air as well as the page. Modish as the post-Thomas cult of poetry readings in the 1950s and 1960s was, first in America and then in Britain, it was salutary in that it counteracted the emphasis put on the poem as a visual object on the page. The established connection between literature and print may not be inviolable, but like another Thomas – the doubting one – we feel the need to *see* for ourselves a work of literature in order to be convinced of its status. The most obvious and important characteristic of radio as a medium of verbal communication is its irreducible spokenness and heardness, and this does much to explain why the idea of a radio literature has presented problems and has not won much acceptance.

Radio drama is not in its infancy (neither is it in its dotage as some might argue) but the study of it is in its early stages. This book cannot hope to do more than scratch a few surfaces, but if it does that it will have accomplished its purpose. The more one looks into the subject, the more complex and many-sided it becomes. One has to consider its relationship with stage drama, with literature, and with radio as a mass medium, including forms of entertainment classed as Variety rather than Drama although, as in the case of the Goons, they may illuminate the nature of radio drama particularly well, as Frances Gray demonstrates. One also has to consider the huge subject of radio adaptation since so much radio drama is derived from preexisting sources, whether literary or dramatic. One has to look at the experience of various countries and different broadcasting systems to understand how these can affect radio drama. And one must always remember that radio drama really exists as performance, as words and sounds on the air. In his recent book, *Radio: A Guide to Broadcasting Techniques*, Elwyn Evans, formerly Head of the Radio Training Section of the BBC, stresses the crucial, if often invisible, role played by the Producer in radio drama and of the extent to which the Producer is responsible for the finished product. It is therefore appropriate for a distinguished BBC radio producer, John Tydeman, to lead the way.

Chapter 2

The producer and radio drama: a personal view

John Tydeman

'What do you do?' It's a question we are all asked at some time or other. It is usually asked by a stranger who has been forced by circumstance into a position of sudden, sometimes unwanted, intimacy. The answer can create ice – or break it. 'Oh, I direct plays.' 'That must be interesting. And where do you do them?' 'For the BBC.' 'Television?' 'I have. And for the theatre too, but essentially I'm a radio producer, I direct plays for radio.' The confusion is there – producer? director? Before you are assailed with the 'Oh, I heard a radio play once' or the 'Oh, I love plays on the radio – you can use your imagination so much more', or you are asked to look at some bottom-drawer script written by a deceased oh-so-talented aunt, or you are asked if you know so-and-so-who-works-at-the-BBC-but-he's-in-television, the overwhelming question has to be answered. 'What is the difference between a producer and a director?' You explain; or try to.

The term 'producer' has different meanings in different media, but it is the film world's use of the word that has come to be the current one. The producer is the overall organiser of a production. He raises the money and is responsible for the disposal of funds. He provides the means for the production and is responsible for marketing it. The producer selects the director and hires him. Although the director appears to be the one who engages the actors, it is the producer who is responsible for their payment. And, necessarily, the director must consult the producer about his casting, just as in the visual media he must have consultation about the choice of set designer, costume designer, lighting designer, etc. If the producer is some kind of High Admiral, then the director is captain of the ship. He is directly responsible for the mechanics of creating the show, for the artistic and technical process that turns words upon a page into a period of entertainment to be enjoyed by an audience.

In the case of the large television-producing organisations, the functions of the producer are delegated to an individual, an Executive Producer. He has the right to interfere in the artistic process if he feels the result of everybody's labours is not going to come up to expectations. But experience will have told him that that right should be exercised sparingly and diplomatically. The best producer, certainly in the theatre and television, is not only a splendid organiser but also a tactful adviser, an encourager and a protector. It is not an easy job. It has to be a very unselfish one.

The radio-drama producer is in a different position. Radio production, because of its relative simplicity and cheapness, has no need to surround itself with a machine of great executive complexity. Moreover the process of making a radio play is so quick, the immediate concentration demanded so intense, the relationships so briefly intimate, that the involvement of too many people would sink the fragile craft. Hence the person who makes a radio play tends to be both captain and High Admiral, director and producer both. Unlike the television director, he is to a large extent his own script editor, being ultimately responsible for the words on the page before they reach the actors' lips and for any changes that need to be made to them thereafter.

To some extent the BBC, at present, has a monopoly in the production of radio drama. There are only about thirty animals known as 'Producers, Drama, Radio' (BBC nomenclature) in the British Isles. Any description of individual experience has to be related to that fact. Consequently it must not be imagined that the radio producer is *sole* master of his production. The BBC management, acting as overall producer, has the right to interfere if it is not satisfied with the artistic standards of a production, or if it feels that actions depicted or language used exceed acceptable limits. The director of a play has the solace of being able to seek advice from superiors, just as theatre or television directors can ask for guidance from their producers. The prime master, however, in any dramatic endeavour is the audience. Ultimately it is the members of the audience whom we serve. They will soon tell us if they do not like what we assume they want. They will switch off. They will not come to the theatre. They will stay away from the cinema. The absence of an audience is terrible. It is failure.

Having mistily managed to distinguish between a producer and a director (and having put up a good pretence at being interested in your reply), the questioning stranger will certainly go on to say, 'Yes, but what does a director actually *do*?' 'In radio, do you mean?' 'Yes that too, but in anything? I suppose you tell the actors how to say their lines, where to move and so on.' Try *telling* actors that, one thinks. *Suggest*, yes, so that the idea seems their own. And, basically, it will be their own.

Generalisations about the various methods of directing a play are impossible. It is a subjective business and each director is as unlike another as one person is unlike another person. It is the result that counts, and the method by which it is reached is as individual as the individual. Generalisations about the qualities a director needs are possible. Often, I think, it is not so much what the director *does* as what he *is* that achieves a certain result. He is the catalyst. He hopefully, through chosen actors, interprets the intentions of an author's script and presents them truthfully to an audience. He must be literate, patient, childlike but never childish, firm but not commanding, decisive, enthusiastic, energetic. He needs to be a bit of a psychologist and something of a politician. He needs to be stage-struck without being overstricken, to be authoritative without being authoritarian, to have a sense of fun but to know when to be serious, to have a sense of excitement without excitability. He is, as Tyrone Guthrie once said, the chairman of a committee. He is, as Colin Davis once said of the function of the orchestral conductor, someone who creates an atmosphere in which a certain number of people brought together at a certain place at a certain time *agree* to give a certain performance. He is, as Maxwell Perkins said of the editor's function in publishing, someone who releases energy. He also needs to know how to control that energy. The director presides over a game of carefully rehearsed tennis. He is the host at a party, aware of everything and everybody. He must not let the party get out of hand. He must avoid self-congratulation, egotism and self-indulgence. He should not be afraid of compromise when it is inevitable – and a certain amount of compromise always is inevitable.

The director needs to have a very sharp sense of Time in its many dimensions. In a radio studio the clock is the tyrant on the wall, telling you how much you have done, how much you have yet to do, and how quickly you must do it. The time allocated by a director for the rehearsal and recording of a radio play is the product of an equation that has to take into account such factors as the duration of the play, its technical complexity, the degree of character penetration required and the likely speed of the actors in realising their characters happily and truthfully, and, of course, the budget. Time is also money.

In the visual media, actors have to learn their lines and feel so at home with them that they actually *become* their own. They have to accustom themselves to lights, props, costume, furniture, set – the space in which they live and move. In radio, the actor does not inhabit space. Essentially he has to create the picture of how he looks, where he is, and his spatial relationship to others, inside his own mind. Through his speech he transmits that picture to the minds of his listeners. Not an easy task of concentration – and the director must *help* him in doing it. In a radio play the actor holds his script whilst he acts his role; he does not need to put his lines to memory. But he must feel just as much at home with what he speaks as the actor in the theatre. He must be 'comfortable' and the director is responsible for creating that comfort. Without it, all would seem like lying, and the microphone is like a microscope – a great detector of truth. On radio you cannot get away with indifferent acting: the microphone, and consequently the listener, will find you out.

Because the medium makes fewer demands in terms of time, a play on radio that would need three to four weeks rehearsal for television or the theatre can be achieved in as many days. Certain stage plays with a duration of approximately two hours that I have recently produced on radio give some idea of the time spent on them in the studio: Stoppard's *Rosencrantz and Guildenstern Are Dead*, five days; Pinero's *The Magistrate*, four days; Shaw's *The Doctor's Dilemma*, five days. Most ninety-minute plays have an allocation of three to four days in the studio; sixty-minute plays, two to three days; thirty-minute plays, one to two days. Three fifteen-minute episodes of the daily serial, *Waggoners' Walk*, are produced in a single day. It is all *very* quick!

The speed at which things happen in a radio studio demands extreme accuracy in casting. In fact the ability to cast well should be one of a radio producer's prime qualities. There is no time to teach an actor how to act (impossible anyhow!) and there is no time for displays of temperament and the occasional row. With a certain amount of ego massage and understanding, a conflict of personalities during rehearsals for a stage play can be overcome in a few days. By the time that had happened, a radio production would be complete. Everybody on a radio production realises the pressure of time and appreciates that at every moment one is dealing with the very essence of the drama. There is no opportunity at all for a relaxation of attention, and a day in the studio is exhausting for all concerned. But it is exhilarating, rewarding and civilised.

Actors seem to enjoy the challenge radio creates for them. They like to work hard and to be 'stretched'. Often they have the opportunity to play parts for which nature has not physically designed them – the thin man inside the fat man can realistically escape, the short actress can achieve Junoesque proportions, the snub-nosed actor can play Cyrano de Bergerac at last! But most times a director will look through the two plates of glass dividing the mechanistic Control Room from the human area of the studio and say, 'Yes, they could all play the parts they are now cast as on the stage.' An accident?

Writers, somehow, seem more satisfied with the results of a radio production than with productions in the visual media. The reasons are obvious: fewer things can go wrong; there are not so many distractions, fewer positive statements. The appearance of an actor on the stage may in no way measure up to the author's imagined projection of his character. The set may be nothing like the one he had painted in his mind, and the costumes can be entirely wrong. A radio production will be far closer to the writer's mental picture of his play when he penned it than any other realisation. Of course it may not *sound* the same; often it will sound better. Actors and director may have discovered depths and nuances which the author had not *consciously* realised were there.

Another possible reason for the writer's satisfaction with a radio production of his play is that he is generally accorded the pre-eminence due to him. The word, on radio, is paramount. And the words being spoken are his, the intentions being interpreted are his. No private exhibitionism, no petty egos come between him and his audience. Occasionally a director will attempt to overdress a scene with sound effects or music. He does so at his peril. Firstly the audience will sniff him out and turn him off; secondly the writer, if he is present, will slap him down.

The writer of a new play should be present for all or part of a rehearsal period. In radio drama this is usually the case; a conscious effort is made to see that the writer is involved in the production process. 'What do you mean by that?' asks the actor. 'I mean . . . ' explains the author. But with an absent writer – 'What do you think *he* (or *she*) means by that?' 'Well what I *think* is meant by that . . . ' suggests the director. Not so satisfactory. With dead writers, directors really have to earn their living, and what a lot of mistakes we make! Translations of foreign writers, particularly if you don't know the original language, are perfect hell. No sound saps a director's confidence more quickly than the continual flutter of the leaves of eleven different versions of a Chekhov play held in the hands of eleven different actors. And there simply isn't *time* for the ensuing discussion.

The most painful thing, perhaps, that a writer can be asked to do in a studio is to cut his script or, if he relinquishes that responsibility to the director, to have it cut for him. Cutting is a difficult craft and in broadcasting, where plays are scheduled into given slots of predetermined length (ninety, sixty, thirty minutes, etc.), it can seem as arbitrary as shoving a beautiful body remorselessly onto a Procrustean bed. Flab has to go (and that is usually sliced away before the script reaches the production state) but occasionally good flesh is cut into and blood leaks out. It is decoration, which usually means fine writing and sometimes texture, that has to be lost when a play is cut for time. The plot, obviously, has to remain intact, though the temptation to cut in that area is often great. Unfortunately it is not always the best bit of dramatic writing in a play that promotes its plot.

Ideally, when a producer knows he is going to direct a new play by a living writer, they should be in contact with each other as soon as possible. If the ideal situation does not occur at an early date, it probably means the producer is overpressured. At any given point the majority of BBC radio-drama producers are involved with six or seven plays in various stages of production. An output of twenty plays a year (not including serials or readings) would be a producer's average output, and the demands this makes on the imagination and energy level of even the most chameleon-like director is not inconsiderable.

'How do you get your plays to do?' asks the enquiring stranger, not yet having caught the eye of somebody better to talk to. 'Well . . . ' You pause. You think. How?

There are always the classics, which it is any broadcasting organisation's duty to reflect, represent and interpret. And there are those plays that have proved their success with audiences in other media. And there are dramatisations of fiction. But the most exciting venture in the directorial business is the production of an original play. If it is a *first* play by a new writer, so much the better. Plays usually arrive on the desks of theatre managers from the offices of a literary agent who specialises in drama. If it comes from an agent whose judgement you respect, then the heart leaps and you know you are going to read something worth considering. Some agents oversell their clients or fail to recommend rewrites prior to submission. This sort of agent loses credibility and subsequently will lose outlets and, probably, clients. A number of scripts are solicited by the management – that is to say, they are commissioned either on the basis of a draft or synopsis or from a writer with a proven track record. A certain number of scripts arrive unsolicited. It is generally amongst this number that the new first play will be found.

The situation is the same with the BBC and the television companies, though the majority of TV plays and film scripts are commissioned. This apparent cautiousness is caused by the heavy investment of money and the wide range of resources involved. Radio's relative cheapness allows it the freedom to take risks. This taking of risks is virtually denied to the commercial theatre manager who has to think of box-office receipts and consequent financial returns to the play's backers. Radio, which measures the success or failure of a play against audience size and researched appreciation and which, anyway, has an enormous dramatic output, can afford the occasional calculated failure. There is no better encouragement that can be given to a writer in whom one has faith than to produce his play. A wide Rubicon is crossed when a writer without a produced play becomes a playwright with just one professional production to his credit. Radio can also afford to judge a play on its intrinsic merits as good drama. Many a play has been turned down for the stage because it is not 'box office', because it would be too expensive to mount, or because it is of an awkward duration.

Essentially the director is like the actor in so far as he has to be *asked* to do a play by the producing agent. Like the actor he can suggest a play he would like to do. If the suggestion is taken up, he still has to be *requested* to direct it. All plays reaching the BBC Radio Drama Department are, at some point, considered and sifted by the script editor, who is, in turn, served by subeditors and readers. In the instance of a new first play, the script editor will send the script to that person whom he deems to be the most capable and sympathetic director for it. At this stage he is something of a marriage broker. If the director likes the play and is prepared to work with the author on it, then a marriage is on its way to being formed. These are not always happy or long-standing, but the success ratio is infinitely higher than with marriages contracted in the social sector.

Because he subsequently became well known through his theatre plays, the events surrounding the production of Joe Orton's first play stand as a good example. They are interesting, not because of Orton's subsequent fame, but because the case was a typical one. An unsolicited script called *The Boy Hairdresser* arrived and was read by two readers, who were not, in 1963, in tune with the intense originality of the style. Also it rambled. It was looked at by the script editor, who thought there was 'something there' and passed it to me. There was decidedly something there, a new voice that was hard to define. It seemed a play full of originality and potential. But would an unproved writer about whom nothing was known be able to tackle the necessary job of rewriting, cutting and reshaping? One had to find out and an interview was arranged. Orton's personality was unexpected, but he approached the problems immediately and as a professional. *The Boy Hairdresser* didn't seem a good title for the play and a change was suggested. *The Ruffian on the Stair*, an apt phrase culled from a little-known poem by a minor poet (W. E. Henley), was offered as the new title. It seemed brilliant and applicable. After two rewrites the play was accepted and, with the director's enthusiasm behind it, got on the air fairly quickly. But only *fairly* quickly. With a vast number of accepted scripts awaiting production at any given time, the period between acceptance of a play and its ultimate production can seem disconcertingly long to the director involved and, more especially, to the writer. For the writer it can feel as though he has been consigned to a kind of limbo.

That this was not the case with Joe Orton is ancient history. At our second meeting he mentioned to me he had a stage script with him called *Entertaining Mr Sloane*. I looked at it, thought it did not have possibilities at that time (1963) as a play we could do on radio and, since he then had no agent, suggested he should show it to Margaret Ramsay. She read it, immediately perceived its quality, and passed it to one of the few theatre managers prepared to take the risk of backing up his acute judgement, Michael Codron. The play was on the West End stage in a matter of weeks. Very quick.

The point behind this part of the story is that neither the director nor anyone connected with the production of drama lives in isolation. There is a general concern with the production of good drama and little pursuit of the petty operation of self-interest. Scripts are for ever being passed between radio, television, theatre and cinema, and recommendations are for ever being made about writers – and actors, come to that. In the pursuit of and encouragement of talent, nobody can afford to remain an island. All are part of the main.

Unfortunately it is difficult for a writer to make a name for himself as the writer of radio plays. Rhys Adrian, the author of some twenty-three plays for radio and winner of two major international prizes, is familiar to few but the cognoscenti. I have directed seventeen plays by him and would rank him with Pinter as a dramatist. Yet he remains little known because, apart from a number of television plays, he has not written for the theatre. And there are several others one could name in that category. But the fault lies not with the writer but with an intelligent society that does not sufficiently value the worth of the radio play. Of course there are reasons for this: a lack of proper publicity, the relatively small size of the audience (though numerically far greater than that for any one production in most theatres), the almost total absence of published texts (how unlike the Continent, where radio plays are frequently available in published form), and, of course, the ephemeral nature of the medium. Any director cares deeply for the reputation of an author with whom he is associated, but he shouldn't lie back and just let those who are paid to do the job do all the beating of the drum. He, too, is part of a Barnum and Bailey world and a share in publicising a production is one of his many responsibilities. That brash Barnum and Bailey world can, alas, often seem remote and removed from the protective atmosphere of the beige halls and padded studios of Broadcasting House.

So, the director has been asked to direct a play for radio. Let us assume it is a new play and a first play. He has met his author; the script has been discussed and formalised. They are on the honeymoon slopes of their relationship. But (at the risk of sounding a little like Mrs Elvsted in *Hedda Gabler*) they are on those slopes with a child – the play. Like a child, a play moves further and further from its parent author at every stage of its growth and development. The relinquishment can be painful, but it is inevitable. The first remove is when it is transmitted from the original, overfamiliar manuscript into typescript or playscript form ready for the actors and technicians to work from. A foreignness has entered; the play is not entirely possessed by its author. The second remove is at the read-through, when the author actually hears his words for the first time. From then on a gift is made. The lines become the property of the actor; the character suggested through print becomes the living creation of a specific actor. 'Oh I don't think *I* would say that. I think it would be better if I . . . ' the actor says. Director consults author (if present). Adjudicates, interprets, filters. It is best, usually, if the director is the exchange point between actor and writer, if they speak to each other *through* him. There should only be direct contact with the director's knowledge and acquiescence. This is not a matter of self-importance but of good, sound sense. The director has to know *everything* that is going on; he has to consider how something said to one actor may affect another actor's performance; he also has to ensure that the information is conveyed in the right kind of way for that particular actor. There is often no consistency in the way a director will address different members of a cast — for one actor a few grunts, noises and hand gestures can provide a golden key to a door that opens to reveal vistas of understanding; for another actor something approaching deep analysis combined with a genealogical exposition back to the Garden of Eden may be necessary. The simplest words are, however, the best – 'quicker', 'slower', 'louder', 'softer'. Unless the director is an

exceptionally bad actor (and sometimes even then), it is extremely
unwise to demonstrate a point by acting out a speech or a character.
Time stops, the cast is embarrassed, exhibitionism has taken over, and
there has been a breach of good manners.

Because radio deals so precisely in words and the accuracy of the
way in which they are spoken, the director of radio plays develops an
extraordinary acute ear for acted speech. Detailed attention to the way
things are said is, by and large, not so frequent in theatre and television
plays where there are so many other distractions for both director and
audience. Care has to be taken, however, not to be overpedantic or
overprecise lest the result seem unreal. There is a terrible tendency,
stemming either from pressure of time or verbal inadequacy, for
directors of radio plays to give an actor the *stress* of a word lazily,
hoping he may thereby achieve the sense of a line. An actor needs to
know the meaning of a speech. When he comprehends that, he will
make sense of it. 'Say it like *that*!' should be used only in the last snappy
resort.

A script will have been finalised six to eight weeks before it is taken
into the studio. Generally a cast will have been engaged three to four
weeks before the studio date. It is part of any director's job to have a
wide knowledge of the various talents available to him in a hugely
talented and unfortunately overcrowded profession. There is no such
thing as a 'radio actor', but there certainly are actors who can respond
more quickly to a role than others; there are actors who may lack a
physical potency in the theatre but whom the microphone favours (and
vice versa). Auditions for a specific role occur less frequently in radio
than they do in the visual media. The extent of the requirements is not
so broad – appearance is not a factor. In radio there are no casting
directors as in television, the cinema and, occasionally, the theatre.
The radio producer uses his own knowledge, relies upon his own
memory, has his own files. He is often, and not unjustifiably, accused
of being parochial in his casting, of not widening the net. Actors often
accuse BBC radio drama of being 'a closed shop'. It isn't, but neither is
it as open as some of the other drama 'shops'. There is a not unnatural
tendency for any director to work again with the actor whom he knows
and whose work he admires. Because of the brief time allotted for the
rehearsal of a radio play, it is of inestimable help to have experience of
the qualities and quickness of a particular artist. A kind of easy
friendship can help in cutting corners and assist in the immediate
creation of the right working atmosphere. Too close a friendship can
destroy both of these. Moreover it must be borne in mind that all
actors look unalike, but that they do not sound unalike. That narrows
the field somewhat.

With decisions over script and cast behind him, the next decision the
director has to make is how best to employ the short time available to him.
Will he rehearse the play and then record it in one take, or will he
rehearse and record it in short scenes, rather in the way one would

make a film? Such a consideration did not arise when everything was broadcast live, and it hardly arose when everything was recorded onto gramophone records. But tape exists and is easily edited. Actors know this, and some of them prefer to rehearse a scene closely and then record it immediately. Others prefer to consign what they absorbed during a day's rehearsal to that splendid silent director – A Good Night's Sleep. More importantly, playwrights also know that tape exists. They know the flexibility it offers in the writing of scenes of great technical complexity, which would be impossible to realise without the ability to stop, restart, edit and play back into the show. Developments in stereophony, quadrophony and binaural recording have added to the problem and have made continuous recording harder to entertain as a viable means of work.

So the two considerations to be taken into account are the technical requirements of a play and the demands it makes upon the actors. The acting must come first. If there is a play in which the slow growth and development of character is of such pre-eminent importance that the actor needs time and repeated continuous rehearsal to familiarise himself with his role, as well as continuity of performance in which to render it, then, whatever the technical complexities, that play must be recorded without breaks, not broken up into segments. The technical requirements will have to be simplified to suit the requirements of the performance. Performance, result, is all.

One example of the need for continuity of performance is *Othello*. After the first act the play rolls as Iago's poison works, and the central character has the problem of holding back the moment of his breaking until as late as possible. The rhythm, the fine tuning of the performance, is vital. The central character in *Hamlet* does not have these problems, so that the play can happily be broken into quite large sections for rehearsal and recording. A play like *The Comedy of Errors*, relying more upon plot than upon character development, can easily be chopped about and can be rehearsed and recorded out of sequence. But when this happens, it is imperative that the director keeps a picture of the play as a whole in his head or he will end up with a very strangely, possibly evenly, paced production. A film editor can alter pace by intercutting various shots. On sound tape this is not possible.

'Yes, I understand about the problems of actors', says the inquisitive stranger, trying hard to remember the story of *Othello* and being utterly confused in trying to remember anything about *The Comedy of Errors* except that it requires two sets of twins, which must be tricky on radio if you can't see them – or is it easier? 'But what are these "technical" considerations you talk of? Surely if you want a dog barking or a bird singing or a sea surging you just have to bung on a record of one. And if it's a case of footsteps in snow you crunch a packet of salt, or for fire you crackle a piece of cellophane close to a microphone, and for stabbing someone you thrust a knife into the heart of a cabbage and drop a sort of sandbag to make the noise of a body falling. And as for horses' hooves . . . ' Yes, it's true, all of it. But it's not quite as simple as that. Perhaps you've got all those sounds going on at once – a maiden burning at the stake near the sea on a snowy day with winter birds singing. A dog barks to alert the executioner of the approach of our hero on horseback. He arrives and stabs the villain, who falls to the snowy ground, dead. Our hero snatches the heroine from the stake in the nick of time and rides off with her into the sunset. (There is no recording of a sunset – the author's lines must tell us about that.) Forty-five seconds that scene took. Busy. And what sort of birds were they? Do they sing in winter in Norway, where our scene is set? What kind of dog is it? How far away is it? And the horse's hooves on snow, how quickly do they arrive? And, in stereo, does the horse come from the left, the right or the centre? And the horse must have a bridle that jingles, and perhaps it snorts frothily on arrival or perhaps it rises on its hind legs and whinnies, afraid of fire. And the actor, when he speaks to tell us about the glorious sunset, must sound as though he is high up on a horse, and the heroine when she thanks our hero, before swooning into his arms, must sound as though she is with him. She wears a long gown – just a little burnt. And isn't the villain wearing some kind of Viking armour, which clanks when he falls? And wouldn't the faggots of the pyre make some kind of sound as the maiden is rescued from the stake? And what kind of sea is it? What kind of shore – rocky, sandy, pebbly – is it coming into? There are a great number of recordings of different types of sea from which to make a selection. A director is always asking questions, choosing between alternatives, making decisions. In radio he has to do this very quickly.

To help him in the studio the director will have three technical assistants and one secretary. Apart from trying to keep him relatively sane, the secretary keeps an eagle eye on her stopwatch to see that the speed (not pace) of the production is as planned, that it is not underrunning or overrunning, and she will mark her script with precise timings for future use in editing. She will make a note of any changes to the script made in the studio; note commercial recordings of music for future copyright payment and time their duration; keep a list of various takes of a scene and make sure they can easily be retrieved from the pile of anonymous-looking tape spools; act as the director's extra ear and make a note of any mistakes or misreadings of the text; keep an eye on the studio clock to ensure that rehearsals are running to schedule; answer telephones, queries from actors, questions from technical assistants like, 'What scene does he intend to do next?'. She will restrain belligerent workmen from noisily rebuilding Broadcasting House throughout a recording, run errands, provide sweets, empty ashtrays and, if she is kind and you are very nice to her, fetch you a cup of coffee when you need one. Above all she will keep her head when all about her are losing theirs and blaming it on *you*. And it is only right that they should blame it on you, for the responsibility within the studio is entirely the director's. Nobody else's.

The three technical assistants have three distinct functions. The senior amongst them operates the control panel and is ultimately responsible for marrying all the sources of sound at varying levels of volume into a unified whole which, subject to the director's agreement, is transferred to magnetic tape and will become 'the programme'. In consultation with the director, he is responsible for the selection of microphones to give the best required effect, and he creates the most suitable acoustic area for a scene to be played in. He will 'treat' voices to the director's specification (the most obvious of these are the telephone distort or the 'thinks' voice) and will advise the director on all technical matters. He also has dominion over a minor mythological nymph known as 'Echo', who is very useful if you are in a large empty church or trapped amongst the mountains or given to dreams. He needs to be both engineer and artist – and very patient.

The other two technical assistants work to the director through the panel operator. One of these is placed in the studio and is responsible for its smooth running. He (or she) creates the 'spot' effects, those noises made with the actors live in the studio at the time of recording: the snowy footsteps, the cellophane fire, the cabbage stab. The spot-effects person has to be in complete sympathy with the motivations, feelings and thoughts of the actor for whom he is making the sound. To time a teacup going down, to pour a measure of whisky with a squirt of soda, to close a door, demand knowledge of the character for whom you are making the sound. Mistime the action and you can upset the performance. It is a job requiring quiet professionalism and artistry.

The third technical assistant fulfils a function that on the face of it may seem more attractive. The power is his, the noise is his. He could bring down Valhalla and flood in the Rhine without recourse to Wagner's music; sink the Titanic, recreate the Blitz, wipe out Pompeii, without ever leaving his turntables. Just by playing records, simply by running a tape. In the average drama studio the gram and tape operator has at his disposal about eight turntables and four tape machines. With these he mixes his palette and paints the scenery. He has a vast library of specially recorded effects to choose from, and his knowledge of that library and of the idiosyncracies of any particular director will help him in the selection he offers for aural scrutiny. Tricks and deceits are his, and he would be well advised not to tell the director that the sound he has offered as an anchor being weighed in 1868 is in fact a 1975 recording of a piece of factory machinery. The innocent director, like the innocent listener at home, will believe what he is told to believe, hear what he is told he is hearing. After all, one of the functions of any director is to be like an objective member of the audience.

In radio production in Britain, all the sounds added to an actor's speech are generally controlled and recorded in the studio at one and the same time. In America and on the continent of Europe, the usual custom is to add extra sound to the actor tape in an editing channel. This takes a great deal of time and hence costs a lot more money. It admits of far more trial and error, a greater leeway for mistakes in the actor's performance, and the result can often have a higher degree of *technical* perfection to it. But the result can seem mechanistic and dehumanised. The actor can often seem divorced from his environment, since Captain Ahab may be shouting from the bridge of the *Pequod* in a tempest or King Lear may be telling the winds to blow and rage without having any idea of the elemental battle with which he is competing. And it is just as difficult for the couple in the family saloon to know precisely how to pitch their voices or their performance.

Where the post-production addition of sound can be useful is with music. Should an actor chance to make a mistake whilst music is playing simultaneously against his words, the production has to be halted and everybody has to return to that point in the play before the music began. Boring, destructive, costly. Speech over music cannot be edited. If music is to be specially composed for a production – and the selection and commissioning of the composer is another of the director's responsibilities, as is the recording of the music – then one is advised to have it written after the speech tracks have been laid down and edited. Timings can then be exact, and the director is not forced into the situation of having to fit the words (of primary importance) to the music (of secondary importance).

Certain sounds cannot be achieved by on-the-spot recording. Sounds from the past we can research, envisage and recreate. But sounds of the future exist only in our imagination, as do the fantasy sounds of an author's invented creation – trolls, spectres, mermaids, inanimate objects to which speech is given, etc. We do not *know* how certain things sound; we can only imagine them. Such sounds can only be made mechanically, by treating the human voice, by treating man-made sounds, or by creating them electronically.

The BBC radio-drama producer can call upon the resources and imagination of the BBC's Radiophonic Workshop for the making of weird sundry noises and for the provision of entire music scores for a play. In my production of *Hamlet*, for instance, I required the sound of swirling mist on the battlements, something to suggest the Ghost, and a strange 'holy' sound for when Claudius was at prayer. Because this was to be the context of the production, I also wanted an unusual sound for the cannons and a not precisely recognisable musical sound for the arrival of Fortinbras at the end of the play. Malcolm Clarke of the Radiophonic Workshop provided all of these – including the mist. I talked to him, as I often talk to composers of conventional music, in terms of colour and of shape. He seemed to understand me, as have the composers.

Radiophonic sounds can be used subliminally as well as interpreta-

tively. A recent production of *Macbeth* I directed for RTE in Dublin
had a prolonged sound score that heightened the sense of evil
throughout the play but never intruded into the action. And only
radiophonic sound could successfully interpret the following requirement made by David Rudkin in *Cries from Casement As His Bones Are
Brought to Dublin:*

*Long long upcurving electronic anthropoid cry, breaking at last at peak into a
frisson-percussion collapse like opening of vast pores, cold . . . Sound
modulates to high slow-throbbing whine, suggesting pain.*[1]

I blanched when I read that, but it was all in a day's work for the
Radiophonic Workshop and the instructions were splendidly realised.
Rudkin also demanded that the bones of Crippen talk to the bones of
Casement from the limepit at Pentonville, where they possibly lay
together in death, and that whilst talking the bones be wrenched apart.
Achieved. His request for *'Opening of Mahler V – Funeral March,
scored for Military Winds, Percussion: unblended, eldritch, hard'*[2] was
not achieved. We tried to realise his intentions radiophonically, but it
proved impossible and there was not the budget to engage musicians
with musical instruments. However, a *'deep moaning of cold wind,
comfortless, reminding of the Wind of Time: no Gothick'*[3] was easy
fare.

   Dr Who, with its music, its special aural effects and, most
particularly, the popular Dalek voice, is for the Radiophonic
Workshop what the *Pomp and Circumstance March* was for Elgar.
This is what they are best known for, yet it is neither the most inventive
nor original of their creations. Science fiction is the most obvious area
for the deployment of radiophonic sound, but the range of possible
sounds is strangely limited and there is a danger of rapidly reproducing
an auditory cliché.

   Not all plays are recorded in a studio. Encouraged by the 'new
naturalism' in television and the cinema, which was itself hastened by
the development of more advanced technical equipment, and
employing mobile recording machines, a number of directors and
writers conceive their productions in terms of being made entirely on
location. As in film, a scene in a church will be recorded in a church,
while for a boat scene on the Serpentine a boat will be hired on the
Serpentine. It need not actually be the Serpentine, for listeners cannot
see the scenery, but it will be a pleasure lake sounding *like* the
Serpentine. There are advantages to this method of recording – and
disadvantages.

   The advantages are that being away from a studio, certainly in
realistic plays, *can* have a liberating effect upon the actors, who
respond spatially to each other and are able to relate to the actuality of
the scene. There is a tendency for location productions to approximate
more closely to the patterns of real speech, to sound less formalised,
less stagy.

The chief disadvantage of location recording is that the director does not have full control over the environment. In art, one has the ability to select what is dramatically necessary, to unclutter, to refine, to remove unwanted sounds and reproduce only those adding positively to the dramatic picture. For example, everybody is aware of the situation of a radio interview recorded in somebody's office – typewriters clatter away, traffic sounds can be heard through the window, phones ring, an unwanted character may enter the room, etc. These intrusive sounds impinge on the essence of the exercise – to hear what the interviewer and interviewee have to communicate to the listener. Editing can remove some of the blemishes – the phone ring or the entry of a secretary – but the director has no control over the nature and volume of the background noise. Location recording can be cumbersome; it is slow; it can distract an actor's attention rather than assist it; it will always demand a great deal of editing. Although it is not creating under-the-line budgetary costs by tying up a studio, it has special expenses of its own in terms of travel and subsistence for the personnel involved. I often wonder whether actors and directors do not derive a pleasure and an excitement from going 'on location' that is not related to the pleasure and enjoyment derived by the listener who hears the play and has no concern for the *way* in which it was recorded. For a small number of plays, demanding a high degree of naturalism, it is the best means of doing them. And it is also right that at all times we should experiment judiciously with new methods and techniques.

However, modern technology has advanced to such an extent that there is the danger that the machines will master the men, that they will determine how we should achieve our results. Being aware of the possibilities that new techniques in recording offer us, there is a temptation to explore and exploit for the sake of the exercise itself. Thirty-two-track recording exists, so let us use it! Oh, Beware! So much emphasis can be placed on the means of achieving an effect that the *matter* that brought the whole process into operation can get lost and forgotten. One of the reasons for the poverty of our dramatic literature in the nineteenth century was the exploitation of and an indulgence in the wonders of splendidly versatile stage machinery. Splendid spectacles, yes, but what happened to the words? In theatre, cinema, television and radio, there are an increasing number of new toys; but if it is true that the director, like the actor, still has rather too much of the child about him, then he must be persuaded not to play with the toys too much of the time. And that is not being Luddite.

Once a play has been recorded the editing begins. Since the director is dealing with sound alone, this is an infinitely simpler and speedier task than the editing of film or video tape. A quick slice with a razor blade and blemishes are removed, and the various takes of scenes are joined to each other. A director is someone who must not only make up his mind quickly but also know his own mind. He should know when he needs to compromise between what he wants and what it is possible for him to get with the resources available in the time at his disposal. To lumber himself with umpteen takes of a scene, which he has taken, retaken and then taken again in the hope that it will magically get better, is to indulge himself in unprofessional ludicrosities. After a certain number of takes, the scene will only get worse. To leave the decision-making as to which take is best to the time of editing is tiresome and time-consuming – and expensive.

The finally edited tape, with any additional sounds now mixed onto it, is given a rough playback in the hope that all the calculations about its total duration are accurate. A certain amount of cutting for duration can always be left to the editing stage, for a hearing of the play in its totality can let you know where the 'slack' is – if there is any. Essential cutting of the tape at this stage can be as painful for the director as the previous cutting of the script in an office or the studio was for the playwright. By now he will have thought about, talked about and justified everything that is recorded. But, except for those plays broadcast on Radio 3 that are allowed 'to find their own lengths', each play has its own specially sized bed and there must be no overhang or overrun. So chop! No whining, no false dramatics.

One hopes the author approves one's work; one hopes the audience will appreciatively receive what the author has written and the actors have performed. One hopes the *way* they have performed will be appreciated as well. One hopes the listener will not have noticed the direction. The greatest compliment that can be paid to a director is when the play and the players receive the credit and plaudits.

When a radio play is completed there is a sense of anticlimax. Since the radio play takes place in the mind of the listener, there is no getting in there with and sharing his reactions. A play on the stage lives only in actual performance, in that moment of communion between actor and audience. It is an act of participation in which the director can also share. A silly joy, perhaps. But nice.

Neatly packaged, properly promoted for publicity purposes, the programme notes written, a production printed onto a certain number of tapes waits on a library shelf for the day of its transmission – and its reception. For the director? Tomorrow, another play.

The stranger you began talking to so very long ago has already decided to adopt a different opening conversational gambit in future. The glass is empty, the legs are weak, most of the guests have departed. 'I hope we meet again.' (Not true.) 'Your job – very interesting.' (Do I detect a trace of the Rowan and Martin's *Laugh In* mock-Germanic?) But yes, yes it *is* interesting.

Notes

1. *Cries from Casement As His Bones Are Brought to Dublin*, London 1974, p. 73.
2. *Ibid*, p. 69.
3. *Ibid*, p. 76.

Chapter 3

British radio drama : a survey

Horst P. Priessnitz

Anyone who embarks upon an analysis of the British radio play will be struck at once by the paradox that, despite its more than fifty-year-long history, it still represents, as a literary form, one of the most neglected areas of research. Although the English radio play belongs without any doubt to the field of interest of the writer of literary history, and although, given the quality and the quantity of the plays produced, one might legitimately expect a critical corpus with some claim to comprehensiveness, the form has passed almost unnoticed in the pages of literary criticism and scholarship. From its earliest days the history of the radio play has been one of complaint at the inadequacy of its public image. The meagre review columns of *The Sunday Times, The Observer, The New Statesman, The Listener, The Guardian, Plays and Players* and *Theatre Quarterly* are evidence enough of this sorry state of affairs. Confined to the most important broadcasts and generally based on little more than personal preference, the discussions one finds there are symptomatic, in the sterility of their approach, of the widespread lack of interest that has been so inexplicable a hurdle to author and producer alike:

Frankly I am at a loss to know why national newspapers particularly don't devote more space to radio criticism. Radio may be a transitory medium but despite this it's an increasingly influential one in the world of drama as a whole.[1]

The fact that even the larger newspapers and periodicals allow 'room for only the most perfunctory of comments'[2] seems particularly incongruous when one compares the number of theatre reviews with those of radio plays. It has been calculated that the 'combined audience for *Saturday Night Theatre* which goes out on a Saturday night and is repeated on Monday afternoon would fill a West End theatre for ten years'.[3] And still the radio play has to fight for its acknowledgement:

This is just one of the perversities of the popular press. I have nothing against it, except that it is a wrong valuation to put on things.[4]

Martin Esslin's well-founded criticism is corroborated by a remark of

Irving Wardle's drawing attention to the consequences such perversities can have on the writer of radio plays:

Radio, despite its continued role as the source of tomorrow's dramatists, remains the critic's Red China; large, potent, simmering with expansionist ambitions, and ignored . . . Audiences for *Saturday Night Theatre* still may top 750,000; a production on the Third may net 100,000. But what good does it do? The author's only contact with them will be a handful of abusive letters. And he will be extremely lucky if he gets a three-line mention in any national newspaper. The indifference of newspapers to radio productions is a subject in itself. It amounts to a kind of blindness . . . I can't explain this.[5]

The indifference on the part of the major periodicals and the national press may be responsible for the fact that authors constantly seek other outlets for their work, rewriting their radio plays for the theatre or television in order to gain the acknowledgement that is their due. Indeed, the adaptability of many such works to TV, film or stage is a characteristic feature of the English radio play, and one that may well be thought to have its origins in this precarious situation.

The attitude of professional literary criticism is no less puzzling. Here, the television play seems to have exercised an extraordinary fascination, while the far older radio play has been left as the Cinderella of literary history. Anyone interested in the English radio play will find himself referred by the BBC to publications from the 1930s: Lance Sieveking's book, *The Stuff of Radio* (1934), was in 1961 still considered the standard work on the subject.[6] The latest BBC bibliographies[7] support Martyn A. Bond's assertion that almost all the English contributions to this field are from the time before or shortly after the Second World War.[8] Leaving aside for a moment Martin Esslin's hardy efforts to demonstrate the existence of the genre and its quality, one is left with Val Gielgud's *British Radio Drama 1922-1956* (1957) and Donald McWhinnie's *The Art of Radio* (1959) as, with Sieveking's work, the most important attempts to come to terms with the British radio play as an art form, though in neither case are the criteria those of literary criticism.

The available material on the subject could be classified under six headings, according to its comprehensiveness. In the first group would come the occasional reviews and critical notices of the various newspapers, rarely representing more than a personal approach to a particular broadcast. Secondly one should mention the BBC's own publications: their annual handbooks provide valuable facts and figures, though these, of course, in no way reflect literary considerations. A third group consists of memoirs and histories of broadcasting, which have the advantage of authenticity, but which, precisely because of their personal slant, do not always give an objective picture of the genre, let alone one that might be relevant to literary criticism.[9] By far the largest body of writing on the subject consists of advice and instructions composed for potential radio playwrights by experienced broadcasters, based on their own practice. Useful though this may be for the actual playwright, it sheds very little light on the British radio play. Forewords, important either for the history of the genre or for their theoretical insights, together with analyses of specific texts, form another identifiable group, in which McWhinnie's and Esslin's work must be given a special place. The last and most informative section comprises the handful of strictly scientific contributions to the subject, among them individual essays by Esslin and, above all and still unsurpassed, Armin P. Frank's book *Das Hörspiel* of 1963. While Esslin's brief but rewarding comments represent a patient one-man campaign for the radio play as a literary form, Frank's analysis of the American and European scene is, despite the enduring value of his insights into the English radio play, on the whole simply too large an undertaking for him ever to have found a successor. The British production alone is so problematic in its range and its types that an attempt to cover the whole field of the American and European radio play must necessarily remain sketchy. A noteworthy though not always entirely accurate contribution of more recent date comes from David Wade, who, however, confines himself to a brief summary of the genre after 1967.[10]

One of the reasons for the neglect of the radio play by literary critics and the academic world can perhaps be found in the very small number of such plays that have ever been published: one might well conclude that as a literary form the radio play is of marginal interest only. And this is indeed the issue on which the rival camps divide. On the one hand one finds the opinion – a hardy survivor from the crisis years of the 1950s – that the radio play is at the end of its days. Martyn A. Bond fathered the notion that the radio play in England has capitulated in the face of the competition from television[11]; it was no more than a typical and transient phenomenon of the postwar period. These remarks are of especial interest in view of the fact that Bond wrote three years after Frank had drawn attention to the immense possibilities of British radio drama.[12] Likewise McWhinnie's references to the audiences of these plays, still a matter of millions,[13] and again the readily accessible data of the BBC handbooks published since 1960 seem to have escaped Bond's notice. Three years later we find Bond seconded by W.H. Auden, paradoxically enough in a BBC publication. In his Foreword to a selection of Louis MacNeice's radio plays published by the BBC, Auden complains 'that, since the advent of television, radio drama is probably a dying art'.[14] There can be no doubt at all that such judgements originate in a simple ignorance of the situation as it is, and they are as simply and emphatically refuted by the statistics of the BBC.

If one follows with care the data regularly published by the Corporation, one will notice a steady rise in the production of radio plays since 1955; the variation in the figures quoted serves only to hinder any determination of the *absolute* growth. In 1952-3 Val Gielgud pointed to the 'insatiable demand' of the Radio Drama Department, which was at that time threatened in its very existence by the novel impact of television: 'Already', he writes, 'no less than 250 full-length plays are called for every year.'[15] The 1955 *BBC Handbook* reports that

the output of the BBC's Sound Drama Department averages about a thousand productions a year, consisting of single plays varying in length from fifteen minutes to three hours or more, and serial dramatizations, both weekly and daily.[16]

At variance with these figures are those given by Burton Paulu, who states in the same year that BBC readers receive some 200 – 300 scripts every month,[17] a figure recurring in the *BBC Handbook* of 1957.[18] For 1960 the number of productions is given as 375.[19] In 1965 the statistics for the radio play output of all BBC programmes quotes a figure of 999 hours.[20] The corresponding figure for 1964 is '775 new play productions',[21] of which Esslin describes 395 as having been written especially for radio.[22] Elsewhere Esslin reckons the annual figure at approximately 1,000.[23] According to Richard Imison, the weekly volume of manuscripts submitted in 1965 was 'about 200'[24]; in 1955 this was the monthly quota. In 1969 the annual production, according to the Central Office of Information, amounted to 'some 300 new plays on the radio, many of them specially written for the purpose'[25]; and in 1971 Esslin, in his latest essay on the subject, gives 500 – 700 plays as the annual production quota of the BBC.[26] This confusing whirl of figures is rooted in the imprecision of the concept 'radio drama', which includes at its widest not only all the dramatic, quasi-dramatic and 'feature' programmes, but also the serialised dramatic readings, as well as the whole spectrum of dramatic adaptations broadcast on the radio.[27] The figures, therefore, vary according to the sector to which the source refers. One would not, however, be all that far from the truth if one were to set the mean at about 300 plays per year, which alone would make the BBC one of the largest producers of radio drama in the Western world.[28]

In the light of these figures, it is astonishing how few radio plays ever get into print. One has to go to the Play Library of the BBC to obtain a convincing picture of the discrepancy between actually available radio-play material and the number of plays – in comparison almost negligible – that are ever published. In this Library alone there are some 40,000 manuscripts,[29] and this refers only to the period since 1946. Bond's figures, quoted in 1966, are in principle still valid today:

Since the war there have been about fifty books published in England, giving either the text of individual radio plays or anthologies (normally of the broadcast work of a particular author) to the interested reading public. And of these more than half appeared before 1950.[30]

The BBC editions of radio-play texts,[31] despite the greater seriousness with which this matter is now pursued, have done little to alter the state of affairs. Even now, as then, only about one in every hundred plays in England appears in print, whereas in Germany the figure, for all its shortcomings, is closer to one in eight.[32] It can, then, scarcely cause surprise when literary critics persist in their erroneous opinion that the radio play is scarcely worth serious attention, for its textual impact is minimal, and the scholar who seeks access to unpublished material will come up against an outdated copyright that hinders, if not entirely frustrates, his intentions. Furthermore, if he thinks he can use recordings to acquaint himself with the material, he will be disappointed, for such recordings do not exist.

To the difficulties arising from the situation as described are added problems that themselves shed light on the particular character of the British radio play. A comparison with the German *Hörspiel* soon shows that the simple equation, *Hörspiel* equals radio play, is not entirely correct. The very diversity of the statistical data already quoted shows that the term 'radio drama' is used in England to cover very different fields:

No one has ever established exactly what 'radio drama' includes. It obviously includes a play by Pinter and it obviously doesn't include a reconstruction of the loss of the airship R-101, but in between there are many less definable programmes.[33]

This 'undefinable nature of radio drama'[34] may well have its roots in the time-honoured notion that the radio play is a simple offshoot of the theatre play, with no claim of its own to critical reflection. The constant emphasis on the affinity between the two forms, reducing the radio play at times to a mere shadow of theatrical performance, may have its origins in the fact that the radio play began with broadcasts of Shakespeare's dramas[35] and in fact received its decisive formative influence from the stage. In contrast with the way things developed in Germany, where the *Hörspiel* could at an early date free itself from its connections with the theatre, the English radio play remained for a longer period in close alliance with stage performance, although even here, albeit on a different front, an independent dramatic form began to emerge,[36] and one to which the name 'radio play' could more justifiably be applied. For a long time the lion's share of what was called 'radio drama' consisted of adaptations of works for the stage, to which were soon added adaptations in a similar vein of novels and short stories.[37] The close liaison between the two media, encouraged by wartime conditions, determined the transference of theatrical terminology and expectations to radio drama which, like the stage, was considered to have as its brief the performance before as wide a public as possible of the whole wealth of English and indeed international drama. In 1942 the BBC sketched out the aims of the Radio Drama Department in the following terms:

Briefly, that policy was by broadcast production to maintain interest in classic plays, British and foreign, and especially those of Shakespeare; to provide . . . theatrical entertainment for lovers of drama cut off by circumstances from the theatre itself; and finally – perhaps the most important of all – to encourage the writing of new plays specifically designed for the medium of broadcasting. In this last activity one may reasonably include the adaptation for broadcasting of suitable novels and short stories.[38]

Given these aims, it is understandable that radio should have appeared in the role of a 'National Repertory Theatre of the Air',[39] a role that persisted long after the war had ended. It must have been due to the healthy shock of television that round about 1955 a change began to take place in the policies and terminology of the Drama Department: the voice of the postwar critics of traditional radio drama began to be heard. The BBC was still considered to be the gateway to international drama,[40] but the unsatisfactory ersatz of traditional radio fare became increasingly evident. The 'mere juxtaposition of the words "radio" and "play" was judged to be a 'contradiction in terms'.[41] Television was so much more obviously suited to fulfilling the tasks of a National Theatre that a rethinking of the peculiar role and qualities of radio was inevitable. The opinion was voiced that 'any movement towards the creation of good radio drama should be away from the theatre, and in another direction altogether'.[42] The BBC started to concentrate on the 'original radio play', the 'radio play proper' – a movement in which the German *Hörspiel* had been of some influence.[43] Convinced that radio had for decades been concentrating on tasks better suited to television, the writers of plays for broadcasting began to explore more seriously the real possibilities of the medium:

The theatre still has much value to contribute, but it seems likely, particularly as television spreads, that Sound Drama will tend more and more to concentrate on work specially scripted for the microphone and making full use of radio's unique flexibility, intimacy, and capacity for imaginative and evocative story-telling.[44]

In some degree, attention was still paid to the adaptation of stage works, short stories and novels, but since 1959 or thereabouts authors like Francis Durbridge, Lester Powell, Lionel Brown, Rex Rienits, Samuel Beckett, Giles Cooper, Caryl Brahms, D.S. Savage, James Forsyth, Lydia Ragosin, R.C. Sherriff, N.C. Hunter, Henry Cecil, Philip Levene, James Hanley, Robert Bolt and John Mortimer have given the term 'radio play' the same sort of meaning as the German *Hörspiel*.[45] With the discovery of the innate possibilities of radio, the confidence of producers began to grow, even to the extent that they felt their medium superior to that of the stage:

Gradually, over the years, one's position has moved round to realising that radio is a creative medium in its own right and that far from trying to put on stage plays and having to make up for our deficiencies we can in fact create far more freely on radio than those poor people on the stage who are bound by a great many physical and frequently commercial restrictions.[46]

Even if today the English radio play can still not entirely deny its derivation from theatrical performance – the two forms are above all linguistically very close[47] – it remains an established fact that since the end of the 1950s the concept 'radio play' has undergone a mutation reflecting the development from broadcast drama to original radio work.

It would, however, be quite erroneous to infer from this that prior to 1955 England had nothing that could be called a genuine radio play: proof to the contrary can be found in the existence of the Features Department. The contribution of the feature to the formal development of the radio play has, as yet, scarcely been investigated. What is certain is that in the period when the radio play was still looking to the theatre for its inspiration and material, the feature was steadily developing and applying precisely those elements that were later to become characteristic of the radio play proper. In 1937, stimulated by the Columbia Broadcasting System's Columbia Workshop, the BBC set up an experimental studio to explore the specific expressive possibilities of radio.[48] The experiment ended with the war. After the war the tradition was resurrected by the Features Department and work continued.[49] In this way, the productions of that Department can be seen as an important factor in the genesis of the English radio play.

Like the term 'radio play' itself, the term 'feature' covers a multitude of almost contradictory notions, which can only be reconciled if one looks at the history of this form. In Germany, 'feature' has come to mean the presentation of documentary material in a way that is effective for radio.[50] But the documentary nature of the material accounts only for part of what in England is known as a 'feature'; the term can be applied to a report on elephant-taming in Burma or to Louis MacNeice's *Christopher Columbus* – and this does nothing but increase the riddle. It includes everything from 'documentaries of the past war, to reflections of the economic crisis, to the South Africa of the Royal Tour', right up to 'experimental presentations of such varied classics as *The Dialogues of Plato*, Milton's *Paradise Lost*, and Langland's *The Vision of Piers Plowman*'.[51] The distinction, attributed to Laurence Gilliam, 'Features deal with fact, Drama with fiction',[52] has never been consistently maintained.[53] Lance Sieveking's tentative definition in 1934, 'A "feature-programme" is an arrangement of sounds, which has a theme but no plot',[54] isolates, on the other hand, one of the elements – sheer love of experiment – that have in a decisive manner characterised the

English feature programme. The exploitation of radio as an artistic medium and the experiments in broadcasting technique that had this as their aim have been a cherished concern of the BBC from its very beginnings; in the feature, or in whatever passes under that general term, this commitment has come to fruition.[55]

The development from the feature of Sieveking's day to the experimental radio play of the postwar period might have been one of uninterrupted continuity, had not the outbreak of war brought a second component into play – that of the feature as a publicity weapon:

We soon realized that one of the first jobs of the feature programme in wartime was to explain the enemy, to shake off the polite fictions of diplomacy, and to convert in the public mind 'leading figures of a friendly state' to the gangsters and assassins of a well-armed foe.[56]

The experimental feature of prewar days was therefore converted into the political documentary, the propaganda piece whose efficacy rested on broadcasting techniques already developed, albeit for a different end. In the hands of such authors as Louis MacNeice, Desmond Hawkins, James Hanley, Robert Barr, Robert Gittings, Walter Allen, John Hampson, D.G. Bridson and Francis Dillon, it became 'the "striking force" of radio'.[57] The crisis once over, however, and the enemy no longer an immediate military threat, the writers of feature programmes saw themselves obliged to return to other areas of factual concern. Louis MacNeice was sent off to Greece – the Greece of antiquity – and his *The Golden Ass* gave rise to a series of travel reports.[58] From that point on, the boundaries between feature and radio play began to blur. There was no discernible difference between a dramatised battle scene from *War and Peace* and a feature report on an historical battle. Thus from 1947 onwards, a growing uncertainty could be felt almost everywhere except in the BBC as to the precise scope of the term 'feature' and its definition *vis-à-vis* the radio play. Rose Macaulay admitted in that year, 'Where drama ends and feature begins, I scarcely know'[59]; and in her 'Author's Note' prefacing the collection of short stories and radio plays, *Voices at Play* (1961), Muriel Spark expressed similar sentiments, affirming that she had 'never quite grasped the distinction between dramatic features and plays'.[60] Nor has the public ever taken much interest in the conceptual subtleties involved in distinguishing two such similar forms: 'Classifications such as play, radio report, feature programme, etc., mean much in Portland Place, but by the time they reach our chilly hearth they mean less than nothing.'[61]

It is not unimportant for the history of English radio drama that a large number of accepted radio plays were not categorised as such by the BBC but produced under the rubric 'feature', and this is the title under which they appear in the catalogues. MacNeice's *Christopher Columbus* is dramatised history and poetic radio play at the same time, inasmuch as the author deviates freely from an actual historical account of the events concerned. MacNeice's *The Dark Tower*, *The Careerist* and *One Eye Wild*, Dylan Thomas's *Under Milk Wood*, John Mortimer's *The Dock Brief*, Muriel Spark's *The Danger Zone*, *The Dry River Bed*, *The Interview* and *The Party Through the Wall*, and Barry Bermange's experimental tetralogy, *The Dreams*, *Amor Dei*, *The After-Life* and *The Evenings of Certain Lives*, were all of them produced by the Features Department. Rayner Heppenstall, Jennifer Wayne, Laurie Lee, Terence Tiller, Robert Gittings, W.R. Rodgers, V.S. Pritchett, Elizabeth Bowen, Henry Reed, Patric Dickinson, J.B. Priestley, Eric Linklater, John Betjeman, George Orwell, Viola Meynell and Sir Herbert Read can all be cited in support of the view that the feature was 'the radio's most natural expression'[62]: it was *the* art form proper to radio:

> If radio can claim to be an art at all, it must base its claim on its features. Here the sound medium is used in an original, positive, even 'creative' way. The feature, in fact, *is* the radio art-form.[63]

The fact that between 1949 and 1955 every British entry for the coveted Prix Italia came from the Features Department[64] suggests that the genuine radio play existed at this time – and probably also before the war – in the form of the feature.

The English radio play comprises, however, not only the radio play proper and certain types of feature: during the war, dramatic broadcasting assumed a number of different roles. It took the place not only of the straight theatre but also of the variety performance, that marriage of verbal humour and music we call the 'show'. *The Goon Show* in particular, brought into being by Spike Milligan, Harry Secombe and Peter Sellers, developed a form that set it off from any comparable undertaking, in that it used radio not as a makeshift or surrogate for the live, visual performance, but as the authentic medium for an entertainment and for a humour whose effect lay entirely in language and its sound accompaniment. Conceived from the start in purely acoustic terms, it made its mark as 'really pure radio'.[65] Grotesque and surrealistic as it was, it achieved so perfect a blend of language with the innate possibilities of radio that the listener, left to himself, would never regard the restriction to a single, acoustic medium as in any sense an impoverishment. As such, *The Goon Show* unquestionably falls within the compass of the term 'radio play', albeit as a variant of the genre, and one whose sole concern was entertainment.

Leaving aside for the moment the dramatised readings, bordering on the monologue radio play, the dramatic pieces composed specially for school broadcasts, the series and serials,[66] and above all the broad field of adaptations, which often possess qualities of the radio play, it is, then, legitimate to conclude that as a genre the radio play in England is composed not simply and solely of the radio play proper, nor of the feature, nor of the show. It is identical with none of these forms, but comprises all three.

Another factor distinguishing the English radio play from the German *Hörspiel* is the way in which a particular play will be directed to a particular audience. This is rooted in the constitution of the BBC, which as a 'public service' is obliged to tailor its programmes to the interests of the social group it serves[67] – a directive applying to the radio play as it does to every other programme. And, of course, the cultural demands made by British audiences on the broadcasting media vary according to the social class and educational level of the audiences concerned. Thus the BBC, in its diverse reforms, has always sought to provide for as wide a socio-cultural spectrum as possible, catering for 'the needs of all segments of the public, with reference to minority as well as majority tastes'.[68] Until 1939 the Corporation had two Programmes at its disposal, the National and the Regional, which, as their titles suggest, provided material of local as well as of more than local interest. With the outbreak of war, the two Programmes were fused into one, renamed the Home Service. But when a British Expeditionary Corps was sent to Africa, a special Programme for soldiers was seen to be necessary; thus the year 1940 saw the birth of the Forces or General Forces Programme as a complement to the Home Service. Postwar reorganisation was built on the concept – by no means an unproblematic one – of 'a broadly based cultural pyramid slowly aspiring upwards'[69]; this resulted in three Programmes, the Light, the Home and the Third, each envisaging a different social class as audience. Despite the many criticisms to which it was subject,[70] this structure held for almost twenty-five years. The latest reform, that of 1970, dispensed with the socio-cultural basis for these differentiations, although, as before, different audiences were still to be provided with qualitatively different fare. The division of what had been three Programmes into what were now four, Radios 1-4, was founded on the realisation that television had had a decisive effect on audience behaviour, as well as on the desire to reflect in the pattern of broadcasting the decentralising trend in society and in politics. Thus local radio stations were instituted with small and specifically local audiences in mind.[71]

The most important of these reorganisations – certainly the most decisive for the radio play – was that of 1945-6. True to the concept of the cultural pyramid, it provided for two mass-appeal Programmes (the Light and the Home) and an intellectual minority Programme (the Third). In this way it affected the majority of radio plays written in England, for since 1936 intensive audience research had established parameters of taste that could be used as definitive guidelines with regard both to the formal construction and to the content of plays, which from their very inception, therefore, were tailored to the different but always more or less homogeneous preferences of a particular social group.

The Light Programme, with its origins in the Forces (or General Forces) Programme, was concerned solely to provide relaxed and relaxing entertainment. A BBC directive of 1947 puts it thus:

The Light Programme is there to entertain in the widest sense of the word. And to do so it draws upon the whole profession of entertainment.[72]

This does not, however, exclude all seriousness:

The title 'Light' Programme does not mean that everything broadcast in it must necessarily be frothy or frivolous. It does mean that the over-all content of the daily or weekly programme contains a higher proportion of sheer entertainment than either the Home Service or the Third Programme . . . more 'easy listening' in general . . . This does not exclude a proportion of more serious items . . . But these items will always form a minor element in the programme as a whole.[73]

Thus radio drama on the Light came to include a large number of thrillers and comedies. The detective play tended to have a happy ending, expressing confidence in a system of values that, though it had at times been destroyed, could yet be restored. As in the fairy story, the good were rewarded and wicked received their just deserts. However tangled the complex of events, a good fairy was always there to straighten them out at the end. One cannot avoid the impression that the world of the thriller was modelled more on wishful thinking than on any attempt to come to terms with reality. Indeed confrontation of this sort was positively avoided: any problem that might have disturbed the listener's placid enjoyment was skilfully side-stepped, excluded from the argument, or suppressed. Inner conflict, verbally expressed, was a rarity. Directed as it was to acoustic entertainment, the play generally made use of exciting, fast-moving events where an excess of activity together with appeals to the sentimentality of the audience would serve to conceal what might otherwise have led to conflict.

Comedy, with its rigidly defined limits, was open to greater variation in formal structure and choice of theme. Some comedies indeed – they might be called realistic comedies – even ventured into areas where the audience no longer received a pat solution. Incipient social criticism coincided with an assault on the untarnished world of the thriller. A more surrealistic variant of the genre invoked the workings of mysterious and unexplained forces in the everyday world without rationalising away the implicit threat. While the realistic comedy generally dispensed with the more specifically radio-inspired means of expression, the surrealistic form made full use of sound and music to achieve a vivid evocation of the transcendent and the occult.

With the exception of realistic comedy, the Light Programme radio play was characterised by the striking wealth of its 'happenings'. The listener was presented with protagonists busy in many fields at once. Outward activity was frequently a substitute for inner. Primacy of the material element, the *Stoff*, was perhaps the characteristic mark of radio drama on the Light, which over and above this, however, was often conducted in a day-to-day language of grinding monotony. Scarcely a sentence was spoken that revealed more sense than could be expressed in the bare conjunction of subject and predicate. What was said conveyed simple information: monofunctional utterance devoid of all semantic polyvalence. For whole passages, the language was the naked vehicle of the 'happening'. Despite this, it would be unjustifiable to consign the drama production of the Light without more ado to the realm of the trivial. A more nuanced judgement would have to take account of the BBC's efforts in the direction of more demanding plays aimed precisely at Light Programme audiences with a view to modifying the normal run of their expectations. Signs of this can be seen in the occasional production on the Light of plays by authors who otherwise wrote mainly for the Third.

The Home Service directed its programmes to the broad middle stratum of the population, its guideline in this – applicable also to the radio play – being a conscious and explicit reference to reality:

It [the Home Service] sets out to be not an exclusive but an inclusive programme – one which reflects as much as possible on the life of the community in which we live, and does what it can to satisfy the tastes and curiosities and mental and spiritual needs of the members of that community.[74]

Aimed, then, at the many and diverse needs of this 'broad middle section of the community', the Home Service overlapped 'to a certain extent with the Light Programme on one side and the Third Programme on the other'.[75] Its 'determinedly middle-brow standard'[76] called for a 'middlebrow radio play',[77] though this term should not necessarily be taken in a pejorative sense. In comparison with the two main forms of Light Programme drama, the Home Service revealed a notably wider spectrum, formally as well as thematically. It included comedy, social satire, self-critical mono- logue, political Utopias and 'fantasies', all of which had in common a critical undertone not drowned in an excess of action. Social institutions, marriage, the family, special events such as weddings and funerals, public bodies like the church, the universities, the forces, all were subjected to the same sort of critical appraisal.

Where the Light Programme was typified by the dominance of narrative material, the Home was distinguished by its predilection for the discussion of problems. Acts of interpersonal communication condemned to sterility were examined with an eye to the conflicts they conceal, and in the same way ethical and moral principles were tested out in particular situations to see if they still held. The Home Service radio play was marked not only by a disciplined restraint of narrative material in favour of verbal confrontation with problems, but also by its more honest answers to the questions posed. The element of fable and fantasy, restricted to the realm of palpable experience, was seldom used as a cosmetic evasion, the straightforward answer often being preferred, even here, to the ideology of the happy ending. Hesitation in the use of experiment can be seen in the whole gamut of Home Service productions; sound and music were employed as a semantic counterpart only when the strict reference to reality was loosened and freer formal structures took its place.

The Third Programme, founded in 1946, represented in every sense of the word a singular construct. Not only the audience but also the level to which it aspired set it off consciously from the other two Programmes. If the Light and the Home were designed for a mass public, the Third regarded itself as

a programme for minority audiences; that is to say, for those comparatively few people whose tastes, education, and mental habits enable them to derive enjoyment from closely attentive listening to essentially serious programmes.[78]

Openness of mind and receptivity should be the characteristics of the Third Programme listener. Plays, then, should be able to demand an audience

whose standards were aesthetic and academic, as opposed to domestic; an audience which would accept the morals of Hellas as a matter of course, the philosophy of Existentialism as a matter of interest, and the behaviour of the characters of Restoration Comedy as normally incidental to a historical period.[79]

It is not for nothing that American critics have liked to refer to the Third Programme as 'the deep freeze of British culture'.[80]

Although far fewer productions took place than on the Light and the Home, the radio play on the Third enjoyed a greater formal and thematic scope. The division of the repertoire, impracticable in any other Programme, into more conventional and more experimental works shows that the initiators of this Programme sought in practice to achieve the aesthetic norms they had themselves established. Thus radio drama on the Third fell into several different categories or groups. In the first instance, one can distinguish plays concerned with individual questions of social reality from those focused on personal relationships, plotting them in the various fragile stages of their rise and fall. Other plays concentrated entirely on the psychogram of the individual or on exploring new fields of semantic relevance in the *démontage* of language. Social criticism in the plays of the Third Programme differed from that on the Home in the stricter formal consciousness that employed production techniques in the service of the theme, forming the utterance itself to express the critical intention. Thus a refined linguistic structure was used to mark barriers and social distinctions, and the ensuing picture was thereby enriched in a way that would not have been possible in a production on the Home or the Light. Discussions of art and the artist grappled with the very norms on which the Third Programme itself was based.

Apart from the manifold expressions of social life, the main interest of Third Programme playwrights seems to have been the world of interpersonal relationships, the microcosm that, carefully examined, reveals forces determining the life of the social whole. Typical stages of approach and alienation were depicted, and the failure to communicate was not always set at the door of a defective environment: the parties themselves were not absolved from their own personal responsibility. A favourite theme of the Third Programme radio play was the isolated, utterly encapsulated individual. Cut adrift from all social bonds, this figure became the symbol either of metaphysical abandonment or of a more purely human loneliness, unable in either case to be touched by any alleviating impulse of society. The journey into an inner reality, into a world of desire and dream alienated to the point of unrecognisability, was achieved in dramatic forms to be found only on the Third. That the Programme had no real comedy of its own was less important, inasmuch as the comic element in its plays generally took the form of a subtle linguistic satire.

While the other two Programmes laid themselves open to criticism for the way in which they were working, a strict compliance with the dramatic laws of radio was taken for granted in the Third Programme. Characters and events reflected the awareness of radio as a dramatic mode. The play was never weighed down with material or suffocated by detail. Language, not action, dominated; language was, indeed, the showplace where the action happened. No other class of radio play could exhibit so nuanced a handling of speech. Whether it was the carefully chosen and skilfully controlled idiom of everyday or the language habits of a certain class, the diction of poetry or the sentence fragment cut loose from the rules of syntax, the verbal happening always took precedence over the external act. Third Programme playwrights were given freedom to exploit conventional forms right up to the limit of their viability, and at the same time to evolve new modes of dramatic presentation and put them to practical test.

With the Programme reform of 1970 and the division of the accepted triad into four, renamed Radios 1 to 4, the principle of the cultural pyramid, which till now had determined the content of radio drama, ceased to be binding. The ultimate criterion of Programme policy remained, however, the different needs of different social strata in the listening public. Qualitative distinctions are avoided in the sober numbering of the four Programmes, but this outward equality represents little innovation. In place of 'the principle of mixed programming . . . that of the specialised network, offering a continuous stream of one particular type of programme'[81] has been established. Radios 1 and 2 are devoted to light entertainment, Radios 3 and 4 to serious programmes of music and the spoken word. But the fear that this new system would destroy the traditional balance of broadcasting levels has proved unfounded. So far as drama is concerned, Radio 3 has shown itself to be the successor of the Third, Radio 4 of the Home. In the whole field of radio-play production very little, in fact, has changed: 'In quantity', one speaker remarked, 'we'll hardly notice the difference.'[82] Qualitatively, too, there is scarcely a noticeable break. The production of Radio 3 and Radio 4 embraces, as it did previously, adaptations, thrillers, comedies and experimental works. The decisive factor for the quality of the play is now no longer the Programme as such, but the time at which it is broadcast, this being calculated with the interests of a particular group of listeners in mind. Peter Porter testifies to the 'excellent programmes' on Radio 4.[83] All things considered, 'the general standard seems . . . much what it used to be'[84]; the only difference is that since 1970 'the whole spectrum from . . . lower middlebrow to . . . *avant garde*'[85] has been compressed into two Programmes. Proof enough that the BBC has not substantially altered its policy comes from the Corporation's Director of Programmes, Douglas Muggeridge, who, replying to a reader's letter in *The Observer*, affirms

that there has been no change in the BBC's policy over such important elements in the radio drama output (and no diminution of that output either, despite the current very real need for economy).[86]

One development that seemed to have serious consequences for the BBC and for the English radio play was the growth of commercial radio stations since 1973. However, the competitive struggle that they inaugurated and that is being conducted at the present time does not appear to have endangered the role of radio drama in Britain as 'a vehicle for a serious poetic exploration of the human mind'[87] and to have led to its decline, as it has in the United States, into an intermezzo between the ads.

The stipulation that broadcasts should correspond to the needs of the listener – itself a principle fundamental to the constitution of the BBC – has, over the years, given rise to a firm framework of theoretical attitudes and dramatic practices whose presence in the contours of the English radio play is unmistakable and whose resistance to change derives from the hard-and-fast demands or refusals into which public expectations have been crystallised. For a matter of decades research has been going on into listening patterns, with questionnaires being sent out to listeners of every class and age group; the results, formulated as clear parameters for majority- and minority-oriented plays, are passed on as guidelines to the author who is interested in achieving public success.[88]

Plays of the first category must possess 'a well-defined plot which unfolds to a climax',[89] the theoretical basis for this being the conviction that the radio play is a variant of 'the age-old human instinct *to tell a story*'.[90] Furthermore, the play must not offend against the principles of clarity and transparency of structure:

Obscurity masquerading as depth – or even perhaps that which, while being profound, is yet ostensibly unconcerned to reveal itself for what it is –; this, together with excessive length, or undue laboriousness of style, or indeed a learning that is worn too obviously, is, therefore . . . treated with disdain . . . The lighter a dramatic work appears to the listener . . . the better it is.[91]

Tension and 'dramatic' writing, with explicit reference to action-packed verbs,[92] are also features whose importance the would-be author is recommended not to overlook:

If you want to sell your first radio play, give it plenty of action. Do not let your characters stand in a bunch and just talk at each other. Bring in new people. Change the scene, vary the tempo, make things happen.[93]

In addition to this, the author must take care that the reality of his play corresponds in every detail to that of life. Events must be convincing, probable, authentic, even though they are to lead to the happy ending that at this level is indispensable: 'What they [the public] want is a naturalistic story, the conflict conventionally resolved with detection and exposure, a death or marriage, a victory or reconciliation.'[94] The drive for authenticity reveals itself above all in the detailed treatment of place and character. But the author must not forget, either, the correct reproduction of language habits, avoiding the twin pitfalls of vulgarity and of too stylised a poetic idiom.[95] Embarrassing or depressing themes are excluded. The three 'Red Lights along the would-be author's road' are, according to Val Gielgud, 'sex, politics and religion'.[96] Finally, the playwright is advised to exercise extreme caution in his use of ancillary sound; if he uses it at all, it must be with technical perfection.[97]

In the minority-oriented radio play the author has more room for creative probing and greater liberty in form and structure. If the BBC makes any stipulation at all, it is that of qualitative excellence. Clarity and overall intelligibility remain welcome assets, but stylistic and formal experiment within a single play are regarded as a legitimate expression of creative freedom. This, then, is the true home of the experimental radio play, in which the author can shake off the fetters of a universally optimistic world-view. Tolerance here of what is otherwise taboo is quite striking. Nor, of course, is the element of entertainment entirely missing; it generally emerges, however, from a nuanced handling of speech:

. . . the listener's pleasure in detecting the tell-tale word or expression, the false vowel sound which betrays the not-so-lofty origins of an otherwise faultlessly affected speaker; the misunderstandings which arise when two people from different social spheres simply fail to communicate – these are the chief sources of enjoyment . . . in the English radio play.[98]

The concentration on linguistic subtleties has resulted in the genesis of a poetic level quite peculiar to the dramatic form in question. Metaphor, imagery, the unspoken content of language has its place here too, but the principal area of interest is the 'unfolding of deep psychological levels of consciousness in the characters'.[99] The minority radio play also encourages the author to explore the possibilities of the medium: Louis MacNeice advises playwrights to think 'studio-minded',[100] to observe the laws of radio and benefit from the opportunities it offers. The only limitation here is that the play should not entirely preclude performance in other media. This is still regarded as a necessary precaution.

If one compares these two sets of mandatory guidelines, one is struck by the sheer range of the contrast between restrictions on the one hand and far-reaching liberties on the other. It would need, however, an individual analysis to show the actual extent to which an author has bowed to the rod of public taste or has made use of the freedoms granted.

(Translated from the German by J. T. Swann)

Notes

1. Richard Imison, 'Drama at the BBC', *Plays and Players*, **13**(3) (Dec. 1965), p. 9.
2. Donald McWhinnie, *The Art of Radio*. London 1959, p. 13.
3. Imison, op. cit., p. 9; see Martin Esslin, 'The mind as a stage', *Theatre Quarterly*, **1**(3) (July-Sept. 1971), p. 6.
4. Martin Esslin, 'Drama at the BBC', *Plays and Players*, **13**(5) (Feb. 1966), p. 65.
5. Wardle, 'Introduction', *New English Dramatists 12 : Radio Plays*. Harmondsworth 1968, p. 10.
6. Robert Collison, *Broadcasting in Britain*, National Book League Reader's Guides, Fourth Series, 9. Cambridge 1961, p. 6.
7. *British Broadcasting : A Bibliography 1958*. London 1958, pp.11–16; *British Broadcasting 1922-1972 : A Select Bibliography*. London 1972, pp. 26–30.
8. Bond, 'Hörspielproduktion in Deutschland und England', *Rundfunk und Fernsehen*, **14**(1) (1966), pp. 46–7.
9. For example Peter Black, *The Biggest Aspidistra in the World*. London 1972; John Snagge and Michael Barsley, *Those Vintage Years of Radio*. London 1972.
10. 'Radio writers', in James Vinson (ed.), *Contemporary Dramatists*. London and New York 1973, pp. 857–66; also 2nd ed., 1977, pp. 901–11.
11. Bond, op. cit., pp. 46–7.
12. *Das Hörspiel : Vergleichende Beschreibung und Analyse einer neuen Kunstform durchgeführt an amerikanischen, deutschen, englischen und französischen Texten*. Heidelberg 1963, p. 40.
13. McWhinnie, op. cit., pp. 14, 16.
14. 'Foreword', in MacNeice, *Persons from Porlock and Other Plays for Radio*. London 1969, p. 9.
15. 'Education and radio drama', *BBC Quarterly*, **7**(4) (Winter 1952-3), p. 202.

16. 'Drama : sound', *BBC Handbook 1955*. London 1955, p. 64.
17. Paulu, *British Broadcasting : Radio and Television in the United Kingdom*. Minneapolis 1956, p. 207.
18. 'Drama : sound', *BBC Handbook 1957*. London 1957, p. 78.
19. 'Drama : sound radio', *BBC Handbook 1960*. London 1960, p. 65.
20. 'The radio services', *BBC Handbook 1965*. London 1965, p. 52.
21. Imison, op. cit., p. 8.
22. 'Radio drama today', in BBC, *New Radio Drama*. London 1966, p. 7.
23. 'Das Hörspiel in England', in Norddeutscher Rundfunk, *Hörspiele im Sommer 1967*. N.p. n.d., p. 5; see *The BBC and the Arts*. London 1968, p. 21.
24. Imison, op. cit., p. 8.
25. *Sound and Television Broadcasting in Britain*, COI Reference Pamphlet 61. London 1969, p. 35.
26. 'The mind as a stage', op. cit., p. 6.
27. Esslin, 'Das Hörspiel in England', op. cit., p. 5n.
28. Imison, op. cit., p. 8.
29. Anon, '"Gold mine" of 40,000 scripts', *Ariel : BBC Staff Journal*, 20 Apr. 1973, p. 7.
30. Bond, op. cit., p. 48 (translation mine).
31. Manfred Erdmenger, 'Bibliographie des englischen Hörspiels', *Anglia*, **95** (3/4) (1977), pp. 454–69.
32. Bond, op. cit., p. 49.
33. Paul Ferris, 'Drama at the BBC', *Plays and Players*, **13**(4) (Jan. 1966), p. 51.
34. Esslin, 'Drama at the BBC', op. cit., p. 65.
35. Esslin, 'Das Hörspiel in England', op. cit., p. 4; Val Gielgud, *British Radio Drama 1922-1956*. London 1957, p. 17; Roy Walker, '"We'll hear a play . . . ": a note on broadcast drama since the war', *BBC Quarterly*, **8**(4) (Winter 1953-4), p. 225.
36. 'The early days: Val Gielgud, talking to Peter Roberts', *Plays and Players*, **13**(3) (Dec. 1965), p. 11.
37. *Ibid*.
38. 'Radio drama', *BBC Yearbook 1942*. London 1942, pp. 40–1.
39. 'Drama: sound', *BBC Handbook 1955*. London 1955, p. 64; see Val Gielgud, 'Policy and problems of broadcast drama', *BBC Quarterly*, **2**(1) (Apr. 1947), p. 19.
40. Roy Walker, 'Short measure', *The Listener*, **59**(1514) (3 Apr. 1958), p. 595; Ian Rodger, 'Our only national theatre', *The Listener*, **62**(1599) (19 Nov. 1959), p. 899.
41. Gielgud, *British Radio Drama 1922-1956*, p. 85.
42. Sewell Stokes, 'Radio drama as I hear it', *BBC Quarterly*, **5**(3) (Autumn 1950), p. 165.
43. Christopher Holme, 'Arbeitsbericht', in Deutsche Akademie der Darstellenden Künste/Hessischer Rundfunk, *Internationale Hörspieltagung Frankfurt 1968*. Frankfurt 1968, p. 300.
44. 'Drama: sound', *BBC Handbook 1955*. London 1955, p. 64-5.
45. 'Drama : sound radio', *BBC Handbook 1958*. London 1958, p. 85.
46. Imison, op. cit., p. 8.
47. Wardle, op. cit., p. 15.
48. Gielgud, *British Radio Drama 1922-1956*, p. 69.

49. *Ibid.*
50. Gero von Wilpert, *Sachwörterbuch der Literatur*. Stuttgart 1969, p. 257; Lutz Besch, 'Bemerkungen zum feature', *Rundfunk und Fernsehen*, 3(1) (1955), pp. 94-102; Alfred Andersch, 'Versuch über das Feature', *Rundfunk und Fernsehen*, 1(1) (1953), pp. 94-7; Holme, op. cit., p. 300.
51. 'Radio features', *BBC Yearbook 1948*. London 1948, pp. 77-8.
52. Quoted in Gielgud, *British Radio Drama 1922-1956*, p. 48.
53. Paulu, op. cit., p. 209.
54. *The Stuff of Radio*. London 1934, p. 26.
55. Esslin, 'Das Hörspiel in England', op. cit., p. 4.
56. Laurence Gilliam, 'The radio documentary in wartime', *BBC Yearbook 1945*. London 1945, p. 56.
57. 'Radio documentary', *BBC Yearbook 1942*. London 1942, p. 38.
58. 'Features department', *BBC Yearbook 1946*. London 1946, p. 67.
59. 'If I were Head of the Third Programme', *BBC Yearbook 1947*. London 1947, p. 23.
60. *Voices at Play*. London 1961, p.v.
61. Philip Hope-Wallace, 'Man of destiny', *The Listener*, 37(947) (20 Mar. 1947), p. 439.
62. Henry Reed, 'What the wireless can do for literature', *BBC Quarterly*, 3(4) (Jan. 1949), p. 219.
63. Hugh Ross Williamson, 'Reflections on radio features', *BBC Quarterly*, 6(3) (Autumn 1951), p. 157.
64. Black, op. cit., pp. 182-3.
65. 'Variety and light entertainment: sound', *BBC Handbook 1957*. London 1957, p. 82.
66. BBC, *Writing for the BBC*. 5th ed., London 1977, pp. 24-6.
67. Francis Williams, 'Public service broadcasting', *BBC Yearbook 1949*. London 1949, p. 10.
68. Paulu, op. cit., p. 143.
69. *Ibid*, p. 147.
70. For example D. A. N. Jones, 'What's the point?', *New Statesman*, 71(1826) (11 Mar. 1966), pp. 349-50.
71. BBC, *Broadcasting in the Seventies*. London 1969, pp. 2-3, 6-7.
72. 'The Light Programme', *BBC Yearbook 1947*. London 1947, p. 36.
73. 'The Light Programme', *BBC Yearbook 1946*. London 1946, p. 54.
74. 'The Home Service', *BBC Yearbook 1946*. London 1946, p. 51.
75. 'Sound broadcasting services: Home Service', *BBC Handbook 1959*. London 1959, pp. 33-4.
76. Val Gielgud, '"No mood to bother with the radio play?"', *BBC Yearbook 1945*. London 1945, p. 54.
77. N. P. Furbank, 'Middlebrow suspense', *The Listener*, 70(1810) (5 Dec. 1963), p. 957.
78. 'Sound broadcasting services: Third Programme', *BBC Handbook 1959*. London 1959, p. 34.
79. Gielgud, *British Radio Drama 1922-1956*, p. 185.
80. Quoted in Harman Grisewood, 'On leaving the Third Programme: some personal reflections', *BBC Quarterly*, 8(1) (Spring 1953), p. 14.
81. BBC, *Broadcasting in the Seventies*, p. 3.
82. Jeremy Rundall, 'Radio drama', *Plays and Players*, 17(6) (Mar. 1970), p. 14.

83. 'Playlets', *New Statesman*, **79**(2031) (13 Feb. 1970), p. 228.

84. David Wade, 'Radio drama', *Plays and Players*, **17**(10) (July 1970), p. 12.

85. Sean Day-Lewis, 'Radio drama', *Plays and Players*, **18**(6) (Mar. 1971), p. 66.

86. 'Radio drama defended', *The Observer*, 29 Feb. 1976, p. 12.

87. Esslin, 'The mind as a stage', op. cit., p. 11.

88. BBC, *Writing for the BBC*, pp. 3-4.

89. Dick Kevin, *Radio Play Writing*. London 1947, p. 4.

90. Val Gielgud, *The Right Way to Radio Playwriting*. Kingswood, Surrey 1948, p. 20.

91. Esslin, 'Das Hörspiel in England', op. cit. p. 4 (translation mine).

92. Howard Thomas, *How to Write for Broadcasting*. London 1940, p. 73.

93. *Ibid*, pp. 87-8.

94. Jones, op. cit., p. 349.

95. Janet Dunbar, *Writing for Radio*. London 1954, p. 24; Thomas, op. cit., p. 69.

96. *The Right Way to Radio Playwriting*, p. 23.

97. Val Gielgud (ed.), 'Foreword to authors', *Radio Theatre*. London 1946, pp. xii-xiii.

98. Esslin, 'Das Hörspiel in England', op. cit., p. 5 (translation mine).

99. *Ibid*.

100. 'General introduction', *The Dark Tower and Other Radio Scripts*. London 1947, p. 17.

Chapter 4
The nature of radio drama

Frances Gray

And softly my little space begins to throb again. You may say it is all in my head, and indeed sometimes it seems to me that I am in a head . . . But thence to conclude that the head is mine, no, never. A kind of air circulates . . . and when all goes still I hear it beating against the walls and being beaten back by them. And then somewhere in midspace other waves, other onslaughts, gather and break, whence I suppose the faint sound of aerial surf that is my silence.

(Samuel Beckett, *Malone Dies*)

'To begin at the beginning: It is spring . . .'[1] To many listeners, this *is* radio drama; for them, understandably, *Under Milk Wood* (1954) represents a perfection to which all future radio dramatists should refer and aspire. This is an attitude that the paucity of critical work on radio has served to reinforce by making *Under Milk Wood* a legend as well as a play, one of the few pieces for radio that everyone knows and has read about. But to stop the discussion at this particular point of perfection is like analysing the nature of film with *Citizen Kane* as the only possible criterion of quality. Films, and life, have moved on since then; and those opening words from Llareggub ushered in not so much the beginning of radio drama as what might be termed the end of the beginning. The play is the fruit of nearly thirty years' accumulated experience of the medium: experience of the tools it provides and of their strengths and limitations; and experience of using them in one kind of way, a way dictated as much by the *zeitgeist* of the first half of this century as by the exigencies of tape and microphone, and a way that, while still valid, is now a way to be consciously chosen rather than the only one known.

As I have said, there are few books on the subject of radio drama, and it might be as well to clarify the intentions of this chapter. It does not propose to deal with the technical aspects of radio as such, attempting only to cover matters of technical necessity as they impinge on the playwright rather than the engineer. Nor will it examine the role of the BBC, although this has been crucial in shaping radio drama as we know it, from the question of subject-matter to the listening-time and channel that dictate the nature of the audience. It seeks instead to isolate the factors that make the experience of radio unique, and to look at the work of writers of varying stature and merit who have one thing in common – a determination to shape and control that unique experience.

Of the few works of radio scholarship so far produced, many reiterate a point that may itself explain the paucity of their number: the fact that the printed page cannot do full justice to a radio work, that the listener, when forced to be a reader, finds the mind's ear inadequate to the voices and music and silence of the realised text and has to content himself with the barest of bones. I would like to open this chapter with a more optimistic thought. I would like to invite the reader – who, after all, has probably tried mentally to stage a few productions, otherwise he or she wouldn't be reading this – to consider the major advantage of studying radio drama: he carries the stage around with him.

A box set stands on a proscenium-arch stage. It represents the Library at Styles where the Body was found. The criminal is discovered; he is led offstage by Hercule Poirot to, presumably, a police station, from which he will subsequently go to court, to prison and, in the tradition of the British Retributive Thriller, to the gallows, after which his progress ceases to interest author or audience. Now all of these are in some sort of relationship to the onstage action: firstly, a spatial one – from the Library we deduce a country house, a village, and ultimately England; secondly, what we might call a reality relationship – in assenting to the physical reality of that Library, we are also, temporarily, assenting to the reality of the Law, the judiciary and the class system. We also acknowledge this reality at the expense of other possibilities. We know that no god will descend on a cloud to reverse a human decision and that no character will vanish into the air and prove a dream; there will be no demon king and no good fairy.

When an Elizabethan actor played Faustus, he was operating in terms of a different reality. His stage was sometimes Rome, sometimes Wittenberg, and at the end of the play he went to a visible Hell. His audience assented not only to the story of one man but to the nature of the universe summed up by the physical shape of the stage, to a God in his Heaven and a Devil in his Hell, and to the possibility of living commerce between them. The power of that physical image was such that what it represented could even be questioned or undermined, as it is in *Dr Faustus*, while still keeping the received world-picture steadily in the mind of the audience.

Both the Elizabethan and the proscenium-arch stages are pictures of the spiritual world of their audience and their playwrights. The stage of radio is darkness and silence, the darkness of the listener's skull. On it the dramatist can bring anyone or anything without the trouble and expense of a scenic artist. This is the first stage that most of us encounter, the stage of the bedtime story on which we create, with assistance, an alternative reality. The process of building it is simple; the words are spoken, and we become designers, producers, scene shifters, and the theatre itself. A cosmic traveller not unlike Faustus analysed the dual role of the mind in *Paradise Lost*:

The mind is its own place, and in itself
Can make a Heaven of Hell, a Hell of Heaven. (I, 254–5)

The inside of the head, in other words, is both the agent that creates the exact image from the words provided, and the place in which that image performs. Llareggub is inside our heads; we build it to specifications:

To begin at the beginning:
It is spring, moonless night in the small town, starless and bible-black . . .[2]

This is a very precise invocation. Something is going to begin; therefore we may infer that it will have shape and structure, a beginning, a middle and an end. And that beginning, although put into the mouth of the First Voice, is not put into the first person, but into the anonymous infinitive. Who, then, is to make that beginning? Not the First Voice alone; nor the listener, although the listener will be addressed, given orders to come close and to listen. This opening establishes the radio play as an act of co-operation between speaker and listener. Gradually, we are told what to construct on the stage of the skull. It is spring; this arouses a mass of associations, quickly modified by 'moonless night' – now we have an exact sense of time, which is instantly followed by one of place with the reference to 'the small town'. By now, too, the rhythm of the voice will have told us that this small town is in Wales and nowhere else. 'Starless' intensifies the depth of that night, preparing us to be taken into the very dreams of the characters, and 'bible-black' suggests one of the forces that circumscribe their waking lives. Dylan Thomas may indulge in verbal pyrotechnics in the body of the play, but not until he is sure of his audience, who first have to create their own town in which to hear them.

But to begin at the beginning: this sure-footed expository economy is the result of a developing tradition of radio whose roots are in the 1920s. To go back to, say, the early experiments of Tyrone Guthrie is to see radio embark on its voyage of self-discovery, to see the first figures move on the dark and silent stage. Guthrie rapidly established two major facts about the medium, facts that are closely related. The first is the sheer flexibility of the sound stage. It can create Ancient Greece or the planet Mars simply by mentioning them, and the listener can be transported from one to the other in seconds. It can move forwards or backwards in time. We can look at a character's past or future – we need only to be told which, in words or by the use of a sound signifying this temporal shift; the microphone eliminates the need for elaborate make-up or transformation scenes. In his story of a young clergyman drowning on his way to a mission in China, *These Flowers Are Not for You to Pick* (1930), Guthrie moves from present

to recent past and from childhood to the present, just as he shifts from
the sea to the nursery and from a moonlit lake to a Belfast parish,
simply by, as he puts it in his Introduction, providing

the listener with the material to create his own décor. For the 'Robbers' Island'
scene, for instance, I have indicated that it is evening, that there are trees on
the little island; a glassy lake, shadows, reflections of trees, birds, and sunset,
two people in a little row-boat, the first star. The detail of this picture, its
composition, colouring, the stress laid on this feature and on that, becomes a
matter of individual selection.[3]

The willingness of the audience to participate in a creative act is largely
owing to the second major fact about radio – its intimacy. Like a
bedtime story, it whispers in our ear. Without visual distractions the
smallest subtleties of the voice become apparent and seize the
imagination; a snatch of song or the rustle of leaves takes on a
significance impossible in the theatre or on film. As soon as we hear a
word in a radio play, we are close to the experience it signifies; in fact
the sound is literally inside us. To submit to this kind of invasion, to
allow another's picture of the universe to enter and undermine our
own, is to become vulnerable in a way we do not when we watch a film
or a play, where the alien world is demonstrably outside. The courage
demanded by our closeness to the playwright's world and characters –
to put our own internal vision of reality temporarily, but totally, aside
– is perhaps only bearable in view of the permission given, in Guthrie's
phrase, to create our 'own particular brand of moonshine'.[4]

These Flowers Are Not for You to Pick takes us directly into the
mind of the hero at his point of crisis. The sound of waves establishes
his plight in the water, and the closeness of his voice, nearer than any
other character, means that we will see what he sees. The sense of
intimacy is reinforced by the pattern of the play. Guthrie grasped that
radio does not move in space but almost wholly in time, even though it
can, by sounds and descriptions, give the illusion of place, and even
though voices can be heard from near and far, depending on their
relationship to the microphone, to give the impression of depth. It
cannot give us a precise picture of characters grouped in a room – one
reason why Chekhov's plays, which often convey complex emotional
undercurrents through spatial relationships between characters, rarely
succeed on radio. Stereo has made some changes in this respect, but
spatial subtleties are still rare. Radio's true element is rhythm. Guthrie
imposes order on Edward's chaotic experience by a simple rhythmic
pattern; although he makes jumps in time and space, the action moves
all the time towards a specific goal. We are taken through each stage of
Edward's development – childhood, school, first love, vocation. This
development and its relationship to the framework of the story,
Edward's struggle in the waves, is made coherent by a pattern: each
stage in his life is marked by a scene culminating in a decision, which is
always 'no', spoken with increasing intensity as problems grow more

painful and complex, until the final step, the 'yes' that sends him out to China to die. The 'yes' is inevitable, but the pattern does not need hours of conventional exposition to demonstrate it. The imagery too is carefully orchestrated so that the play is a shapely whole rather than a linear progression. Two things are kept in our consciousness throughout – a pair of spectacles, which symbolise for the hero his own incompetence and inadequacy, and water – the sea in which he is drowning and the lake on which he declares his love. The spectacles finally sink, uniting the two symbols, and Edward loses the ridiculous dimension of his being with them; at the end, we see him as a man of true integrity.

Guthrie found it necessary to preface his plays with an announcement. A speech about Edward's plight sets the scene for *These Flowers Are Not for You to Pick*; in *Matrimonial News* (1928) he informs the listener:

What follows is supposed to be happening in the mind of Miss Florence Kippings, – who is sitting alone in a cheap restaurant in the Strand in London. The time is about a quarter to twelve, midday. She has ordered a cup of coffee . . . Remember, you are overhearing her thoughts – she is alone . . .[5]

He was perhaps aware of the possible reluctance of an early listener to commit himself so closely to the creative act of radio without those reassurances implicit in words like 'supposed to be'. Nor could he rely on a trained ear ready to pick up the information that Edward was struggling in the sea merely from the sound of the waves; although Guthrie had no doubt of the *emotional* effect of the sound of water, he had to make painful efforts to clarify the actual physical picture. But by 1942 Louis MacNeice took for granted an audience sitting at home ready to be taken into the mind of the hero in *Christopher Columbus*:

DOUBT: No, it cannot be done, it cannot be done.
                 Here on the shore of the final sea
                 Our windows open on unreality,
                 The bitter rubric of the sinking sun -
                 Ne plus ultra. This is the Western edge
                 Of the established world, the ocean wall
                 Beyond which none may pass. To pass
                 Would lead to nothing at all. . . .

FAITH CHORUS: West of Europe lies a world
                 Never heard of, never seen,
                 But the sails that still are furled
                 Soon shall reach a new demesne.
                 All the things that might have been -
                 When we cross the Western Sea,
                 All those things shall be, shall be.[6]

Confident that he can take the listener directly into the mind of a complex man, MacNeice uses the device of splitting a mind into different voices, a device only radio can exploit without difficulties of staging. He imparts through them a considerable quantity of information, sure that the by-now-sophisticated radio ear will process it: first, that the play is not about geographical discovery alone but about faith, about the conflict between two world-pictures, the flat earth and the round, and their concomitant religious beliefs; second, that the land to the west means to Columbus the resolution of countless frustrations and the fulfilment of dreams. Columbus is a myth-maker as well as a sailor; and from the pat rhymes we discern that this is a well-worn treadmill of thought, the hundredth repetition of arguments that can only be resolved by action.

MacNeice can also impart information by sound alone; in the developing iconography of the medium, a guitar is enough to tell us that we are in Spain. He seldom wastes words on the air, despite the poetic cast of his plays. As he points out in the Introduction to *Christopher Columbus*, a radio writer sometimes has to abandon 'literary' techniques of fine writing, but also gains enormously from the very *spokenness* of his words, since a voice can colour a cliché just as certain contexts can invest cheap music with profound significance. In fact, the writer 'can count on his words regaining those literary virtues which literature itself has lost since it has been divorced from the voice'.[7]

MacNeice vividly articulates his own development in the prefaces to his published radio plays, a development that could serve as a paradigm of the history of radio drama in the 1940s. His best play, *The Dark Tower* (1946), shows the medium turning to its roots, the tale told in the dark, a tale of magic quests and dragons. It uses all the resources discovered over the previous two decades – acoustic variety (notably in the desert scenes, which have a dead acoustic conveying a stuffy dryness), evocative sounds (such as the hero's lonely heartbeat as he finds himself alone with his awful task), poetry, and music that feeds the imagination rather than just sounds pleasant. MacNeice's attitude to these resources is embodied in a speech by the Soak that amounts to a declaration of faith in their strength:

All right, all right;
If you won't come to the Tavern, the Tavern must come to you.
Ho there, music!
The orchestra strikes up raggedly – continuing while he speaks.
That's the idea. Music does wonders, young man.
Music can build a palace, let alone a pub.
Come on, you masons of the Muses, swing it,
Fling me up four walls. Now, now, don't drop your tempo;
Easy with those hods. All right; four walls.
Now benches – tables – No! No doors or windows.
What drunk wants daylight? But you've left out the bar.
Come on – 'Cellos! Percussion! All of you! A bar![8].

However, despite the undoubted *brio* of passages like this, there is also a slight air of self-satisfaction about them, with something a shade proprietorial in phrases like 'masons of the Muses', as if the Muses had indeed joined the BBC club and ensured that radio drama had no further to go. In fact, new territory remained to be charted, worlds that, paradoxically, MacNeice and writers like him failed to discover because of their very skill.

The Dark Tower creates a whole world on the sound stage. Roland lives for us and we willingly build up his environment in our minds. But the evidence we have for the existence of that environment is, quite literally, hearsay – and, as the law has always known, hearsay evidence is notoriously unreliable. A few sounds enter the ear: the words 'the sea'. At once we see the sea, but the words that have evoked that image are gone; they have entered the head and there is no external evidence that they ever existed. When MacNeice puts Roland on a boat, he has to keep him afloat by constantly supporting our imagination:

ROLAND: The sea today is drunken marble.
NEAERA: The sea today is silver stallions.
ROLAND: The sea today is – Tell me, steward:
            Where's all this floating seaweed come from?
STEWARD: I imagine, sir – forgive me mentioning it –
            That we are approaching land.
ROLAND: Land!
STEWARD: Yes, sir – but *you* won't be landing of course.
            The best people never land, sir.
ROLAND: No? . . . (*to himself, fatalistically*) I suppose not.[9]

The passage does, of course, advance the plot and illuminate character, but fundamentally it is doing the same job as the sound of a throbbing tractor engine or repeated allusions to the landscape in *The Archers* – it is keeping before our inner eye a reality that it wants us to accept as consistent; it is stopping the sea from disappearing. In less accomplished hands, the barrage of motiveless sound effects and pointless reminders of location can be vaguely reminiscent of the last legionnaire in *Beau Geste* firing from behind a row of dead comrades to suggest vast reinforcements. MacNeice succeeds brilliantly, but he is working against the bias of the medium in trying to impose on sound the same consistency of perception that vision has – a film of *The Dark Tower* could keep the sea before us as long as the director wished it to be there.

The Dark Tower is fantasy – it contains dragons and magic rings and a heroic quest; it is also allegory, in that the desert and the dragon symbolise certain spiritual states. Things appear and disappear, by magic and music – the Tower itself, for instance, comes to vivid life 'like a wart coming out of the ground',[10] aided by Britten's 'Tower' theme; and there is a suggestion that this can happen only when the self-doubting Roland has come to believe in it and in his ability to destroy it. But although the story contains many elements that are not literally true, the reality it presents is a consistent one. Roland may doubt many things, but the listener never doubts Roland's world – we are convinced, as the Tower rises out of the desert earth, that it is real and that he is not deceiving himself. The whole fantasy has a solidity and a reality that MacNeice establishes against all the radio odds; it moves in Euclidean space.

MacNeice described the Browning poem that inspired his play as having 'the solidity of a dream',[11] and commented several times, especially in *Varieties of Parable* (1965), on the links between dream and allegory. This speaks volumes not only about his attitude to the poem, and hence his play, but also about his attitude to dreams – as if they, too, moved in Euclidean space. An actual dream rarely has this consistency, although an account of a dream, an attempt to convey its quality to a listener, might have some kind of order imposed upon it. C. G. Jung, in an essay roughly contemporary with *The Dark Tower*, prefigured the way in which the second half of the twentieth century has, on the whole, seen the world of dreams, and perhaps, in doing so, provided a way of looking at and understanding the hearsay world of radio:

To inquire into the *substance* of what has been observed is possible in natural science only where there is an Archimedean point outside. For the psyche, no such outside standpoint exists – only the psyche can observe the psyche . . . The honest investigator will piously refrain from meddling with questions of substance . . . he will then be in a position to appreciate the phenomenological standpoint of modern psychology.[12]

MacNeice, in providing a consistent world for *The Dark Tower*, is attempting to provide such an Archimedean point. His fairy-tale world is rather like that of Perrault; people are placed in magic situations and have magic help and magic enemies, but the way in which they behave is the way in which, on the surface, real people behave. Roland has to choose between his girl and his quest; Cinderella stays too long at the ball: our everyday imagination is supported during the fantasy. (The same might be said of Francis Dillon's appealing radio fairy tales.) But both Perrault and MacNeice were polishing and making coherent dreams that, in their original, primitive form, had a rather different flavour. In the Grimm version of the Cinderella story, a version closer to its roots, irrational things happen; life is not consistent, reality changes; the Ugly Sisters dance minuets at the ball and go home to mutilate their feet to fit the slipper; birds peck out their eyes; Cinderella's mother speaks to her in the form of a tree. Here we have no Archimedean point; we have simply to accept what we hear, even if our picture of reality is made to shift and change. Here we are closer to the world of dreams – and to the world of radio unmitigated by the careful guiding hand of a MacNeice or a Guthrie. And here too we are perhaps closer to a world-picture for the second half of our century.

As I said before, a stage is the reflection of the universe of its time. The Second World War changed the received view of the universe; it publicly split the atom and exploded the ordered world of Euclidean space; it proved that man could, suddenly and inexplicably, descend to the moral level of Vlad the Impaler. The relativistic universe became a part of the popular imagination, just as the three-layer world of Heaven, Middle-Earth and Hell had been part of the psychic equipment of every medieval peasant. Science fiction boomed in the 1940s; and in the 1950s the Theatre of the Absurd came to Britain. Suddenly, radio's major weakness, its failure to present a consistent reality, became a major strength.

This change can be best understood by examining a radio play of the 1970s that takes for granted the relativistic world-picture and the ability of radio to depict it. Like *The Dark Tower*, Angela Carter's *Vampirella* (1976) draws on myth and folk tale. It does not, however, pretend that these elements are part of an apprehensible world; rather it plays a phenomenological game with its listeners, presenting us with a giddy series of possible realities. The plot suggests a simple confrontation between them: Dracula's daughter meets a young subaltern on a cycling tour in the Carpathians. But the play's disturbing little prologue implies that it is about links rather than confrontation:

COUNTESS VAMPIRELLA: Can a bird sing only the song it knows or can it learn a new song . . .
HERO: . . . said the lovely, lonely lady vampire, running the elegant scalpel of her fingernails along the bars of the cage in which her pet bird sang.[13]

There is a tension set up from these first moments. The content of Vampirella's speech suggests that people on all planes of reality – including vampires – are confined to being what they are. The fact that she and the hero share a sentence indicates that they can meet and make a difference to each other. Dracula's opening words,

Endlessly, I attend my own obsequies; softly, enormously, across all my funerals, my fatal shadow rises again,

seem to fix us securely in the world of myth, a world of stakes through the heart and the virgin boy on the virgin stallion who alone can track down the vampire to its grave. The next sound is that of bicycle wheels, identified for the listener and given their full symbolic value by the prosaic hero:

The North West Frontier, far more barren, far more inimical . . . damn' deserts never scared me so . . . to ride a bicycle is in itself some protection against superstitious fears since the bicycle is the product of pure reason applied to motion . . .

Even as he does so, however, we are simultaneously informed by his *naiveté* and his historical context that here indeed is a virgin riding a virgin velocipede, the latest thing on two wheels – in short, that he is potential myth himself. The play explores the attempts of reality and myth to come to terms with each other. The hero sensibly offers his beloved vampire-countess a context in which to be loved; he wants to take her to Vienna – where presumably Freud, who destroyed one lot of myths only to set up another, would psychoanalyse her out of existence after a dentist had fixed the fangs that deter the hero from taking her straight home to Mother. She claims that she cannot exist in a context of reality at all:

I am not a demon, for a demon is incorporeal; not a phantom, for phantoms are intangible. I have a shape; it is my own shape, but I am not alive, and so I cannot die. I need your life to sustain this physical show, myself.

Only on radio can this kind of non-being be given a body without some kind of filmic illusion falsifying its nature; only on radio can the conflict between the everyday world and the dream world be expressed so effectively as to form the theme of an entire play and to make the games Carter plays with existence not only possible but central.

Vampirella explores Einstein's space, which 'is no longer the stage in which the drama of physics is performed: it is itself one of the performers'.[14] Carter's combination of myth and history creates a whole new dimension in which it is possible for them to mix. She uses figures from various points in the past – Elizabeth Bathory, Henri Blot the necrophile, Sawney Beane the cannibal – all of whom flaunt their own improbability at us and become part of the legendary structure surrounding Castle Dracula. Some of them, like Beane's devastatingly respectable relict, now Vampirella's governess, have a part to play; others find their way in simply as analogies, like Henri Blot – but this does not stop him from discussing himself at length. All the characters, whether they affect the action or not, present themselves largely through extended soliloquy; there is little dialogue in the conventional sense, but rather a series of narratives occasionally cutting into one another. The hero tells his story in the past tense, though sometimes it is brought alive into the present, with described characters speaking. Blot tells his story, and his courtroom drama is enacted before our ears; but he has no physical or spatial relationship with anyone else in the main narrative. We are the only consistent audience; our consciousness is the one fact that remains constant throughout. What is remarkable is that we do not miss what we tend to think of as the very stuff of drama: confrontation scenes in which characters act and interact, and in which they touch and change one another. Here every character stands in his or her personal space. Listening to the play is like being present at a trial; evidence is brought before us, and the court is the only place in which those characters and those circumstances could ever coincide. What is on trial is reality, and at the end it proves totally inextricable from myth: the hero spends the night with his vampire-love and kills her by his purity and reason. Then:

HERO: So I sped through the purged and rational splendours of the morning; but when I arrived at Bucharest, I learned of the assassination at

Sarajevo and returned to England immediately, to rejoin my regiment.
Drumbeats. Above, the Count's dreadful posthumous chuckle.

COUNT: The shadow of the Fatal Count rises over every bloody battlefield. Everywhere, I am struck down; everywhere, I celebrate my perennial resurrection.

It is no coincidence that the play is set at the time when our conception of the universe began to change, when the face of Europe became unrecognisable, and when the disciplines of physics and psychiatry began their assault on the old world-picture. And radio is perhaps the only medium that could fully articulate these changes.

If *Vampirella* works as an entertaining play as well as an intellectual game, this is largely owing to its power in conveying sense impressions that bring the action alive. It gives us vivid pictures of the castle bathed in moonlight, and puts over the unique taste of human flesh as Sawney Beane praises the delights of a crisply roasted aristocrat. But all these impressions are conveyed through the narrators; they are second-hand hearsay. This is the great radio paradox: that it is, on the one hand, a deeply sensual medium – Marshall McLuhan found this sensuality its most distinctive feature:

If we sit and talk in a dark room, words suddenly acquire new meanings and different textures. They become richer, even, than architecture . . . All those gestural qualities that the printed page strips from language come back in the dark, and on the radio. Given only the *sound* of a play, we have to fill in *all* of the senses, not just the sight of the action.[15]

On the other hand, it deals with experiences having no parallel in reality at all, as in one of *The Goon Shows*:

BLOODNOK: Eccles, stand on my shoulders and pull me up.
ECCLES: I'd like to see them do this on television.[16]

One might term this the sensuality of the physically impossible. This essential radio contradiction has never been more creatively explored than by the Goons.

It is interesting to note the difference in ethos between *Vampirella* and *The Dark Tower*. There is about MacNeice's work a kind of 'literary' flavour that is not merely a function of his poetic talent. His play is technically sophisticated and knows it; it marries poetry with sound and is full of its own experimental self. Beside it, Carter's play seems strangely casual about its medium. The effects are there – the strange music made by the bars of the lark's cage, the leaps in time and space – but we are also aware that they are there simply because they are needed and that the plainest of techniques will suffice where they are all that Carter needs. Much of the play sounds as if she has wandered among her characters with a cassette recorder; the simplicity serves to show up the extraordinary nature of the material, rather as a hand-held camera can add impact to film by its very crudity.

There is no attempt to compensate for the lack of visual stimulus by giving the ear a feast of imagery – a tendency certainly apparent in some of the verse dramas of the 1930s and 1940s.

This casualness owes a great deal to the liberation of radio through comedy, of which the Goons represent the zenith. Although radio techniques had been fully explored by the time they were working, it took *The Goon Show* to banish the slightly reverential air that hung about them. The Goons carried to its logical conclusion a tendency clearly present in shows such as *ITMA* and *Take It From Here*, in fact a style common to all comics whose art is grounded in the music hall. As Brecht knew, the realistic theatre and the variety artist are separated by what he called the alienation effect, the awareness of the theatricality and artifice of the act of performance and the acknowledgement of it to the audience – like Archie Rice's admonition in Osborne's *The Entertainer*, 'Don't clap too hard, it's a very old building.' With the Goons, this awareness manifested itself in complex ways. They made jokes about the audience and the script of the kind we are familiar with in *The Morecambe and Wise Show*, and allusions to the quality of the humour and the nature of the ending typical of performers like Frankie Howerd. But there are also jokes that are more specifically radiophonic; the iconography of the medium is ruthlessly sent up. The tramp of marching feet and the sound of soldiers whistling, which has provided 'atmosphere' for every dramatised radio war since D. G. Bridson's *The March of the '45* (1936), features in a story about Roman legions – who, however, whistle *Lili Marlene*; a frenzied medley of sea shanties is topped by the words, 'and so we joined the army'; Big Ben establishes London at midnight – but after the build-up chimes, the hour chime itself is replaced by an impotent little plink. This kind of parody makes possible a more casual use of sound techniques by making it clear that they *are* only techniques; it takes the tools out of the hands of the 'masons of the Muses' and puts them on the shop floor.

This is true too of radio's relationship with physical reality. The Goons made its ambiguity into a major strength. Instead of constantly supporting the imagination, they controlled it, let it range free, reined it in, showed it they had been fooling all along. Their world shifts and changes. Objects appear when needed for a quick laugh:

DR LONDONGLE: Silence – don't move, any of you, or I'll shoot.
SEAGOON: Fool – put down that tin of potted shrimps.
DR LONDONGLE: And starve to death? Never.[17]

They disappear with equal speed, for in this world nothing is certain, not even the body itself. 'How dare you come in here when I'm changing me knees?' snaps a Colosseum gladiator.[18] 'Min, stop wallpapering my trousers while I'm straining with the trowel', says Crun.[19] The experiences conveyed by these remarks might well be termed sensuous, even though they do not refer to the world of nervous sensation precisely as we know it.

The Goons triumphantly established the reality of nothingness, the positive impact of the uncertain. Their relationship with the ear has been taken up by countless radio writers, and we are now used to having our imagination controlled rather than supported, to having our expectations pandered to and also betrayed – sometimes in the same broadcast. Donald McWhinnie has written of the ear's expectations and of how false they can be:

In the production of Walter de la Mare's *The Return*, the sound of the tiny weir by the churchyard, poetically evoked by the text, was rendered by a recording of the Zambesi Falls, which corresponded exactly to the imaginative conception.[20]

Many excellent plays still make use of sound in this way. They establish a code with the ear and send all their messages in it; the soft roar of water indicates 'tiny weir' in this iconography and the listener gets along very nicely imagining it. One wonders whether the Archers' tractor might not be a Rolls-Royce; but as long as the words confirm its tractorness, it will do its job anyway. Goon logic, however, demanded that the relationship between ear, tiny weir and Zambesi Falls be explored. We can see this logic at work in the plays of many young radio writers today. Bo' Rider, hero of Ian Dougall's radiophonic hymn to the Old West, *Garrison Halibut* (1977), describes his ride for the Pony Express to appropriate music:

Ah approached the ridge, feelin' that sumt'n special wus imminent. *(Pause)* An' it sho' was. *(Music gathers momentum)* Befo' ma eyes lay the lowlands o' Nebraska *(Orchestra in full flight)* rich, fertile plains fer as far as the eye could see, fields o' golden corn. Bronzed, laughin' homesteaders' sons . . . Oh, we rode thru' towns ah'd only read the names of in books, over mountain passes high as the sky. *(Pause. He says, louder)* Over mountain passes as high as the sky! *(Orchestra hurriedly switches to appropriate music).*[21]

Dougall's orchestra is a fully living presence, complaining about the food, producing children, getting bored with the journey, and eventually going home. Similarly a signpost performs the kind of iconographic role it would have in a film, indicating to us and the hero where he is going; it becomes a comic role when translated into the logical radio equivalent, speaking information such as 'Garrison Halibut, forty-seven miles' – but once it can speak there is every reason for it to develop as a character and discuss its feelings about its circumscribed role:

SIGNPOST: *(on verge of tears)* No one thinks of me. Passes me by! I've got a lot to offer, you know?
RIDER: Sho' yu' have, sho' thing.
SIGNPOST: Oh yes, a lot to offer. T . . . tokyo, 3128 miles. P . . . p . . . paris, 5250 miles. N . . . New Y . . . York *(bursting into tears)*

The ability to negotiate the line between fulfilling and confounding the listener's expectations can lead to vivid experiences of alienation for the receptive ear. Stephen Davis's *The Dissolution of Marcus Fleishman* (1976) begins by setting up expectations. We know from the outset that the narrator is dead. 'Things have not been easy for Zelda since I died',[22] he tells us, and we are prepared to accept his reminiscences of the concentration camp in which he was killed as remembrances in tranquillity. Then we learn a fact that the blindness of the medium has hitherto concealed: Fleishman is alive in a new incarnation – he is a monkey and is being vivisected in a laboratory. We have allowed ourselves to accept cruelty easily, and our response to the concentration camp in the past has to be reassessed.

It is perhaps clear from the plays just discussed that radio provides what is in many ways a natural home for the Theatre of the Absurd – more natural, in fact, than the theatre for which writers like Ionesco, Adamov and Mrozek actually wrote. It has become a commonplace that writers who attempted, as Sartre and Camus did, to show a universe without logic using a box set as consistent with nineteenth-century realities as anything by Pinero were being illogical. But even plays such as Ionesco's *Rhinoceros* and *The Chairs* are forced, once clothed in stage flesh, to make all manner of tacit pronouncements simply because physical circumstances force them to. When we *see* the old couple in *The Chairs* arranging rows and rows of empty chairs, we know them to be empty; we have, in the theatre, to make the judgement that they are hallucinating; there is no question that *we* might be. The director of *Rhinoceros* has to decide whether the characters really are turning into animals or whether they merely think they are; he cannot leave the matter open, cannot be ambiguous. A stage playwright, in fact, can postulate any number of realities, but the onstage presence of props and costumes and actors forbids him from implying that reality is not consistent. Radio's reality is never consistent; it is perfectly adapted to the portrayal of an absurd universe. And the theatre of the skull does not display those little signs that twinkle so comfortingly in the theatre during the most despairing analysis of the world – the ones that say 'Exit'.

The impact of the Theatre of the Absurd in the 1950s and 1960s had a shattering and in some ways permanent effect on the British theatre as a whole. If we examine the work of British dramatists who were so influenced, say N.F. Simpson and Harold Pinter, we find a clear determination to establish the roots of the action in everyday reality. The smooth surface of the boarding house in Pinter's *The Birthday Party* and the solid do-it-yourself mania that leads to the building of the Old Bailey in the Groomkirby household in Simpson's *One Way Pendulum* provide a kind of earth to the bizarre horrors that disrupt them, and render these at once more credible and more frightening. Radio's habit of building up realities only to knock them from under the listener's feet made it an excellent medium for the distinctive nature of British absurdism. In *No Quarter* (1962), Barry Bermange does it quite literally, creating an apparently ordinary hotel that disintegrates and leaves the inhabitants stranded in the dark, trying to relate themselves to a hostile and shifting world:

QUIET MAN: You may confess your sins to me – not now. Later. When we are settled. Meanwhile . . . let us consider ourselves in relation to the Universe as a whole . . . determine in which direction lies the North. (*Pause*) Once we know this, we will know where Hornsey lies . . . (*Pause*) And Bethlehem.[23]

The most astringent and perceptive of the radio absurdists is without doubt the late Giles Cooper. He negotiated the Hornsey-Bethlehem-Universe road without a shadow of the pretentiousness inherent in such overt statements of the fact. Plays such as *The Disagreeable Oyster* (1957) and *Under the Loofah Tree* (1958) were to a large extent responsible for the setting-up of the BBC Radiophonic Workshop and the expansion of remaining technical frontiers. The technical demands he made reflected his special vision of a reality that shifts and changes, yet is never divorced from an everyday *Gestalt*. In *Under the Loofah Tree*, for example, the hero takes an existential buffeting in a homely situation. When the play begins he is in his bath, enjoying the operatic possibilities of the acoustics and playing with his son's boats. He has a distinct propensity for the little unacknowledged rituals that add a dimension of magic to the dullest and most rational lives:

(*The clockwork runs down*) Oh. (*Disappointed*) They don't make them like they used to. How many waves to sink her? (*Sloosh*) One . . . (*Sloosh*) Two . . .(*Sloosh*) She's listing. (*Sloosh*) The passengers are running for the boats . . . (*Sloosh*) The bulkheads go . . . (*Sloosh*) And now she sinks. (*Pause*) Why not? She should have sunk. This time! (*A bigger sloosh*) Sink you damned tin toy! (*A tidal wave*) Oh, sink! (*His voice changes from anger to peevish fear*) If I don't sink her this time nothing will ever go right again. I shall die, go broke, be hanged. Sink![24]

Here microphone intimacy facilitates extreme naturalism (while the theatre of the 1970s can face the fact that people are naked under their clothes, it lacks the close focus needed for the acknowledgement of private silliness of this sort) alongside a dimension of fantasy; the slooshing of the water takes on some of the dramatic sound it has in Edward's mind. This combination of verisimilitude and distortion enables us to explore the furthest reaches of Edward's being. We hear him as the hero of his own life in a nightmare version of *This Is Your Life*, which he peoples with characters who come to praise and stay to condemn; meanwhile, events outside the bathroom take on their own paranoia. Cooper cuts between them with verve, but maintains a discipline of form that prevents the play from degenerating into incoherence. Incredible imaginings have a Shandean logic, one always springing out of the previous one; the wildly improbable is grounded in homely fact. And we have a touchstone by which to judge this fluctuating ego – a plastic duck, first simply an alternative to the toy submarine, but which we soon learn to identify as the voice of truth, quacking through Edward's dreams of an heroic death to force onto the mental stage the figure of his old Sergeant:

At 18.15 hours he proceeded to inform the Company Commander that he had been delayed by encountering an enemy patrol. There was no longer any need for reinforcements as the enemy had attacked in strength at 17.45 hours, capturing the position and killing the defenders, I myself having been wounded, tied to a tree and bayoneted. It was a painful death. Sir!²⁵

This prompts Edward to suicide by drowning, an episode in which his life flashes past in radio shorthand in about a twentieth of the time Guthrie needed in *These Flowers Are Not for You to Pick*. And as Edward rises in joyous self-assertion from the water, Cooper raises questions about the nature of truth in the homeliest way imaginable. Edward puts away the bathtime equipment: 'Soap, sponge, frog, boat, submarine, duck. (*Quack*) . . . Loofah . . . loofah.'²⁶ It was at the Battle of Loofah Corner that his act of cowardice took place. His dwelling on the word makes us wonder whether the whole pattern of self-glorification and abasement occurs every bathtime. The way in which he passes over it so lightly as the water gurgles happily away suggests that the incident might be fantasy only; the farewell quack implies that the bathroom contains more truth than the world outside. The sounds and voices, so slightly but clearly distorted, show us what the mind can encompass, but not what the facts are; this is a picture of a personal world, which is, as Cooper puts it, 'neither fact nor fiction, neither prose nor poetry', and which has 'no being at all except on the air'.²⁷

Cooper also exploited the existential mobility of radio in plays that transcend characters' personal fantasies and show the nightmare dimensions of our own world. It is interesting to note that the more complex the balance between illusion and reality becomes, the more closely he adheres to the formulae of myth and folk tale that MacNeice also found essential to what he had to say on radio. *The Object* (1964), for instance, depicts a space capsule landing in the garden of a young London couple in desperate poverty. Cooper austerely avoids detailed description, allowing our imagination to build on the smallest details, then suddenly confronts us with a brutal and irresistible image:

MILL: There's something in there.
GARY: I didn't think it was empty, did I?
MILL: Some sort of fish, look – floating.
GARY: Eh?
MILL: There, when it steadies, look. It's like a fish sort of, got kind of little arms, kind of little legs, all hunched up. Do you see? And it's alive, look where its heart's beating!²⁸

This violence is not arbitrary; it crystallises all manner of questions about the governors and the governed, the freedom of those who send up the foetus and of the couple who can't even make a few illegal pounds out of the capsule because they are trapped in their own ignorance. The questions can invade us because of the disciplined structure – the story is the old one about the poor man and his wife who get three wishes and fritter them away because poverty has placed crippling limits on desire. The events might, just, be real; again, they might be the products of the characters' dreams and wishes.

The same might be true of Cooper's masterpiece, *Mathry Beacon* (1956), which draws on the Ark story to depict a group of soldiers guarding a secret weapon in the Welsh hills, who create a community so potentially perfect that their leaders keep them in ignorance that the war is over. Cooper shows the forces that keep society together and those that break it; the power of the play comes from the interplay of different sounds and languages. The community is built up convincingly by the use of seasonal rhythms. They discuss the weather and the birth of piglets, and after the death of the NCO the growth of a five-cornered marriage and the arrival of group children follow naturally and credibly. At the same time these life rhythms are counterpointed with military jargon; this stems from the presence of Gann, the NCO who lives his life in the cradle of King's Regulations:

Stand still with the thumb in line with the seam of the trousers, so. Those that don't have a trouser put their thumbs where there would be a seam if they had, those that don't have thumbs indent for them in triplicate on army form two-o-five-o.[29]

For that matter, his death, too, conforms: 'Turn to the right, face the wall, expire.'[30] This may make clear the possibilities open to a stylised parlance of this kind. It can slip from the everyday to the surreal without perceptible shift. It can join with the more matter-of-fact rhythms of the farm to embody the tensions that are at once its strength and its weakness:

GANN: . . . Nobody. Guard, turn out! And a pause, two three and the lantern at the gate and the feet on stone . . . and the walls, thick walls. Nothing grows on those.[31]

Most of the characters in *Mathry Beacon* operate on the level of instinct; uneducated, they cannot put their dreams into ordinary speech. But this linguistic mix makes it possible for them to take off into near-poetry while still allowing us to accept them on a mundane level.

The sound balance is equally subtle. The secret weapon, the Watling Deflector, gives off a strange humming whine, always present in outdoor scenes. This serves several functions. It fixes location and reminds us of the cliff on which it stands, over which the group scapegoat is hounded at the end. It is also a complex symbol of the group spirit. In part, it is Gann's will incarnate, holding the group together by reminding them of their common purpose. It also symbolises military discipline, against which is set another aural symbol. Jake Olim, the negro trumpeter, takes the Deflector sound and builds on it a jazz improvisation called 'Deflector Rag' – which is, of course, anathema to Gann, who orders that

you will either blow tunes of a military nature or in a slow and melancholy manner, not calculated to inflame the passions of personnel.[32]

After the death of Gann, jazz trumpet succeeds Deflector whine, until the weapon is finally smashed. Cooper uses the two sounds to indicate a necessary harmony and tension. The Deflector sound alone kills not only the passions of personnel but the very spirit of life; the group pines in isolation until the arrival of living things to care for. But the Deflector also means order. While one man has to guard it, there can always be a man for each of the two women and one out of the way. Once they realise the weapon is useless and the war over, they cannot bear the futility of guarding it – but they are then driven to kill Blick, the educated soldier, to keep the sexual balance. 'Deflector Rag' closes the play; but by now it is not merely a symbol of freedom but of its misuse. The group is seized by greed for the army pay that has accumulated for them during the 1940s and 1950s. They see their return to the world as a liberation, rejecting the experience of their potential paradise. While the play deals in rhythms and values that are eternal, it also enshrines the 1950s, both the grey postwar years almost indistinguishable from the war itself and the eventual materialism outlined in Harold Macmillan's well-known paean, 'You've never had it so good'. Its use of language and sound to make fantasy incarnate, while never losing sight of the everyday world dreaming the fantasy, has seldom been bettered.

Cooper explored more fully than any radio writer before him the infinite number of worlds that can be created inside the head. For Beckett, however, it is the inside of the head itself that is there to be explored. His characters, whether in fiction or drama, are haunted by voices that may or may not proceed from their own skulls, as in *The Unnamable:*

. . . it has not been possible up to date to determine with certainty, or even approximately, what it is, in the way of noise, or how it comes to me, or by what organ it is emitted, or by what perceived, or by what intelligence apprehended . . .[33]

John Berger found one reason for the rise of non-representational art after the First World War in the development of mass communication – film, radio, TV, the aeroplane - which eroded 'the rigid distinction between absence and presence'.[34] What precisely is the relationship between the listener and the voice that comes from the radio set and enters his head? He controls it, if he has access to the on-off switch; but while it is on, he may allow his being to be changed or extended or modified by that voice, perhaps more profoundly than by a person in the same room. He is, as I have said, vulnerable; as long as the mind is surrendered to the voice in the head, the boundaries of the self will become slightly faint at the edges. Even in his earlier and more apparently conventional works for radio, *All That Fall* (1957) and *Embers* (1959), Beckett's exploitation of this vulnerability is unique, in that his characters are struggling with the problem of existing in their own voice-haunted skulls. Our heads are invaded by other heads, which are invaded . . .

Beckett's work is pervaded by a theme expressed outright in his preface to *Film*:

Esse est percipi. All extraneous perception suppressed, animal, human, divine, self-perception maintains in being. Search of non-being in flight from extraneous perception breaking down in inescapability of self-perception.[35]

This is a fair summary of the situation of both Maddy Rooney in *All That Fall*, perpetually jerked back into a hostile world from her self-absorption and longing to be 'in atoms', and Henry in *Embers*, with his endless recital of stories to keep the self at bay. To express this flight from self-perception in radio terms is in itself a paradox, because the radio writer has to make our perception of his imagined figures possible. The imagination has to have something with which to co-operate, even if only a particularly vivid instance of this flight from being. Beckett once wrote a perceptive review of O'Casey's *Windfalls* in which he praised a quality he called 'dramatic dehiscence' – the ability to show in farce the universal tendency towards disintegration, to show 'the triumph of the principle of knockabout in situation, in all its elements and on all its planes, from the furniture to the higher centres'.[36] The principle at work in Beckett's radio plays is the converse. He conjures up in the darkness and silence of the listener's skull those of the protagonists; the effect of their despairing flight inward turns the stage of radio into a Black Hole, in which all matter turns endlessly in upon itself.

But even as being shrinks inwards it is also expanding outwards. In his *Three Dialogues* with Georges Duthuit, Beckett speaks of art turning from the depiction of reality to

the expression that there is nothing to express, nothing with which to express, nothing from which to express, no power to express, no desire to express, together with the obligation to express.[37]

All the major figures in his radio plays experience the tension between self-flight and self-expression. This is of course true of other works; in his trilogy of novels, *Molloy*, *Malone Dies* and *The Unnamable*, we are often aware of the struggles of Malone and the Unnamable to find *le mot juste* for their sufferings. The radio plays, however, have that immediate awareness of themselves as artefacts noted in *The Goon Show*. In *All That Fall* Maddy and Dan are intensely preoccupied with language:

MRS ROONEY: No no, I am agog, tell me all, then we shall press on and never pause, never pause, till we come safe to haven.
Pause

MR ROONEY: Never pause. . .safe to haven. . .Do you know, Maddy, sometimes one would think you were struggling with a dead language.

MRS ROONEY: Yes indeed, Dan, I know full well what you mean, I often have that feeling, it is unspeakably excruciating.

MR ROONEY: I confess I have it sometimes myself, when I happen to overhear what I am saying.[38]

They are aware that it is primarily language that keeps them alive, and this awareness extends to a kind of half-awareness of the medium in which they are being presented. In the most extensive passage of scene-setting in *All That Fall* – one of the most precise bits of location-painting in the whole of Beckett – Mrs Rooney makes clear that there is a relationship between this description and her presence. She prefaces it with a remark that pinpoints the problem of the radio dramatist dealing with a large number of characters (as indeed Beckett does here, rather perversely in view of his small stage casts), almost as if she were aware that she had 'no being at all except on the air', to use Cooper's phrase. 'Do not imagine', she remarks, 'because I am silent, that I am not present, and alive, to all that is going on.'[39] This is a radio character speaking to us; and she goes on to describe something of the tension set up in a mind that is at once the place in which the action happens and the agent that creates it:

The entire scene, the hills, the plain, the racecourse with its miles and miles of white rails and three red stands, the pretty little wayside station, even you yourselves, yes, I mean it, and over all the clouding blue, I see it all, I stand here and see it all with eyes. . . (*the voice breaks*) . . . through eyes . . . oh if you had my eyes . . .you would understand . . . the things they have seen . . . and not looked away . . .[40]

   Throughout *All That Fall*, we are in Maddy Rooney's consciousness. In her self-absorbed walk to the station, we hear extraneous things only as they impinge upon her – often to comic effect, as when Tyler's bicycle bell comes as a noisy bolt from the blue or Connolly's van sends Maddy and Tyler flying into a ditch. In both cases, the sounds used in production were grotesquely distorted, aural slapstick, suggesting their impact on Maddy and the indignity she feels rather than treating the situation objectively. Similarly Miss Fitt, the only character apart from Dan to draw our attention away from Maddy for any length of time, was still presented as a figure in her consciousness. As the director, Donald McWhinnie, describes, this was done

by making Miss Fitt play her monologue in long perspective and therefore at a disadvantage in relation to Mrs Rooney (the character closest to the microphone is always dominant). Reverse the positions of Miss Fitt and Mrs Rooney in this scene and Mrs Rooney would evaporate, Miss Fitt become the central figure. And yet it becomes tiresome to the ear to listen for any length of time to a voice in distant perspective; we solve this . . . by slowly moving the focus onto the speaker, so that she is in near close-up for the centre of the speech, then withdrawing.[41]

Sometimes, Maddy's consciousness seems to be governing what we hear, to be composing reality and transmitting it to us, not only in obviously descriptive sections like the racecourse passage or what Dan calls his 'composition' about events in the train, but also when dealing with apparently extraneous noises:

All is still. No living soul in sight. There is no one to ask. The world is feeding. The wind – (*brief wind*) – scarcely stirs the leaves and the birds – (*brief chirp*) – are tired singing. The cows – (*brief moo*) – and sheep – (*brief baa*) – ruminate in silence. The dogs – (*brief bark*) – are hushed and the hens – (*brief cackle*) – sprawl torpid in the dust.[42]

In part, this is straightforward parody of radio technique, like the famous *ITMA* door; it also creates a strange paradox in our minds. Maddy is calling up these creatures while negating their existence, or at least their vitality; but the noises are intimately linked to the consciousness that does this calling up. In both BBC productions (1957 and 1972) they were human in origin, not recordings of real animals, reinforcing the impression that here we have a mind at once creating and running away from itself.

Embers provides a similar experience. When we hear the sound of the sea, Henry has to identify it for us: 'I mention it because the sound is so strange, so unlike the sound of the sea, that if you didn't see what it was you wouldn't know what it was.'[43] This is common enough in radio, and here it makes us instantly aware of Henry as a creator in our heads as well as someone telling himself stories in his own. (It occurs to me as I write that a remarkable number of the plays referred to so far contain the sound of the sea and that in most cases this is linked to a character whose consciousness we share for much of the play – Edward in *These Flowers Are Not for You to Pick*, Edward in *Under the Loofah Tree*, Roland in *The Dark Tower*, Captain Cat in *Under Milk Wood*, Columbus in *Christopher Columbus*. Perhaps because it sounds like the pounding of the blood in the head or the waters of the womb, the sea seems to draw us instantly inwards.)

The effect of this relationship between listener, protagonist and external world is to convey a sense of the helplessness of those protagonists in the face of a world they at first appeared to control. Henry initially seems to be summoning up the ghosts of his past and composing stories about them. Soon, though, we are aware that the ghosts do not obey him, that, in Francis Doherty's vivid image,[44] they are like gramophone records that are wearing out. So his part is not fixed; even that cannot be relied upon. He expends much care in getting the details of his story precise and even beautifully phrased:

Holloway with his little black bag, not a sound, bitter cold, full moon small and white, crooked trail of Holloway's galoshes, Vega in the Lyre very green.

(*Pause*) Vega in the Lyre very green. (*Pause*) Following conversation then on the step, no, in the room . . .[45]

But no amount of care can prevent the suffering he experiences as the story, which, we conjecture, is his own, reaches its conclusion; nor does it seem able to keep the ghostly Ada there to listen to it. Similarly Maddy Rooney's linguistic (and radiophonic!) facility serves largely to counterpoint with its fertility the theme of sterility and decay on which she dwells. Her self-description contains the poignant twisting of a cliché that for Louis MacNeice was one of the great strengths of a spoken art:

Oh I am just a hysterical old hag I know, destroyed with sorrow and pining and gentility and church-going and fat and rheumatism and childlessness.[46]

In this context we expect the word 'child-bearing', and her grief for little Minnie becomes all the more powerful for that. The theme is reinforced by the hinny, the sterile hybrid of horse and donkey, the dead leaves in the dust, and Dan's desire to 'nip some young doom in the bud'.[47] When, at the end of the play, we learn that a child has been killed beneath the wheels of the train, we are left with the possibility that Dan may have killed it – a possibility many of Beckett's critics find an irritating enigma. But it is a part of the texture of Maddy's experience that fits with all we know of her; she can, in the end, express, but not create. While she seemed to summon the animals, she only clarified their non-being. She and Dan can suffer for their childlessness, but even this regret turns the image of the dead child into one of another sterile being – 'little Minnie' is described as one who would now be 'girding up her lovely little loins, getting ready for the change'.[48] The desire to create is constantly broken by the greater power of destruction, and the need to express is in perpetual conflict with the longing to withdraw from existence, so that permanent tensions are set up in our own skulls.

So far it is almost exclusively of the skull as private theatre that I have spoken. Some of the most notable theatre of the 1970s has been that of the marketplace rather than that of introspection. Edward Bond sees the change reflected in both plays and the theatres that express them:

The bourgeois theatre set most of its scenes in small domestic rooms, with an occasional picnic or a visit to the law courts. It thought it understood the world and believed that nothing in it needed to be changed very much . . . But we need to set our scenes in public places, where history is formed, classes clash, and whole societies move. Otherwise we're not writing about the events that most affect us and shape our future. The Olivier stage is ideally suited to this sort of theatre. It's like a public square or the meeting of several roads or a playing field or a factory floor . . .[49]

Hitler and Churchill both knew how to use the theatre of the skull; during the war, radio held the European Underground together; it continues to shape history. When it comes to political drama, however, radio must use the tools it has. It cannot, on the whole, cope with public places. This is clear if one listens to a broadcast of *Julius Caesar*. The crowd is represented in sound terms by the cobbler with his jokes about bad soles and later by some more or less organised rhubarb, which does no more on the air than make it clear that the mob is present and responding to Antony's speech. Without the visual dimension we lose the metamorphosis of the mob, the point at which they cease to be cobblers and carpenters and become a single violent entity. We miss the contrast between public and private violence, the uncontained 'tear him for his bad verses', and the closeted intimacy of the triumvirs compiling their list of proscriptions.

It is possible, however, to appreciate a radio broadcast of *The Tempest*. We are close to Prospero throughout the action, all of which he either controls or has to think out. Through him we are involved in a creative process; through him we learn experientially about the business of good government. The play is his vision, his dream. When we hear him with the conspirators or with Caliban, we are made aware that history may be made in public places, but it does not begin there; it begins in the head, with cool political thought or with uncontrollable anger.

The point at which one's personal 'history' begins, the reception and absorption of a political idea, is a uniquely disturbing experience, quite separable from the translation of that idea into action; and the precise quality of that disturbance owes much to the means by which the idea is transmitted originally. Queen Victoria disliked Gladstone's addressing her like a public meeting; anyone who has listened to Hitler on radio can appreciate that this might be more than snobbish resentment at a commoner's presumption. Quite apart from the ideas, or lack of them, being expressed, the delivery is singularly unnerving. It seems to be trying to elicit responses like those made by the crowds at the Nuremberg Rallies, and yet the context remains private; the listener is painfully invaded in terms of both public and private identity.

Two plays of the 1970s have coped admirably with public issues while satisfying the technical and emotional demands of radio: David Rudkin's *Cries from Casement As His Bones Are Brought to Dublin* (1973) and John Arden's *Pearl* (1978). They are very different in style and impact, and the strongest surface similarity is that of subject-matter: both deal with the matter of Ireland, perhaps the one political issue that, for the English, partakes of the quality of myth, of a knowledge they carry inside themselves. They also share a complicated relationship with the idea of time; and a concern that whatever political awareness is conveyed should establish itself by involving the audience, as does *The Tempest*, in a creative process and a highly personal vision.

Cries from Casement is about a historical figure; and it is not biography. It is Rudkin's vision of the man, and he makes use of all kinds of social and political hindsight. He is therefore at pains to make this clear by presenting a Casement with no earthly reality, and after the short introductory section the play opens in the grave itself, the Pentonville limepit where Casement lay buried with the remains of Crippen until 1964. In this way, Rudkin at once establishes a figure who is capable of thinking forward and backward in time, of encompassing contemporary perspectives on Ulster and his own sexuality without losing the sense of the nature of those burdens as they lay on him in 1916. 'Because it was to be heard in a box,' writes Rudkin, 'I set most of the action *in* a box.'[50] The intimacy of presentation means that, although the tone may be polemical, we are not addressed as a public meeting but invited to consider the pain of Ulster as it is incarnated in this one man – or rather, this one corpse. We are always made aware that Casement *is* a corpse – for example, we experience vividly the tearing of his bones as they pull him out of the limepit (together with bits of Crippen) – and this renders him helpless at a crucial and tragic point in his story, his reburial as a hero in Dublin. For Casement the Ulsterman this is a bitter irony, and to hear the dead man himself articulate it makes it uniquely clear that the events of 1916 are not safely in the past but are still shaping the course of English and Irish history:

Relevance on relevance, me in my life a symbol of Ireland's seceding, a token of her fracture in my death: an exile even in my grave. Am I to have no rest from paradoxical significance?[51]

The play is an exploration of what it means to be an Ulsterman and of how people define their social, political and sexual selves. The play opens with Casement and Crippen mutually surprised by the gap between their public images and the real selves lying in their common grave:

CASEMENT: I thought Crippen was a quiet-spoken doctor of a man.
CRIPPEN: We fought Casement was a gentle parfit knight.[52]

The inextricable Crippen is present through much of the play to bring Casement the hero-figure down to earth; by calling attention to his deflationary role – 'I am wiv you alway', he tells Casement, 'a puncturin voice'[53] – he also stresses the fact that he is a dramatic device, a radiophonic convenience, which is doubly ironic since Crippen had little reason to love radio. We are always aware that this is a play, an act of creation in which masks and identities will be assumed and discarded. In fact Crippen prepares the way for the introduction of Rudkin himself. The author presents the Author (with Rudkin's own Ulster-tinged voice) struggling with the problem of how to write a play on Casement.

Thus, although Casement is a figure from the past, he can be presented in the here-and-now as an essentially dynamic figure; his identity is still undefined. The Author finds him an enigma; we listen to him striving to understand his hero, by research, by giving lectures (to which the audience response, both Ulster and Southern Irish, is largely hostile, uncomprehending and even violent), and by roughing out scenes for the projected play. The effect is rather like watching a fresco take shape; the lines may alter their shape, the picture may change, and there will be false starts which, however, still contribute something to the finished whole.

The presence of the Author allows Rudkin great freedom of presentation, as when, for instance, he shows fragments from the Author's play depicting alternative Casements. We hear him, an urbane and elderly peer chatting to Joan Bakewell, as the man Casement might have been if he had chosen a conformist and pro-British identity. We hear too a detailed discussion of the so-called 'Black Diaries'. Extracts are read from them in a voice subtly differing from that of Casement himself; so we are able to draw our own conclusions as to whether Casement was in fact the author of those diaries. We are convinced that this is the case by the passionate advocacy of the Author rather than by having the conclusion forced on us in an underhand way. And we hear scenes from the 'play' that clarify Casement's personality although they have no factual base – for instance, a powerfully erotic scene in which Casement, bestridden by his black lover, makes a choice of national as well as sexual identity, a scene whose balance between sexual power and objective political thought only radio can convey. Throughout the whole of the play's first half we are intimately involved with an ego in the throes of creation and birth:

Through horror, sickness, danger, sodomy, farce, he hacks out a new definition of himself. For that, is he a hero: and not for Ireland only. For Ireland today, of course, he has a more immediate, pressing relevance: with which of us, Ireland or England, must the Ulsterman Protestant in the end throw in his Red Hand? But Casement has a relevance to all mankind. He recreates himself in terms of his own inner truth.[54]

Before we see the living Casement's final choice of identity, Rudkin provides a fast panorama of Irish history and the British part in it. On television, with the usual style of documentary presentation, there would be a danger of this scene becoming a pendant to the whole, a programme in its own right; on stage, the eye would need compensation for the lack of action. On radio, the scene admirably serves its purpose of pulling together the alternative realities of Roger Casement. It gives us a factual background, after which we can be confronted with the historical Casement in full possession of the reasons underlying his actions. The Author is heard no more after this; we hear only the dead Casement on his journey back to Ireland from Pentonville and the Casement of 1916 – first in Germany, then, as Rudkin depicts the corpse's arrival on Irish soil, in Ireland. Rudkin's

Casement and the Casement of history become one. He movingly
narrates his own arrest and trial, in a monologue rarely interrupted,
which breaks off at the moment of the drop.

We have been so close to Casement in his process of self-creation
that the following scenes come as a profound shock. Casement the
man has found himself; now Casement the corpse has to face the
realisation that he has been brutally misunderstood. Slowly it dawns
on him that he is not to be buried in the North. The scene slips into
surrealist comedy with a cutting edge, as Casement cries out from his
grave and the Cardinal presiding over the ceremony snaps, 'Balls to
your specific dying wish, we've got you now.'[55] In some nowhere
beyond the grave, the play closes with an exchange between Casement
and an unborn Ulsterman, confronting together the problem of
Northern Ireland. Casement is, at the end of the play, still an alien, still
far from home.

Rudkin specifically wished that the voice of the unborn patriot
should be a voice new to the listener. This typifies the play's concern
with linguistic subtlety; Rudkin took full advantage of the fact that
radio's sound palette is capable of the most delicate shadings. He
exploits the contrast between the syrupy stage-Irish voices of the
aircrew flying the corpse to Dublin and the almost Paisley-like Belfast
accent of Casement in his genuine anger, and the contrast between the
clipped English voices expressing uptight value systems and the
relaxed rhythms in which Casement explores the Irish language:

The Perfect Tense. Irish has no direct way of inflecting its verbs to denote past
action. We do not say 'We lost the battle' but 'That battle is lost for us,' usually
Anglicised as 'We are after losing' etcetera. 'It is had at me'; 'I am after having'
. . . How many lads are after having me this year so far? Denis, Pierre . . .
Fred, Ernest, Fanti . . . Five. The Yid, Welsh Rarebit, Laurens of West India
Docks . . .[56]

Language becomes in itself a method of self-definition. Rudkin's
careful nuances coupled with the intimacy of the microphone make it
possible for him to achieve a perfect balance, depicting the many
different and sometimes even contradictory realities that go to make
up Casement the man, Casement the dead hero, and Casement the
eternal surd in the Irish equation.

Pearl, although originally conceived for the stage, takes full
advantage of the ambiguity of a hearsay medium to present parallel
realities. Its base is not in fact, but in alternative history; it demands
that we consider the possibility of an alliance against the Crown in the
1640s between English Puritans and Irish Catholics – and in particular
that we consider the role the creative imagination might play in
shaping such an alliance. The instrument to persuade the Puritans is a
play composed by Backhouse, a dramatist in the Ben Jonson tradition,
and the lady Pearl, an agent of mixed blood who has come to negotiate
the alliance. It is a version of the Esther story, at the end of which Pearl

intends to step out of her role and appear dressed in contemporary clothes to call for the impeachment of the King's deputy in Ireland and, if she can carry the audience with her, of the King himself. The plan was thwarted by Royalists, who force an alien interpretation upon the play, break up the performance to force Priapic humiliations on Pearl, and ensure that the Puritans will be alienated from the theatre for years to come.

Arden and his collaborator, Margaretta D'Arcy (whose name, incidentally, means 'pearl'), have written feelingly about the seemingly wilful misinterpretation of one of their own plays, *The Island of the Mighty*.[57] Arden has also written of the double focus discernible in Shakespeare's *Henry V*, the jingoistic overlay and the 'hidden play' betraying a disgust with war and the way in which the English were currently waging it in Essex's Irish campaign – a disgust apparent in the opening scene with the wily bishops and in the unresolved conflict between Henry and the soldiers, Bates and Williams.[58] The ambiguity of radio makes it possible for us to imagine simultaneously the true play and the distorted version, to see the theatre through the eyes of Pearl, the Royalists' cynicism, and the Puritans' wondering suspicion.

As with *Cries from Casement*, we are close to one character throughout. *Pearl* is also the title of a medieval poem, the subject of which is bereavement and the role of the beloved dead as intercessors. Like her namesake, Arden's Pearl acts as a mediator. We share her excitement at the creation of a play, both in terms of its political potential and the sheer joy of the act of composition, augmented by the growing love she feels for Backhouse. Much of the play is spoken by Pearl directly to herself and to us. In production the actress, Elizabeth Bell, spoke Pearl's private thoughts in a special studio of her own with a different acoustic; the effect was to bring the listener even more emphatically into Pearl's head. Our closeness to her provides, not an objective 'Archimedean point' from which to observe the action, but a point from which we can appreciate simultaneously the need for Puritan revolution and the necessity that it should be accomplished without the overthrow of the old Jonsonian imaginative values. Pearl has suffered in Ireland and in the colonies, and her political sympathies are with the preacher, Gideon Grip; but when she speaks of the theatre and her part in it, her voice melts into verse so that we experience its power for her.

The ending of the play is a radio *tour de force* – so much so, indeed, that it is hard to imagine any other medium presenting it with such power. Arden uses a kind of alienation effect with shattering force. We have become accustomed to Pearl narrating the story in the present tense. As the play is destroyed, as the Royalists sweep backstage to murder Backhouse and mutilate Pearl's face, the narrative switches suddenly to the past. The play has sustained throughout the excitement of potential success; the Esther play, an ironically triumphant echo of Pearl's own story, has suggested what the theatre can achieve coupled with Puritan values. Then, suddenly, we realise that we have been listening to something that never happened. The reality is much harsher; it begins with the physical pain of civil war, symbolised here by the agony of Pearl:

She drove the point deep into both of my eyes. And she split my top lip to the division of my nostrils. She cut notches into my cheeks and my ears.[59]

It ends with a damage that is both physical and spiritual:

Every theatre throughout the land was closed down by Act of Parliament: and from that day to this the word of the Common People of England, most powerful in the strength of the Lord, had little or nothing to do with the word of their tragic poets or the high genius of their actors. You might say this did small hurt to the body and bones, but deeper, within the soul . . . Let them live with it.
As for myself, made ugly and made blind,
I had to live the best way I could find.
(She chants) 'For the mercy of Christ give a penny to the poor blind woman.'[60]

We hear her in a howling wind, tapping her stick on the stones. Her voice is different. We are no longer in her head but on the outside, observing a picture of historical reality, of a suffering that is not, like the joyfully created Esther play, a might-have-been, but real. We have been so close to Pearl that her voice has been inside us, and we have accepted the Pearl who had hopes of the alliance and who helped create the play as real. Suddenly Arden forces us to see that, if a Pearl should exist, she would do so at this level of blind beggar in the true historical context of the Civil War – and perhaps in the present civil war in Ireland too.

Twenty years ago, Donald McWhinnie expressed, in one of the best studies of radio ever written, *The Art of Radio*, the hope that radio would survive the impact of television and perhaps even profit by it. It now seems extraordinary, in view of plays of the stature of *Pearl* and *Cries from Casement*, that its non-survival could be contemplated. It seems, too, even more important that it should go on surviving.

Time passes. Listen. Time passes.
Come closer now.[61]

The shape of the stage inside the head is changing and will go on changing.

From where you are, you can hear their dreams.[62]

As Jung said, there is no 'Archimedean point' from which to study the dream. It is in the mind, and only the mind can study itself. But the dream can leave the head of the writer and become part of the head of the listener. The listener becomes yet another link in a chain, which Peter Brook has described from the point of view of a stage actor:

A word does not start as a word – it is an end product which begins as an impulse, stimulated by attitude and behaviour which dictates the need for expression. This process occurs inside the dramatist; it is repeated inside the actor.[63]

And then, in radio, it is repeated inside the listener. The listener's mind is at once the ground of the action and the instrument that gives it life. The stage actor has to perform on a stage that may, with luck, reflect the universe of his playwright; but it may not, given the antiquity and eccentricity of some of our playhouses. The theatre inside the head is exquisitely responsive; the listener creates not just the flesh of the play but the whole world-system in which it takes shape, a universe as varied as the men and women who create for radio. 'From where you are, you can hear their dreams.' From where you are, you are the only thing that gives their dreams life.

Notes

1. Dylan Thomas, *Under Milk Wood*. London 1976, p. 11.
2. *Ibid*.
3. *Squirrel's Cage and Two Other Microphone Plays*. London 1931, p. 10.
4. *Ibid*, p. 9.
5. *Ibid*, p. 87.
6. *Christopher Columbus*. London 1944, p. 21.
7. *Ibid*, p. 8.
8. *The Dark Tower and Other Radio Scripts*. London 1947, p. 39.
9. *Ibid*, p. 47.
10. *Ibid*, p. 65.
11. *Ibid*, p. 21.
12. 'The phenomenology of the spirit in fairytales', *Four Archetypes*. London 1972, p. 85 (first published, in German, 1948).
13. Quotations from *Vampirella* are taken from the script in the BBC Play Library, Broadcasting House, London.
14. Edmund Whittaker, *Space and Spirit*. London 1946, p. 102.
15. *Understanding Media*. London 1964, p. 303.
16. Quotations from Spike Milligan's unpublished script, *The Histories of Pliny the Elder* (1957), are taken from the script in BBC Written Archives.
17. Spike Milligan, *The House of Teeth* (1956), in *The Goon Show Scripts*. London 1972, p. 186.
18. *The Histories of Pliny the Elder*.
19. Spike Milligan, *The Scarlet Capsule* (1959), in *More Goon Show Scripts*. London 1973, p. 94.
20. McWhinnie, *The Art of Radio*. London 1959, p. 80.
21. Quotations from *Garrison Halibut* are taken from the script in the BBC Play Library, Broadcasting House, London.
22. Quoted from the script in the BBC Play Library, Broadcasting House, London.
23. *New English Dramatists 12 : Radio Plays*. Harmondsworth 1968, p. 88.
24. Cooper, *Six Plays for Radio*. London 1966, p. 187.
25. *Ibid*, p. 204.
26. *Ibid*, p. 207.

27. Quoted by Desmond Briscoe in his introduction to the second production of the play by the BBC Radiophonic Workshop (25 Mar. 1972).
28. *New English Dramatists 12*, p. 44.
29. Cooper, op. cit., pp. 19-20.
30. *Ibid*, p. 45.
31. *Ibid*, pp. 42-3.
32. *Ibid*, p.28.
33. *Molloy, Malone Dies, The Unnamable*. London 1959, p. 392.
34. *The Moment of Cubism*. London 1969, p. 6.
35. *Film*. London 1972, p. 11.
36. 'The essential and the incidental', *The Bookman*, **87** (Dec. 1934), Christmas Review Supplement, p. 111.
37. *Proust and Three Dialogues*. London 1965, p. 103.
38. *All That Fall*. London 1965, pp. 34–5.
39. *Ibid*, p. 23.
40. *Ibid*, pp. 23-4.
41. McWhinnie, op. cit., p. 145.
42. *All That Fall*, p. 32.
43. *Krapp's Last Tape and Embers*. London 1965, p. 21.
44. *Samuel Beckett*. London 1971, p. 109.
45. *Krapp's Last Tape and Embers*, pp. 23-4.
46. *All That Fall*, p. 9.
47. *Ibid*, p. 31.
48. *Ibid*, p. 12.
49. 'Us, our drama and the National Theatre', *Plays and Players*, **26**(1) (Oct. 1978), p. 8.
50. *Cries from Casement As His Bones Are Brought to Dublin*. London 1974, p. 81.
51. *Ibid*, p. 77.
52. *Ibid*, p. 10.
53. *Ibid*, p. 16.
54. *Ibid*, p. 24.
55. *Ibid*, p. 76.
56. *Ibid*, p. 30.
57. 'Playwrights on picket', *To Present the Pretence*. London 1977, pp. 159-72.
58. 'Playwrights and play-writers', *To Present the Pretence*, pp. 195-208.
59. *Pearl*. London 1979, p. 75.
60. *Ibid*. p. 76.
61. Thomas, op. cit., p. 12.
62. *Ibid*.
63. *The Empty Space*. Harmondsworth 1972, p. 15.

Chapter 5
Icon or symbol: the writer and the 'medium'

Jonathan Raban

The inverted commas are essential. At a conference on Radio Literature (and the word 'literature' should have been similarly isolated for close cross-questioning) held at Durham University in 1977, there was a great deal of talk about the 'medium'. An eavesdropper might have concluded that the assembled delegates were there to discuss not radio at all but some new advance in the field of psychical research. Was this 'medium' Madame Sosostris? Madame Blavatsky? Mr Sludge? I listened to the talk with care and steadily mounting scepticism. If it were ever to be taken seriously, it would – I am convinced – severely limit rather than expand the possibilities of writing well for radio. That the possibilities exist is proved by a large archive of excellent plays. *Under Milk Wood* was written for broadcasting; so was *All That Fall*; so was *Mathry Beacon*; so was *Artist Descending a Staircase*. Talk of the 'medium' is hardly more relevant to a discussion of the particular merits of works like these than a discourse about the medium of print would be to a consideration of, say, *David Copperfield* or *Ulysses*.

Yet there is something about radio, especially radio today, that does invite such talk. Radio plays, despite international commissioning systems designed to persuade some of the best-known dramatists alive to write for the wireless and despite the introduction of little trophies for the 'best single play of the year', do not make the public splash they did in the 1940s and 1950s. The radio play is a minority form. It has its addicts and enthusiasts – a small, attentive, critical audience. Its larger public consists of passers-by who drop in to listen casually. They are doing the washing-up, sitting stalled in traffic jams, making love, trying to gag the baby, or going at the walls of their living rooms with electric drills.

It is hardly surprising that radio producers and radio writers, who have put as much imaginative effort into their work as any theatrical director or stage playwright does into his, should feel afflicted by what sociologists call status anxiety. Television has robbed the radio people of the inert millions who can be clocked up on Jictar ratings. Nor are they compensated by the respect shown by arts-features journalists on newspapers to exponents of lunchtime theatre or to authors of novels that sell a meagre fifteen hundred copies. Anyone working on radio is doing something too 'mass' to be treated as art, too 'coterie' to be a significant public event.

It is out of this sense of loss, this appeal for dignity, that the talk about the 'medium' has emerged. If only, goes the wistful refrain of what is in fact, if not in intention, an elegy on a death, if only we could have *pure radio*. . .

The idea has an immediate allure. *Pure radio* is about sound. It aspires to the condition not of music, but of noise. It will be recorded with the highest and strictest technical fidelity known to man. It will employ instruments like the *kunstkopf*, a plastic head with ears modelled in wax, containing microphones set in the exact position of real human eardrums. It will be received in quadrophony with four vast Goodman speakers surrounding the listener in what should ideally be a darkened room.

Imprisoned in the dark between walls of expensive technology, the radio listener will be subjected to the same techniques that military regimes use to make suspect citizens tell all they know. Sensory deprivation is the most basic and effective form of torture. So the listener will be sensorily deprived. There will be nothing to look at, nothing to smell (except for the peculiar thin odour of the technology itself). The listener will be all ears. Having voluntarily blinded himself with science, he will be free to wander among the noises reverberating in his head, alone with the 'medium'.

Then, runs the *pure radio* line of thinking, every fade and swelling of the volume, every silence, every crackle of a leaf, every cry of every seagull, and every crunch of gravel under the tyres of a fictive car arriving up a ghostly fictive drive, will take on an oppressive and exaggerated reality.

I don't doubt it. If I am ever unlucky enough to find myself in the position of the ideal radio listener, I shall have confessed all before the announcer has finished with the titles and before the introductory blast of music has begun. I see myself kneeling before my torturers crying, 'Anything – do with me what you will – but not, please not . . . not, oh God, the Medium!'

This is not simply tilting at windmills. The technical advances made over the last twenty years, a period corresponding exactly with the radio play's steady decline in public esteem, have given the Medium a dangerously effective collection of racks and screws. Studio technicians have become expert at producing brilliant synthetic imitations of the noises of the outside world; and if we embrace the notion of *pure radio*, that is what the radio play is going to become – an arid, technically dazzling piece of aural mimesis.

In 1978, one such radio 'play' did bring back to radio some of the publicity it had lost to television. Days in advance of its transmission, there were items about it in the newspapers and on news and current-affairs programmes on radio and television. It was attended by perhaps half the brouhaha that waits on a new production at the Royal Court or Open Space theatres. Measured simply in terms of the tattle surrounding it, *The Revenge* was a vindication of the doctrine of pure radio. At last, a radio play had made news.

The Revenge was a wordless sequence of noises. Twigs crackled. Lumps of earth crumbled underfoot. There was a great deal of heavy breathing. Doors opened and closed. Someone, it became apparent, was on the run. *Grunt. Grunt. Aargh!* (Sound of footsteps on stairs, bottle falling from table, the noise of a boot being painfully slid from a swollen, thick-socked foot, etc.) Pure radio. Here was the 'medium' being exploited to the hilt – *kunstkopf redivivus*.

The play was a well-puffed curiosity, and it succeeded in attracting an unusually large audience for a BBC Drama Department production. It was given a rapid sequence of repeat performances, and there was a notable lightening of the atmosphere around the Corporation: radio drama was on the up and up again.

I was curious to hear Andrew Sachs, the author of the piece, interviewed on a magazine programme. He said that the idea of *The Revenge* had come to him after listening to Tom Stoppard speak in a symposium on the radio play, which had been broadcast on Radio 3. Sachs said that Stoppard had inspired him with the notion that radio was, at heart, really about sounds. So he had written what amounted to a set of directions for an extended sequence of sound effects. Its characters were necessarily limited to 'the pursuer' and 'the pursued'; its plot was just a chase – but it was undeniably a collection of evocative noises. In Stoppard's own terms, therefore, should it not be the purest piece of radio drama ever conceived?

In fact, Stoppard had been pointing out some of the special opportunities that radio affords the writer – the aural pun, for instance. Take the sound of horses' hooves on a street – the clippety-clop of a pair of coconut shells being banged together under a microphone. Suppose, Stoppard said, that you reveal these to be not horses' hooves at all but someone abroad armed with a pair of coconut shells. Who is he? What is he doing? How did he come by his shells? Pure radio.

So it is. Stoppard's concept of the pun-in-sound is tantalising; his example of such a pun was convincing and funny. Sadly, it led one of his listeners straight up a cul-de-sac of the other sort of 'pure radio', at whose end lie only the terrible engines of the Medium. Far from taking advantage of a possibility inherent in that curious situation of *just listening to* a play, Andrew Sachs has embraced one of the limitations of the situation like a half-blind man gouging out his other eye in order to become a pure blind man. The 'blindness' of radio is not necessarily a disease or an affliction at all; and it should certainly not be thought of as the one quality distinguishing radio from all other media. If we do accept that argument, then radio turns into the beggar of drama, earning a meagre living by putting its empty sockets on public exhibition.

Blindness has been cited far too frequently as radio's unique attribute: so, 'The radio play turns its listeners into temporarily blind men; they have to find their way through its dramatic world on the evidence of their ears alone.' The sentence was a mistaken attempt of my own at coming to a definition of radio drama: one version or another of the same sentence crops up again and again in what discourse there is about the nature of radio as a dramatic medium.

Very few plays turn their listeners into blind men. The only example I can think of is *The Revenge*. Most plays, though, are reports from a world in full possession of its senses to a listening world equally well endowed. It is perfectly true that blind people are able to enjoy radio plays in a way that they cannot enjoy theatre or television. That is not the point. Radio does not render the listener blind any more than print renders the reader blind. We cannot literally see Bloom's kitchen on the page as we work our way through the print of Joyce's *Ulysses*; the typography is there to be decoded, symbols to be translated into sights, sounds, smells, textures. The medium itself may be pica, élite, roman, italic, Bembo, Fournier or what you will. Yet after staring at these spoors of black hooks and squiggles, the reader will be able to describe how Bloom 'removed the saucepan to the left hob, rose and carried the iron kettle to the sink in order to tap the current by turning the faucet to let it flow'.

So it is with radio. Writer, producer and actors create a skein of sound – noises, voices, music – which exists in order to be unravelled in terms of our own memory and experience. Much of it will be visible in the sense that Bloom's saucepan is visible: the sound of a radio play, like the typeface of a book, invites the listener to exercise all his senses.

In this context, writing for radio is much closer to writing for the printed page than it is to writing for television or the theatre. Unless one is plagued by a bonnetful of bees about the 'medium', one has at one's disposal a form as flexible as the short story or novella. Gone are the dramatic unities – the restrictions on casts and sets. Much more importantly absent is the rigid literalness of the television screen and the lighted stage. Characters and places have room to grow in the space between the listener's ear and the pattern of coded symbols being transmitted from the radio receiver. No one listener may see a radio character in quite the same way as any other listener (any more than my Leopold Bloom exactly resembles yours); this does not mean that the character is invisible. Far from it. He has, rather, the extended symbolic visibility denied to characters in other forms of drama but enjoyed by those in prose fiction.

'Radio', I once heard a particularly sonorous Corporation executive say, 'is, essentially, an aural medium.' That is true only to the extent that print is a visual medium. You must be able to see in order to read;

you must be able to hear in order to listen to a radio play. Neither statement says anything at all, though, about what should be written for the radio set rather than for the printed page. The implication of the first statement is often taken – by the 'medium' enthusiasts – to mean that radio drama should, in some way, be *about* sound. The consequence of this assumption is that radio is threatened with a future equivalent to that of concrete poetry: a series of ever more ingenious experiments with what is really only the typography of radio, not its deep structure.

For the writer, this is a depressing prospect. It suggests a future of sound effects, of radiophonic workshop toys, where words are an impure additive to the medium. Fidelity to the mere sound of life is a naturalistic trick. The early enthusiasts of stereo gramophone equipment used to spend much of their money on records that made the Royal Scot disappear into a tunnel at one end of their living room and emerge, whistling, at the far end, just past the bit on the wall where the china ducks were. Too much recent British radio has succumbed to this trifling amusement, on the grounds that it represents an important advance 'in the medium'. It doesn't.

This may sound like waspish generalising. Let me be more particular. Over the last eight or nine years, all plays recorded by the BBC for transmission on Radio 3 (most plays, in other words, regarded as 'serious', 'literary', 'experimental', or whose characters use language of too colourfully expressive a kind to be thought suitable for family listening on Radio 4) have been produced in stereophony. The characters in them have been allocated positions in space; no longer merely creatures in a code of sound, they have become figures in the air of the living room. They cross the fireplace; they hover over the coffee table; they move, with awful intent, upon the sleeping cat.

This is high infidelity. To a small handful of plays, stereophony adds a quality of dense, subtly textured realism unavailable in a mono production. Stereo is an excellent tool for fleshing out certain atmospheric situations; it can bring the illusion of all the sounds of a particular event into the listener's own room. Some plays are enhanced by it, but for many stereo is a straitjacket. It tends to impose a mechanical naturalism on everything it records. It keeps sounds 'out there', making it very hard to create the special, intimate, 'in here' quality that was once the hallmark of radio drama.

Captain Cat, Polly Garter and the rest of the citizens of Llareggub were – in the original 1954 production – characters who entered one's head as if one had dreamed them. The whole dramatic logic of the play is in the realm of the *in here*; like Thomas's poems, *Under Milk Wood* is obsessively private in its means and movements. Mono radio did not violate that privacy; it handed the dream onto the listener intact, still ravelled.

In 1978, *Hi-Fi Theatre* mounted an elaborate stereophonic

production of the play; and several critics noted a curious, and generally inexplicable, diminution in *Under Milk Wood*'s power. Much of the language sounded arch and stilted when placed in the context of a 'real' Welsh village constructed with faultless naturalism by the studio technicians. The dream stopped short of the listener's head and took place instead on his carpet. *Under Milk Wood* was turned into a cross between a film shot on location and a ghostly stage play in which one was prevented from seeing the actors as one heard them moving around the stage. Radio does not make one blind; stereo can, and often does.

By giving radio plays a 'right-hand' and a 'left-hand' side (let alone all the further discriminations offered by the *kunstkopf* and quad), stereophonic production has created a 'sound screen' which must be filled with audible texture. All the small, distracting, realistic sounds of life find their way onto this screen to compose something like the background of *trompe l'oeil* painting. The play is no longer a code to be deciphered as one deciphers print; it has turned into something like an unrolling tapestry of sound pictures, before which the listener remains a detached, and often puzzled, spectator.

Two quite separate habits and traditions lie at loggerheads in contemporary radio, or so it seems to me. On the one hand, there is the ambition of the radio producer and the studio manager to manifest an illusion, a form of sound cinema. On the other, the literary roots of radio (and they go deep – Thomas, MacNeice, Beckett, Cooper, Reed, Spark) have caused the radio play to grow as a kind of audible version of the printed page. The producer makes icons; the writer, symbols. The one product is complete in itself, requiring only an audience to witness it; the other demands an active readership, or listenership, which will do its own share of the creation.

I do not think that the opposition between these two points of view is adequately recognised. In a boat as relatively small and unfavoured as that of radio drama, it is not in the interests of any crew member to rock it. Until recently, largely because of a happy accident (the lack of sophistication of radio technology; crackle and splutter, tweeter and woof), radio was without doubt a 'writer's medium'. Words ruled, because words were the easiest objects to transmit clearly. Sound effects were essentially symbolic – the seagull, the creaking door, the crunching gravel. They demanded reinvention and elaboration in the listener's head. That has all changed. With VHF, stereo, *kunstkopf* and quad, radio has begun to manufacture its own iconic version of reality; and in radio iconography it is the technician, not the writer, who is much the most important creator of the drama.

This passion for reproducing the audible surfaces of life does answer to the need which afflicts radio people – the desire to be *sui generis*, to be able to do something quite different from practitioners in any other literary or dramatic field. The move from symbol to icon, from 'in here' to 'out there', from mono to stereo, from the writer to the director, is evidence of one thriving brand of radio purism. Yet the preoccupations I have tried to describe affect only a tiny area of the grand conspectus of radio. They are the concern of that band of devotees who talk about the 'medium'. In Britain, they are evident mainly in the 'serious' plays transmitted on Radio 3, and do little more than brush against the dramatic output on the other channels. It is in this large, unpretentious province of the BBC's Drama Department that the writer is likely to find most to reassure him that the medium (no inverted commas) really can work as a place where words count and powerful fictions flourish.

There is a lot to be learned from workaday radio drama of the kind that goes out week after week, careless in its freedom from the attentions of serious criticism. Here, much more than in the self-conscious efforts of *Drama Now* and *Hi-Fi Theatre*, traditions and techniques are laid down like sedimentary rocks. This is where conventions of writing for radio become established; and for that reason I want to concentrate in some detail on *The Archers*, radio's own demotic *Iliad*.

For *The Archers* embodies an important contradiction. Of all radio programmes involving imaginary characters, *The Archers* has much the strongest claim to providing its listeners with a fiction readily accepted as being 'real'. When Grace Archer died in a fire in the 1950s, Britain came close to going into national mourning. As recently as 1979, when Chris Archer married a divorcee in a church ceremony, the Bishop of Truro wrote a protesting letter to *The Guardian* (and began a long and acrimonious correspondence), and other newspapers fought with each other to leak the secret of whether or not the vicar of Ambridge was going to find it in his conscience to marry the couple. If realism has anything at all to do with persuading people that imaginary characters lead lives of serious consequence (and may, indeed, be written to, telephoned, or stopped in the street), then *The Archers* is the most realistic radio programme ever to have been produced. Orson Welles's radio version of *The War of the Worlds* produced a flurry of panic in the streets; but *The Archers* generates the kind of continuous gossip and moral comment we normally reserve only for close friends and members of our immediate families.

Yet listening to any fifteen-minute episode of this extraordinary serial, one is instantly struck by its studied unrealism. In radio terms, it is highly stylised, as formal in its dealings with the world as the most precious of Christopher Fry's verse dramas. It positively abhors the technical realism that has come to mark the drama output of Radio 3, preferring to operate instead in a highly elaborate and ritualised dramatic code. It is a supreme example of symbolic rather than iconic radio, yet it is accepted by its listeners as an entirely credible fiction.

One quality distinguishes all the inhabitants of Ambridge: they are compulsive narrators. If spring has come to the village, Doris Archer will sit at her window and tell her husband exactly which flowers are currently blooming in the garden. Dan Archer, sitting in the chair opposite, can presumably see these flowers for himself; nevertheless they must be named, and a complete inventory of the garden is sedulously compiled. One important reason why Dan frequently appears to be suffering from some form of sleeping sickness is that his wife's function as a key narrator of the serial leaves him little to do except doze irritably while Doris continues her illicit relationship with the listener.

For the first fifteen years or so of its twenty-five year life, *The Archers* had an official narrator in the character of Tom Forrest, the gamekeeper. At one time, he alone used to speak directly to the audience, filling them in on the main events in the village. Narrators, though, went out of radio fashion, and the job was broken down and distributed among half a dozen of the villagers – characters who are privileged to take time out and monologue with all the solipsistic disregard for the presence of other people of Lucky in *Waiting for Godot* or Aston in *The Caretaker*.

Genuine monologue is not a convention available to *The Archers*; it would probably strike the writers and producers of the programme as pretentious and alienating. Another character always has to be present at these recitals to the audience. Nearly always it is the wife or husband of the soliloquist, which tends to give most Ambridge marriages a distinctive edge of long-suffering, patient tension. If we hear a wife in bed with a husband, one or other of the couple will be so preoccupied in talking to us that he or she will have no time at all for their spouse.

If they are inveterate storytellers, the people of Ambridge are also insatiably curious about their own latest news. If Dan Archer and Brian Aldridge are busy relaying to the listener some piece of information provided by the Agriculture Ministry (*The Archers* is a semi-official source of real farming news), they are bound to be interrupted by Tom Forrest breaking in at the end of their conversation with a line like, 'Listen! What's all this about Joe Grundy and Tony?'

So the narrative proceeds, by a highly artificial system of strategically placed cue questions, formal monologues and stories, and brief sketches of dialogue – dialogue which is there not as the centre of the serial but as a device to establish atmosphere and set scenes. Climaxes and crises happen in dialogue, but a remarkable proportion of each episode is given over to what is in effect a direct colloquy between a character in the serial and the listener on the far side of the radio set.

The texture of sound in the programme is of the same stylised kind. One episode, chosen haphazardly, yielded six separate scenes involving ten characters altogether. Three of the scenes were set outdoors, three indoors. Every outdoor scene was signalled by the same symbol: the sound of wood-pigeons cooing, followed by a burst of mixed birdsong including sparrows and finches. Much of the talking took place without any background sound at all; these effects were used first to cue-in scenes, then repeated intermittently to remind listeners of the location. The three indoor scenes used just three sound effects: the noise of someone knocking on a door (no one in Ambridge seems to have a bell); the clink of teacups; and the sound of a telephone being replaced in its cradle.

The producers and writers of *The Archers* are masters of an extremely effective, if mundane, form of radio drama. Everything is vested in cues, signals and symbols. No attempt is made to create a realistic aural surface; such imitations of reality as are absolutely necessary are given in economic semaphore, then dropped as soon as the listener has been equipped with whatever basic clue he needs. The language of the programme is, by the standards of naturalistic drama in the theatre or on television, artificial and functional. It also has a remarkably flexible range. A single episode is likely to accommodate a rhapsodic passage on the changing seasons (Doris Archer) and a barely disguised Ministry hand-out on swine disease (Phil Archer). Between monologues, the programme can take teenage love affairs conducted in the argot of *Company* and *Seventeen*; gardening tips; politics; even the occasional detective story. *The Archers* is a grab-bag of different styles. It has much of the content of a magazine programme like *Today*, while never losing the essential veneer, at least, of dramatic fiction. It is pure radio.

The Archers surely provides an object lesson for the radio dramatist. One may be quick to jeer at the essential banality of its fictional world and at the mechanical cursoriness of much of the writing that goes into the serial, although the occasional episode is just as imaginatively written as many plays transmitted in more prestigious circumstances. Most importantly, *The Archers* recognises that radio as a medium is a mongrel form. Radio is not like paint or bronze, or like the theatre; it is more in the nature of a corridor through which the whole world passes. Even by comparison with its sister medium of television, it is chaotically eclectic in the hospitality it affords to different kinds of language. The formal rhetoric of Churchill's wartime speeches would surely have sounded phoney if one had been able to watch him making them on television; radio allowed them their necessary distance and resonance. At the other end of the scale, the introduction of the phone-in programme a few years ago soon made one accustomed to hearing voices on the radio speaking as informally, often as inarticulately, as if one had heard them drifting through one's window from the street. In the course of an hour spent as an idle radio listener, twiddling between stations, one drifts from the most elaborate and carefully scripted language through every shade and tone to the most unofficial and unrehearsed grunts and squawks. On radio there is no median register, no particular way of speaking that could be said to represent the medium in neutral gear, ticking over. (There is such a dialect on television, as there is on the stage.) Radio is by turns gossipy, authoritative, preachy, natural, artificial, confidential, loudly public, and not infrequently wordless. Its languages bleed into one another. Even the identities of particular channels are constantly being eroded. The Third Programme did provide a recognisable social and intellectual context for its programmes; Radio 3 conscientiously – I presume – does not.

For the dramatist trying to think about the medium in which he has to work it makes bewildering listening, this concatenation of noises and voices. He can at least take from it the consolation that, if radio provides no obvious context, there is almost no imaginable form of writing that will sound obviously out of place on it. Stage plays transfer comfortably onto radio. John Arden's *Pearl*, written for the stage but not performed there, made one of the most memorable radio plays of 1978. Ian McEwan's short story, *Conversation with a Cupboard Man*, was published first in a magazine, then in a book, then turned, with only a few words of revision, into another fine radio play. As I write, I notice that this evening Tom Stoppard's *Professional Foul*, written for television, is being broadcast as a radio play. In such an easy-going open house, it is extremely hard to discover what the house rules are. If there are any. It's said that children who come from households run by determinedly permissive parents begin to yearn for discipline and fixed bedtimes. Radio playwrights suffer from much the same problem. Some of them find the rigour they seek in the notion of 'pure' radio; as I have tried to show, I think there are strong reasons for regarding that particular route as a dull dead-end.

So far, I have been trying to write as a critic – a critic, admittedly, with a fairly evident bias. As a sporadic practitioner in the medium (seven plays in as many years), I should perhaps come clean about my own ambitions as a playwright for radio.

When I began to write for radio, its messy eclecticism seemed wonderfully hospitable. I was very doubtful as to whether I could write a proper 'play' at all. Plays, as I understood them, had to work entirely through their dialogue. Everything had to be 'shown', in Henry James's sense; nothing could be 'told'. Two plays for television (grubby efforts which only just passed muster for transmission) had taught me that my camera directions, my descriptions of sets, my italic asides on what my characters were supposed to be thinking as they spoke their lines, were stronger pieces of writing, on the whole, than the stretches of dialogue they were designed to frame.

Radio, it seemed, would permit me to incorporate the frame into the main body of the play. I wanted the excitement of performance, in which actors and director would take over my characters and give them independent lives. I also wanted the privilege of commentary and description – the freedom to intercede and make footnotes that is normally the prerogative only of the writer of prose fiction. Radio struck me as a unique medium in that it allowed me to do both things.

Of course the Narrator, who used to guide the listener through the plot of the radio play in its early days, was an outmoded figure. As a character, he was the 'Voice of the BBC' or the 'Voice of the Home Service' in an era when both the Corporation and its individual channels had a recognisable identity and social authority. He belonged, in fact, to a much more rigidly structured society than the one I was familiar with in 1972. The Narrator was a fossil from the England of Chamberlain and Churchill; and his forced exile from radio drama was based on good social reasons.

Yet there was, and is, no shortage of narration and commentary on radio. Documentaries, magazine programmes, quizzes, discussions, all use a figure who enjoys a specially intimate relationship with the listening audience. He can arbitrate between the other characters in the show, he can participate in the action himself, and he can be pig-headed, opinionated and often wrong. I felt that it should be possible to borrow this useful character from magazine and current-affairs radio and let him loose in radio fiction. It seemed natural to write plays in which one character was, as it were, a kind of host, announcer or compère.

It also seemed right to listen to what else was happening on radio, quite outside the productions of the Drama Department. The format of the radio phone-in provided me with the basic shape of one play; the stance and language of the sports commentator allowed me to tell the story of a suicide in another. I am wedded to the notion that radio drama can find nourishment in the conventions used by other kinds of radio programmes; and much as I admire the radio work of Beckett, Cooper, Pinter and Stoppard, I suspect that I have more to learn as a dramatist from listening to *Start the Week*, *Checkpoint*, *The World at One*, *The Living World*, *Tuesday Call* and all sorts of bits and pieces having nothing to do with official drama. Radio does not offer the writer very much in the way of a formal tradition – what tradition he needs is probably best found in the theatre or in literature; but it does have an enormous, bottomless reservoir of conventions and techniques in which he can fish, without a licence and out of season, for whatever he needs to fill his own particular pot.

It is from the most ordinary of radio programmes that the dramatist can learn most about the one piece of technology that must seriously concern him – the microphone. When one writes for television, the precise control of the camera does not fall within one's province as a playwright. In radio it is different. The writing of every line entails an exact calculation about the distance of the speaker from the microphone, and about the way in which the volume of that speech will be controlled from within the studio. It is in these calculations that the real flexibility of radio as a medium emerges.

Six inches away from the microphone, we are in the territory of interior monologue, where the fictional character is in closer collusion with the listening audience than he is with the other people in the studio. Three feet away from the microphone, he is intimately engaged with the other characters in the play. Increase the distance, bring up the volume, and he is preaching, haranguing, free to use all the rhetorical figures of public address. On radio, more than on any other dramatic medium, one can shift, on the instant, from public to private, from the most formal to the most intimate, through every nuance of syntax, vocabulary and tone between pillow talk and the Reichstag.

One need only listen to a few minutes of a news bulletin to see how rapidly and intricately these shifts are made, even in the most basic and functional of radio's many forms. The news announcer has his own distance; the recorded speech of a public figure is cut into the programme on tape; a reporter makes his comments; a studio guest is interviewed. In one short item, the perspective of the microphone will be constantly changing, now lengthening, now foreshortening. How much more flexible an instrument is it when placed in the hands of someone constructing a deliberate piece of radio fiction.

Given the immense elasticity of microphone distance and volume control, it is no strain on the medium to make someone speak his thoughts as quietly as if they were rolling round, unspoken, in his head. Radio is peculiarly kind to interior monologue, just as it can cope comfortably with the ranting of a demagogue in the full flight of oratory. In television and on the stage there are 'optimum distances' at which a certain register of speech sounds 'natural' and beyond which language tends to sound artificially formal or artificially familiar. Radio has no such distance, and the dramatist is free to wander in the more-or-less limitless linguistic expanses opened to him by the microphone.

I began this chapter by trying to isolate the word 'medium'. Without wishing to make the page into a rainstorm of inverted commas, I believe that we should also isolate the word 'play'. In my own work for radio, I have found myself writing pieces that have not really been plays at all. Is *Under Milk Wood* really a play? Or Beckett's *Embers*? They are certainly radio fictions; but to call them plays is to use a loose metaphor. They are both original forms. They have a good deal in common with printed prose. They have something of the theatre in them. They owe a great deal to the conventions and the technology of radio itself. The world of radio fiction is a great deal baggier, more inclined to telling rather than showing, more hospitable to the ruminant storyteller, than that of any other kind of drama. There are plays on radio, but they compete for airspace with pieces of fiction whose only real claim to being plays is that they require actors to read them.

To the writer whose ambitions on radio extend beyond seeing it as a convenient place to work out an apprenticeship for television or the theatre, the great lure of the medium lies in this possibility of creating an eclectic fiction. For all its lack of critical prestige (much the most dispiriting feature of the business), radio affords the writer a unique stretch of open territory. There are recent signs that its openness is endangered. The doctrine of 'pure' radio is one threat. Attempts to draw up a list of conventions of the 'radio play' is another. The insistence with which the BBC tags the word 'theatre' onto its series titles (*Thirty-Minute Theatre*, *Afternoon Theatre*, *Saturday Night Theatre*, *Hi-Fi Theatre*) is a further bad omen. For my own part, I would far sooner write a radio programme that was a work of fiction than a 'play'. I also hope that in its basic structure it would more resemble the symbolic, eclectic radio represented by *The Archers* than it would the iconic purism of *The Revenge*.

Chapter 6
Popular radio drama

David Wade

What is popular radio drama? Let me start with a statement which I shall immediately have to dismantle: it is what you hear on BBC Radio 4. Radio 3 can safely be said not to be in the popular drama business and, with the exception of Radio 2's *Waggoners' Walk*, the other two BBC networks have nothing to do with drama at all, while the local stations, both BBC and independent, have made only the most tentative incursions into the field so far.

This, then, is my subject: the plays, the serials and all the other forms of drama put out by Radio 4, plus *Waggoners' Walk*. Perhaps the first thing to be said is that, with the exception of that one daily serial and about fifty new productions a year mounted by Radio 3, the whole of radio drama is to be heard on Radio 4 – that is to say, something like five hundred productions annually. Is this single chapter to attempt to cover that? Mercifully no. For one thing – and this is where the dismantling begins – while virtually all popular drama occurs on Radio 4, not by any means all of that channel's output could be termed popular, in the sense of being accessible to and followed by the largest audiences radio can currently assemble. In fact, if that were my sole criterion for inclusion, this chapter would have to limit itself to a detailed study of just two items. *Waggoners' Walk* and the perennial *Archers*. No drama anywhere on radio can begin to compete with the first of these when it comes to that sort of popularity: the size of its Radio 2 audience exceeds that of the greatest agricultural show on the air by roughly two to one, even though in the less heavily patronised domain of Radio 4 *The Archers* still pulls, by the standards prevailing there, a very large audience indeed. So, if I am to deal with other categories of drama, that criterion for popularity will have to be a little less exigent.

What other categories are there that might be classed as 'popular'? The question may appear to have been answered for me by the way in which, over the years, radio drama has divided up its own repertoire: *The Monday Play, Saturday Night Theatre*, the various *Afternoon Theatres, Thirty-Minute Theatre*, as well as – both late 1978 innovations, these – *Hi-Fi Theatre* and *Just Before Midnight*. These have been Radio 4's 'theatres' for plays proper, even if work not originally conceived in play form has often found its way into a number of them: adaptations of novels, for example. Apart from them, we have the 'Sunday Serial', always of a novel, usually a famous classic; occasional other serials, thrillers or the more domestic kinds (*Dr Finlay's Casebook* is one instance, borrowed – for radio is not above trading on established reputations – from television); and the annual collection of documentaries and what these days pass for features, containing sequences in some kind of dramatic form.

So much for the major categories of radio drama; but before considering them, let me first try to expand my so far rather sketchy definition of the word 'popular'. Whether or not a production draws, by radio's standards, large audiences is something that can more or less be measured, but what about accessibility? By this I mean a play that will not put up any very great barriers of language or production technique, such as might be erected by verse or poetic prose or the extensive use of radiophonics. Listeners will understand what is being said to them – in a quite literal sense – and will know where the action is taking place in terms of their own experience – and again I am using 'experience' in the more literal sense of what has actually happened to people at first hand or, at a slight remove, what they have heard about often enough for it to have acquired the same kind of immediacy. Popular drama, like radio drama as a whole, offers its listeners a myriad of themes. When it deals in social or moral issues, which it often does, it will tend to present these in a recognisably topical way and in a contemporary setting; it will be high on 'relevance'. In fact a great deal of its work as regards theme, construction, language, characterisation and direction will be at or near the level of the two daily serials – a remark I should immediately follow up by saying that, far from being derogatory, it implies a standard of professionalism, especially when applied to *Waggoners' Walk*, which many authors of single radio plays would do well to try to match.

Perhaps this expanded definition of 'popular' will serve to be going on with. I hope to be able to sharpen it as we proceed, but immediately the question is, 'Where in the categories of Radio 4 drama is work of this kind reliably to be found?', and confusingly the answer is, 'Everywhere and nowhere in particular.' Of course, there are certain places where you would expect to find it either very infrequently or not at all. *The Monday Play* is one of them; on its early form *Hi-Fi Theatre* appears to be another. Otherwise the popular repertoire is scattered throughout the network so that, as a generalisation, drama on Radio 4, both within its 'theatres' and as a whole, forms a continuum from the humdrum to the major work. *Afternoon Theatre*, for example, which incidentally also offers repeats of *The Monday Play* and *Saturday Night Theatre*, ranges from the most ordinary domestic drama or comedy to Pinter and the like. In fact the continuum extends outside Radio 4: work originating on Radio 3 now commonly repeats on Radio 4, and the reverse applies as well. In other words, the considerable gap

– intellectual, emotional, literary and artistic – that not so many years ago divided Radio 3 from Radio 4 has now virtually been closed. The two dramatic repertoires have merged almost seamlessly.

The broad picture of radio drama, then, is of a vast diversity of material and of a very great deal of it, which resists categorisation but shades away by imperceptible degrees from the most difficult, not to say forbidding, work into what at least approximates to – and sometimes descends lower than – my groping definition of 'the popular'. Given such a state of affairs, it seems to me that the only way to proceed is both rather arbitrarily and by example, and this is what I now intend to do.

I wrote just now that the gap once dividing Radio 3 from Radio 4 has virtually been closed. This would suggest that, unless the standards of Radio 3 have fallen, those of Radio 4 have gone up. There is no doubt in my mind that this is so and that Radio 4 now finds itself able to present work very much more taxing of its listeners' understanding and experience – even in the other than literal sense – than was the case in 1965, when I first became a professional listener. At that time *Afternoon Theatre*, for example, was a byword for reliable mediocrity from end to end. Standards have risen with the introduction of material at the less popular end of the repertoire, and you might expect that this process would have dragged the lower end up with it. That is precisely what has occurred. Let me illustrate, and in doing so I shall be bringing in certain other topics that stem from this phenomenon.

Here is an excerpt from an *Afternoon Theatre* broadcast in 1966, selected by going through the reviews I then wrote for *The Listener* and picking out plays that had incurred some critical displeasure – a method providing me with no lack of choice. The particular script from which this illustration is taken merely happened to be the first I picked up. I do not intend to identify it further in view of what I have to say about it: why should one author take the rap for the failings of so many others? For the sequence is all too typical of a very ordinary play of a period rich in very ordinary plays. From now on I shall refer to it as 'Exhibit A', and in the following scene a daily help, Mrs Osborne, is talking to her employer, Dorothy, a single lady who has recently given houseroom to a rather difficult teenager.

MRS OSBORNE: Is this what you ordered, Miss, 3lb of stewing beef and a whole leg of lamb?

DOROTHY: Yes, that's right, Mrs Osborne. I'll put the stewing beef on now.

MRS OSBORNE: Might I ask if it's a boy or a young lion you're keeping?

DOROTHY: Is there much difference except that you have to cook the meat for the boy?

MRS OSBORNE: Humph. What with the back room all cluttered up with saws and oilcans and bits of wood, this place has changed overnight and no mistake. But if you don't mind me saying so, you want to be careful, Miss.

DOROTHY:	How do you mean?
MRS OSBORNE:	Boys are very peculiar. You and Mr Bennett [the boy's uncle] may think you've got the measure of this one, but boys can be very unexpected at times.
DOROTHY:	I daresay they can – can't we all?
MRS OSBORNE:	Not to the same extent. He's growing up and he don't care a fig for anyone, he don't really, Miss. Not even his poor dead parents, that's my belief. So don't you and Mr Bennett go expecting too much, will you now?
DOROTHY:	I . . . I'm not awfully sure what you mean . . .[1]

The listener, however, is only too sure what Mrs Osborne means. He has, as it were, been heavily nudged in the ribs by the author who has used one of the oldest gambits in the business: after servants discussing their masters, there can be no more well-worn dramatic cliché than the servant who presumes to instruct or warn his employer. Then consider the dialogue, the actual phraseology: it would be difficult to maintain that no one ever spoke any of the sentences assembled here, but there is something about them in the aggregate which identifies them as the language of playspeak (or to be cruelly exact, radio playspeak), a condition aggravated by the fact that, even if they do not spell out the precise nature of the impending crisis, they are still woefully overexplicit. I must confess that this is a particularly grim and concentrated example of late 1960s domestic. In the rest of the play it is more diluted, but its spirit still clouds the entire work to the point of killing the slightest interest in its no doubt very worthy and topical theme, which I take to be 'the generation gap' or some such fiction. It is from this kind of pit that popular radio drama has had to climb.

How far has it climbed? Here is another exhibit, this time from a *Saturday Night Theatre* play, which is so much more recent that, quite apart from the fact that I do not want to be so damning of it, I think it had better be identified. What follows is the opening of Charlotte Hastings's *The Soft September Air*, first broadcast in October 1978. That this excerpt also features an employer in converse with her daily treasure is pretty much an accident, but it makes for a reasonably meaningful comparison, as does the fact that the subject of their remarks turns out to be another lodger, also of the younger generation.

Garden of Linnets Cottage, evening. September birdsong in the background.

MRS BEVIL:	(*calling*) I'm off now.
LINDSEY:	(*calling*) Thank you, Bev.
MRS BEVIL:	And there's no call for you to be on your knees to them weeds. Bev'll be up Saturday.
LINDSEY:	I'll just finish this border. Saturday we'll lift the dahlias.
MRS BEVIL:	We don't never lift ours. Bevil don't hold with it. Your supper's in the oven and there's a mousse in the fridge – you said you fancied chocolate, but I think lemon's better.
LINDSEY:	Thank you, Bev.

MRS BEVIL:	And George Billing just brought up the late post – two bills – one's the 'lectric. I put 'em on your desk.
LINDSEY:	*Thank* you, Bev.
MRS BEVIL:	And I reckon this one's from your sister.
	Paper noise
LINDSEY:	Oh dear, so it is. How tiresome.
MRS BEVIL:	Ah, she'll not be best pleased when she knows what you're up to. And I'll get gone before this long-haired layabout arrives.
LINDSEY:	Bev, students are not all necessarily long-haired layabouts.
MRS BEVIL:	(*forging on*) Worst thing they ever did, putting that university in the town. All them up there living off social security.
LINDSEY:	And student grants are not social security.
MRS BEVIL:	I don't know why we bother to vote. Bevil says what we need now is a collision government.
LINDSEY:	Oh *Bev*.
MRS BEVIL:	And we don't want one of them lads up here spoiling all the peace and quiet.
LINDSEY:	I cannot be alone at night in this isolated house any longer. And one boy studying quietly in his room is not going to disturb anything.
MRS BEVIL:	(*darkly, going*) Thass as maybe. See you in the morning.[2]

This is surely something of an improvement on 'Exhibit A'. Its expository role, though still plainly visible as a piece of mechanics, is a great deal less heavy-handed, being carried along by the author's interest in the relationship between the two women and by some nice touches of humour. I do not want to overrate its fairly modest virtues and shall be correcting any tendency in that direction within the next few pages; but in comparison with my 1966 specimen, this one seems to me altogether easier, more realistic and interesting. While still employing a stock situation, it makes the listener less aware of it as a cliché; nor does the author's signposting so completely kill all interest in what may be going to happen. In one corner of the field of popular drama, at least, it may be taken as typifying a general and very necessary improvement in the standard of basic radio playwriting during the ten years up to 1979, an improvement that could be matched by examples from plays of many other kinds.

Why should there have been an improvement and how has it come about? After all, by 1966 radio was deep in the depression induced by the runaway success of television, at which time it was even forecast that sound broadcasting was finished except as a medium for purveying news, current affairs and music. Certainly, and even at its lowest ebb, radio drama always declared its interest in raising standards and improving its audience's taste, but at the level of *Afternoon Theatre* that interest tended to wane somewhat as the audience declined. Yet paradoxically it appears to have been television itself which in the end woke radio out of its sleep, and it did this partly for the negative reason that it proved not to be as all-pervasive as had been expected, partly because in some respects it set new standards, which radio has been forced to meet.

From one point of view, television is a very much more lifelike medium than radio. Because the viewer can see what is happening, can read expressions, gestures and other physical actions just as he does in daily conversation, there is no need for so many words. Consequently television dialogue has less difficulty being 'like the real thing' than its radio equivalent, which tends to be preoccupied with the problem of compensating for the listener's 'blindness'. An episode of, say, *Crossroads*, which is economically and realistically written, makes the point well enough. Not surprisingly, anyone who acquires an ear for television dialogue is likely to find the 1966 radio style of 'Exhibit A' a little quaint – to say no more. In addition, characters with some sort of visible appearance, like those of *Crossroads*, are going to find it harder to behave in ways that strain or even slightly stretch the viewer's credulity than those who exist in voice alone.

Rather to the initial astonishment of the makers of radio programmes, viewers turned out to be the same people as listeners. What differentiated them, and still does, was time of day. Your viewers, broadly speaking, exist only from some point in the early evening until 10.30 or so at night. Before that, and especially on weekdays, they are – if they are anything – listeners, and it is thought that they may transmogrify themselves back into listeners again, those who don't go straight to bed, from about 10.30 on. Hence the introduction of Radio 4's *Just Before Midnight* series. Hence, more importantly, the fact that in the television era listeners have become afternoon people and radio drama has turned into what is predominantly an afternoon activity, explaining why the *Afternoon Theatres*, particularly if you add to them the repeats of evening productions, have come to include virtually the entire range of radio plays available. I want to return to this topic, the effect of time of day on radio-drama listening. For the moment, the point I want to make is that when viewers revert to being listeners they bring their television ears with them, and almost from the start these must have told them that, in terms of natural-sounding speech and credible, absorbing action, much of what they heard on radio in the late 1960s and early 1970s was really very poor. The standards of those years would no longer do; and so between them, the audience and the radio dramatists – using the term to include script editors, producers, actors, as well as the writers themselves – have combined to create a popular radio drama that is no longer as woefully contrived and dead as were so many of the specimens I have listened to.

In using *The Soft September Air* as an example, I said I did not wish to overrate it. Indeed that should apply to the situation as a whole, but let me refer to Ms Hastings's play again, as well as to 'Exhibit A', to make clear what I am saying. While Charlotte Hastings is plainly better at the job of radio playwriting than her anonymous predecessor, it must be obvious that both these plays are in the very same tradition. I do not mean that both are rooted in middle-class settings: many plays could be found to show that that is not a necessary distinguishing mark of popular BBC drama. What I do mean is that each takes an issue of some contemporary social interest and each, according to professional ability and the differing standards of the day, *manufactures* a play out of it. In doing this, each, it seems to me, owes a great deal to that famous model of so many playwrights for so many years past: the well-made play of the slightly more serious kind. Here the ancient convention of more or less barefaced exposition was accepted, even encouraged; so was the step-by-step, signposted build-up to some crisis that the last act would resolve. What was often missing from the species was any sense of a play growing of itself, from the inside, by an almost organic compulsion. That sense was certainly missing from 'Exhibit A' and, despite its greater accomplishment, was also missing from *The Soft September Air*. Because of this, not all the art of Flora Robson in the leading role could persuade this listener anyway that his experience had been in any way enlarged – which is what I take to be the point of the whole radio-dramatic enterprise.

What is a radio play like when it is not deficient in this way? Let me produce a third exhibit, saying only that yet again and by another act of chance this too presents an encounter between servant and employer: Dot, a companion-nurse-housekeeper, and Sybil, a very ancient lady. They are characters in Jehane Markham's *More Cherry Cake*, which like *The Soft September Air* was first broadcast in October 1978 on *Afternoon Theatre*. Here is the opening sequence:

SYBIL: Thomas and I with the boys on the beach at Seaford . . . before the war. Thomas is wearing white flannels. The wind blows the cloth against his legs. It is hot. We sit with our backs to the breakwater. Tar melts between the cracks of the bleached wood. The children drink lemonade out of bottles with straws.
Pause. Title of play announced.
DOT: (*murmuring*) Butter in curls in butter dish. Jam in a pot with long-handled spoon.
Opens door
Did you have a nice rest?
SYBIL: I heard that baby again.
DOT: Have you been worrying?
SYBIL: Not really worrying.
DOT: You've been upsetting yourself again. What's the problem?
SYBIL: I heard a baby crying quite distinctly.
DOT: There aren't any babies for miles around here. I've already told you. It's your ears playing you up again. You know what Dr Williams said.
SYBIL: If only his father were still alive, he knew how to put everything right.
DOT: Shall we get tidied up now?
SYBIL: I'm not a piece of furniture.
DOT: You know what I mean. Do you want to pay a visit?
SYBIL: No thank you.
DOT: Quite sure? You know what happened last time.
SYBIL: What are you talking about?

DOT: What happened last time you sat out in the garden.
SYBIL: I don't know what you're talking about.
DOT: Come on, up you get. That's it.
SYBIL: Don't fuss. I'm up now.
DOT: Slowly does it.
SYBIL: As if there were any other way.[3]

Can there be any doubt that this is in a different class of writing from my first two examples? Consider the opening short soliloquy; at once the scene springs to mind – an old lady gazing at an ancient seaside photograph. We are not told that this is what she is doing because we do not have to be. The writer has selected half a dozen images which at once identify it, and these will find their parallels in the memory of almost anyone over a certain age who has ever been to the seaside. In doing this, she establishes a pattern of interior reminiscence and reflection which will be a hallmark of her play. The short speech that follows is remarkable for its economy: 'Butter in curls in a butter dish. Jam in a pot with a long spoon.' We know at once that this is teatime and tea for a special occasion – which indeed it is: Sybil's son and her granddaughter are to visit. We also know that this is a household where that style of presentation is expected and where there is someone whose job it is to see to it. Then by the kind of shorthand that radio not only allows but thrives on, a door opens and the next scene is launched. Here too the dialogue is economical, with its terse non-expository sentences, so much closer to how people speak than anything I have already cited. The upshot is that we actually learn more about the situation the play will explore than the expository method could have told us in twice the time. We know this old lady and her nurse and how it is between them; the play is already alive and burgeoning.

Of course, I must not give the impression that it is all a matter of dialogue. That scene change into 'Did you have a nice rest?' shows an immediate grasp of how to write not just a play but a radio play; so does the opening soliloquy (and note that it is not a device, not a talking-to-oneself which happens to be overheard), for it takes us straight into the interior, private world, where radio drama, as this author clearly knows, is at once most penetrating and most at its ease. Radio is a private medium, heard by each of its listeners as if he were its sole recipient, and it can therefore address us at a level of intimate personal reflection in a way not open to television, theatre or the cinema. When it does that, it is exercising a unique ability and, if we had not recognised the fact before, we suddenly know that we are gaining from it something not easily available elsewhere. This is the key distinction to be made between *More Cherry Cake* and *The Soft September Air* together with its ancestor 'Exhibit A'.

A niggling question arises at this point: is Ms Markham's play an example of what this chapter is supposed to be about? Can it in my expanded terms be described as popular? From many points of view of course it can. Its theme is an experience, or more properly a variety of experiences, most of which not one of us can avoid – growing up, growing apart, growing reluctantly dependent, growing old, facing death. Its characters are ordinary people; they speak and think as many of us do, middle-class or no. There are no very complex ideas for the listener to cope with, nor any radiophonic pyrotechnics – which does not at all stop the piece being a genuine play for radio, as opposed to a play that just happens to be broadcast. As a whole it does the job of conveying information, images and feeling with, to put it no higher, immense efficiency – far beyond the average. If this is so, why are there not more plays like *More Cherry Cake*? Why do the listeners whom television educated to demand a standard of radio writing better than 'Exhibit A' not now rise up and declare that the standards of *The Soft September Air* are no longer good enough either?

There are various reasons, and several of them have to do with the way things are now arranged and seem likely to remain. *More Cherry Cake* is what I have described as 'alive and burgeoning' – in other words it conveys that sense of organic growth, from the inside, and this is not a quality which can be called into existence just like that. It is amongst other things the product of inspiration and of talent, neither of which is in plentiful supply – certainly not enough to ensure that any but a small proportion of creative work in any medium will be more than fair-to-middling. This alone seems to me basic, but radio as a dramatic medium labours under two other burdens. First, the whole structure of the Radio 4 network puts it under an obligation to find some five hundred new and original scripts every year, while the total of all productions passing through the Department comes to something like eighteen hundred annually; a necessity such as this is going to spread even the richest vein of talent pretty thin. Second, radio has established itself as the one medium in which a quite untried playwright can hope to see his work performed. This, of course, is admirable and I have personal cause to admire it, but first plays, even performed first plays, can be pretty dire. These two burdens combine in such a way that, even today and despite all improvements, radio drama at its worst becomes unique for quite the wrong reasons: it puts out a number of plays too weak to survive in any other medium. At less than its worst, a high proportion of it is extremely ordinary.

According to some people, this situation would be much improved, if not altogether mended, were radio able to pay its writers better money – the current rate for a radio play is a good deal less than half what the same amount of work would earn from television. There is some force in this argument, but probably not as much as its supporters claim. More money would do little or nothing to increase available talent; it would merely lure some of it to radio, either anew or for the first time. Unfortunately there is no guarantee that the successful writer in another medium will be the slightest use to radio except as a great name: work by the late Sir Terence Rattigan and by William

Golding exists to prove it. First-class radio writing demands a rather special brand of creative ability, either alone or as an adjunct to whatever other talents a writer may already possess.

Yet, in spite of all I have said, it might still be expected that radio writers at all levels would show a greater interest than the evidence suggests they do in employing what might be called the grammar and syntax appropriate to radio. There is, at least up to a point, the work of the Old Radio Masters to refer to. Professional interest alone might surely recommend exploration of the techniques of the medium in which one happens to be working, not to mention the pleasure in it – which is considerable – as well as the fact that such exploration might actually suggest original creative ideas. That this does not happen to anything like the extent it might, points to another aspect of television's influence, but one that is not so beneficial. As it has been explained to me, writers fight shy of writing 'pure' radio for the very understandable reason that they tend to write for television first and, when rejected as most of them will be, to use radio as a longstop. This is probably compounded by the fact that neither the BBC Drama Department nor the audience is actually going to demand such writing from them. A radio producer, for example, given a script, will ensure that its performance will be comprehensible in sound alone, but he will not feel under any obligation to ask the author to recast it in a way that *only* sound will be able to convey.

As regards the audience, perhaps in this respect it has no influence – and indeed in discussing all broadcasting it is quite common to imply that the listeners-cum-viewers are a sort of inert mass on whom the broadcasters impose whatever their contempt or intellectual pretensions dictate. The response of radio drama to its audience's interest in better writing suggests that this is not at all the case, and indeed broadcasters always seem to be haunted by an image of 'the listener' and 'the viewer' – perhaps, ironically, because he can hardly ever be seen and has to be imagined. For myself, I have always been much struck by the way in which broadcasting and its audience, like twin stars, revolve around and substantially determine each other. It is, I think, worth looking at some of the traits of the audience to try to see in what ways it influences and forms the drama fed to it, though first I should make clear that it is highly misleading to write as I have done about '*the* audience'. There are audiences – plural – and in radio these are for different kinds of music, different kinds of magazines, different styles of news, and therefore also different kinds of plays.

What are these audiences? Despite what I have just said of their diversity, there are in fact certain respects in which they behave in a highly unified fashion. One such behaviour I have already mentioned: the radio-drama listener is above all a creature of the afternoons, and the degree to which this is so is obvious from the listening figures. The 'Sunday Serial', for instance, when transmitted just after 9.00 p.m., usually attracts less than half as big an audience as its Tuesday

afternoon repeat. The same goes for *The Archers*, but somewhat back
to front: originating in the early afternoons it attracts roughly
three-quarters of a million pairs of ears, but that number drops to three
hundred thousand for the evening show. When the omnibus edition
went out on Sunday morning some million people heard it; moved to
Sunday evening the figure was down to three hundred thousand.
Waggoners' Walk, by contrast, which is first heard in the morning,
loses only about a third of its one and a quarter million listeners when it
repeats at teatime. Here, then, is one way in which audiences impose
on broadcasting, and implicit in it is the really rather discouraging
message to radio dramatists that their success (as measured by
audience) is only partly related to the quality of what they do; it is as
much or more a function of the time of day.

Success of this kind also varies with the wavelength. One of the
deadliest blows to *The Archers'* listening figures was delivered when in
1966 the serial moved from the Light Programme to the Home Service
and lost a million or something like a fifth of its audience. That the
1979 audience for *Waggoners' Walk* is double that of *The Archers* may
be as much a measure of its place on Radio 2 as of any superior
qualities it possesses. These are less important – and again how
cheering for the dramatists – than the fact that such a large percentage
of the total audience goes for Radio 2's style of easy music and chat and
will consume whatever comes with it. To a very great extent listeners
patronise wavelengths not programmes, somewhat as shoppers
patronise a particular supermarket and are content to take what it
stocks. They are probably confirmed in this behaviour by an apparent
difficulty, most peculiar in a nation of our technical competence, in
mastering how to retune a radio set.

There is another general characteristic of daytime audiences: few of
their members will be at leisure. The chances are they will be doing
something (cooking, cleaning, driving, painting the ceiling), but they
will be able to listen to the radio no matter what, thanks to the
existence of the portable transistor. What all this has done for radio
listening is to turn it into a secondary activity, and here again the habits
of the listeners have imposed themselves on broadcasting. In all
departments of radio a very large number of programmes are now
devised on the assumption that they will not have and cannot be made
to have their hearers' full attention. Drama, like it or not, is part of this
situation. A proportion of every afternoon audience will be looking for
something secondary, a diversion to ease an hour spent, say, at the
sink. Whatever such a listener is to hear and understand had best not
be too unfamiliar in form or content. Even in the cinema, the theatre
or in front of the television set, where at least in theory the watcher can
give his attention to little else, nothing succeeds like the stock
situation. There is an immense and really very interesting gratification
in seeing the same routine, or a near variation of it, played over and
over again. How much more must this apply to radio, where whatever

is happening must be grasped from fleeting speech and sound alone and in competition with, let us say, the muffled rattle of wet dishes. If we consider the illustrations I have given, then it is fairly obvious that a play like *The Soft September Air*, explicit and expository as it is, must meet criteria of instant comprehensibility a good deal better than *More Cherry Cake*, which demands that you listen to it as something more than a secondary activity. I really doubt whether most listeners want that sort of demand from their radios, and this is surely one good reason why the 'pure' radio play is not more common than it is.

What is it, over and above the elements which have already emerged, that drama audiences do want? I assume here that, to a large extent, want corresponds to what is already there, otherwise it would not continue to survive; and one immediately identifiable want is for a substitute theatre. There must be hundreds of thousands, possibly millions, of people in this country who cannot reach a live theatre or cannot afford it if they are able to reach it. Accordingly a substantial part of the radio-drama repertoire consists of stage classics, old and new, adapted for sound. Because they were always conceived to be seen in a theatre, they survive the transition with varying degrees of success, and as a general rule those that find it hardest to live within the confines of a stage come off best. *Peer Gynt*, though hardly a popular piece, will indicate what I mean. However, a substitute theatre, usually with first-class actors, is certainly better than none.

The need for a substitute literature is somewhat harder to understand, but the number of plays adapted from established novels leaves no doubt that there is an audience for it. Here adaptation always takes its toll: the author tends to disappear with the prose and cannot generally be recreated in the dialogue that has to do duty for it. If the author happens to be Henry James, the loss will be a savage one, but from another point of view there is a certain natural sympathy in radio for the novel form. Both can take all sorts of liberties with time and place, and both are interested in the interior world of human beings. An adaptation can be a great work seen afresh, and the best of them are.

It seems plain that audiences also want the plays they hear to feature the issues of the day – or at least those recognised to be so; and they look for interesting information about the world. Radio's response to this second want might seem to be contained in the dramatised documentary, although in my experience the dramatic element in documentaries so very often falls below the standard even of 'Exhibit A' that it may actually inspire rejection of what it hopes to communicate. In any case the informative role of drama is very much more all-pervading than that. *The Archers*, for example, was for many years of its existence as much a means of telling the public about agriculture as it was a dramatic entertainment, and the public was happy to be told. It is said that the foreign ways and customs of *Waggoners' Walk*, which is set in Hampstead, exercise a great fascination in the working Midlands and North, pointing to an enormous appetite for information about how other fractions of the population live: their jobs, lives at home, relationships within the family and without, values, attitudes. Details of this kind are the stuff of radio plays of every kind; by listening widely it would be possible to build up a very full picture of the various nations we are. To put it another way, much of radio drama offers an opportunity to spy on one's neighbours, near and far, to indulge in one of the enduring pleasures of human beings but to do so without any of the attendant risks, like having to go and look or getting caught in the act of looking. It offers a related pleasure too: it holds up a mirror to one's own existence – one which may reveal things the owner of the mirror image did not know about himself before, but not necessarily with greater penetration than that achieved by seeing a photo or a cine picture of oneself. It is, after all, extraordinarily beguiling merely to hear oneself 'played back', and this is certainly part of the want, the fascination, particularly as regards the daily serials – the encounter with lives and problems so very like one's own. The whole affair resembles a neighbourly chat, without of course the benefits of human contact, but with none of the pressures either.

On this analysis, as far as it has gone, the audiences' behaviour and their wants suggest patterns of listening which the actual content of programmes does little to modify, as well as a preference in that content for what, in some general sense, they already know. In case anyone should draw such an inference, let me say that I do not for a moment mean to equate the known with the dull or not-worth-doing. There are, after all, degrees of familiarity, some aspects of life that are a good deal better known than others, suggesting perhaps another kind of continuum from the decidedly stale to what, despite repetition, remains interesting and full of possibilities. For example, a glance at any selection of 'Sunday Serial' productions (or, for that matter, of the single plays that started life as novels or on the stage) reveals an immense amount of literary work difficult to exhaust. Has anyone ever known, say, *The Pickwick Papers* to the point at which he feels he has sucked it dry and never wishes to hear the thing again? And yet, from another point of view, even works such as this possess a profound, almost numbing familiarity. They are part of our immense cultural baggage – more than that, part of a national rite – and as such must be heard to a considerable extent for the pleasure of the replay, the recital; or if not that, then because the hearer, seeing them as part of everybody else's cultural-ritual baggage, has not yet made them part of his own and has a guilty feeling that he ought to do so.

What I have been outlining is not, it seems to me, a situation likely to promote the best in radio writing, for it also has to be said that the kind of writing that uses radio's peculiar capacities – even, like Jehane Markham's, in relatively sober fashion – will always tend to wander into a less familiar world. Other examples could be cited: Derek

Raby's *Tiger* (1974) and J.C.W. Brook's *Giving Up* (1978) are two that come to mind, both of them unassuming plays, but the first built round a thoughtful conversation, which explores ideas of freedom, between a small boy and a tiger in a zoo, the other about the effort to give up the smoking habit (or indeed habits in general) as experienced by different organs of the body. This sort of play, unthinkable except on radio, is also quite uncommon by comparison with the rest, the bulk of the repertoire which on the whole has no particular affinity for sound alone. On the basis of my argument that this repertoire represents pretty much what audiences want, the comparative scarcity of the 'pure' radio play, with its unfamiliar, exploratory elements, suggests that most listeners are not really interested in it. Add to this the other factors I have referred to – radio drama's huge appetite for material, its obligations to the beginner, the financial and other lures of television, the shortage of talent that likes, and is able to express itself in, 'pure' radio terms – then perhaps the wonder is that the scarcity is not a total lack.

I wrote earlier that if I took as a criterion of popularity that of 'accessible to and followed by the largest audiences radio can currently assemble', then I would have to confine myself to discussion of *The Archers* and *Waggoners' Walk*. As it is, I have come this far without much more than a passing reference to either. Yet of all radio's dramas, these and their predecessors are undeniably the most obviously, numerously popular there are now or ever have been, so I cannot end without some consideration of them. They may, besides, cast more light on some of the topics that have already emerged.

The first in a line that runs direct through *Mrs Dale's Diary* (later *The Dales*) to *The Dales'* successor, *Waggoners' Walk*, was *The Robinson Family* (later *The Robinsons* – both changes of title, incidentally, bringing very similar waves of protest). I do not recall ever listening to *The Robinsons*, but reactions to it seem to have been very like reactions we have heard since. A child is killed off by the writers and there ensues a small flood of letters of objection or commiseration, some of the latter indistinguishable from those written for real. A new actress takes on the part of Mrs Robinson and provokes the comment: 'The Robinsons may be all right for men listeners, but to me it's infuriating to hear "Maggie" [the character previously played by the actress now playing Mrs Robinson] pretend she's Mrs Robinson and Mr Robinson not seeming to notice any difference.' Both of these are surely pointers to the way in which the daily serial and listeners' imaginations have entered into a conspiracy: not only do they picture the fiction as very like daily life, but some of them do so as if it were that very thing. This suggests that the human imagination, in contrast to claims made for it, is frequently content, indeed eager, to spend itself in visualising the known, the familiar. Is this what happens?

The Robinsons is all but forgotten. The serial that overlapped with both it and *Mrs Dale's Diary* is still a household name, revived in full stereocolour for the BBC's Golden Jubilee and since then enshrined in television: *Dick Barton – Special Agent*. The first transmission went out in October 1946 and by the following April it was reckoned to have some fifteen million listeners. One of them wrote to the show's then producer, Raymond Raikes: 'A young friend of mine aged 10 was at his Sunday School class. The teacher said: "Who made you?" "God, sir." "And who looks after you all day?" "God, sir." "And who would you turn to if you were in trouble?" "Dick Barton, sir!" '[4] Barton had his detractors, too: '*Please* kill Dick Barton soon', wrote a Royal Engineer from Gibraltar. A thirteen-point 'Rules of Conduct' was drawn up for the writing of *Dick Barton*, according to which authors were asked not to include such vices as swearing, lying, drinking, sadism or even the mildest forms of sex. In spite of these rules, and they were moderately well observed, the poor Captain found himself held responsible for outbreaks of juvenile delinquency up and down the land. Oh, shades of things to come . . . In short, this thriller serial displayed many of the characteristics associated with the more domestic kind: intense involvement of a huge audience and an apparently very potent influence on daily life. Did *Dick Barton* affect behaviour? Did young lads go out and bash pensioners after listening to it? Or save them gallantly from being bashed? Perhaps: perhaps not. What *Dick Barton* did was to affect the behaviour of imagining, and making assertions about, what affected behaviour, which is in its turn a form of affecting behaviour.

At this point the question may arise: do I really have the nerve to hold up *Dick Barton* as an instance of imagination spent in visualising the familiar? In spite of Rule 12, which held that 'the theme of the-man-who-wants-to-control-the-Earth creates little impact', a large number of stories – and all three surviving episodes in the BBC Archive – revolved around it, and what could be more improbable? 'Utterly fantastic', wrote one civil-servant listener: he went on, however: 'But very absorbing. Like ivy, it grows on one.' Of course *Dick Barton* was fantastic. So is James Bond, of whom Barton appears as an innocent Boy Scout precursor, and this comparison, I suggest, enables one to see that the realm of the fantastic is one in which the imagination is as prone to take exercise as in picturing the everyday familiar. Both provide it with easy options, one element of which is that both offer a good deal of emotional stimulus. In personal experience, the two, far from being dissimilar, feel rather closely related to one another.

The Dales, or to be more accurate *Mrs Dale's Diary*, is still, like *Dick Barton*, something of a household name, but principally, I suspect, because a great number of people who never listen to radio believe either that it is still running, or that it represents radio as it is, or both. Although not quite as cosy as its critics liked to suggest, it was unarguably devoted to representing a world – a predominantly middle-class one – with which its listeners were in the mass utterly familiar. It generated great audience involvement and response, much of which gave fresh evidence of what had already, in *The Robinsons*, established itself as a basic element in the relationship of many listeners to the domestic daily serial: up to a point, and the point varies with individuals, they believe it to be true. Dr Dale, for instance, complaining of his breakfast kippers – or was it the lack of them? – received kippers through the post. In this case you might say there was an added reason for belief, because the part of Dr Jim Dale was for a time played by an actor called James Dale. However, the history of the most famous serial of all, *The Archers*, has gone to show that no such minor inducements are necessary. The audience is always there and waiting, looking for something to which to anchor its belief.

The power of *The Archers* to be taken for real has always been enormous from the time, quite early in its run, when it became a national institution. This has continued in spite of the fact that at times some of the writing has been such as to make 'Exhibit A' look like the work of Shakespeare. If the desire to believe is there, then it makes little or no difference that the representation is comparatively crude. Admittedly, by the beginning of 1979 there was a good deal to suggest that the audience's level of passionate credulity had fallen off very sharply, but in a contribution to Ray Gosling's study of the soap opera, *Friends and Neighbours*, first broadcast in January 1978, Edgar Harrison, who is the third and newest Dan Archer, was able to report as follows:

I remember a letter I had, not all that long ago – well, time goes by so quickly, it's probably longer than I thought, but you know we publish a paper periodically called *The Borchester Echo* and it's got up like an ordinary paper with adverts and so on. And I had a letter from an old lady living in London – she obviously lived in a sort of concrete block, I should think – saying that she'd seen property advertised in *The Borchester Echo* and did I think I could find them a cottage in Ambridge. She said she was 76, her sister was 78 and they'd very much like to come and live in the country. And what do you say to people like that? I wrote back and said, well, there was property available from time to time – I wrote back as Dan, of course – and said that it was very expensive and I felt at their time of life that it wasn't wise to pull up all their roots and come and live in the country after living in London for so long, but I hoped they'd go on listening to the programme.[5]

It is tempting to wonder how Mr Harrison saw his own identity as he signed himself 'Dan Archer', the more so when one considers a remark in the same programme by William Smethurst, former *Archers'* scriptwriter who went on to be editor: 'If I switch on *The Archers*, they are far more real to me than most people in my own village, far more real to me.' They have, additionally, been far more influential than a great many people of well-attested reality and influence on daily life. The story of how it was necessary for Dan Archer not to go over suddenly from dairy shorthorns to a better milking breed in case the farming nation chaotically followed suit is too well known to need full repetition; could any Minister of Agriculture wield such power? More recently (December 1978) the impending marriage of Christine Archer to a divorced man and a suggestion that the vicar of Ambridge might give it his official blessing was the subject of a disapproving pronouncement from no less a reality that the Bishop of Truro, and this in turn provoked a heartfelt correspondence in the national press. The curious thing is that, in terms of size of audience, *The Archers* cannot possibly exercise the sway it did in the late 1950s. The influence it retains must be by a sort of tradition, now very difficult to change.

It is interesting that *Waggoners' Walk*, with a much bigger audience, has turned its attention not only to the marriage of divorced persons but to other hot topics – homosexuality, drug addiction – without the national emotional seismograph so much as hiccupping. This suggests, perhaps, that the power of the kind of belief that reached such heights with *The Archers* has itself begun to decline, and that some kind of social focus has shifted to other areas. *Waggoners' Walk* has never held its listeners in the kind of trance produced by Ambridge, and in the main they do not seem to be in any doubt that what they are hearing is a fiction. National tastes, values and attitudes have changed; it is far easier for a serial only ten years old to reflect this than for one three times that age.

What has given *The Archers* its extraordinary influence? In most respects the factors that have contributed to it are no different from those affecting any other serial. Like *The Robinsons* and *The Dales*, it has inhabited a very familiar world of human experience, even if the rural setting is outside the intimate knowledge of the greater part of the population: like them, it has been built round the fortunes of one family – a great spur to identification. All serials profit from cumulative effect. The single radio play has come and gone in an hour or so, but the daily serial is there day after day, year after year, and in that respect, of course, it additionally resembles life. Moreover, by a kind of paradox, the longer it runs, the more people get to know the characters until, as in the case of *The Archers*, a simple country family is 'known' in some detail to about a quarter of the adult population of the United Kingdom alone. This ought to annul belief in their reality but actually appears to reinforce it.

Given a good story, well-written and well-developed, the factors I have mentioned are enough to ensure a decent run for any daily serial, but they do not account for the truly magnetic attraction exerted by Ambridge life. This, I believe, has always lain in the very element that has, in one sense, been *less* familiar to many of its listeners: the country setting. That is to say, *The Archers* has been able to play on what is, in another sense, an exceedingly familiar and captivating idea to British minds: the notion, the romance, the fantasy of country life, of living close to the land. Perhaps it was this state of mind and the possibility it offered that the serial's originator, Godfrey Baseley, was able to perceive on that almost legendary day when someone suggested 'a farming *Dick Barton*'. It was a marvellous idea and, like many such, part of the marvel was in its timeliness, coming as it did to a nation which as a result of the war had often become forcibly, superficially, but not always disagreeably acquainted with the countryside, and which in the dreary days of the late 1940s was more than ready for a glimpse of modern Arcady. It may also be that the grip maintained by *The Archers* is exactly what you would expect of a society in which, during the time the serial has been running, the proportion of the population actually earning its living from agriculture has declined to about two per cent. It is hard to imagine *The Archers* going down too well with, for example, the French, whose agricultural population is vastly greater than Britain's and in whom one detects an altogether less romantic attitude toward the land.

At a more practical level, *The Archers* has continued to cast its spell because, with occasional lapses, it has been kept up to the mark. These days it sounds a good deal less like a Ministry of Agriculture hand-out, and this reflects several things – most obvious among them the elimination of some distinctly tired writing by bringing in new hands. Many listeners may still be recovering from the shock occasioned by the importation of Malcolm Lynch from *Coronation Street*, after which, for a brief period, *The Archers* actually did begin to resemble 'a farming *Dick Barton*'. The culmination came when the bells fell down Ambridge Church tower. Life sobered up after that and just as well, but the necessary kick had been administered. New writers and editors quickly appreciated that the departmental hand-out style was finished, not only because it represented poor writing, but because an audience of the early 1970s had acquired a higher expectation of how drama should sound. Over the years farming itself has changed, becoming, as that drop in the working population would suggest, much more businesslike and mechanised. Accordingly, the scripts have changed and now concentrate much less on the minutiae of farming practice. They continue to reflect it, of course, but the fact is that the practice now corresponds even less closely than it did to the English town- or suburb-dweller's dreams of Arcady. Where is the romance in the broiler house or the intensive pig-rearing unit? *The Archers* has turned more to personalities, relationships, issues of a general sort, values, attitudes. The creation of the aggravating Shula Archer probably illustrates this as well as anything – through her character are reflected not only changes in society and in audience expectation, but even in the BBC's attitude to its listeners. By this process, life in Ambridge has come to resemble more closely life elsewhere, and *The Archers* as a serial has come closer to *Waggoners' Walk*. Here, in a community whose only bond is the accidental one of a Hampstead locality, the emphasis has always been on personalities and relationships. *Waggoners' Walk* is very tightly written and constructed, very confident and well characterised; its audience lead over *The Archers* may not be attributable only to its place on Radio 2. Perhaps the perplexity in Ambridge now should be over discovering what familiar things, what fantasies, what gratifications it can offer to a large audience that *Waggoners' Walk* cannot.

The moment has come to attempt, if not a summary, at least a rounding off. Radio, so the story goes, and radio drama in particular, has been and is and always will be the medium of the imagination. The anecdote is quoted time and again, like a Tradition of the Prophet, of the small boy who was asked why he so liked listening. He is reported to have replied: 'Because the pictures are so good.' But what sort of pictures? What sort of work for the imagination?

It is of course perfectly true, in fact unavoidable, that almost any kind of radio listening requires an act of the imagination. What, after all, is more unlikely than that a human voice or the sound of a full orchestra should emerge from a small, knob-encrusted box? Alasdair Clayre quotes a Yorkshire child who, hearing radio for the first time in a neighbour's house, went home and declared, 'Mother, Mrs Buckle's wall is singing'[6] – which might be called the response primitive-magical. To comprehend radio at all, it is first advisable to set aside the idea of a singing or speaking wall and to be able to allow other explanations which may not at first hearing be any less implausible and of which our fundamental grasp may be very slight. Most of us manage if not an understanding then an acceptance.

When it comes to radio drama, without the exercise of the imagination there is nothing at all. Take the most commonplace play you can think of: to grasp even that, the listener must construct out of clues provided by words and sounds the appearance and the actions of the people represented, as well as their environment. No one can deny that this is a use of the imagination, but it is – if I may suggest a parallel – rather like the example of dried milk. We start with fresh milk (representing everyday life and experience), dehydrate it to powder (reduce the basic material to the elements of sound, which is all radio can transmit), distribute (broadcast) it, and by adding water (imagination) arrive at something not quite like what we started with. What I have written leads me to wonder whether radio drama is really doing anything much more advanced than that in most of its manifestations. There can be little doubt that this is the limit of the demand made by those indisputable representatives of the popular, the daily serials. With varying degrees of competence, a vast number of single plays work over the same sort of ground and make the same sort of imaginative demand: that the listener should recreate in his head what he is already, visually or in his experience of human behaviour, pretty familiar with; that he should identify with this material and, up to a point, accept it as 'happening'.

Popular or no, all radio plays are in the same boat: the audience is 'blind', and since this is a necessity it ought also to be made a virtue.

But one characteristic of the vast majority of radio plays is that they seem to feel obliged not to use this blindness but to compensate for it. To return briefly to my three opening exhibits: sheer radio-literary skills apart, what separates Jehane Markham's play from the other two is that, where they seem to be asking the listener to conjure up scenes and appearances for which vision would in fact be an improvement, hers spends part of its time in an area – the inside of the human head – where for the listener to be able to see would be no advantage to him at all, but rather an impediment.

'Popular radio drama' was the title suggested to me for this chapter. Perhaps the true conclusion to be drawn from it is not, as I made out at the beginning, that the creature is hard to pin down and discuss because of an embarrassment of riches; it might be nearer the mark to say that, like the yeti, it is a job to sight it at all. What we actually find on radio are many, many plays on all kinds of topics and of all kinds of difficulty (intellectual, emotional, literary), but probably more of them 'popular' – as I have defined it – than not. For various reasons having to do with the giant's appetite of the medium, the wants and discrimination of its audiences, and the needs, hopes and ambitions of its authors, the majority of these plays have no essential affinity with sound broadcasting: they just happen to have landed there. A popular radio drama – indeed a *radio* drama – in any substantial sense may be something that we do not really have.

Notes

1. Quoted from the script in the BBC Play Library, Broadcasting House, London.
2. Quoted from the script in the BBC Play Library, Broadcasting House, London. A stage version of this play was published by Samuel French in 1979.
3. Quoted from the script in the BBC Play Library, Broadcasting House, London.
4. I am indebted to Raymond Raikes for this and some other information about *Dick Barton*.
5. Quotations from *Friends and Neighbours* are taken from the script in the BBC Documentary and Talks Library, Broadcasting House, London.
6. *The Impact of Broadcasting*. Salisbury, Wilts 1973, p. 11.

Chapter 7

The essence that's not seen: radio adaptations of stage plays

John Drakakis

In a recent newspaper interview, the new Controller of BBC Radio 3, Ian McIntyre, outlined his plans for introducing a measure of 'discipline' into the area of future programming. Rejecting what he considered to be the rather 'wet' practice of beginning major drama productions at times such as 'nineteen and a half minutes past eight', he went on to say, in connection with a forthcoming radio production of Shakespeare's *Coriolanus*, 'eight o'clock's the time you go to the theatre, or seven-thirty. Let's do that.'[1] The image of the Controller as theatrical impresario was not lost upon the interviewer, Paul Ferris, and has come to represent a view of his role that in more general terms the BBC has sought to foster in recent years. Such an image would clearly avoid some of the more contentious issues arising from the now customary identification of 'the medium' with 'the message', and has come to be regarded by some commentators as part of a larger argument in defence of the 'objectivity' and 'neutrality' of the broadcaster.[2]

This attempt to promulgate the notion of the 'transparency' of the medium, which allows radio in chameleon-like fashion to take into itself the habits and, in some respects, the practices of the live theatre, has a well-tried historical pedigree. In the sphere of dramatic production generally, early practice measured itself against that of the traditional live theatre, although early theory, in an attempt to sustain its claim for the unique aesthetic attributes of radio, was at pains to keep the two separate. Paradoxically, these questions of identity and aesthetic validity could be resolved only with direct reference to an already existing canon of dramatic literature, and even though the adaptation of theatre plays for radio has over the years become a major part of the drama output of the BBC, this uneasy duality, present from the outset, has fuelled both the aspirations and the disappointments of successive generations of broadcasters. Indeed, as early as 1929 when the call for a specifically *radio* drama was at its loudest and, with the work of Tyrone Guthrie, Lance Sieveking and L. du Garde Peach, looked like being answered, the *BBC Handbook* could naively assert that the medium was admirably placed to occupy a space in the nation's cultural life left vacant by the absence of a 'national theatre': 'It has the means of spanning the unprofitable dramatic ground which lies between the commercial and the artistic; between the business theatre of to-day and the national theatre of to-morrow.'[3] Moreover, Sir John (later Lord) Reith himself, while regretting the overdependence of early dramatic broadcasts upon 'theatre effect',[4] could also regard radio as a supreme means of 'popularizing' the one dramatist to whom both the theatre and the world of literature could lay equal claim, Shakespeare.[5]

The implications of this apparent contradiction are of particular relevance to the larger theoretical issues involved in the adaptation of stage plays for radio, especially since drama now possesses a dual identity, both as script intended for performance and as self-contained literary text. Indeed, it raises a fundamental question of what precisely is being adapted, since, along with the exhortation to establish its own identity, radio was from the outset encouraged to discharge a wider cultural responsibility to the very corpus of drama, much of which had long been appropriated into the specialist category of 'literature'.[6] Thus Reith's suggestion concerning the popularisation of Shakespeare may be interpreted as a bid to attach radio firmly to an already established pattern of cultural values, thereby upholding and preserving the aesthetic judgements of the very institution it threatened to displace.

This location of the radio adaptation of stage plays within a particular network of values has been sustained with remarkable consistency during the last fifty years. With the reorganisation of radio during 1945-6 and the beginnings of selective listening, which was itself further reinforced in the early 1960s by the programmed juxtaposition of drama and classical music, adaptations, whether broadcast on the Third Programme or the Home Service, were usually associated with minority audiences. Allied to this, the question of 'standards', which has always been part of radio's defensive strategy, began in certain quarters to take precedence over that of 'entertainment' to the point where the Third Programme came to be regarded above all as the repository of cultural and, hence, literary excellence. Writers such as Henry Reed welcomed this segregation on the basis of the principle that 'some listeners are fools and some are not, and . . . we cannot wait for the fools to catch up with their betters',[7] and he went on to affirm that the criterion of excellence for all writing, including that of original radio writing, was its phenomenological (and by implication ideological) durability:

In the last resort, the printed page must become the easily available repository of all good talk and writing; on the printed page dramatic literature remains perennially fresh and possible and reproducible in the mind; we neither need nor want the assistance of the actor every time to provide the human voice.[8]

This mandarin emphasis on the relationship between quality, exclusivity and permanence, with its implied commitment to an 'idealism of the essence'[9] as opposed to that assumed to exist between the popular, the trivial and the ephemeral, served to reinforce the placement of *all* dramatic writing, and especially radio writing, in some sort of platonic relationship to the category of 'literature'. Once having established this relationship, the question of the listener's response was itself axiomatic: the process of 'listening' became analogous to that of 'reading'.[10] Thus, extending the logical scope of Reed's argument, radio adaptation, like theatre performance, need be regarded as no more than a superfluous reaffirmation, ephemeral in its dynamics, of essential truths accessible to broadcaster and listener alike on condition that both parties possessed the requisite taste and imagination. According to this philosophy, the radio adaptation of a stage play could never be more than a pale shadow of a *literary* original, and where theatrical performance represented an intermediate stage – as with, say, broadcasts of Stratford productions of particular Shakespeare plays – a radio adaptation, such as it was, simply became one step further removed from the original.

Although Reed wrote and adapted for radio,[11] he was rather more sceptical than most about the extravagant claims being made for the uniqueness of the medium. Indeed, given the idealist aesthetic motivating his own judgements, such traditional theories of sound as in fact existed could easily be adduced in support of his argument. For example, Rudolf Arnheim, in his book *Radio*, had argued in support of a pristine form of language, an essence, recapturable (in theory) through sound, which is, of course, radio's only attribute: 'we should feel ourselves back in that primeval age where the word was still sound, the sound still word'.[12] Arnheim was, however, quick to point out that the ultimate quarry was *not* sound itself, since 'the concept of a timeless representation of sound is meaningless',[13] but the *reality* lying behind it. Thus, in Arnheim's case, it was simply a question of tracing language back to its epistemological origins, in precisely the same way that, for Reed, literature was held to embody within it a spiritual core. Although Arnheim placed more emphasis upon the intermediate stage of sound – he was, after all, seeking a theoretical justification for radio – the basic philosophical thrust of his argument was similar to that of Henry Reed.

This dual concern with the validation of radio itself and the establishment of a relationship between broadcasting and literature was also broached by Donald McWhinnie, who was appointed Assistant Head of Drama at the BBC in 1953. However, although he sought to establish a distinctive art of radio, the philosophical tenets of his argument drew heavily on an already familiar aesthetic. On the subject of adaptation he was forced to concede that radio and theatre drama shared a certain amount of common ground: 'the affinity between stage drama and radio drama is superficial, though often misconstrued, because dialogue may be an important element in both'.[14] Moreover, he contended, adaptation itself was to be regarded primarily as an act of *criticism* performed upon a particular text, necessarily involving a degree of transliteration: 'interpretation, restatement in a different form, in terms of a different medium'.[15] The process was, however, subject to one overriding validating principle, involving a commitment 'to preserve the essence and at the same time to find a form which, though new, will seem true and unavoidable'.[16] As with Henry Reed before him, McWhinnie's preoccupation was with the literary artefact as opposed to the theatre performance. Moreover, such an argument is logically related to the wider notion of radio as an all but transparent agency through which the 'essence' of the text might be transmitted, hence obscuring the more problematic question of mediating influence. Ironically, the concentration of listener response advocated by McWhinnie serves to place radio on a par with the theatre, both demanding what Terence Hawkes has recently referred to as 'total "reading" absorption'.[17]

The question of the radio adaptation of stage plays effectively resolves itself into two distinct but connected areas of concern. On the one hand, there is the practical question of making a stage play 'radiogenic'; that is, of converting those elements of its structure that depend for their effect upon visual realisation into appropriate aural equivalents, and the inevitable editorial adjustments of the text which such a process demands. On the other hand there are the larger, theoretically-orientated questions involving issues such as the nature of the mediating influence exerted by theatrical and radio forms respectively, the cultural relationship between the two, and the extent to which the one may, in certain circumstances, enter into an 'intertextual' relationship with the other. Within this larger theoretical area of concern, account must also be taken of the extent to which drama has acquired a dual identity, on one side preserving its generic distinctiveness, while at the same time having been absorbed into the larger (and in some ways transforming) category of 'literature'. Here the subsidiary question of *response* becomes an important one, depending, as we have already observed, upon a particular set of aesthetic preconceptions that value 'essence' over 'process' and regard the 'text' itself as a repository of universal truths. In a lucid critique of Russian Formalism, Tony Bennett has recently focused on the implications of this distinction in a way that has particular relevance to the matter in hand. In an attempt to place literary texts within a series of historical matrices, he observes:

One must adopt a 'binocular vision' in relation to the text, studying it as a concrete, historically changing entity subject to different determinations in the different ways in which it is appropriated and the different sets of intertextual relationships in which it is placed during different moments of its history as a received text. To posit the concept of the text outside of such matrices or to speak of its 'effect' – aesthetic or political – independently of such considerations is to fall prey to a 'metaphysic of the text': to a conception of the text as an abstraction which transcends history.[18]

Bennett's objective is to evolve a full historical materialist approach to criticism generally, but his exposure of the ideological purchase made upon literature, and of the various mechanisms whereby this takes place, has some relevance to the question of the way in which a 'text' such as a play changes its identity, so to speak. But before considering in more detail some of these larger questions, it is worth pausing to enumerate some of the practical decisions an adaptor may face in the business of transferring a play from one medium to another.

To begin with, lack of original material, which in the case of radio was to become a perennial concern, meant that adaptation from the corpus of established dramatic literature (and indeed from novels) became a necessary means of preserving a sufficient balance of drama within overall programming schedules. From the very outset radio appealed to both theatre and literature with its broadcasts of what might be termed 'Shakespeare highlights', effectively extending a practice begun by eighteenth-century editors of Shakespeare. For example, during the first full year of broadcasting there were excerpts from *Julius Caesar* (16 February 1923), *The Merchant of Venice* (23 May), *King John* (31 May), *Henry VIII* (7 June), *Romeo and Juliet* (5 July), *A Midsummer Night's Dream* (25 July) and *Macbeth* (18 October).[19] Also during 1923, the first full Shakespeare play to be broadcast was, perhaps surprisingly, *Twelfth Night* (28 May), with Arthur Bourchier as Shylock and a cast including Nigel Playfair, Gerald Lawrence and Cathleen Nesbitt. It was Cathleen Nesbitt, along with Dulcima Glasby, who was responsible for much of the early adaptation of Shakespeare for radio.

The adaptation of Shakespeare consisted mainly of cutting the text, although early on distinctions began to be made between a producer's cuts and what was considered to be a full adaptation. In a note to a BBC Belfast producer responsible for a production of *The Merchant of Venice* in 1932, Val Gielgud made what seems to be a very clear distinction between the two; on the matter of a request for an adaptation fee, he replied curtly:

I must admit that this is most definitely not an adaptation in the special sense: it's merely a producer's cuts that could have been made an hour before rehearsal. There is *no* suggestion – or attempt made – of considering the play freshly from this microphone angle.[20]

But even when readjustments for the microphone were made, the effects could not be guaranteed. For example, after a radio production of *Romeo and Juliet* on 15 February 1949, Leslie Stokes complained to the producer Hugh Stewart that arrangements made to credit the duel sequences were derisory. He had asked that the credit, 'Duels arranged by Charles Alexis', be deleted from the closing announcement on the grounds that, poor reception notwithstanding, 'to give a credit for such a small amount of clatter would sound ridiculous'.[21] Stewart's response was to assert that the playing time of the duels was 'between I think two or three minutes', that 'they seemed of great value from the point of view of authentic sound', and that in a recent radio production of *Hamlet* where the duels had been of shorter duration 'they had a credit'.[22] Stokes remained unconvinced and added a manuscript note to Stewart's reply suggesting that 'credits for duels in sound productions sound rather silly and should be avoided'.

It is rather difficult to determine precisely what Gielgud meant by the phrase 'an adaptation in the special sense'. Inadequate recording technology in the early years severely limited the kinds of sound effects that might be used in a production, and also meant that broadcasts were live – in all but a visual sense resembling theatre performances. Moreover, it was not until 1928 and the invention of the Dramatic Control Panel that crowd scenes could be handled properly, although even then the effect attainable could have nothing like the kind of precision and momentary close focus that one might notice in, say, an Eisenstein film. Thus, from the outset, excerpts from Shakespeare – and indeed from Shaw also – tended to focus on dialogues dominated by a few strong and easily recognisable characters, such as in the quarrel scene from *Julius Caesar* (IV.iii), the trial scene from *The Merchant of Venice* (IV.i.), and the Hubert and Arthur scene from *King John* (IV.i).

The demands of the medium effectively ruled out the adaptation of certain sorts of play, although this in no way inhibited experimentation. From a very early stage it was felt that Shakespeare's *The Comedy of Errors* would not work well on radio because of its reliance upon intractably visual material, although *Twelfth Night*, which utilises a number of comic devices contained in the earlier play and which in a number of crucial respects falls within this category, was the first full-length play to be performed and was also the subject of further experimentation in the *Experimental Hour* series inaugurated by Gielgud in 1937.[23] Gielgud claimed that an earlier similar series begun in 1928 had failed because of its disregard of entertainment value, but it is difficult to see how a production of excerpts from *Twelfth Night* with allegedly authentic Elizabethan pronunciation could have had anything but curiosity value. Other plays considered unsuitable for broadcasting were *Titus Andronicus*, the *Henry VI* trilogy, *The Merry Wives of Windsor* (although excerpts from this play were apparently broadcast sometime during 1923), *All's Well That Ends Well* and *Pericles*. Of non-Shakespearean plays, those of Chekhov were considered unsuitable largely because of the way in which dialogue and action are often made to work at cross-purposes in them. However, for what would appear to have been cultural reasons, these plays found their way into programme schedules. Indeed, there was, from 1932 onwards, some interest in broadcasting the complete works of Shakespeare, a suggestion that has, not uncharacteristically, been revived in relation to radio's natural successor, television, in recent years. The idea was first mooted in December 1932 by Filson Young, who saw it as an opportunity to 'afford the highest kind of entertainment combined with high educative and cultural value'.[24] Gielgud's unusually compromising response to this suggestion offers ample demonstration that the issues at stake were more than merely practical. He replied that the majority of Shakespeare's plays should be broadcast, 'including several of the less well-known plays', but he rejected plays such as *Titus Andronicus*, 'which can only have a curiosity value, and which are neither good plays nor good broadcast material'.[25] Evidently questions of taste were as important as practical considerations.

That Gielgud's attitude was part of a general policy, operated (one suspects) almost unconsciously by those concerned, may be demonstrated in relation to a later discussion (October 1936) concerning the suitability of broadcasting an adaptation of Ibsen's *A Doll's House* on a Sunday evening. The play was adjudged pernicious because Nora's final reasons for leaving set a bad example: 'She is simply saying what many women in Surbiton and Sevenoaks are saying today, and is giving them an admirable excuse for imitating her own rather sentimental cowardice.'[26] But perhaps the most revealing example of this kind of aesthetic-cum-moral judgement in operation is to be found in a memo from R.H. Eckersley to the Director-General in October 1933 concerning the Sunday timing of Shakespeare plays. While acknowledging that no time was ideal – a reflection, perhaps, of a certain uneasiness with the notion that simulated theatre-going of the sort provided by broadcasting on Sundays was permissible – Eckersley went on to report:

From the point of view of those who do not go to church on Sunday evenings, 5.30 to 7.00 is really the most convenient time. Iremonger said incidentally that the type of listeners most likely to be interested in Shakespeare plays would usually be found at morning service and not at evening service.[27]

Apart from the fact that Iremonger's 'incidental' comment soon found its way into the rationale of future policy planning, it also associated Anglican orthodoxy (morning attendance at church) with 'high culture' and hence with all those literary values possessed by persons of 'taste', and non-conformist radicalism (evening attendance at church) with philistinism. These attitudes were themselves fed subliminally into debates about adaptations, and affected not only matters such as choice of play but also practical questions of timing.

What gradually emerged was a dualistic approach to adaptation, involving, on the one hand, judgements about the status of particular works of dramatic literature derived from cultural and orthodox literary critical standards, and, on the other, the intrinsic demands of the medium. A cursory glance at the frequency of performance of particular Shakespeare plays over the years would amply bear this out. Plays such as *The Merry Wives of Windsor*, *Love's Labours Lost*, *The Comedy of Errors* and *All's Well That Ends Well*, which have not generally been considered among the best in the canon, have not received frequent broadcasts. The position with regard to plays such as *Timon of Athens*, *Titus Andronicus* and *Pericles*, for example, is revealed in a response by Gielgud in November 1952 to a suggestion that Shakespeare's Roman plays be broadcast as a cycle:

Frankly, I don't think there is the same cohesion or quality of sequence relevance in the Roman Plays as in the historical dramas, but it may interest Mr Walker to know that *Titus Andronicus* is included in the Third Programme schedule for the first quarter of next year, together with *Pericles* and *Timon of Athens*, both as examples of Shakespeare's plays which are very seldom performed and also as completing the broadcasting of the complete canon of plays.[28]

Evidently radio, like Ibsen's Nora, occasionally had to regard itself as lying back and thinking of England. By contrast, plays such as *Macbeth*, *King Lear*, *Hamlet*, *Richard II*, *Antony and Cleopatra*, *Twelfth Night* and *The Merchant of Venice*, already firmly established with generations of theatre audiences, have received regular radio attention, and in some cases Stratford productions have been broadcast.

It has long been recognised that the dynamics of theatrical performance differ from those of radio broadcasting, even though in terms of creating their audiences each medium seeks to accommodate the *individual* listener and spectator respectively. But even so, there still remain certain fundamental differences. For example, in a theatre an audience is always aware of an actor's presence onstage, whereas on radio reminders of that presence require to be given to the listener from time to time. Very often this is accomplished by means of interjections which take the form either of simple paralinguistic responses such as 'm-m-m' or, particularly in the case of silent servile characters who are acquired to exit at specific points in the action, words such as 'My lord' or 'My lady'. In this way, sound equivalents of visual presences can be established. This creation of a 'sound presence', suggesting to the listener a series of relationships between the characters involved in the action, is a very basic way of solving an obvious problem. Fortunately, in the case of many of Shakespeare's plays, written as they were for a non-naturalistic stage setting, many of the visual gestural responses required of particular actors are described in the dialogue itself. A clear example occurs in *Macbeth*, a play that has proved popular both in the theatre and on radio. At this point in the play Macbeth is suffering from hallucinations intensified by his acute awareness of the horrific murder he is about to commit:

Is this a dagger which I see before me,
The handle toward my hand? Come, let me clutch thee.
I have thee not, and yet I see thee still.
Art thou not, fatal vision, sensible
To feeling as to sight? or art thou but
A dagger of the mind, a false creation,
Proceeding from the heat-oppressed brain?
I see thee yet, in form as palpable

As this which now I draw.
Thou marshall'st me the way that I was going;
And such an instrument I was to use.
Mine eyes are made the fools o' th' other senses,
Or else worth all the rest. I see thee still;
And on thy blade and dudgeon gouts of blood,
Which was not so before.   (II.i.33-47)[29]

This speech enacts, by a kind of reportage, the murder of Duncan,
which is not shown on the stage, and it is one of a number of examples
in the play where action is reported and not demonstrated. Here, as
elsewhere, a theatre audience is placed in the position of a radio
listener, as they imagine the physical presence of the object of
Macbeth's attention and as they construct in advance a series of mental
images of the murder. Moreover, the speech conveys a clear picture of
Macbeth's mental processes, his attitude towards the crime he is about
to commit, and a general sense of the deepening irony of his position,
all of which is focused upon the image of an *absent* dagger. Of course, a
theatre audience can *see* the actor and has access to a greater number
of comparisons that the combination of dialogue and visual presence
forces upon it. But although, for example, the imaginary dagger is
compared with a *real* one – 'this which now I draw' – the radio listener is
in no way disadvantaged since this articulated stage direction makes
possible the very same comparison between the *real* and the *imaginary*
to which a theatre audience has access. Equally, the tone and rhythm
of the actor's delivery, as dictated by the structure of the soliloquy
itself, reinforce the character's own description of his physical
gestures: 'Come, let me clutch thee./I have thee not, and yet I see thee
still.' Indeed, each pause in this soliloquy is described by the character,
so that by the end of it listener and audience alike are given an
unusually vivid picture of Macbeth's state of mind.

This particular soliloquy, utilising as it does a mode considered
generally well-suited to the intimate nature of the radio experience,[30]
functions on the basis of a technique that harmonises the rhetoric of
dramatic construction with the developing psychology of the character
who is the focus of the action. By giving everything a 'voice' on radio
(and in the theatre a *persona*) the medium bestows 'character' upon
each facet of the play's structure.[31] Macbeth casts his own doubts upon
the discrepancy between appearance and reality, and this has the
inadvertent effect of making the *means* whereby this process is
communicated 'transparent', so to speak. Of course, there are
parameters within which the actor works. While in radio the listener is
given the task of creating the setting, of deducing a visual essence, as it
were, from the spoken dialogue, the actor can control that process
without necessarily having access to the kind of photographic
verisimilitude involved in, say, a naturalistic stage presentation. For
example, the adoption of a conversational rhythm will invariably raise
in the mind of the listener certain expectations that will cause him to
adjust his mental image of the play's physical setting.[32] Occasionally

the two will collide unintentionally, so that a tension is created between a colloquial manner and the more densely expressive idiom of, say, a blank-verse speech.[33] Alternatively, and in a much more complex semiotic way, a declamatory style of delivery, as evidenced for example in Donald Wolfit's 1949 broadcast of Shakespeare's *King Lear*, may as easily carry with it a subtextual component that *signifies* 'theatre' of a rather special, culturally overdetermined sort.

Other Shakespeare plays, such as *Othello*, *Antony and Cleopatra*, *The Tempest*, *King Lear* and, in a more special sense, *Henry V*, provide ample opportunity for naturalising thematic concerns in the way that the text of *Macbeth* allows. In so far as these plays succeed on radio, they all do so by transferring what is basically a deficiency of the medium on to the central characters themselves. For example, Othello is made to create in his own mind an image of both Desdemona and himself; and so careful is Iago's manipulation of his victim that cues for visualisation are extraordinarily dense within the texture of the dialogue. Here the play's themes are reinforced by a kind of *absence* that actually determines physical presence, to the extent that the action always drives towards an essence that is not seen but requires nonetheless to be known. Similarly, and despite the fact that the setting does not transfer easily or well to radio, Antony and Cleopatra attempt to imagine a world for themselves, and they seek to create it through a sensuous dramatic poetry whose ultimate veracity the play deliberately leaves open to question. In *The Tempest*, Prospero creates the play for his many audiences, thereby fulfilling the role of personalised narrator; but while in theory the stream-of-consciousness technique often employed in radio seems appropriate here, and does in fact produce a more effective Ariel than is usual onstage, there still remains a certain amount of recalcitrant material that does not withstand the sea change from stage to radio.[34] In *King Lear*, as in a number of original radio plays from Richard Hughes's *Danger* onwards, blindness itself is endowed with a thematic value located in the characters, although again some areas of the play – notably Gloucester's attempt at suicide – require full visualisation in order to be effective.[35] In all these examples, and despite in many cases the spatially panoramic backgrounds, there is ample opportunity for the kind of close focus upon dealings between individual characters that radio can handle so well. However, while it is generally agreed that intimacy is a feature of the medium and that a device such as soliloquy works well on radio, it must be said that the aside (comic or otherwise), which requires rapid spatial adjustment from the listener, is, by contrast, ineffective. Indeed, the creation of a context for dialogue, and the expectations concerning the visual deployment of the participants which flow naturally from it, make it extremely difficult for the listener to accept yet another level of intimacy which is only a momentary violation of the norm he has been persuaded to accept, whereas in the case of soliloquy the sustained context serves to validate the convention.

This problem is, perhaps, another facet of the larger difficulty of expansion and contraction that often lies at the heart of the dramatic rhythm of many of Shakespeare's plays. For example, successive radio productions of *Antony and Cleopatra* have found difficulty in coping with the rapid shifts of scenic location without shrinking the world of the play to a series of playfully intimate dialogues between the two central characters. Again, and in theory, the flexibility of the radio medium, and its nominal freedom from the shackles of naturalism, is admirably suited to the business of rapid scene changing, although particular productions of the play have been reluctant to allow its dramatic structure to stand unsupported.[36] In the 1954 radio production of the play by Peter Watts, which was a broadcast of Glen Byam Shaw's Stratford production, the character of Plutarch was introduced as a personalised narrator whose function was obviously to smoothe the rapid transitions from one location to another. That such a smoothing has the effect of diluting the dramatic conflict seems to have escaped both directors, as the narrator Plutarch's attempt to 'place' the opening dialogue of the play shows:

Music
PLUTARCH: Now while Antonius, being this while in Egypt, was delighting in
            fond pastimes, there came a messenger from Caesar to wait upon
            his pleasure.
PHILO: Nay, but this dotage of our general's
            O'erflows the measure; those his goodly eyes
            That o'er the files and musters of the war
            Have glowed like plated Mars, now bend, now turn
            Their office and devotion of their view
            Upon a tawny front. His captain's heart,
            Which in the scuffles of great fights hath burst
            The buckles on his breast, reneges all temper,
            And is become the bellows and the fan
            To cool a gypsy's lust.
                Look where they come.
            Laughter off
            Take but good note, and you shall see in him
            The triple pillar of the world transformed
            Into a strumpet's fool.
CLEOPATRA: (*approach*) If it be love indeed, tell me how much.[37]

The omission of the character of Demetrius and the consequent elevation of Philo to choric status, combined with Plutarch's overarching narrative presence, establish the strength of the Roman viewpoint from the outset, thus upsetting the delicately balanced dynamics of the play's central conflict. In a play that focuses upon the process of making value judgements, tampering with the mechanism in this way represents a simplification rather than an adaptation. A more recent radio production of the play directed by John Tydeman (30 January 1977), which restricted its adjustments to a fairly judicious cutting of Shakespeare's text and dispensed with the narrator figure in favour of simple musical themes to signify shifts of location, succeeded in reinstating the play's central conflict, thus foregrounding the ambivalent effects of the dramatic poetry and forcing a choice upon the listener. But even here the two worlds of Rome and Egypt receded in terms of their symbolic value as the natural focus of the listener's attention became Antony (played with impressive range and power by Robert Stephens) and Cleopatra (whose seedy beauty was amply conveyed through the faintly cracking voice of Sian Phillips).

Clearly it is the dramatic scope of *Antony and Cleopatra* that creates difficulty for both stage and radio alike. This is not a problem with *Othello*, in which, apart from a few public scenes, the general atmosphere is one of 'a close-shut murderous room',[38] although the black-white symbolism is an important visual effect requiring the attention of the adaptor. John Tydeman's 1972 radio production of the play, with Paul Scofield as Othello, responded well to this close focus. Unlike *Antony and Cleopatra*, in which basic issues such as entries and exits become something of a problem, in *Othello* the listener's attention is so carefully directed that the spatial complications arising in large ensemble scenes are virtually nonexistent. From the point of view of adaptation the most problematical scene appears to have been V.i, where, because of a series of rapid entries and exits involving minor as well as major characters and involving also a series of different perspectives on the action, some attempt had to be made to establish and fix identities clearly from the listener's point of view. Thus the two opening soliloquies of the scene, from Iago and Roderigo respectively, are delivered close to the microphone, while Cassio's entry is marked by Roderigo's "tis he, Cassio' (V.i.23) as against the unspecific ' 'tis he' of the text. Also, the absence of an exit line for Iago at V.i.27 in the text is adjusted in the broadcast script by the insertion of a non-Shakespearean interpolation: 'And now depart.' Iago's later re-entry is already catered for in Shakespeare's dialogue, though the radio script makes a minor adjustment at V.i.56 in order to reinforce the listener's impression of the affected nature of his concern for Cassio, 'O my Lieutenant', as opposed to the more distant irony of 'O me, Lieutenant' of the text. The character of Gratiano presents a minor difficulty in this scene since he has a number of lines to speak, but in terms of creating a clear 'sound presence' they offer little assistance to the listener. Thus at the earliest opportunity, and to avoid later confusion as the scene fills, Lodovico's line at V.i.40 is extended from the text's nonspecific monosyllable 'Hark!', which would be self-explanatory in a stage production, to 'Gratiano hark!', which establishes a presence. Similarly at V.i.104, in order to avoid the confusion that might arise with Emilia's entry at V.i.110, Iago's question, 'What, look you pale?', is extended in the radio script to 'What, Bianca, look you pale?', thus establishing Bianca's presence clearly before the appearance of a second female character.

Virtually all adaptations of Shakespeare's plays require adjustments of this sort, simply as ways of keeping to the fore of the listener's mind distinctions between individual characters. In most cases the objective is to compensate for an absence of visual perspective, thus establishing by implication a framework that has theatrical performance as its reference point. But there are occasions when adjustments in sound alone, at a level below that of the articulated text, can suggest meaning more precisely and economically than is usually possible in the theatre. For example, in a radio production of *The Merchant of Venice* on 3 October 1976 directed by Ian Cotterell, which involved little in the way of explicit adaptation, the use of 'live' sound for Portia's interviews with her three egocentric admirers (II.i and II.vii) effectively underlined the cold formality of her response to their advances, to the extent that the listener could detect a tension between her own wishes and the will of her dead father. Similarly the adjustment to 'dead' sound, without changing the scenic location, for the interview with Bassanio suggested a warmth and a receptiveness that *anticipated* the outcome. Such effects can be used in a sophisticated way to suggest critical perspectives, influencing the listener in a manner not unlike that in which the novelist might influence his reader – by the *style* of presentation as opposed to explicit direction.

Even so, in many radio adaptations, explicit direction in the form of a narrator used to be regarded as the most expedient way of overcoming the problems of translation from theatre performance to radio broadcast. Gordon Lea was one of the first practitioners to realise the value of this device to the adaptor, and in his handbook, *Radio Drama and How to Write It*, he attempted to show how an adaptation of Ibsen's *Peer Gynt* might work using a narrator.[39] But Lea made a distinction between using a narrator and what he called 'the Self-Contained Method' as far as original radio drama was concerned.[40] Here the narrator was regarded as a barrier to the dynamics of the listener-actor relationship, whereas when the illusion remains seamless 'the listener is in direct touch with the player – there is no intervening convention – no barrier. Soul speaks to Soul.'[41] Some ten years later, in 1936, opinions appear to have hardened. H.A.L. Fisher's suggestion that 'in some plays good purpose might be served by means of a narrator giving the setting by way of brief stage directions' was thought to be 'really contrary to broadcast principles since radio plays ought not to depend on any such substitute for vision'.[42] There was, however, a discrepancy between theory and practice. In particular productions of excerpts from Shakespeare's plays, narration of a rather sophisticated sort was being used. For example, a broadcast in April 1941 of excerpts from *Romeo and Juliet* was billed as 'a sequence from Shakespeare's play arranged for broadcasting by Hugh Stewart, with narrative taken from *Tales of Shakespeare* by Charles and Mary Lamb'.[43] But objections to the anti-dramatic role the narrator fulfilled continued, so that in 1945

Edward Sackville-West could pronounce, 'the introduction of the
Narrator's voice, even when disguised as a character in the play,
always makes for a drop in the temperature of the programme',[44]
arguing that music might make a better substitute. Yet some three
years later, an adaptation of *Hamlet* by M.R. Ridley (December 1948)
used narration in every scene. In Ridley's adaptation (used again as
the basis of a new production by Cedric Messina broadcast on 23
October 1960) the narrator's function was to provide an almost
photographic visualisation of the scene for the listener. For example,
I.ii opens in the following quasi-naturalistic manner, with a possible
reference to the Laurence Olivier film of that year:

> *Subdued chatter*
>
> NARRATOR: Claudius, the new King of Denmark, the late king's brother, is
> about to hold a State Council. The Councillors, headed by
> Polonius, are in their robes, and behind them are the courtiers in
> full court dress. Among them Polonius's son Laertes. Sitting a
> little apart, and dressed in plain black, is Hamlet, the late king's
> son. His claim to the succession has been overridden and he is not
> a member of the Council.
>
> *Trumpets*
>
> The king enters . . . (*chatter down*) . . . with his newly married
> Queen, Gertrude, his brother's widow . . . they take their places
> . . . and the king prepares to address the Council.[45]

Non-Shakespearean interpolations of this kind offer an interpretative
context for the action, suggesting a point of view even if the style of the
narration is impersonal. Indeed, the Wolfit *King Lear* used an even
more clipped narration in 1949. But by the early 1950s the narrator had
become part of the overall dramatic illusion, as a comment by Andrew
Stewart to the Head of Sound Drama concerning a broadcast in
August 1953 of *King John* shows. Stewart had wanted the stage
directions narrated in 'a smooth simple piece of prose saying "We now
move to France to the encampment. There the King of France . . .
etc." ', but instead, their apparently bare and staccato presentation
'wrecked the illusion'.[46] But it was Val Gielgud who attempted to
make clear the role of the narrator, in connection with a festival of
Shakespeare's history plays broadcast in 1947 in an adaptation by
M.R. Ridley, and the distinctions he drew then have a continuing
validity:

I am anxious to make perfectly clear the purpose of the narrator in the
Shakespearean Chronicle plays. This is an experiment of Ridley's, admittedly
of an extremely simple kind, to overcome the main difficulty with which these
plays have to contend on the air, the difficulty of disentangling a large number
of small characters who lack any particular idiosyncracies, and the extreme
clarification of the process of physical action. It is clearly important that in the
whole series the handling of the narrator by the various producers should be
approximately the same. I believe that the best way in which to look at the
problem is to consider the narrator as entirely outside the play as a whole, and
to produce him very much after the fashion of a running commentator, and, if

at all possible, to keep him in a perspective different from that in which the rest of the play takes place. The pace should be lively, the approach should be modern. There is absolutely no parallel between the use of the narrator and, for example, the position of the Chorus in *Henry V*.[47]

Relatively speaking, and notwithstanding purist objections, the case of the Chorus in *Henry V* reflects certain aspects of those problems of narration faced by the novelist. In a survey of narrative technique in fiction, Wayne Booth draws attention to Shakespeare's Chorus as the source of a device for effecting rapid changes of scene.[48] In radio (as in the novel) the narrator is often 'transparent' – integral to the scene but peripheral to the action – rather than a grafted-on presence. Bearing in mind the natural propensity of radio towards intimacy, the narrator either employs his soliloquies to set the scene, whose naturalistic detail the listener complements from the reservoir of his own experience, or alternatively he becomes a kind of bardic presence, mediating the action in a more conscious fashion and smoothing its passage between play and listener. Either way, it becomes difficult to transform the narrator into the object of the listener's critical attention without exposing the artifice it is his function to disguise, and hence shattering the illusion. The Chorus in *Henry V* is born out of a firm sense of the inadequacy of the Elizabethan stage itself, and to this extent fulfils a compensatory function, augmenting the evidence of the audience's own eyes. Thus, paradoxically, the Chorus establishes his own sincerity by exposing the artifice of the play, and thereby places himself in what might be termed a natural relationship with his audience. It is exactly this sleight of hand that allows the play to work well on radio, since the Chorus provides an entry point into the action which allows the listener to transcend his own limitations. In Martin Jenkins's 1976 radio production of *Henry V* (broadcast on 18 April) the intimacy of Sir John Gielgud's Chorus helped to focus the listener's response despite the now obligatory opening reference to Laurence Olivier's film of 1945. Whatever the medium, the play displaces its own theatrical point of reference, thereby leaving the action free to generate its own illusion, and in this production, with the listener cast in the role of the Chorus's *confidant*, a degree of complicity was virtually assured. Jenkins's production, like Oliver's film, moved by stages into a kind of pictorial setting, mounting its gradual appeal to an established canon of naturalism.[49] Indeed, generally speaking, even where perfunctory or symbolic sound effects are used in radio to augment dialogue – as in, say, a recent broadcast of T.S. Eliot's verse play *The Cocktail Party* (19 October 1978) – the listener's imagination is invariably stimulated to piece out the imperfections with his thoughts, creating under controlled conditions, and even placing himself within, a setting that is invariably naturalistic. It is rare that the discipline of listening becomes the object of *critical* attention itself in radio in the same way that, for example, the reader's role is often scrutinised in the modern novel.

The role of the Chorus in *Henry V* focuses for us the larger question of distance in relation to certain kinds of adaptation. In most cases the perspective forced upon the listener militates against his adopting a position of complete critical detachment, in exactly the same way that the radio actor cannot but approach his public *directly*. As a result, those plays that generate emotional sympathy for individual characters stand a greater chance of success on radio than those that do not. Moreover, these also tend to be the plays that, in aesthetic terms, are held in the highest esteem. This distinction is implied in a comment Philip Hope-Wallace made in 1949 with specific reference to the radio adaptation of stage comedy:

> Week after week we are astounded how ill the most amenable stage pieces adapt themselves for broadcasting; we discover that the screen scene in *The School for Scandal* falls flat on the air; that the unspoken but so to say 'faced' thoughts of Chekhov's sad ladies by their absence in this medium affect the balance of the play and diminish their creator's fame. We discover that *The Importance of Being Earnest* is not at all funny on the air, because the deadly earnestness with which the characters must play – and the farce would die stone dead if the characters seemed to share the joke with us – is deadly ineffective unless set off by the co-operative laughter of the audience.[50]

Recent radio productions of *The School for Scandal*, *The Importance of Being Earnest*, Shakespeare's *As You Like It*, *The Merry Wives of Windsor*, *Love's Labours Lost* and Middleton's *A Chaste Maid in Cheapside*, all bear ample testimony to the continuing validity of this assertion. All these plays have required major surgery, mainly in the form of cuts of more or less drastic proportions, and a recent Peter Barnes adaptation of Marston's *Antonio and Mellida* and *Antonio's Revenge* (broadcast on 20 February 1977 as *Antonio*, and subsequently staged in 1979) involved a considerable degree of rewriting.

In each case, and particularly with regard to Marston's odd combination of comedy and satiric tragedy, the problem appears to have been that of a failure to establish the correct distance between listener and action, or to co-ordinate verbal and visual detail. For example, a scene such as IV.iii in *Love's Labours Lost* depends in the theatre upon a series of cumulatively visual repetitions which serve to generate comic tension while at the same time reinforcing the spectator's position as arbiter of the gulf opened up between utterance and action. In David Spenser's radio production (22 February 1979) the attempts to excise some of these repetitions and to tamper with the carefully controlled pace of the discoveries, allied to the necessarily imprecise depiction of the spatial dynamics of the scene, resulted in failure of comic impact. Moreover, in the masking scene (V.i) radio proved ill-equipped to deal with the sort of stage business demanded by the action but not always clearly stated in the dialogue. It is not simply that comedy is more visual than other forms of drama, although there is a degree of truth in this; rather, the complicated mechanisms of plot and the carefully modulated rhythms of comedy which require sudden shifts of perspective do not withstand translation easily. A recent adaptation by Tom Stoppard of his own television play *Professional Foul* (broadcast on 11 June 1979) rather reinforces this general point, since, despite Peter Barkworth's masterly portrayal of the donnish Anderson, the adjustments required by radio adaptation effectively suppressed a whole series of intricate semiotic details, thus ironing out a number of the swift changes of pace and focus evident in the television original. It was as though Stoppard was required to place primary emphasis upon depicting the scene for the listener, thus diverting attention away from some of the subtleties of text and television performance.

Nonetheless, what makes *Professional Foul* acceptable as a radio play – and it is a moot point as to how much rewriting or rearrangement of scenes is permissible before an adaptation can be said to have relinquished its dependent status in order to become an original play in its own right – is its focus upon a particular issue and its concentration upon the character of Anderson. The more diffuse the elements of dramatic structure, the greater are the difficulties of adaptation, as radio productions of plays such as *Love's Labours Lost*, *As You Like It* and *The Merry Wives of Windsor* show. These problems, however, are further intensified in the case of the plays of a dramatist such as Bertolt Brecht, and may well be the reason why so few of his stage plays have been adapted for radio. This is perhaps surprising, considering that Brecht 'was fascinated by radio as a medium as early as 1927 and wrote several scripts for radio'.[51] In the case of his stage plays, virtually all the principles upon which radio establishes its identity are inverted. Plays such as *The Threepenny Opera* and *The Exception and the Rule*, both of which have been broadcast recently, violate those very principles of intimacy and sincerity upon which radio has come to depend for its effects, since they demand that the listener maintain a detached critical stance in relation to both character and action. Brecht's plays generally depend upon constant interruptions of the flow of the action in order to reveal what the critic Walter Benjamin called the 'gest' of each incident, with the result that the purpose of his 'epic theatre' was and is that of 'making gestures quotable'.[52] Each Brecht scene, therefore, has a *core* which it is the actor's task to reveal to his audience, and he does so by repetition and mimicking the actions of others; but above all he is obliged to hang on to his identity as an actor. In this way his function is to uncover the underlying conditions of reality rather than simply to reproduce them, thereby making strange, or alienating, what is familiar. In this way Brecht makes a direct assault upon naturalism, which demands the acquiescence of spectator or listener in the illusion that actor and dramatist seek to create.

In terms of their political objectives, Brecht's plays have something in common with the George Bernard Shaw of the Preface to *Mrs Warren's Profession*. But whereas Shaw's method is that of heightened naturalism, which allows his plays to adapt well to radio, the diffuseness of response and the constant adjustments of critical distance demanded by Brecht's make them intractable from this point of view. Or, to put it another way, no adequate correlative has been found in radio for the deliberate aberrations of theatrical form upon which a Brecht play depends for its effects. Even the flexibility of the medium – which can take in tight or episodic structures – cannot cope, since the constant pressure to which it is subjected is that of making the unfamiliar familiar and encouraging the listener's collusion to this end. The result is that the iconoclastic vitality of Brecht's plays, with their constant focus upon form itself, is reduced on radio to series of familiar variety acts, held together by an even more familiar radio figure, the narrator.

In practical terms, each play adapted for radio presents its own set of problems, although there is a sizeable body of evidence to suggest that adaptors generally avail themselves of established devices, while at the same time drawing on familiar assumptions about the listener and the medium itself. Moreover, the choice of plays to be adapted, though often apparently random, is based in part on a number of considerations other than the radiogenic qualities of a particular text: considerations relating to the status of a particular dramatist's work or, in the case of already established dramatic literature, to the larger questions of the BBC's cultural responsibility. Two theoretical issues now remain to be considered. They are, first, the status of a radio adaption and, second, the nature of its relationship to a stage original. The position is complicated by the fact that the aesthetic values promulgated by radio with regard to its dramatic output form part of a larger literary framework that interpenetrates any critical evaluation of adaptations. Indeed, what John Hartley and Terence Hawkes have remarked in relation to television is *a fortiori* true of its predecessor, in that it has 'tended to conceive of itself as merely an adapted version of its predecessors, not as something completely different'.[53] Such a process smoothes over the ground upon which radio mingles with other forms of literary expression, allowing it to become assimilated or naturalised into an existing framework of values and judgements. Successive festivals on radio of the plays of dramatists such as Shakespeare and Ibsen, or educative forays into the history of dramatic forms, such as *The First Stage* (1957) or even *Vivat Rex* (1977), rather support this general view, while the flurry of adaptations of Continental dramatists in the 1950s, along with the perennial resurrection of those plays whose place in the literary pantheon is not secure, may be seen as an extension of an already established canon rather than attempts to re-form it.

This raises certain questions about the status of the relationship between dramatic text and radio adaptation. Leaving aside the complex question of the ways in which modern tape-recording techniques can now transform a radio performance from a live event in time into a text whose semiotic properties are susceptible to analysis, it is clear that problems of relationship and genesis do exist. For example, whatever alterations an adaptor might make to the written text of a stage play – and here questions of cutting, and the concentration of dramatic focus that follows from this operation, have considerable relevance – the process is generally seen to involve the extracting and reproducing of an 'essence' enclosed within the original text itself. Thus what is required is some clarification of the relationship between text and production.

In a provocative theoretical analysis of the problem, the Marxist critic Terry Eagleton observes:

The relation between text and production is a relation of *labour*: the theatrical instruments (staging, acting skills and so on) transform the 'raw materials' of the text into a specific product, which cannot be mechanically extrapolated from an inspection of the text itself . . . The theatrical mode of production in no sense merely 'mediates' the text; on the contrary, its practices and conventions 'operate' the textual materials according to an internal logic of their own.[54]

Eagleton goes on to argue that the relationship between text and production 'is not to be theorised as one between thought and word',[55] but rather along the lines of a quasi-Saussurian relationship between grammar and speech. He rejects the notion of the text as a source of production, 'a threadbare score on which the production improvises',[56] since this would ultimately divert attention away from 'the conditions of a *production*'[57] towards an abstract original of which it was a pale 'reflection'. While such a view separates text from performance for the purposes of analysis, it effectively cuts right across the traditional ways of regarding a dramatic text. Of course, Eagleton regards traditional criticism itself as the vehicle of a cultural ideology, but the issues he raises offer us a way of rationalising questions such as the choice of materials to be adapted for radio, and help to expose some of the larger assumptions by which those choices may be motivated. Or, to put the issue more concretely, it is not that, say, Shakespeare's plays are naturally radiogenic; rather, they occupy a position in our predominantly literary culture that justifies their adaptation time and again. Moreover, the isolation of language, which is an obvious feature of radio, allows such adaptations to foreground Shakespeare's poetry in almost as concentrated a form as might be encountered by a reader of the text. To this extent, the nominally anti-Bradleyan rationale for approaching Shakespeare advanced by L.C. Knights in 1933[58] appears to have received its natural apotheosis in the business of radio adaptation itself.

While practitioners have argued that the focus of any critical concern with radio should be upon certain (one might almost say, aesthetic) elements of what Eagleton has called the conditions of production, we are still left with the intractable fact that substantial amounts of broadcast drama have already been appropriated into the category of 'literature'. Thus, unless one wishes to make a claim for the absolute autonomy of an adaptation, one is left with the view that it stands in a curiously complex *reflective* relationship both to literary text *and* theatre performance. Thus criticism is required to adopt a diachronic as well as a synchronic approach. For example, a radio adaptation of, say, *Measure for Measure* (1976) or *Henry V* (1976, rebroadcast in 1979) could only be evaluated fully in terms of their synchronic relationship to contemporary theatre productions and their diachronic relationship to all previous productions of these plays. But, of course, the primary condition of performance is ephemerality, which makes it impossible, unless one was present at them, to reconstruct past performances either in the theatre or in the case of early radio. Even now, criticism of drama falls back on performance as a way of illuminating facets of a text's *meaning*, hence preserving the very structure of values that critics such as Eagleton wish to attack. The traditional appeal to 'literature' effectively neutralises the threat from the existential ephemerality of performance by focusing upon those *permanent* or universal qualities of the text that it is the function of the *ideal* performance to illuminate. Within this problematic or conceptual framework, which helps explain adaptation as a process of extraction, the recording of performance extends this feature of permanence to an area that was previously inaccessible. Moreover, although a radio adaptation of a stage play may be regarded in itself as an act of interpretation, the curious evenness of most broadcasts has the effect of allowing the listener to regard them individually as sum totals of all possible performances and, hence, as self-contained 'texts' that generate a series of meanings verifiable from within an already existing canon of 'literary' criticism.

This helps to underline the complex 'intertextual' relationships enshrined in the radio adaptation of a stage play, in that although it may have a claim to independence as a 'text' and can therefore be subjected to a formal analysis of its parts, it can never be entirely free from other 'texts'.[59] Thus, although sincerity and intimacy may be regarded as characteristics of radio generally, and in their application to adaptation clearly imply an unmediated presentation of an original, it is unquestionably the case that a radio adaptation *enacts* those values and aesthetic structures which are already in receipt of prior assent. One final example will, perhaps, serve to make the point. A radio adaptation of, say, *As You Like It* (1 January 1978) given a naturalistic setting refers us in the first instance directly to the category of 'realism', which is the dominant style in which 'our particular culture prefers its ritual condensations to be cast',[60] and through this to the proscenium-arch theatre. But closer examination reveals that the *production* of the text does nothing to suppress recalcitrant poetic material, and thus inadvertently parades its fictional quality. Consequently, both the play's theatricality and its literariness cannot but jolt the listener into an awareness of the established duality of its existence. Moreover, since the *value* of a play such as *As You Like It* is beyond question – and one is prompted to wonder to what extent all radio adaptation minimises this question of value judgement – the listener is placed in the position of participating in a ritual that is, in effect, self-validating.

What emerges from this limited survey is the inescapable fact that the role and status of radio adaptations of stage plays is extraordinarily complex. An adaptation functions as a point of convergence, bearing simultaneously the traces of more than one artistic form, yet claiming a straightforward line of descent. Nominally a radio adaptation may be regarded as the production of a particular text – an embodiment of an essence that is not seen – although historically each text is itself the locus of divergent cultural forces. Some years ago, Philip Hope-Wallace noted that it is a little-recognised fact that 'radio drama is not a part of dramaturgy but of "fiction" writing'.[61] Subsequent assertions to the contrary, and the periodic establishment of a host of intermediary positions, simply serve to remind us that radio has yet to establish a clear identity of its own, even though it continues to be possibly the largest single mediator of established literature and drama that we possess.

Notes

1. Paul Ferris, 'Rocking the boat at Radio 3', *The Observer*, 1 July 1979, p. 34.
2. Krishnan Kumar, 'Holding the middle ground : the BBC, the public and the professional broadcaster', in James Curran, Michael Gurevitch and Janet Woollacott (eds), *Mass Communication and Society*. London 1977, pp. 246-7; Philip Abrams, 'Television and radio', in Denys Thompson (ed.), *Discrimination and Popular Culture*. 2nd ed., Harmondsworth and London 1973, p. 123.
3. 'Drama'. *BBC Handbook 1929*, London 1929, pp. 74–5.
4. Asa Briggs, *The History of Broadcasting in the United Kingdom*. Vol. 1: *The Birth of Broadcasting*. London 1961, p. 282.
5. J.C.W. Reith, *Broadcast over Britain*. London 1924, p. 168.
6. Terence Hawkes, *Shakespeare's Talking Animals*. London 1973, pp. 220-1; Terry Eagleton, *Criticism and Ideology*. London 1976, pp. 46-8.
7. 'What the wireless can do for literature', *BBC Quarterly*, 3(4) (Jan. 1949), p. 218.
8. *Ibid*.
9. Louis Althusser, *For Marx*. London 1969, p. 228.
10. Philip Hope-Wallace, 'The unities in radio drama', *BBC Quarterly* 4(1) (Apr. 1949), pp. 21-5.
11. Roger Savage, 'The radio plays of Henry Reed', in John Drakakis (ed.), *British Radio Dramatists*. Cambridge 1981, pp. 158-90.
12. *Radio*. London 1936, p. 35.
13. *Ibid*, p. 24; see Walter J. Ong, *Interfaces of the Word*. Ithaca, N.Y. and London 1977, p. 136.

14. McWhinnie, *The Art of Radio*. London 1959, p. 174.
15. *Ibid*, p. 175.
16. *Ibid*, p. 176.
17. Hawkes, op. cit., p. 220.
18. Bennett, *Formalism and Marxism*. London 1979, p. 60.
19. BBC Written Archives, Accession no. 44986.
20. BBC Written Archives, Accession no. 7845.
21. BBC Written Archives, Accession no. 37859.
22. *Ibid*.
23. Gielgud, *British Radio Drama 1922-1956*. London 1957, p. 69.
24. BBC Written Archives, Accession no. 7845.
25. *Ibid*.
26. BBC Written Archives, Accession no. 44987/1.
27. BBC Written Archives, Accession no. 7845.
28. BBC Written Archives, Accession no. 37922.
29. Except where otherwise noted, all quotations from Shakespeare's plays are taken from *The Complete Works*, ed. Peter Alexander. London and Glasgow 1951.
30. Herbert Read, 'Sotto voce – a plea for intimacy', *BBC Quarterly*, **4**(1) (Apr. 1949), p. 4; Mary Crozier, 'Four radio plays', *BBC Quarterly*, **3**(3) (Oct. 1948), p. 169.
31. Louis MacNeice, 'General introduction', *The Dark Tower and Other Radio Scripts*. London 1947, p. 10; see my 'Introduction', in Drakakis (ed.), op. cit., pp. 1–36.
32. Raymond Williams, 'Recent English drama', in Boris Ford (ed.), *The Pelican Guide to English Literature*. Vol. 7: *The Modern Age*. Harmondsworth 1961, pp. 496-508.
33. One wonders what listeners might have thought of Hugh Stewart's ultimately abortive suggestion, made in November 1952, for an all-Scottish *Macbeth*, justified in the following terms: 'The Macbeths themselves are really a typical product of the Highlands insofar as they have a tough and dangerous courage but are soft at the core, sentimental and vacillating. Lady Macbeth, played with a West Highland accent, would I think be extraordinarily effective particularly in the sleep-walking scene . . .' (BBC Written Archives, Accession no. 37622).
34. In Ian Cotterell's recent production of *The Tempest* for Radio 4 (22 May 1977) with Paul Scofield as Prospero, the 'naturalistic' opening sequence was badly handled; some of the group scenes (e.g. II.ii) and some of the entries were also difficult to adapt to radio.
35. In the celebrated 1949 radio production of the play with Donald Wolfit as Lear, there was simply a pause at the point when Gloucester '*casts himself down*', so that the listener is not certain what to think.
36. See Roy Walker's comments in *Radio Times*, **123** (1588) (18-24 Apr. 1954), p. 7, on Glen Byam Shaw's Stratford Memorial Theatre production of that season, in which he used 'a featherweight permanent setting of which the main feature was the cyclorama. His simple but attractive solution to the problem was that one sky covers all earthly places. So does the air.'
37. Quoted from the script in the BBC Play Library, Broadcasting House, London.
38. A.C. Bradley, *Shakespearean Tragedy*. London 1957, p. 143.
39. The choice of *Peer Gynt* is an odd one, since it seems to have all the ingredients of a play written specially for radio. A recent radio production,

broadcast on Radio 3 on 27 December 1978, dispensed with a narrator altogether, allowing the dream sequences to flow into each other.

40. *Radio Drama and How to Write It*. London 1926, p. 53.
41. *Ibid*, p. 69.
42. BBC Written Archives, Accession no. 449871/1.
43. BBC Written Archives, Accession no. 7807.
44. 'Preamble', *The Rescue*. London 1945, p. 9.
45. Quoted from the script in the BBC Play Library, Broadcasting House, London.
46. BBC Written Archives, Accession no. 37922; see McWhinnie, op. cit., p. 115, rejecting the device as 'part of a novelist's equipment'.
47. *Ibid*; see also in this file M.R. Ridley's own report on the series.
48. *The Rhetoric of Fiction*. Chicago 1961, p. 208: 'The Chorus' flight supports the invasion, as it were. Our imaginations sweep us across the channel in the wake of Henry V's forces.'
49. John Fiske and John Hartley, *Reading Television*. London 1978, p. 161.
50. Hope-Wallace, op. cit., p. 22; see Mary Agnes Hamilton, 'The influence of radio on social life and habits', *BBC Quarterly*, **3**(2) (July 1948), p. 93.
51. Martin Esslin, 'Radio drama today', in BBC, *New Radio Drama*. London 1966, p. 9; see Bertolt Brecht, 'The radio as an apparatus of communication', in John Willett (ed.), *Brecht on Theatre*. New York and London 1978, pp. 51-3.
52. *Understanding Brecht*. London 1973, p. 19.
53. 'Popular culture and high culture: history and theory', Unit 4 of *The Study of Culture 1*. Milton Keynes 1977, a part of the Open University course, *Mass Communication and Society* (DE 353).
54. Eagleton, op. cit., pp. 65-6.
55. *Ibid*, p. 66.
56. *Ibid*, p. 67.
57. *Ibid*.
58. 'How many children had Lady Macbeth?', *Explorations*. Harmondsworth 1964, pp. 13-50.
59. Terence Hawkes, *Structuralism and Semiotics*. London 1977, p. 144; Bennett, op. cit., pp. 59-60; Fiske and Hartley, op. cit., p. 191; Jonathan Culler, *Structuralist Poetics*. London 1975, p. 139.
60. Fiske and Hartley, op. cit., p. 160.
61. Hope-Wallace, op. cit., p. 23.

Chapter 8

Classic fiction by radio

Donald A. Low

The appetite of radio for broadcasting material of all kinds is apparently insatiable. Programme planners and producers have a professional obligation to fill all the hours designated for broadcasting each week throughout the year. If the phrase 'fill all the hours' seems unflattering as a way of describing programme-planning, it is nevertheless realistic, for this is the basic requirement. While the planners must aim for quality, their first responsibility is to provide an unbroken supply of programmes of different types for the listening and viewing public. This places a premium in broadcasting organisations on workable rather than ideal programme plans, on the ability of staff to adjust flexibly and without undue signs of strain to constantly changing commitments, and on deadlines. In broadcasting, as in journalism, yesterday's output normally ceases to be of interest after the event. What counts is always the future, whether that means next year, next week, tomorrow, or what is due to happen in the studio in ten minutes' time.

The broadcasting of classic fiction by radio has to be considered against this background of unremittingly frequent production demands. In other words, although broadcasters in this area may, if they so choose, legitimately think of themselves as contributing to 'high' culture, something other than high-mindedness is involved, as the historic record shows. Novels and short stories were discovered early on by the BBC to be reliable time-fillers. Moreover, the costs of producing programmes based on books were modest, especially where copyright no longer applied. For these reasons, and also because they proved extremely popular with many listeners, readings and dramatisations of fiction – with a bias towards the nineteenth-century English classics and above all towards Dickens – soon became a staple part of BBC radio. They still are today on Radio 4 and, with a subtly different emphasis, on Radio 3.

In common with other forms of 'serious' entertainment on radio – very much the Cinderella of the modern media – such programmes tend to be taken for granted. Yet they make a notable contribution to the nation's cultural life, giving fresh currency and immediacy to the words of great novelists, introducing individuals to books they did not previously know, recreating literary works in a new medium by a process that can be compared to translation. If one makes the experiment of reading the *Radio Times* with an eye for dramatisations and readings from fiction, the average week's tally is remarkably high, amounting to several hours. At one end of the range are full-scale adaptations for radio, to be broadcast either serially or in single programmes, with a substantial number of actors and actresses taking part. At the other are 'penny' readings, often of very high quality, as in *Story Time* and *A Book at Bedtime*. Between these two types of programme are several variant and intermediate forms, including readings for two, three or more voices, and dramatisations of selected scenes from particular novels. All have this in common, that the starting point is a work of fiction, and the avowed aim the communication of auditory pleasure, along with at least some part of the essential meaning and quality of the story.

The story, it seems, is the thing. It would be interesting to have statistical evidence of how often listeners tune in to broadcasts within this broad spectrum of programmes because they wish to be in the company of a particular author, and how often instead they do so out of a desire to 'listen to a tale'. Obviously, both considerations come into play simultaneously when the tale happens to be a familiar one. More often than not, though, the main and habit-forming reason for switching on appears to be the craving for a story – any story – told well, irrespective of who the author happens to be. After all, everyone has an instinctive need to listen to stories, whether or not he takes the chance to gratify it. Enjoyment of character and of subtleties of plot are part of this, no less than of reading. With the disappearance from many homes – hastened, ironically, by radio and even more by television – of the centuries-old practices of oral storytelling and of reading aloud, radio storytelling addresses itself to a sense that may otherwise be starved. It is probable that what characteristically leads radio audiences to listen is not the reputation of authors, whether 'classic' or 'popular', so much as their professional skill in narrative and the skills of those who rehandle their work on radio.

At any rate, the re-creation of fiction is well established on radio in Britain, and classic novelists are seldom off the air for very long. This is not to say, however, that all have been represented equally strongly. Scott, for instance, though regularly broadcast in Scotland, has had far less UK airtime than Dickens. This disproportion reflects among other things the mind of Val Gielgud, who had more influence than any other single individual over radio drama in Britain from 1929 until 1962. Gielgud had strong views on the classic novelists suitable for radio adaptation, just as he had on Shakespeare's plays in relation to radio. The following memoranda were exchanged in 1945 between Andrew Stewart, the then Scottish Programme Director, and Gielgud as Director of Drama. Stewart wrote on 18 December about a possible serialisation of *Rob Roy*, which he was ready to entrust to Moray

McLaren, formerly Gielgud's Deputy and a very experienced producer and adaptor:

I remember that when we discussed the possibility of a Scott Serial you were not on the whole favourable. Such discussions, however, were in terms of the old Home Service, and therefore, speculative; but I think I should now put before you a fairly firm proposition . . . With all respect to your views on Sir Walter's work, I think we could agree that he remains one of the foundation members and that his novels are still read and therefore, that a Scott serial is worth considering. The case, of course, is much more obvious in his own native Scotland; but in his own day he certainly did not write only for readers here. We have been very carefully through the most likely novels and on the whole we believe that *Rob Roy*, while it may not be the best novel, should be the subject for the first broadcast Serial. Moray McLaren has submitted a half-hour treatment for episode one and a synopsis for a series of eight half-hour programmes. What prompts me to write specially, is the approach which Moray McLaren has suggested: you will remember that the Scottish characters and the romantic Highlanders are seen through the eyes of a young Londoner, Frank Osbaldistone, and this is the approach which Moray McLaren has endeavoured to retain and develop; as it were, he interprets the mysterious North. I am not quite sure whether four programmes of an hour's duration each would not make more impact than a series of half-hour programmes spread over two months . . . Scottish Home Service would originate and meet all costs. I should welcome the idea of providing such a serial for Basic Home Service and I believe that it would be popular South of the Border. I should be grateful if you would consider the project and, if you are favourably disposed, then, of course, I should be happy to meet you about starting date, length, duration of episodes.

To this heartfelt plea on behalf of Scott as 'one of the foundation members', presumably of classic British fiction, Gielgud replied discouragingly on 21 December:

I cannot help feeling that, although this will no doubt make admirable programme material for Scotland, it is unlikely that its appeal to an English audience would prove large. The book is not, I think, one of Scott's best known novels compared with, for example, *Kenilworth, Ivanhoe*, or *Quentin Derwent [sic]*. There is also the perpetual nettlebed of dialect dialogue, and I have yet to be convinced of the capacity of any adapter to reproduce the essential qualities of Scott in dramatic form considering that his own dialogue is, from the actors' point of view, very nearly unspeakable and would require almost complete rewriting. Moray McLaren may, of course, have solved the latter problem, and on this point you are better able to judge than I.[1]

Gielgud had a valid point about the difficulty of adapting the Lowland Scots dialect in Scott's Scottish novels in such a way as to preserve the flavour of the original without losing part of the audience: but the challenge was not insuperable, as successful adaptations in the last fifteen years have shown.

Behind the disagreement about Scott, as it happened, there also lay a history of tension between London and the regions over radio drama in general. In the 1930s, Gielgud had more than once aroused the ire of regional directors by his insistence that the main national productions should be concentrated in London. Such a policy of centralisation, he believed, was the best way to achieve excellence. As long as he remained in charge of radio drama, Scott's Scottish novels were largely – although not entirely – confined to the Scottish region; and this particular serialisation was broadcast on the Scottish Home Service, but not in England. Historically, Gielgud's rather frosty reply to a notably enthusiastic proposal is of interest, in that one of the most celebrated of all early BBC broadcasts of classic fiction was a Glasgow transmission of *Rob Roy* in 1923.

While there have been marked variations in the amount of network airtime given to masterpieces of British fiction, the coverage has nevertheless been very wide. Nor has the output been limited to readings and adaptations of novels published in Britain and North America. The best stories have a way of crossing national and linguistic frontiers, and the BBC has often played an active part in furthering the process. In this connection, Val Gielgud was more than once an initiator; and where he was not, he usually lent his support to imaginative proposals from his team of producers and freelance adaptors. When, for example, his colleague Barbara Burnham wanted to undertake an ambitious production of *War and Peace* in 1942, Gielgud helped to gain official backing for the project, as well as solving complicated technical problems associated with it. *War and Peace* was broadcast in eight parts, with two hour-long broadcasts being transmitted on each of four successive Sundays, one in the afternoon and another in the evening. This arrangement, which was Barbara Burnham's idea, did not suit all listeners; the evening transmissions proved more popular than those in the afternoon. However, the overall level of appreciation was very high, as a Listener Research Report of the time shows:

War and Peace, which was an unprecedented broadcasting enterprise, succeeded in attracting and holding exceptionally large audiences. At the very least some 5,000,000 people heard some of it and probably at least 1,500,000 heard it all.

In due course the Controller of Programmes, B.E. Nicolls, wrote to Barbara Burnham and to Gielgud to congratulate them on 'a magnificent success' which 'redounded to the credit and prestige of the BBC'. A long and enthusiastic cable, moreover, was received from the Union of Soviet Writers in Moscow. The reply to this, drafted by Barbara Burnham and Gielgud, reveals the extent to which all broadcasting in wartime Britain was affected by the state of international affairs:

Soviet Writers to accept our profound gratitude for their moving and encouraging message. This will hearten us greatly in tackling immense task before us. Our chief hope in broadcasting version *War and Peace* to contribute something towards increasing friendship and natural understanding between

Russia and Britain, insolubly linked in the battle against the barbarians.

War and Peace had pleased its audience, and it had been acceptable as cultural 'propaganda' of a high order. But the reaction of one listener quoted in the Listener Research Report proves that, artistically speaking, the serialisation had not gone uncriticised. The listener who made these comments had not read the novel and based his criticism on the broadcast version only:

Taking *War and Peace* as it was presented to me, I cannot regard it as one of the great books of the world. The battle scenes were interesting, as almost any account of such tremendous events must be: the family histories much less so. None of the characters, to me, attained that supreme vitality that marks the great figures of fiction like Hamlet or Elisabeth Bennett; but what I felt to be more lacking was the sense of universality that is the hall-mark of all great art, the feeling that the affairs of the Rostovs are important to all men always. They were not so to me: they were a story, like any other. If the book has a dominating theme, a central idea that holds it together, this was not made apparent to me. If there was to be one, Pierre seemed likely to be the mouthpiece of it, but he is himself so puzzled and confused as to be unable to present it clearly. Several times there were hints of it – in his conversion to Freemasonry, in his meeting with Platon, and so on – but nothing definite emerged; the death of Andrew [sic] promised it too, but seemed to have no lasting result. The effect, to me, was that of a set of musical variations without either a preliminary statement of the theme or a coda: the theme could no doubt be detected on analysis of the score, but would certainly not be apparent at first hearing. I think the adapter's first duty should have been to bring out clearly this central theme (if there is one, as the book's fame induces me to believe), and in this, I think, he definitely failed.[2]

The cogently expressed argument of this anonymous listener is a reminder of the complexity of the task facing adaptors and producers of dramatised versions of great novels. Few, if any, adaptors succeed in pleasing everyone, however hard they strive to ensure that the story line remains clear, the characterisation vivid, and the dialogue lively and natural-sounding. Reviewing a recent two-part production of Henry James's *The Ambassadors* on Radio 4, Val Arnold-Foster observed:

Drama adaptations of any novel have to fulfil two major tasks. They have to satisfy the original creator's intentions and please those who already know and love the work. They must also attract and please those who either do not know the original or who have found the original uninteresting: the adaptation must be a successful play in its own right.[3]

While this prescription points valuably to the twin essentials of truthfulness to the original and communication through a new medium with a mixed audience, it can be objected that Arnold-Foster asks for the impossible from adaptors. Certainly, an adaptation must exist and communicate 'in its own right', and this is how it is likely to be judged; but need it have the formal characteristics of a *play*? Again, is it not an incidental rather than a 'major' obligation to 'please those who already know and love the work'? Finally, is it not similarly an incidental rather than a major duty to have in mind the particular category of those 'who have found the original uninteresting'?

In practice, adaptors and their producers go for what they take to be salient characteristics of the work in question, and concentrate on putting these over as tellingly as their knowledge of radio allows. The art is inevitably one of compromise, but this does not mean that gifted practitioners necessarily fall short of conveying the spirit of the original. A dogma of many radio theorists since about 1950 has been that narrators have no place in adaptations. Narrators, they argue, belong to books, and plays are different. But the experience of listening to adaptations, both of books that are already familiar and of unknown books, strongly suggests that it is a mistake to lay down the law too firmly on this point. There are novels that, when adapted, benefit unmistakably from the use of a narrator, just as there are others that do not. To insist on conformity to a notion of dramatic form that always necessitates the elimination of a narrator is to be guilty of a lack of due flexibility. It is rather like demanding the Three Unities instead of being content to reinterpret a work of art with as much openness and sensitivity as possible towards both it and the audience. Or it might be compared to the excess of zeal that for a time threatened to stifle invention in 'Directors' Theatre'.

Provided that words and meaning are clear, the ear adjusts readily to forms of radio that, strictly speaking, may be hybrids: so narrators need not be banned for evermore. Drama and an allied pleasure in listening – as distinct from the conscious awareness of 'a play' – can be created by more means than one on radio. A reading of a short story may achieve a greater degree of dramatic impact than an elaborate well-made radio play (whether original or adapted) that does not quite come to life. It is no exaggeration to say that the finest radio readings of fiction, and of much else besides, are intensely and superbly dramatic in effect. The voice of one man or woman may suggest several characters, a clash of points of view, an end or a beginning. In group readings, and also in dramatised adaptations, such effects are orchestrated and multiplied.

If one asks why this should be so, the answer that immediately suggests itself is that the best writers have known their job, and a large number of the actors and actresses who have lent their talents to BBC radio have known theirs. Essentially what takes place in the radio re-creation of classic fiction is that words of beauty and power that tell a story are spoken with clarity and distinction. In performance, what comes over as vital is the apt rendering by the human voice of a memorable narrative. A sparing use of sound effects, and well-chosen music, may heighten the pleasure of listening.

Too much can be made of the kinship between literary tradition and print, and of the differences sometimes alleged to amount to incompatibility between the novelist's commitment to writing, and by implication to silent reading, and the medium of sound broadcasting. It is of course perfectly true that from the seventeenth century onwards novelists have written primarily for a silent reading public, and this has significantly shaped both their art and the conditions for coming to terms with it in its original form. But on the other hand, some of the greatest novelists, including the major Victorian figures in Britain, have kept in mind the widespread practice of reading stories aloud. One reason why Dickens is so well suited to radio lies here. He thoroughly enjoyed giving public readings from his work, and quite clearly conceived of fiction as capable of being dramatically 'performed'. His own dramatic readings did, in a sense, complete his communicative art.

It is easy to be mesmerised by post-McLuhanite dicta on the long connection between literature and print into forgetting that, in Ian Gordon's words, 'the continuity of English prose is a continuity of spoken English'.[4] The language of the classic novelists may at times be cast in elaborate descriptive or narrative patterns, and their dialogue is not as a rule close to a 'transcript' of actual talk, with all that this term implies by way of broken sentences, pauses, interjections and redundant phrases. But for all that, the language of the novel is speech-based. This is borne out by narrative, description and authorial commentary, and above all it is exemplified by dialogue. 'Voices' have a central place, however disguised. As Ian Gordon puts it:

The movement of conversation at various social levels, articulated into the narrative with varying degrees of literary sophistication, is the heart of the English novel, from Richardson and Fielding to Joyce and Virginia Woolf . . . Dialogue – one need look no further than Jane Austen – consistently echoes the accepted speech of the day.[5]

Whatever its complexities and obliquities, the novel habitually draws on and gives full play to the resources of the spoken language, and in this way it shares space with radio. It took a poet and brilliant radio professional, Louis MacNeice, to adapt Virginia Woolf's *The Waves*. His success in doing so shows that interior monologue, even in a highly developed form, remains recognisably close to the speech of its time. 'Stream of consciousness' may be thought of as a typically *literary* technique. In one sense it is, yet it, no less than the very different style of, say, Fielding, carries over the energies, rhythms and idioms of actual talk. Even in the most boldly experimental twentieth-century English fiction such as Joyce's *Ulysses*, there is a speech-based element in the language which the words 'oral residue' do not adequately describe. And, for at least some listeners, radio performance can clarify the meaning of a 'difficult' novelist's words by engaging the imagination. In the case of *Ulysses*, this may be illustrated from a Listener Research Report on 'a performance of two episodes from the novel arranged for broadcasting and produced by

Peter Duval Smith' on the Third Programme in 1954. The two episodes in question were 'Paddy Dignam's Funeral' and 'At the Newspaper Office'; each programme lasted one hour and was repeated within a week. Reaction to the first programme was particularly positive:

. . . well over half the sample commented in enthusiastic terms. Many thought the task of transcribing this section of the 'difficult' *Ulysses* had been accomplished with amazing success. One listener who had read the original described it as 'a great achievement to have translated so faithfully the feeling of the book to sound radio' and one who had not regarded the broadcast as 'an astonishing and interesting experiment'. In fact several readers (or would-be readers) of *Ulysses* said they found Joyce much easier to assimilate in this medium; two or three even thought his style enhanced. And several who for one reason or another have never been able to bring themselves to tackle this book, now feel encouraged to do so. Generally those listeners considered 'Paddy Dignam's Funeral' a particularly remarkable episode, illustrating just the sort of thoughts and odd reflections, the 'free associations', that occupy the idler moments (perhaps the major part) of everyone's mind. It was a morbid episode, they granted, but it was 'striking in its very morbidity', 'terribly real and graveyardy'. Their interest never flagged during that long journey to the cemetery; they could imagine themselves being trundled along the road to Glasnevin; Bloom's thoughts could have been their thoughts.

However, two or three listeners noticed an occasional unnecessary alteration in the text:

'I must complain of some hacking of the original', wrote a Clergyman. 'For example, Mr Bloom chapfallen we heard as Mr Bloom crestfallen. As if Third Programme listeners would be unfamiliar with the word.'[6]

The purist deserves his say. Like every other form of imaginative literature, the novel depends upon the exact word. What matters most of all, if adaptation is not to be a cheapening of one art by another, is that those who carry it out should care greatly for the work they decide to 'translate'. Val Gielgud was right to claim in *Years in a Mirror* that 'the only real basis for satisfactory adaptation is genuine love of the original'.[7] To this may be added Donald McWhinnie's contention:

The best kind of adaptation will stand comparison with its original; it will also exist as an entity in its own right, without relation to the original. And it can only do this if it has been conceived poetically, in other words if the adaptor has hammered out an artistically satisfying form to contain what to him is the essence of the original. It follows that the kind of novel which is most likely to provoke a memorable radio performance is that which itself exists on more than one plane, which has overtones of atmosphere, emotion and meaning which will vibrate in a new way, given a fresh instrumentation.[8]

Radio has fallen on comparatively lean times, but the broadcasting of excellent programmes based on novels and short stories is itself a classic tradition, and one that deserves to be honoured.

Notes

1. BBC Written Archives, Accession no. 7838. (I wish to thank Jacqueline Kavanagh and her colleagues at the BBC Written Archives Centre, Caversham, for their valuable help, and the BBC for permission to quote from documents in their keeping.)
2. BBC Written Archives, Accession no. 7955.
3. 'Wit and polish', *The Guardian*, 20 July 1979, p. 12.
4. *The Movement of English Prose*. London 1966, p. 9.
5. *Ibid*, pp. 8, 162.
6. BBC Written Archives, Listener Research/54/1062.
7. *Years in a Mirror*. London 1965, p. 179.
8. *The Art of Radio*. London 1959, pp. 176-7.

Chapter 9

Organising the imagination : sociological perspectives on radio drama

Graham Murdock

This chapter sets out to review the available sociological work on radio drama and to suggest areas where a more comprehensive perspective might be developed. I want to focus particularly on the interplay between individual choice and structural constraint, and to explore some of the connections between imagination and social organisation.

Radio drama in a dramatised society

The fact that the mass media have made drama an ubiquitous and insistent part of modern experience has prompted Raymond Williams to suggest that we are now living in a 'dramatised' society.[1] Despite the dominance of television, radio continues to make an important contribution to this 'dramatisation' of contemporary life.

Table 9.1. Network drama production on BBC Radio: 1968-1978[2]

	Total hours of drama broadcast on:				*Drama production as a % of total output on:*			
	Radio 2	*Radio 3*	*Radio 4*	*All channels*	*Radio 2*	*Radio 3*	*Radio 4*	*All channels*
1967-8	254	202	827	1,283	4	13	13	6
1977-8	124	172	912	1,208	2	2.5	13	4.8

As Table 9.1 shows, the BBC broadcast well over 1,000 hours of drama on the main network channels during 1977-8, and this excludes the contribution of the BBC's local and regional operations and of local commercial stations. However, the network output alone was some 150 hours more than the combined drama output of ITV and BBC TV in 1978. As Table 9.1 also shows, 90 per cent of the BBC's network productions are transmitted on Radios 3 and 4. Radio 4 takes the lion's share with, for example, *Saturday Afternoon Theatre, Saturday Night Theatre* and *The Monday Play*. It also carries most of the dramatisations of novels and *The Archers*, with Radio 3 mainly concentrating on classical and *avant-garde* drama. Although Radio 2's share of total output has fallen by half over the last ten years, it continues to broadcast the highly successful daily serial, *Waggoners' Walk*, which goes out in the commuter slot of 5.05 p.m. to 5.20 p.m.

In terms of audience size, the heyday of radio drama came with the Second World War and more particularly with the Blitz. During the blackout, *Saturday Night Theatre* reached an estimated 30 per cent of the total population. The figure has fallen sharply since, but even now the Saturday broadcast and the Monday repeat can pick up half a million listeners. The audiences for drama on Radio 3 average about a tenth of that at 50,000. Nevertheless they would comfortably fill one of the bigger football grounds. In terms of listening figures, radio drama's biggest successes remain the two daily serials, with *The Archers* averaging about 1½ million and *Waggoners' Walk* 3 million. By television standards these figures are not particularly startling – *Coronation Street* regularly picks up about 10 million viewers and *Play for Today* around 4 million. In terms of theatre audiences or book sales, however, radio-drama audiences are still impressive. As Richard Imison has pointed out, the average audience for the two broadcasts of a *Saturday Night Theatre* play would fill a fair-sized West End theatre for ten years.[3] And even the more *avant-garde* offerings on Radio 3 are heard by a good many more people than managed to see the original production of *Look Back in Anger* at the Royal Court Theatre in 1956. They would certainly be sufficient to make a serious modern novel into a modest best-seller. Radio, then, remains important for a full understanding of fiction and drama in contemporary society and of the pressures that shape it.

Pressures on production

Sociologists who have looked at drama production in television have highlighted the way in which the organisation of production and the economics of costs and budgeting restrict the range of content and form, nudging them towards the already acceptable and popular.[4] So far, we lack equivalent studies of radio production, but the available evidence suggests that the financial pressures are considerably less and the room for creative manoeuvre and experiment correspondingly greater.

The present Managing Director of BBC Radio, Aubrey Singer, has recently described radio as a 'cottage industry',[5] and certainly compared with the Corporation's television operation it remains reasonably small-scale and relatively cheap. As Martin Esslin, the former Head of Radio Drama, has pointed out:

in planning a radio play we think in terms of hundreds of pounds. On television one thinks in thousands. In the theatre one thinks in tens of thousands. In the cinema one thinks in hundreds of thousands. Really, then, we are the most economic dramatic medium there is.[6]

This relative cheapness means that there is a good deal less at stake if a production does not quite come off or if it fails to attract a respectably sized audience. And this in turn, Esslin argues, means that it is

possible to venture on out-of-the-way experimental material with far less heart-searching than any television programme, even one addressed to a minority audience, could tackle.[7]

This sense of experiment can be seen in several ways. The Radio Drama Department has been in the forefront of translating the work of contemporary *avant-garde* writers from Europe and elsewhere and introducing them to British audiences. It has also made a point of seeking out new native writers and original plays. Robert Bolt's *A Man for All Seasons*, for example, started out as a radio play on the then Home Service. Similarly, John Arden's work received its first public performance when he won a playwriting competition sponsored by the North Region. Radio was also responsible for relaunching the career of Harold Pinter after his somewhat inauspicious début in the commercial theatre. Tom Stoppard narrowly missed becoming one of the regular scriptwriters for *The Dales*, but several of his most notable early works were first performed on radio, including *If You're Glad I'll Be Frank* and *Albert's Bridge*, which won the 1968 Prix Italia. And Alan Ayckbourn served his dramatic apprenticeship as a BBC producer.

The openness to experiment and new writing encouraged by low production costs is reinforced by the relative simplicity of the production process itself. Compared to the cumbersome, segmented and bureaucratic nature of drama production in television, radio remains surprisingly intimate and compact. At the same time it is technically sophisticated, with writers able to call on the full resources of the Radiophonic Workshop and stereo transmission. This combination of simple production and the availability of complex aural effects has a number of advantages. First, it gives authors much greater scope in choosing settings and subjects. Whereas in television the escalating costs of sets, costumes and location shooting impose severe limits on what can be done in a normal production, in radio it is feasible to contemplate doing an epic subject involving numerous scenes without thinking in terms of a budget appropriate to a Hollywood blockbuster. There are pressures on content from other directions, however.

Unlike theatrical performances, which were subject to the Lord Chamberlain's censorship until 1968, the BBC has always been in the peculiar position of acting as its own censor.[8] In order to preserve this autonomy, however, the Radio Drama Department, along with other sectors, has traditionally avoided themes likely to cause public or political offence. Under Val Gielgud's headship, these included 'obviously propagandist problem-plays' and 'plays dealing with physical disabilities – cancer, stammering, tuberculosis'.[9]

Many of these prohibitions have since lapsed as public taste has become more liberal. Cancer, for example, is no longer a taboo subject. Indeed, *Waggoners' Walk* recently featured a death from the disease. The caution over politically contentious material remains, however. According to one of the country's leading younger playwrights, Howard Brenton, the BBC turned down his radio play, *Government Property*, because it dealt with the internment policy in Northern Ireland and its effect on the British Army and public life.[10] Yet the question of British intervention in Ireland has been broached elsewhere in recent radio drama, most notably in John Arden's *Pearl*, set in 1640. Arden is well known for his fierce opposition to government policy, and *The Non-Stop Connolly Show*, which he wrote with his wife Margaretta D'Arcy, is one of the most passionately polemical pieces on 'The Irish Question' in the modern British theatre. Although *Pearl* approaches the issues more obliquely, there is no mistaking its contemporary relevance or its political stance.

Characterising trends in output in terms of particular examples is not, however, a very useful way of mapping the range and limits of present-day radio drama. This requires a more systematic analysis of the whole of the current output to see which areas of social, political and personal life are excluded, which aspects are emphasised, and how they are treated. So far we lack such a survey. A full analysis would also need to look at the scripts that were submitted or commissioned but that were never produced, to see if they differed from those broadcast in the kinds of issues and situations they focused on and in the ways they approached and dealt with them.

If content is still subject to certain restrictions, radio nevertheless allows the writer almost unlimited freedom as regards form. One of the long-standing complaints of writers working in television is that the need to maintain a constant flow of images tends to pull everything back towards naturalism.[11] In contrast, radio allows much greater scope for modernist forms. It is particularly good at handling interior thought, dreams and fantasies. In addition, the fact that radio is a medium that trades in sounds and language considerably upgrades the relative status of the writer. Together with the compact nature of production, this gives authors a good deal more control over their work. Unlike the usual situation in television, they can follow the production through and be present at every stage. Although most welcome this situation, some see the cosiness as leading to a certain narrowing of vision. As one disgruntled writer put it: 'it's the feeling of being in Croydon instead of London W1, and the day after finding that your friends watched TV to a man'.

The relatively low costs of radio-drama production have a negative as well as a positive side for writers, however. While it means that they are likely to have more creative elbowroom than they would in television, it also means that they are considerably less well paid for the same amount of work. As Table 9.2 shows, within each category of drama the fees for television work are roughly three times as high as those for radio.

Table 9.2. Agreed rates for different categories of radio and television drama (Spring 1979)[12]

	Established writers			Beginners		
	ITV (£)	BBC TV (£)	BBC Radio (£)	ITV (£)	BBC TV (£)	BBC Radio (£)
Play	1,815	1,950	660	1,362	1,475	420-90
Serial episode	1,320	1,500	495	1,240	1,125	315-67
Dramatisation of prose	1,100	1,125	396	825	850	189-294

Most writers would get the going rates shown in the table, although the better known and more successful would negotiate above the basic fee. The comparison with television, taken in isolation, can be misleading, however. If radio fees are compared to likely earnings from theatre plays, they appear in a rather better light.[13] For the first stage performance of a short play lasting up to an hour, a writer stands to get a maximum of £300, which is considerably less than the £420 minimum fee for an hour-long radio play by a 'beginner'. A full-length stage play outside the West End will earn £750, providing it runs for a minimum of ten performances. Once again this is rather less than the fee for a two-hour radio play. Even so, most full-time writers have to look elsewhere for the bulk of their income, as a recent survey of Writers' Guild members showed.[14] Of the 153 full-time writers surveyed, only 13 per cent said that radio work was likely to contribute half or more of their 1978 earnings. Most relied on film, television, and book publishing, supplemented by newspaper and magazine work. Almost a half had written a radio play in the past, however, and just under a third (31%) said they would like to write more sometime in the future. Radio was more important to part-time writers, who supplemented their authors' earnings with other jobs. Almost a third of this group (30%) said they were likely to get over half their 1978 writing income from radio.

Overall, radio drama appears to be relatively free from the kind of financial pressures that beset production in film and television. Yet there is one area where 'the dreary, but permanent, conditions of economics', as Val Gielgud called them,[15] exert a rather more insistent influence; and that is in the rapidly expanding sector of local radio.

Local radio and local culture[16]

The last decade and a half has seen a renaissance in local theatre, as the space left vacant by the demise of provincial repertory has been increasingly filled by local-authority funding topped up by Arts Council grants. In some cases, such as Manchester's Royal Exchange Theatre, existing buildings have been adapted and renovated; but in most, brand-new auditoria like the Leicester Haymarket and the Sheffield Crucible have been built in the city centres. Alongside these municipal theatres and their resident companies, there are the theatres built on the campuses of the new universities such as Sussex and Warwick, and the community-theatre groups and touring companies supported by the Arts Council. As a result of these various public investments, people living in most of the country's major cities and fair-sized towns are now able to see a range of live professional theatre reasonably easily. It is against this general background of provincial revival and expansion that local radio and its contribution needs to be set.

Local radio was launched in Britain in November 1967 when the first three BBC stations opened in Leicester, Liverpool and Sheffield, with Independent Local Radio (ILR) finally arriving in 1973 after a long campaign by the commercial lobby. At the time of writing there are thirty-nine stations on the air, split more or less equally between the BBC's twenty and the ILR system's nineteen. However, this figure is likely to move fairly rapidly into treble figures in the 1980s as the current development plans for both systems are put into operation. Consequently, any future study of radio drama will need to look quite carefully at local broadcasting and the possibilities it opens up. In the space available here, though, I can only offer a very preliminary sketch of some of the factors that have shaped developments to date.

Most of the successful ILR franchise bids included at least some plans for drama. In practice, however, these intentions have increasingly run up against the hard edges of accountancy, with the result that, in many stations, drama programming has been cut back, postponed or shelved altogether. As a senior executive in one of the medium-sized stations somewhat bluntly put it:

the only dramatic intentions we expressed in our application to the IBA for the franchise had to do with a local soap opera. Mainly for economic reasons we have not yet got around to starting this and I cannot forsee when we will begin.

The first and most important of these 'economic reasons' is that radio drama, although relatively inexpensive compared to film or television, is still costly to produce compared to the staples of local programming – the record-request show and the phone-in. Authors have to be paid for original scripts or adaptations or for the rights to perform their existing work; and under the present Equity agreement, actors' fees are the same for performing on local stations as for a BBC network broadcast. For a station operating on relatively tight profit margins, even a modest outlay represents a risk they are reluctant to take, as a senior producer at one of the smallest stations related:

Joining the station in 1975, I submitted a pilot script for a daily 5 minute serial of the *Waggoners' Walk* type – based on a local housing estate. The then Head of Programmes budgeted out the recording costs, studio time and actors' fees – and the cost of £30 [sic] per week plus made it unviable.

In addition to these direct costs, drama also entails substantial 'hidden' costs. It ties up studio time and production facilities that could be used for more popular programming, and it requires the kind of specialised experience and expertise that only the largest stations can afford, as one programme controller explained:

The basic problem in the presentation of drama on Independent Local Radio is cost, not only in terms directly attributable to the employment of actors, commissioning of writers and so on, but also the tremendous demand it places upon technical resources and production talent. Radio drama is a highly specialised technique demanding talent at all levels which is not easily available and not easily employed in other aspects of broadcasting operations. At the present time we could not consider for instance setting aside 3 days of studio time to record a 90 minute play as might happen in the BBC.

Direct production costs can be substantially reduced by getting listeners to submit scripts and by employing local amateur actors. However, this strategy may well turn out to be counter-productive since it often entails even greater hidden costs than on a professional production, as one producer graphically pointed out:

The station's first full scale attempt at a drama production came just over a year ago. *Under Milk Wood* was produced as a joint venture by one of our engineering staff and a news lady who happened to be Welsh – and an ex-actress who is currently a member of a local amateur dramatic society. Faces still go white when the title of the work is mentioned. The finished product was very professional and polished, but the process of achieving that finish, with the limitations of studio facilities not geared to drama production, and using amateurs used to projecting their voices sans microphone and with a lot of movement, can hardly be imagined. With dubbing, cutting, recording, rehearsals etc., etc., it was estimated that the engineer involved and the news lady both spent a hundred hours plus each of their 'spare time', not counting discussion meetings and out-of-studio rehearsals etc.

There are problems too with using material submitted by listeners. A recent playwriting competition sponsored by the BBC station, Radio Brighton, in conjunction with South East Arts produced, according to the station manager, 'no result whatsoever, i.e. none of the plays submitted were up to the standard that we were prepared to broadcast'. This clash between the professional standards of the broadcasters and material originated by audience members has been noted by researchers studying other participatory situations in broadcasting. However, it is by no means a one-way movement. If producers are chary of transmitting material that falls short of their standards of excellence, listeners used to polished and technically sophisticated productions are apt to find programmes done by non-professionals on a shoestring budget 'sloppy' and 'amateurish'. Moreover, in an effort to guess what producers may want, would-be writers are quite likely to look to already successful styles and to write as though they were scripting *The Archers* or as though they were Tom Stoppard. As a result of this pincer movement, most of the material that reaches the airwaves tends to work within rather than outside the already accredited themes and forms. The relationship between organisation and imagination operates on two dimensions, then: directly through the material constraints on production, and indirectly through the prevailing assumptions of what constitutes 'good', 'entertaining' and 'exciting' drama. However, even if listeners do submit scripts that are generally 'up to standard', there may still be considerable problems with knocking them into a suitable shape for broadcasting, as one producer recounted:

I decided to try out a community involvement project two Christmases ago, which would involve listeners writing their own half hour play on an Xmas theme. Response to the project was very encouraging, with over fifty listeners taking on the task of writing a play for no financial reward. The problems became clear when the scripts arrived, as obviously writing to time and for a particular medium like radio is not as easy as many imagine. However, we rewrote the winning entry and produced the play . . . the whole project involved literally hundreds of unpaid hours of work for all concerned. The result was, to be charitable, not very rewarding for either those involved in production – or the listeners. We have not repeated the project.

There are, therefore, constant tensions between the station's need to make a profit, the broadcasters' desire to produce polished, professional programmes, and the ethos of audience participation and community involvement that underpins the public rhetoric of local radio. The phone-in offers an ideal solution to this dilemma. It is cheap, it is participatory, but it remains firmly under the control of the professional presenters and producers.

In contrast, the situation at the larger, more affluent stations in the ILR system is in some ways rather more open. Having survived an initially shaky start, the stations operating in the revenue-rich major cities are all showing a healthy profit. According to their latest annual reports, London's general station, Capital Radio, made taxable profits of £1.86 million in 1977-8; Piccadilly Radio, the Manchester station, made £600,000; with Radio City in Liverpool showing a balance of £337,000.[17] Profits of this order, together with a sizeable audience, have given the big stations a firm base from which to launch out, and all three are currently in the process of building up their drama output. Capital are developing a new daily serial, *Double Trouble*, and a series of monthly one-off plays. Piccadilly have already produced two original science-fiction series, *The Last Rose of Summer* and *Hunter's Moon*, and are planning a number of one-hour plays, while Radio City have recently commissioned six thirty-minute plays from well-known local dramatists such as Willy Russell and Alan Bleasedale. There are developments, too, in some of the other larger stations, notably Metro Radio in Newcastle (currently the seventh most profitable station in the ILR system). So far, it has produced a daily serial, *City*, based on a local football club, and a weekly situation-comedy series, *Slatey Drift*, about the activities of a local working-men's club. Metro also had the distinction of being the first commercial station to move into 'classical' drama when it produced August Strindberg's *Miss Julie* as a contribution to the Newcastle Festival.

However, projects like these are well beyond the means of the smaller stations. As one of the programme controllers emphasised, they 'simply cannot afford the technical resources or the budget that would be necessary to produce drama of an adequate standard'. It appears, then, that a split is currently developing within the commercial-radio system, which parallels the division within the commercial-television system, with the larger companies covering the whole range of programming including drama production, and the smaller stations concentrating on record shows, local news and topical phone-ins, and occasionally buying drama programmes from the major operators. According to one senior producer, this tendency is likely to accelerate in the future with

the larger more affluent stations taking on ambitious and worthy production, which they will play in the evenings for those who wish to take advantage of them, then offer round the Network to the smaller stations like ourselves, who will or will not take them, depending upon suitability and space.

Although a network system makes obvious financial sense, the search for 'suitable' material for syndication may well be at odds with the idea of *local* radio. The hope of recouping costs by selling across the network is likely to nudge the originating companies towards certain sorts of drama. It may mean going for writers who are already well known and popular outside the local area, and opting for themes that will have a widespread appeal and that can be sold over a reasonable time span. This in turn means looking for material whose attraction is not limited by too heavy a reliance on local reference and topical allusion. Hence the drama offered on the network is likely to have a general rather than a local appeal. Moreover, for the purchasing stations, inserting syndicated material into the evening schedules may well mean dropping local-interest programmes on, say, fishing or gardening. This dilemma of balancing service to the locality against the chance to expose audiences to the range of contemporary and classical drama is not peculiar to local radio, however. It is also shared by the municipal theatres, where the claims of locally originated productions (such as the Crucible's *Stirrings in Sheffield on a Saturday Night*) are balanced against revivals of the classics, box-office hits, and plays by leading modern dramatists.

In contrast, the BBC's local-radio stations are explicitly 'committed to reflect the musical and artistic life of the community', including its literary and dramatic life.[18] At first sight, however, the financial pressures besetting this ideal appear even greater than those on the commercial stations. According to one authoritative estimate, for example, the projected 1979 income from the nineteen ILR stations is likely to be in the region of £40 million, which is nearly half the total budget for the whole of the BBC's domestic radio operations.[19] However, the BBC local stations have several advantages in this unequal financial struggle. In the first place, they can draw on the specialised expertise and production facilities of the Corporation's regional studio complexes. The winning entries in the recent playwriting competition organised by Radios Birmingham, Derby and Stoke, for example, were produced at the BBC's Pebble Mill centre in Birmingham by an experienced network drama producer, and then broadcast over the three stations. Similarly, the stations in Manchester, Blackburn and Liverpool sponsor an annual playwriting competition in conjunction with the North West Arts Association. This is now in its third year, and as well as receiving their share of the £1,000 prize money, all the winners have their entries broadcast on the BBC's stations in the North West.

While the pooling of budgets and resources goes some way towards alleviating the financial constraints on drama production, by operating at a regional level it again poses problems for the ideal of *local* radio. Not least, it means that the BBC is to some extent competing with itself. The alternative is to try to find co-sponsors for specifically local productions, and to this end a number of stations have developed links with other public agencies involved in promoting local cultural activity. In several instances, stations have collaborated with local arts festivals. The most notable example is Radio Brighton, which has produced an original radio play by a well-known writer every year since 1973 as part of the Brighton Festival. The first production was Jeremy Sandford's *Oluwale*, with Paul Scofield. Subsequent contributions have come from Alan Plater, N. F. Simpson, and Mary O'Malley, who wrote this year's play, *I've Only Got the Large One Dear*. Other stations have received direct grants from local authorities. At Radio Sheffield, for example, an annual grant of around £1,000 from the South Yorkshire Metropolitan County Council has enabled the station to put on two series of short plays by local writers for the past three years. However, as the producer involved stressed, the station would not be able to continue the project if the grant was withdrawn and money from other 'outside agencies' was not forthcoming. For other stations, these outside agencies have included educational institutions and municipal theatres. For example, Radio Solent's serial, *A New Life for Brenda*, which dealt with the problems of a woman returning to work after raising a family, was funded by the Adult Education Department of Southampton University. In view of the renaissance of subsidised theatre, it is perhaps surprising that there has been so little collaboration between local stations and the theatres in their transmission areas. Some obvious forms of joint venture are ruled out on the grounds of cost. Direct outside broadcasts from theatres, for example, would be prohibitively expensive for a local station. Studio broadcasts of local productions are more feasible, however. In 1977, for example, Radio Derby combined with the local Playhouse company to broadcast *The Peartree Conspiracy*, a one-hour play originated by the company and dealing with a little-known local plot to assassinate Lloyd George.

Even so, these instances remain the exception rather than the rule. In the absence of outside subsidies, the BBC local stations are subject to much the same financial pressures and constraints as the smaller ILR stations with much the same result – that drama makes a negligible or non-existent contribution to their programme schedules. As one producer forcefully reiterated:

Drama is one of the most expensive forms of broadcasting, and one of the most time-consuming in terms of personnel, equipment and time, so although a station manager might like to do more drama, it is probably out of the question for these reasons.

Other executives argue strongly for recognising the economic facts of local-radio life and concentrating on what the station can do best, leaving drama to the BBC's regional and network centres. As one station manager put it: 'We are in the main a news and information station with some music, and drama is broadly beyond us.' This view is likely to gain ground in the future as the reduction in the BBC's local-broadcasting hours coupled with the cutbacks in local-authority expenditure put even greater pressure on drama production and lead to a further contraction in output.

Turning from production to consumption we find a rather subtler but no less powerful set of pressures organising the imagination of listeners. They do not stem from straightforward economic constraints, since, with the abolition of the radio licence and the spread of cheap transistor sets, radio has become the least expensive and most widely available of all the mass media. Rather, they come from the 'invisible' pressures on participation and response rooted in the social organisation of personal experience and aesthetic judgement.

Exploring audience responses

Systematic social scientific research into radio audiences began in earnest in America in the late 1930s. By then, radio had become firmly associated in both popular and academic commentary with persuasion and propaganda. Not only was it a key arm of Hitler's ideological machine, it had also emerged as a major channel for commercial advertising. Altogether, it appeared as a medium of unparalleled reach and power. The pundits' worst fears were amply confirmed by the reaction to Orson Welles's 1938 broadcast dramatisation of H. G. Wells's *The War of the Worlds*. Delivered in a documentary style and interrupted at intervals with convincing-sounding news flashes, the transmission caused widespread panic. According to a contemporary study conducted by the eminent psychology professor, Hadley Cantril,[20] over a quarter (28%) of the estimated six million listeners actually believed that an invasion was taking place, and a number of those living near the supposed landing-site got into their cars and drove into the night in an effort to get as far away as possible. The event added further fuel to growing fears about the effects of radio, and it was this same concern that had prompted the Rockefeller Foundation to set up the Office of Radio Research at Columbia University in the previous year. Under the direction of the Austrian social psychologist, Paul Lazarsfeld, the Office set out with the brief 'to study what radio means in the lives of listeners'. The results of their work still provide the most comprehensive set of studies of radio ever undertaken outside audience-research departments and advertising agencies.

The work on radio drama focused primarily on the daytime serials or soap operas (so called because one of the first sponsors was a soap manufacturer). They were among the most successful and ubiquitous of all radio programmes, and by careful channel-switching it was possible to listen to them end-to-end throughout the day. Lazarsfeld's team looked at the themes and plots of these serials and at their impact on the imagination of the women who listened to them.

According to the detailed content analysis carried out by Lazarsfeld's co-worker, Rudolf Arnheim,[21] the serials concentrated almost obsessively on domestic happenings and studiously avoided wider social problems and political events. Their dominant message was: 'no matter how bad or unjust things seem, everything will finally turn out happily for those who deserve it'.[22] This fatalistic view of the world, it was argued, taught women to accept their subordinate status and limited horizons, and encouraged them to make the best of a bad job. This analysis fitted easily with the pessimistic views of another distinguished refugee from Hitler's regime, Theodor Adorno. He saw radio and the rest of the modern 'culture industry' as instruments of mass deception bolstering the interests of dominant groups, whether a political élite, as in the Third Reich he had fled, or big business, as in the America he had come to. (As if to confirm his fears, one of the most successful serials was called *Big Sister*, which carried connotations of manipulation and control even before Orwell.) Although Adorno reserved his strongest criticism for the popular-music shows, he and his collaborator, Max Horkheimer, saw the same dynamics operating across the board:

From . . . every broadcast program the social effect can be inferred which is exclusive to none but is shared by all alike.[23]

Adorno saw the sponsors' desire to maximise audiences as leading inevitably to bland content and standardised programme formats, which conditioned listeners' tastes and expectations so that they came to want only more of the same. As he put it:

Standardization, moreover, means the strengthening of the lasting domination of the listening public and of their conditioned reflexes. They are expected to want only that to which they have become accustomed.[24]

Adorno saw no need to test this argument empirically, since he believed that listeners' reactions could be inferred from the programme formats. Lazarsfeld, on the other hand, insisted on the need for detailed studies of response. Unlike Adorno, he saw listening as a dynamic process in which people actively reworked and interpreted the material on offer in line with their social experiences and views of the world. Before asking what people got out of the serials, however, it was necessary to find out who in fact listened to them by conducting general audience surveys.[25] The results were much as expected: the bulk of serial fans were working-class women with a minimum of formal education and generally conservative political views. There were exceptions, however. One or two of the serials did attempt to break with the standard formula and try to link personal struggles to wider political events and issues. The most notable example was probably *Against the Storm*, which centred on a girl whose brother was fighting with the Danish resistance and who was in love with a man traumatised by his experiences at the front. The audience for this was markedly better off and better educated than for most serials. The links between class, education and taste that are hinted at by these findings open up some interesting questions, which we shall return to presently. But unfortunately they were not explored by the Columbia team. Instead they concentrated on finding out what people got out of their serial listening and how their imaginative involvement with the plots and characters was integrated into their everyday life. They were not interested in what the serials were doing *to* listeners, but in what listeners were doing *with* the serials.

The two major studies of 'uses and gratifications' (as they are now called) were conducted by Ruth Palter[26] and Herta Herzog.[27] Both involved detailed personal interviews with a small sample of women, and both stressed the way in which serial-listening was actively integrated into housewives' strategies for getting through the day and coping with their domestic lives. By providing a constant stream of interesting events, many listeners claimed that the serials helped to break the monotony of their domestic round and fill their 'empty lives' with content. Others stressed the way the serials broke down their sense of social isolation by supplying 'imaginary friends'. As one of Ruth Palter's respondents put it: 'It's nice to have company. But if you don't, it's nice to have the radio.' The serials also offered their listeners convenient recipes for coping with unlooked-for problems. As one of the women Herzog interviewed explained: 'If you listen to these programs and something turns up in your own life, you would know what to do about it.' The examples they mentioned ranged from how to discourage an unwanted admirer, to how to comfort a bereaved relative and how to cope with a law suit.

Altogether, listeners emerge from these studies as active rather than passive, participants rather than dupes. Even so, it is activity that remains confined by the limits set by the imaginative and ideological world presented by the serials, and from this perspective Adorno's general thesis begins to look a little more credible. The serials do indeed appear as vehicles for dominant and largely conservative values. Although the audiences were mainly working-class, the serials concentrated on the doings and attitudes of the upper class and the better-off sectors of the middle class. They therefore provided a powerful conduit for the downward transmission of dominant views and assumptions.[28] These views in turn were embedded in a social vision that celebrated the stable lifestyle and solid virtues of clean, Christian, small-town America. Change, if it appeared at all, came in the form of problems and threats to this vision. The world of the serials was a world whose inhabitants were engaged in a 'desperate defence of a status quo, the value of which' was largely taken for granted.[29] It was this same conservatism that fuelled Senator McCarthy's witch-hunting campaign and led to the infamous 'black list' that banned a number of scriptwriters from working in broadcasting for a good part of the 1950s.

With the advent of television, researchers tended to desert radio for the new medium, with the result that there have been relatively few successors to these early studies. The work of Jay Blumler and his colleagues is a notable exception, however. They followed up some of the leads provided by the Columbia work in a study of the audience for *The Dales*, conducted just before the programme was finally 'killed' in 1969. Their research was based on intensive interviews with a cross-section of women in Leeds. The results confirmed the findings of the Lazarsfeld group. Like the American serial fans of the 1940s, followers of *The Dales* were 'markedly conservative in social and political outlook'.[30] Their lives were firmly centred around domestic activities and they saw *The Dales* as a confirmation of traditional family life. It seemed to speak for stability and the old verities in a

Britain buffeted by social and moral change. Not surprisingly, they were particularly antagonistic to the dramas of contemporary life represented by *Play for Today*. Although the last episode of *The Dales* was written by the same scriptwriters who were working on the first episodes of its successor, *Waggoners' Walk*, the social worlds of the two serials were very different. The early *Waggoners' Walk* focused on a group of office girls sharing a flat in London. Where *The Dales* celebrated the family and social stability, *Waggoners' Walk* offered images of what it was like to be young and single in the London of the late 1960s. Moreover, it set out to break with the accepted taboos and formulas by 'dealing with subjects which soap operas on the whole didn't touch'.[31] It was exactly the kind of imaginative world that *Dales* fans felt most distanced and alienated from. They felt betrayed, and they deserted in droves, as the original scriptwriters remember:

A whole lot of people never tried it. They switched off *The Dales* and went into mourning . . . Something like three million people listened to Mrs Dale's end, but no more than a million wanted to know *Waggoners'*.[32]

Blumler's sample was no exception. Out of the original seventy *Dales* fans he interviewed, only five became regular followers of *Waggoners' Walk*. Their place was taken by different, younger, more working-class listeners. Followers of the traditional family serial, however, still had *The Archers*, which continued 'to avoid the trivial and the trendy' and 'to concern itself with the yearly round of country life' and 'the enduring things of human life and love and death'.[33] As Norman Painting, who plays Phil Archer and contributes regular scripts, has recently re-emphasised, *The Archers* is

not full of the things the newspapers are full of; we don't reflect 100 per cent the permissive society. I think we much more represent the silent majority. That's not to say we don't present life as it is, but we don't dwell on a certain minority section of it, so you won't find sex and violence and rape and abortion and the pill thrust down your throat.[34]

The Archers, then, is definitely not the place for an aspiring writer to push 'across the problems of a single parent or a token women's libber or a gay'.[35] However, by no means the entire *Archers* audience is composed of middle-aged and retired conservative ladies living in the shires. Like *Coronation Street*, it commands a sizeable following among the intelligentsia, which raises an important point about the determinants of preference and response. Clearly, as the existing studies show, tastes are strongly connected to social experience and general views, with people tending to opt for drama that connects with their own preoccupations and assumptions. But this is not a complete explanation. It ignores the part that cultural forms and aesthetic codes play in shaping tastes and reactions. One point of entry into this knotty but crucial area is provided by the work of the French sociologist, Pierre Bourdieu.

Audience-research studies have consistently shown marked social divisions in the audiences for different types of drama.[36] Why is it, for example, that the audiences for *avant-garde* works tend to be concentrated among the non-manual strata in general and those who have been educated beyond the minimum age in particular? Bourdieu's answer is that although radio and television appear to make contemporary culture equally available to everyone at the touch of a button, understanding and enjoyment of, say, a modernist play depends on being familiar with the conventions and codes employed.[37] Without this knowledge it is likely to seem unintelligible, confusing and boring. A good example is provided by *The Cookham Resurrection*, a kaleidoscopic impression of the life of the artist, Stanley Spencer, broadcast on Radio 3. According to a BBC study of reactions, although most listeners welcomed it as a vivid evocation of Spencer's private world, 'a substantial number' found it 'so "chaotic" in form as to be quite incomprehensible'.[38] Access to the necessary interpretative frames is not available to everyone, however. On the contrary, Bourdieu suggests, it is systematically maldistributed through the class structure. The differences begin, he argues, with the family.

Families hand on what he calls the primary 'habitus'. This consists of 'a system of schemes of thought, perception, appreciation and action' which provide the basic frames through which people approach the cultural domain.[39] These habits of thought are acquired surreptitiously through observing the way parents relate to cultural artefacts, through language learning, and through involvement in everyday social interaction. Research on child socialisation has shown that all these features of family life differ markedly in different social classes, and these differences, Bourdieu suggests, feed through into the way people come to approach the world of art. For example, children from homes where the parents consume a wide range of culture and take the trouble to explain their choices and judgements are much more likely to be familiar with the less popular cultural forms and the rudiments of criticism from an early age. Similarly, children from families where patterns of personal interaction are fluid rather than rigidly structured according to age and position are more likely to feel at home with the relative openness and indeterminacy of modernist works. Moreover, recent work suggests that both these features are particularly characteristic of child-rearing patterns among the educated middle class, who are the major audience for modern works.[40] As yet we know very little about how these connections actually work, but they are clearly well worth exploring.

According to Bourdieu, the initial inequalities in cultural competence, stemming from differences in family upbringing, are further cemented by divisions in schooling. As numerous studies have shown, children from non-manual homes tend to fare better within the education system, and this success gives them access to a different kind of aesthetic training. As Bourdieu points out, any cultural artefact, 'from cookery to dodecaphonic music by way of the Wild West film, can be a subject for apprehension ranging from the simple, actual sensation to scholarly appreciation'.[41] However, it is only towards the top end of the education system that children are systematically trained to intellectualise their responses. A vivid instance of this is provided by the story of the eminent professor of American Literature who is reported to have spent fifteen minutes 'explaining how Joe Grundy [in *The Archers*] was obviously based on a character in Trollope's *An American Senator*'.[42] As this example makes clear, a person's cultural and aesthetic training determines not only the kind of drama he will listen to, but also the *way* in which he relates to it. There is evidence, for example, that many listeners find the plotting of *The Archers* somewhat contrived and unrealistic and the characters generally unlikable.[43] However, while the traditional audience probably remains loyal *despite* these features, it is likely that at least some of the 'intellectual' audience are attracted *by* them. Stylisation and failed seriousness, for example, are part of that 'camp' sensibility that has underpinned a good deal of recent art and criticism.[44] It is precisely this sensibility that is celebrated on television in *Monty Python*'s merciless send-up of the soap-opera form and in such American pastiches as *Soap* and *Mary Hartman, Mary Hartman*. It is no accident that all three have achieved cult status among sixth-formers and college students. This is, however, an exception; significant, certainly, but an exception all the same. Overall, the social distribution of drama audiences is remarkably stable in both the theatre and broadcasting, and crossovers between radically different forms remain relatively rare.

Moreover, this social distribution of taste tends to be self-reinforcing, as particular forms become associated in people's minds with particular social groups. To express a preference, then, involves not only the making of an aesthetic choice but also the declaration of a social affinity or identity. Radio 3, for example, has a markedly middle-class and well-educated audience. Most working-class listeners do not consider tuning in, or even looking to see what is on. For them the channel is indelibly associated with intellectuals and highbrows, and seen as not for ordinary people like themselves. These channel identities and differentiations have been reinforced still further by the recent moves towards 'streamed' output.

An important part of the BBC's original cultural policy involved building bridges between the different cultural domains to allow listeners to 'progress smoothly, in their own time, from the known to the unknown, from "Grand Hotel" to Beethoven, and perhaps even from Beethoven to Schoenberg'.[45] This was achieved by mixing different levels of culture on the same channel so that 'millions of people, sitting in their homes of an evening, would turn on to Tommy Handley, and then would by accident hear Beethoven'.[46] However, with the introduction of television and the increasing competition from 'offshore' stations like Radio Luxembourg, the Corporation began to shift towards a policy of streaming by category. It became, in a favourite BBC phrase, a matter of 'horses for courses'. The first step was to give particular programmes a positive identity. Under Val Gielgud's regime at the Drama Department, for example, *Saturday Night Theatre* became the slot that offered 'family entertainment on the lines of a popular West End play', with *The Monday Play* providing 'either a classic or an intellectually stimulating play by a living writer'.[47] Because audiences knew what to expect from each slot, the argument ran, they were able to avoid listening to something they did not want. A favourite analogy was with magazine publishing. As Martin Esslin put it: 'No one buying a highbrow literary periodical will expect to find popular fiction in it, no housewife buying a woman's magazine will expect experimental writing.'[48]

More recently, the streaming principle has been extended to the channels themselves so that each becomes identified with a particular range and type of programming. This policy was laid out in the BBC document, *Broadcasting in the Seventies* (1969), and has underpinned the BBC's radio policy for the last decade. The results can be seen in Table 9.1. Drama is now almost exclusively the province of Radios 3 and 4, the only significant exception being *Waggoners' Walk* on Radio 2. Both Radios 3 and 4 have a distinctly skewed audience profile, however, with the bulk of listeners coming from the older age groups and the higher socio-economic groups. Those in professional or managerial occupations, for example, listen on average to three times as much Radio 4 programming and six times as much Radio 3 output as those in manual occupations.[49] Instead of breaking free from established patterns of cultural stratification, then, the channel-streaming policy has meant that, with the notable exception of *Waggoners' Walk*, the audience profiles for radio drama have moved closer and closer to the known profiles for theatre-going and the readership of serious literature.

Within this general pattern there are some interesting variations, however. As mentioned earlier, *The Monday Play* is the BBC's radio equivalent of *Play for Today*, and as such it tends to favour the tougher, more contentious areas of contemporary drama. The recent transmission of Tom McGrath's *The Hardman*, based on Jimmy Boyle's harrowing account of his criminal career and his period of long-term imprisonment, is a case in point. This emphasis on contemporary experience is reflected in the fact that *The Monday Play* attracts rather more listeners in their twenties than is usual for Radio 4. In fact the constitution of the audience is much more like that for fringe theatre than for mainstream commercial or subsidised drama. *Afternoon Theatre*, on the other hand, still finds the majority of its listeners among the over-fifties. However, the recently appointed young editor, Penny Gold, has declared her intention of trying to change this situation by attracting 'more of the young women who are at home looking after kids or on shift work'. And to this end she is commissioning plays that deal with contemporary problems and with the situation of women in a more 'political and socially-concerned' way than is usual in daytime domestic drama.[50] Certainly, the authors she has signed up cover a wide range of British women writers. Some, like Shelagh Delaney, belong to the first wave of postwar English realism; others, like Pam Gems, have emerged out of the current feminist movement; and others again, like Elaine Feinstein, are established novelists who so far have not written for radio. Whether this attempt to alter the popular tea-and-crumpets image of *Afternoon Theatre* will succeed in capturing a broader audience remains to be seen; but judging from the experience of similar initiatives in television drama, it is unlikely to make more than a smallish dent on ingrained patterns of cultural socialisation. It seems more probable that, although radio will continue to offer an enormous range of contemporary and classical drama, the bulk of potential listeners (particularly the young and the working-class) will continue to see it as an offer they can comfortably refuse.

Although suggestive, the evidence we have so far on audience dynamics is disappointingly thin and sketchy, and a great deal more is needed before we can begin to unpack the connections between social and cultural stratification with any degree of precision. But I would suggest that the work deserves to be done, not only for what it may contribute to our understanding of radio, but for what it may tell us more generally about the ways in which social organisation impinges on imaginative life.

Notes

1. *Drama in a Dramatised Society*. Cambridge 1975.
2. Data taken from the *BBC Handbook 1969*. London 1969, p. 62, and the *BBC Handbook 1979*. London 1979, p. 107. In both cases the respective years run from March to March.
3. 'Drama at the BBC', *Plays and Players*, **13** (3) (Dec. 1965), pp. 8-10.
4. For a general review of sociological studies of mass-media production, see Philip Elliott, 'Media organizations and occupations: an overview', in James Curran, Michael Gurevitch and Janet Woollacott (eds), *Mass Communication and Society*. London 1977, pp. 142-73. The pressures shaping drama production in television are explored in Graham Murdock, 'Fabicating fictions : approaches to the study of television drama production', in Edizioni RAI, *Organization and Structure of Fiction Production in Television*. Turin 1977, vol. 1, pp. 183-98; and in Graham Murdock and J.D. Halloran, 'Contexts of creativity in television drama : an exploratory study in Britain', in Heinz-Dietrich Fischer and Stefan Reinhard Melnik (eds), *Entertainment : A Cross-Cultural Examination*. New York 1979, pp. 273-85. The present chapter draws on a wider study of

broadcast drama being conducted by the author at the Centre for Mass Communication Research, University of Leicester.

5.   Singer, 'Radio in the eighties – art and utility', a speech delivered to the Edinburgh International Radio Seminar, 23 Aug. 1979.

6.   'Drama at the BBC', *Plays and Players*, **13** (5) (Feb. 1966), p. 65.

7.   *The National Theatre of the Air*, BBC Lunch-time Lectures, Second Series, 4. London 1964, p. 4.

8.   Geoffrey Robertson, *Obscenity: An Account of Censorship Laws and their Enforcement in England and Wales*. London 1979.

9.   Gielgud, *British Radio Drama 1922-1956*. London 1957, p. 185.

10. Letter to *The Guardian*, 14 Sept. 1977, p. 12.

11. Troy Kennedy Martin, 'Nats go home: first statement of a new drama for television', *Encore*, **11** (2) (Mar.-Apr. 1964), pp. 21-33; John McGrath, 'TV drama: the case against naturalism', *Sight and Sound*, **46** (2) (Spring 1977), pp. 100-5.

12. The figures quoted are taken from the 1979 agreements negotiated by the Writers' Guild of Great Britain. Rates are based on running time. BBC rates are based on sixty-minute segments, ITV rates on fifty-two-minute segments (to allow for advertising inserts).

13. John Bowen, 'Making a living: the playwright's problem', *The Author*, **90** (1) (Spring 1979), pp. 3-10.

14. My thanks to Elaine Steel, Marie Banks and the staff of the Writers' Guild for their help in getting the survey off the ground, and to all the members who took time off to answer my questions.

15. 'The early days: Val Gielgud, talking to Peter Roberts', *Plays and Players*, **13** (3) (Dec. 1965), p. 11.

16. Except where otherwise stated, all quotations in this section are taken from direct communications to the author. I would like to thank all the staff in the various BBC and ILR stations who provided me with information and comment.

17. *Investors Chronicle*, 18 May 1979, p. 589.

18. BBC, *Serving Neighbourhood and Nation*. London 1978, p. 27.

19. Singer, op. cit.

20. Hadley Cantril, Hazel Gaudet and Herta Herzog, *The Invasion from Mars: A Study in the Psychology of Panic*. Princeton 1940.

21. Arnheim, 'The world of the daytime serial', in P.F. Lazarsfeld and F.N. Stanton (eds), *Radio Research 1942-1943*. New York 1944, pp. 34-85.

22. H.J. Kaufman, 'The appeal of specific daytime serials', in Lazarsfeld and Stanton (eds), op. cit., p. 88.

23. Max Horkheimer and Theodor W. Adorno, *Dialectic of Enlightenment*. London 1973, p. 127.

24. *Prisms*. London 1967, p. 124.

25. Herta Herzog, 'What do we really know about daytime serial listeners?', in Lazarsfeld and Stanton (eds), op. cit., pp. 3-33; Kaufman, op. cit., pp. 86-107.

26. 'Radio's attraction for housewives', *Hollywood Quarterly*, **3** (3) (Spring 1948), pp. 248-57.

27. 'On borrowed experience', *Studies in Philosophy and Social Science*, **9** (1941), pp. 65-95.

28. W. Lloyd Warner and William E. Henry, 'The radio day time serial: a symbolic analysis', *Genetic Psychology Monographs*, **37** (1948), pp. 3-71.

29. Arnheim, op. cit., p. 78.

30. Jay G. Blumler, J.R. Brown and Denis McQuail, '*The Dales*: a "uses and gratifications" investigation of a daytime radio serial', in Television Research Centre, University of Leeds, *The Social Origins of the Gratifications associated with Television Viewing*. Leeds 1970, p. 8.
31. Rodney Challis, 'Still walking', *Radio Times*, **223** (2893) (21-7 Apr. 1979), p. 15.
32. *Ibid*, p. 14.
33. Norman Painting, *Forever Ambridge: Twenty-five Years of The Archers*. London 1975, p. 244.
34. Quoted in Ray Gosling, 'Friends and neighbours', *The Listener*, **99** (2542) (12 Jan. 1978), p. 48.
35. Vicky Payne, 'Ladies of Ambridge', *Radio Times*, **224** (2914) (15-21 Sept. 1979), p. 17.
36. B.P. Emmett, 'The television and radio audience in Britain', in Denis McQuail (ed.), *Sociology of Mass Communications*. Harmondsworth 1972, pp. 195-219.
37. 'Outline of a sociological theory of art perception', *International Social Science Journal*, **20** (4) (1968), p. 594.
38. BBC, *Annual Review of BBC Audience Research Findings, Number 3, 1975/76*. London 1977, p. 31.
39. Pierre Bourdieu and Jean-Claude Passeron, *Reproduction in Education, Society and Culture*. London and Beverly Hills 1977, p. 40.
40. Basil Bernstein, *Class, Codes and Control*. Vol. 1: *Theoretical Studies towards a Sociology of Language*. London 1971.
41. 'Outline of a sociological theory of art perception', op. cit., p. 593.
42. Payne, op. cit., p. 14.
43. BBC, *Annual Review of BBC Audience Research Findings, Number 2, 1974/75*. London 1976, p. 34.
44. Susan Sontag, *Against Interpretation and Other Essays*. New York 1967.
45. Frank Gillard, *Sound Radio in the Television Age*, BBC Lunch-time Lectures, Second Series, 6. London 1964, p. 7.
46. Ian Trethowan, *Radio in the Seventies*, BBC Lunch-time Lectures, Eighth Series, 4. London 1970, p. 5.
47. Esslin, *The National Theatre of the Air*, p. 11.
48. *Ibid*.
49. *Annual Review of BBC Audience Research Findings, Number 3, 1975/76*, pp. 17-18; Emmett, op. cit.
50. Quoted in Anne Karpf, 'A theatre in transmission', *Time Out*, 495 (12-18 Oct. 1979), p. 11.

Chapter 10

Radio drama and English literature

Peter Lewis

In Germany, it is not at all uncommon for the radio play (*Hörspiel*) to be taught as a form of dramatic literature at both secondary and tertiary educational levels. The *Hörspiel* did, in fact, attain academic respectability some time ago, and radio drama is consequently accepted as an entirely legitimate area of serious literary and dramatic study in Germany. In Britain, on the other hand, and indeed in the English-speaking world as a whole, how many radio plays have ever appeared on literature courses and reading lists in schools, colleges, polytechnics and universities? How many have been put on the syllabuses for O-level, A-level and degree examinations in English Literature? Can you count them on the fingers of one hand? Two hands? Three hands? The fact that the best-known and most popular of all radio plays has appeared at every level, including the postgraduate, all over the world serves to draw attention to its uniqueness. *Under Milk Wood* is very much the exception that proves the rule. Many courses on modern poetry include some reference to Louis MacNeice, but in how many cases is it even pointed out that he spent his professional life as a BBC staff member, writing and producing for the Features Department, let alone that quite a lot of his literary, indeed *poetic*, output was intended for radio? Muriel Spark is a likely contender for any course on contemporary fiction, but are her radio plays ever mentioned? Is it even known that she has written radio plays? Everyone with literary interests knows that Richard Hughes wrote *A High Wind in Jamaica*, but how many people know that a few years earlier he wrote the first original radio play, *Danger* (1924), something that ought to be of considerable interest to literary historians?

Under Milk Wood is not, of course, the only work for radio to receive academic attention or to turn up on English Literature syllabuses, but plays that receive this accolade almost invariably do so because their authors are famous for other forms of writing which are the primary source of critical interest. This is obviously the case with Samuel Beckett, for example, or Harold Pinter, or Tom Stoppard. Beckett's *All That Fall, Embers, Words and Music* and *Cascando* are among the chosen few radio plays to stimulate English critics into activity and to be brought to the attention of literature students, but the centre of attention is inevitably elsewhere: *Waiting for Godot* perhaps, or the *Molloy, Malone Dies, The Unnamable* trilogy. Beckett's radio plays are of interest because they are by Beckett, not because they are for radio. No one, it is safe to assume, has constructed a course on Beckett around his radio plays, whereas many courses on Beckett, even those on him as a dramatist, have omitted any reference to his radio work.

What this indicates is that the guardians of English Literature have, for the most part, turned both a deaf ear and a blind eye to radio drama. It is manifestly not the case that radio drama has been brought to the Court of Criticism, placed in the dock as a defendant, subjected to intensive cross-examination and scrutiny, found wanting, and sentenced to everlasting perdition in the penal colony of subliterature. There has been no investigation. No trial has taken place. The prisoner has, it seems, been overlooked, left in the vaults of Broadcasting House to pine away and die of neglect. If, in connection with radio drama, we served a writ of habeas corpus on the literary establishment, it would probably deny any knowledge of the alleged detainee. Ignorance of the law is said to be no excuse, but it is equally clear that no excuses are offered by literature specialists for ignorance of radio drama.

Of course, the arrival of television on a large scale at the beginning of the second Elizabethan age, ironically coinciding with the completion and first production of *Under Milk Wood*, the biggest single boost radio drama has ever received in Britain (Orson Welles's adaptation of H.G. Wells's *The War of the Worlds*, and the widespread panic it caused in America, is another story), encouraged people to think of radio as old-fashioned and unable to compete with the new medium – perhaps on a vague analogy between broadcasting and film, since the arrival of the 'talkies' rapidly killed off the silent cinema. With television seeming to sound the death-knell of radio drama, the latter could, to some extent, be written off as a has-been, despite *Under Milk Wood*. Indeed, Dylan Thomas's 'play for voices' could be seen as the end of a cultural phase, a culminating and concluding efflorescence, a kind of grand finale to the era of radio, rather than as a new beginning, especially as he himself died at this symbolic moment. At the very time when, in the wake of *Under Milk Wood*, radio drama might have been expected to attract literary scholars, several factors, notably television and the anti-1940s (including the anti-Thomas) attitude of the young literary turks of the Movement, the 1950s novel and the new wave of drama (although they were far, far too English to be called even metaphorical 'turks'), militated against this. Introducing a posthumous edition of some of MacNeice's radio scripts, W.H. Auden argued that because of the impact of television 'radio drama is probably a dying art',[1] a common enough opinion of the 1960s whatever the realities of the situation. From this point of view, radio drama was a fairly short-lived phenomenon, born in the 1920s, coming of age in the 1940s, and destined for an early, though perhaps lingering, death. It was being overtaken and supplanted by technological development in the form of television drama and was about to become something that might be nostalgically recollected in the tranquillity between television programmes. Even the critic with an interest in the media, when apparently faced with a corpse or a terminal patient, felt no obligation to perform an autopsy, euthanasia or a hopeless act of resuscitation. He could pass by on the other side, his eyes glued to the small screen, his intelligence seduced by the glamour of the new medium.

Yet during the quarter-century of the television era, radio drama has shown no signs of dying. Far from it. Those gloomy prognostications of the death of radio from a thousand television cuts have turned out to be much too pessimistic, and the idea of 'the fall of the house of radio' is assumed a little too readily. For example, D.G. Bridson's admirable 'personal recollection' of broadcasting, *Prospero and Ariel* (1971), is subtitled *The Rise and Fall of Radio*, and in the Introduction to his 'personal celebration of fifty years of the BBC', *The Biggest Aspidistra in the World* (1972), Peter Black describes the third part of his book as being about 'the rise and fall of radio as a mass entertainment'.[2] Shortly before his premature death in 1963, Mac-Neice wrote in his Introduction to an edition of two of his last radio plays:

These two plays were both written for what some think an obsolescent medium. Obsolescent or not, sound radio, in Britain at least, is not the *mass* medium it used to be, television having stolen most of its public though it cannot take over most of its territory. Sound radio can do things no other medium can and, if 'sound' dies, those things will not be done.[3]

Writing at a time when radio was often condescendingly and even sneeringly called 'steam radio', MacNeice had grounds for his fears and apprehensiveness, but he need not have worried overmuch. We may not have reached the stage of 'steam television', despite all the hot air the medium has generated during its existence, but the so-called 'threat of television' has proved to be more illusory than it once seemed when it had the advantage of novelty and was not the utterly mundane medium of mass communication and entertainment it is now. Photography, we should remember, was once thought to be a threat to painting and, indeed, to spell the beginning of the end of fine art, but it proved to be not a competitor but a liberator of painting, encouraging it to move in new directions. Radio drama has shown an admirable ability to adapt to circumstance, and although it has changed somewhat it shows no signs of obsolescence. Indeed, in the 1950s television was one of the factors encouraging radio drama to move in new directions, since it made both writers and producers rethink the relationship between drama and the medium in which they were operating. Radio drama may pass unnoticed in the literary and dramatic journals, and almost unnoticed in the review pages of the 'quality' newspapers and weeklies, but it has been thriving in spite of the critical neglect it suffers from, and the large output of the BBC Radio Drama Department (now about one thousand broadcasts a year) is surely a sign of health and vitality rather than obsolescence. Inevitably, much of this output is not of the kind or the artistic quality to have much interest for the student of dramatic literature, having more to offer the historian and sociologist of mass communication and popular culture, but every year a body of original radio drama appears that is just as worthy of serious attention as many of the novels, stage plays and television plays that receive it, and most of this is very lucky to receive as much as a passing mention somewhere in the dailies or weeklies.

Full many a gem of purest ray serene,
The dark unfathom'd caves of ocean bear:
Full many a flower is born to blush unseen,
And waste its sweetness on the desert air.
(Gray's *Elegy*, 53-6)

The flowers of radio drama are not, of course, unheard, and do not waste their sweetness (not, perhaps, *le mot juste* when you think of writers like Giles Cooper and Rhys Adrian) on the air, because there still is a huge audience for radio plays, but not, it would seem, in the literature departments of our educational institutions, where 'the desert air' prevails.

Why should this be? Why is the artistic status of radio drama so low in Britain that after nearly sixty years of life, almost as long as the BBC itself, it is almost totally ignored in the groves and concrete campuses of academe? Interestingly enough, it is from Germany, where the *Hörspiel* (including the contemporary experimental and radiophonic *das neue Hörspiel* [new radio play]) enjoys a much higher status, that scholars and critics have been coming to pioneer the systematic study of British radio drama from a literary viewpoint as something of considerable artistic value and meriting the attention that English criticism reserves for stage plays and orthodox literary forms such as the novel. Of the few books and pamphlets published in England that deal, either wholly or in part, with radio drama, most have been by BBC personnel and are written from the perspective of a producer, author-producer or producer-administrator, not a critic. There are the various guides aimed at writers interested in the medium, the most recent being Elwyn Evans's excellent *Radio: A Guide to Broadcasting Techniques* (1977); the memoirs of people in the thick of the BBC, such as D.G. Bridson's fascinating and illuminating *Prospero and Ariel*; the histories written from the inside, notably Val Gielgud's invaluable *British Radio Drama 1922-1956* (1957); and a couple of attempts to define the nature of radio as a dramatic medium, the major one being Donald McWhinnie's *The Art of Radio* (1959). Books about certain authors who have written for radio, such as Dylan Thomas, Beckett and Pinter, sometimes include discussion of their radio writing, and the same is true of books surveying modern dramatists, but in neither case is the interest in radio *per se* hardly ever more than incidental. To find scholarly studies that take radio as their starting point, one has to turn to German publications, such as Armin Frank's monumental *Das Hörspiel* (1963), Horst Priessnitz's *Das englische 'radio play' seit 1945: Typen, Themen und Formen* (1977) and the large collection of essays he edited, *Das englische Hörspiel: Interpretationen* (1977), covering work by Richard Hughes, Louis MacNeice, Dylan Thomas, Giles Cooper, Samuel Beckett, John Mortimer, Harold Pinter, Muriel Spark, Ted Hughes, Alan Sharp, Barry Bermange, Caryl Churchill, Ian Rodger, Rhys Adrian, Joe Orton, Alan Plater, Tom Stoppard, Don Haworth and John Arden.

If German scholarship and criticism can find so much to admire in the English radio play, why can't its British equivalent? One can't help thinking of the old joke about German *littérateurs* claiming Shakespeare as their own because he is too important to be left to the English. In the light of the German interest in and enthusiasm for our radio drama, it is tempting to put the whole blame for its widespread critical neglect in England on the conservatism, narrow-mindedness and snobbishness of the academy, but this may not be altogether fair. There are a number of obstacles, including an archaic law of copyright almost designed to make research difficult, in the path of the British student of radio drama – more than in the case of the German student of the *Hörspiel* – that act as deterrents, and these can be summed up in the word 'accessibility'. Although a repeat of a BBC radio play or adaptation or serial is not uncommon today (the *Saturday Night Theatre* play is repeated as Monday's *Afternoon Theatre*, for example, and if you miss *The Archers* in the evening you can hear it the following afternoon, and if you miss that there is always the omnibus version on Sunday mornings), most radio plays and features during the history of the BBC have been broadcast only once. This is why radio drama has acquired the reputation of being ephemeral. Whereas one usually has plenty of opportunities to see a new film or stage play, a radio play unheard or a television play unseen will most likely remain unheard or unseen. Multiple broadcasts, except in the case of *Under Milk Wood*, are very rare, and new productions of plays already produced, except in the case of Shakespeare, some other stage classics, and *Under Milk Wood* (now with four radio productions behind it), are almost unknown. Furthermore there is, with a couple of exceptions, no alternative source of radio plays in a fully realised version.

Good stage plays are likely to turn up at a theatre not too far away in productions by a touring company, a local repertory group, or an amateur dramatic society. Good films can be hired on 16mm at reasonable cost for teaching purposes, and are also shown regularly at film societies, specialist cinemas, and branches of the National Film Theatre throughout the country. But good radio plays do not enjoy any comparable outlets. You can't expect to tune in to the neighbourhood amateur radio dramatic society giving MacNeice's *The Dark Tower* a run through on your local radio station. You can't buy or hire radio plays on either gramophone records or cassettes, unless you want *Under Milk Wood* or *Embers*. The release of Douglas Cleverdon's 1954 production of *Under Milk Wood* on Argo discs in the same year certainly made history, but it was a precedent without successors. The Audio-Visual Centre of London University has recently been pursuing a policy of making its own productions of outstanding radio and television plays in order to hire them out for educational purposes, but this is on a very modest scale and is in its infancy. It is ironic that many stage plays, intended for the eye as well as the ear, are now available to the public on record or cassette, while radio plays, intended for the ear alone, are not. The only solution to this problem for the student of radio is to record programmes off-air, either licitly or illicitly, and build up his own library, but unless the student has been doing this for a long time it is of very limited value, since it does not solve the problem of access to past material, including the acknowledged radio classics. The contrast with film is striking, and it is hardly surprising that film studies have prospered while radio studies have not.

On top of this problem of the unavailability of most radio drama in a form that can be listened to, there is the added complication of its unavailability in a form that can be read. During the history of the BBC, thousands upon thousands upon thousands of scripts of a dramatic nature have been broadcast, many of them original radio plays, but only a minute fraction of this enormous output has ever been published in book form. Much of it, no doubt, does not deserve to be perpetuated in print, but on the other hand some of it is of very high quality indeed and merits publication much more than, for example, the many mediocre and even downright poor stage plays that have had no difficulty in finding publishers after being on the boards. Except in the case of writers who have established reputations for themselves in other genres, commercial publishers have shown very little interest indeed in radio drama, and until fairly recently the BBC did not take it upon itself to counteract this almost total indifference. *Under Milk Wood* was in print within weeks of its first broadcast, Beckett's radio plays appeared fairly soon after their productions, MacNeice published a number of his radio works during his lifetime, and Stoppard's radio plays became available soon after he was adopted by critics and academics alike as the great white hope for the English theatre in the 1970s. But what about writers who have committed themselves wholeheartedly to writing for radio and television, or those who have written well for radio but have not excelled as poets, novelists or stage playwrights? Most likely, their scripts remain in typescript in the Play Library of the Radio Drama Department in Broadcasting House, which is not, it should be added, a public reading room, although *bona fide* researchers are generously allowed access. Fortunately, BBC Publications have been coming rather belatedly to the rescue, otherwise some of the finest and most memorable radio plays since *Under Milk Wood*, from the best work of Giles Cooper in the late 1950s and Henry Reed's contemporary Richard Shewin–Hilda Tablet saga to one of the finest works of the 1970s, David Rudkin's *Cries from Casement As His Bones Are Brought to Dublin*, would probably still be sitting patiently, or impatiently, on the shelves of the Play Library, surrounded by equally patient, or impatient, scripts yearning for the light of day *outside* Broadcasting House.

With the BBC's current policy of publishing more new plays, the position is improving, but it could not have been much worse. It has been calculated that only 1 per cent of broadcast British radio plays ever appear in print, whereas in Germany the figure for the *Hörspiel* is over 12 per cent; still low, of course, but so very much higher than the British figure. Considering the high regard accorded to the printed word, as opposed to the spoken word, in our culture, any literary critic approaching radio drama without much knowledge of it could not be blamed if, on the basis of these figures, he drew the conclusion that the standard of radio drama was very low, too low to justify the honour of print except in very isolated cases. Yet scholars who have investigated international radio drama are impressed not only by the staggering quantity produced by the BBC but by its quality, the sheer excellence of its best work. It is commonly assumed that *Under Milk Wood* is at least head and shoulders, and perhaps a good anatomical bit more, above other radio plays, but for anyone who has explored the canon this is manifestly not the case. The truth is that *Under Milk Wood* is by far the most fortunate of a sizeable number of brilliant and original works. And the most regrettable consequence of the neglect of radio drama is that these other brilliant and original works are so little known and so systematically undervalued. Ask someone to name a play by David Rudkin, and the answer will almost inevitably be a stage play, probably *Afore Night Come*. Yet his radio play, *Cries from Casement*, has a strong claim to be considered his finest achievement. Giles Cooper is one of the very best British dramatists since the Second World War, yet he remains much less familiar than many of his contemporaries and successors, such as Beckett, Osborne, Wesker, Pinter and Bond, and the reason is surely that he concentrated less on the stage than on radio and wrote his best work for the medium. In talking about his interest in writing for television, Cooper once said that 'it took me a long time to live down the slur of being a radio writer'.[4] Rhys Adrian is even less well known, although a dramatist with few equals or superiors during the last twenty years; it is not surprising, therefore, to find that he, even more than Cooper, has devoted himself almost exclusively to radio. One thing the committed radio writer can obviously reconcile himself to is lack of public recognition and critical acclaim, as well as fat cheques: radio does not pay as well as television, the cinema or the stage (as long as there is a moderate run), which explains why a number of gifted writers, having served their apprenticeship on radio, change their allegiance. The television playwright is much more likely to achieve fame, not to mention fortune.

The more we consider the whole problem of accessibility, especially the dismal publishing record of radio drama, the more we are forced to consider the reasons for this appalling state of affairs. It is easy for the academic world and the literary establishment to excuse its massive indifference to radio drama and therefore free itself from any blame or responsibility by pointing to the lack of published texts, but the argument is, of course, circular. One could, I suppose, claim that God, having a grudge against radio plays not by Welsh poets, ordained it so, or that the structure of the universe is inimical to radio drama, but for most of us the answer lies much closer to home. The availability or unavailability of radio drama in recorded or printed form is not something determined by mysterious forces beyond human control. One of the most common descriptions of radio drama is 'ephemeral', but this so-called ephemerality is not a necessary, inherent and inevitable feature of radio drama, as it is often assumed to be, but a direct consequence of its inaccessibility. If you could borrow records, cassettes and texts of radio plays from your public liberary, as you can of poetry and stage plays, radio drama would immediately cease to be 'ephemeral' – or, since most art is ephemeral (*ars brevis, vita longa*), it would be no more ephemeral than any other medium or genre. It really is very hard to believe that radio drama would have remained as inaccessible and 'ephemeral' as it is had there been genuine critical interest in it. If there had been a demand, the demand would have been met, just as in the eighteenth century, when the reading of plays became very popular, publishers quickly supplied the reading public with what they wanted, including unperformed plays. So the defence that the lack of interest stems from the absence of published material rings hollow since the absence of published material is in fact a result of the lack of interest. The case is not like the proverbial chicken and egg, because there can be only one answer to the question, 'which came first?': radio drama. The response has been silence. And the silence explains the rest: the inaccessibility, the unavailability, the ephemerality, the nonpublication. The BBC probably could have done more to promote the publication of radio drama, either through commercial publishers or its own resources, but it would be most unfair to criticise the BBC for not acting as a publisher's agent or a publisher when it has fulfilled its task of producing radio plays so well.

But this still leaves the question of why radio drama has suffered so much neglect not fully answered. Why, indeed? In the first place, there is the newness of the medium. It is a truth universally acknowledged that any really new artistic development, such as the emergence of a new genre, takes time, often a long time, to be accepted as being the equal of older and more familiar forms. It may no longer be the case that scholars, when faced with new forms, reach for their *Poetics* to find out whether Aristotle vouchsafed for it (God help it if he didn't), but even so the acquisition of artistic respectability is one of the things that is not instant in our supersonic, conspicuously consuming society. In a marvellously witty and entertaining paper delivered to the Radio Literature Conference in 1977 called 'Sound drama before Marconi', which was subsequently broadcast on Radio 3, W.M.S. Russell drew attention to Seneca as a precursor of modern writers of plays for voices, but for all his ingenuity not even Russell could claim Seneca as a classical precedent for *radio* drama. So like the novel, radio drama is having to prove itself and, despite the pleas of Fielding, Jane Austen, and other major novelists, it took the novel between one hundred and fifty and two hundred years to be accorded a literary status comparable to that of poetry and poetic drama rather than be regarded as an inherently lower form of popular entertainment.

If the newness of radio is against it from a literary viewpoint, so is its mass appeal. Writing before the advent of television, MacNeice had this to say (n.b. the final parenthetical sting in the tail, drawing a parallel with the Elizabethan theatre and its great 'literature'):

What the radio writer must do, if he hopes to win the freedom of the air, is to appeal *on one plane* – whatever he may be doing on the others – to the more primitive listener and to the more primitive elements in anyone; i.e. he must give them (what Shakespeare gave them) entertainment.[5]

In the twentieth century, most new artistic developments, from Cubism to sound poetry to electronic music, have been associated with *avant-garde* experiment and have been met with the outraged cry of philistinism – or good sense: 'You don't call this art, do you?' Radio drama as a new development is manifestly not in this category and is really at the opposite end of the scale since it has to defend itself from the charge of pandering to the lowest common denominator as a popular, mass medium. And literary criticism, with its élitist assumptions and its preoccupation with excellence, has always been very wary, to put it mildly, of popular forms and the mass media. Why else did MacNeice feel it necessary to insist in his important Introduction ('Some comments on radio drama') to *Christopher Columbus* that the radio play is 'a popular art-form which still is an art-form'?[6]

The comparison between film and radio is illuminating in this respect. Film began as an entirely visual and nonverbal medium, and even after the coming of sound it has remained a predominantly visual medium with its own nonliterary iconography and semiology. Consequently literary criticism has not been able to claim film as its own, and this has been fortunate for film as an artistic medium since it has remained free from many literary preconceptions; film has been able to develop its own criticism rooted in a conception of a distinctive film language and grammar. It is because of this independence from traditional critical categories and assumptions that film has gradually been able to win artistic and academic respectability, despite being a mass medium of entertainment. Radio, on the other hand, has not surprisingly always been regarded as a writer's medium, even more than the stage and certainly more than television, because the word – the spoken word – has more or less reigned supreme, unimpeded by visual distractions and with only the BBC seagull, the music-and-effects assistant, and the sound wizards of the Radiophonic Workshop as company. In the circumstances, radio writing has inevitably found itself under the umbrella of Literature, and although this might originally have seemed a distinct advantage over film, in practice it has been the opposite. Radio has not been able to develop its own critical system in the way that film has, and literary criticism, instead of succouring the new offspring, has largely ignored or even disowned this upstart of the mass media.

All public-service broadcasting must obviously cater for majority tastes and cannot be expected to provide a nonstop diet of high culture for the intelligentsia, but especially through the Third Programme and subsequently Radio 3 the BBC has done as much as any broadcasting system to cater for minority tastes and an intellectual élite. Even so, radio drama has often been branded as 'middlebrow', which with the possible exception of 'bourgeois' is the ultimate insult in the critical vocabulary. In the nature of things, much radio drama must be middlebrow and only a small part of the output can be highbrow, and an even smaller part experimental or *avant-garde*. Radio drama is, after all, a distinctly nebulous term, covering everything from *The Archers* to Andrew Sachs's nonverbal experiment in pure sound, *The Revenge* – lowbrow, middlebrow, and highbrow: serials of various kinds, what used to be known as features, adaptations of stage plays, fiction and even television plays, as well as original scripts written for the medium. The result is that works that would be of interest to serious criticism are lost sight of, smothered in the cloud of uninterestedness that literary criticism snobbishly exudes towards radio drama, except when established writers of other forms are involved. MacNeice pinpointed this intellectual snobbishness very accurately when he argued that in writing for 'the Man-in-the-Street' or 'the Ordinary Listener' ('The writer . . . must make his work, if not intelligible, at least interesting to the millions') the radio dramatist is not abandoning artistic standards and committing himself to what MacNeice calls 'vulgarity', because 'I refuse to believe that men and women in the street are as insensitive or as emotionally atrophied as is sometimes assumed by the intelligentsia'.[7]

Another and related reason for the low critical status of radio drama is that it is commonly regarded not as an alternative to orthodox drama, and therefore a distinct form in its own right, but as an inferior substitute, very much a second best. From the birth of the BBC there has always been a strong connection between the theatre and radio drama: the first broadcast of dramatic material consisted of scenes from Shakespeare. In the early days there were broadcasts of plays direct from theatres, which were obviously not satisfactory, while today it is remarkable how prominent the word 'theatre' is in *Radio Times*: almost all of the regular series put out by the Drama Department on Radio 4 have a title incorporating 'theatre'. Long before the National Theatre was built, radio was called things like 'the National Theatre of the Air' and 'our only National Theatre'. Radio was certainly much more deserving of the title than the edifice on the South Bank, since in its heyday radio drama could regularly attract audiences measured in many millions, and for its more popular offerings can still hold the attention of hundreds of thousands, sometimes even a few million, whereas only a small percentage of the population has ever set foot in the physical National Theatre. In 1971 Martin Esslin calculated that a play performed in a full, thousand-seat theatre would take five years to gain the same size of audience as a radio play broadcast on Saturday evening and repeated on Monday afternoon.[8] Yet all the kudos belongs to the live theatre, not least because we have been effectively brainwashed by a superb public-relations exercise into believing that the period since *Waiting for Godot* and *Look Back in Anger*, the second Elizabethan age, is the greatest period of both English theatre and English drama since the first Elizabethan age. Be that as it may – history, with its air of scepticism, is already beginning to put the myth into perspective – it is obvious that all stage plays produced in London and many produced in the provinces receive plenty of coverage in the national dailies, Sundays, weeklies, and monthlies, however appalling both play and production and however small the total audience it reaches, whereas good radio drama, reaching vastly more people even with the competition from television, goes unnoticed. This may seem grossly unfair to radio, but on the other hand a radio drama that insists on being 'theatre' cannot complain too much if it is thought second-best, because it often is.

A stage play or a play written with the stage in mind – many broadcast plays were intended for the stage but failed to make it, and others are written for radio but in orthodox theatrical terms – achieves its fullest realisation in the theatre, and except in the rarest of cases radio cannot hope to compete. The same is true of adaptations of classic novels, many of which make excellent listening but all of which inevitably lose a great deal in the transformation. This is not to depreciate the efforts of the Drama Department: Shakespeare heard on radio is much better than Shakespeare not heard at all: but few people would disagree with the opinion that Shakespeare on radio is not as rich an experience as Shakespeare on the stage, where he belongs. Similarly, a radio adaptation of, say, *Bleak House* or *The Ambassadors* may illuminate the book in unexpected ways as well as being a pleasure in its own right, but it can never hope to be Dickens or James in all his prose glory. What is unfortunate and grossly unfair is that this sense of radio drama being second-hand and second-best rubs off on the entire output, including the relatively small but still substantial amount of radio drama that is imaginatively conceived for the medium, that is not easily transferable (perhaps not at all) to another medium, and that has its proper existence in sound terms just as *Hamlet* and *Rosencrantz and Guildenstern Are Dead* have theirs on the stage. This more purely radio work has never achieved enormous popular success, except in the documentary or quasi-documentary form of the feature and, of course, *Under Milk Wood*. Ever since Lance Sieveking produced his radiophonic experiment *Kaleidoscope I* in 1928 and Tyrone Guthrie wrote his three innovatory 'microphone plays' in the late 1920s,[9] it has been evident that what the listening public really wanted from radio drama were stage plays, plays like stage plays, and dramatisations of novels and short stories, rather than the more imaginative dramatic explorations of the medium that the BBC has always encouraged and provided, as Val Gielgud observes:

I don't think it took intelligent producers interested in a new medium long to realise that while many stage plays – notably the classics – made excellent broadcasting, the normal modern stage conventions tended to handicap, as opposed to exploit, the particular qualities of the studio and the microphone . . . Certainly by 1930 the original radio play – I need only cite the names of Lance Sieveking and Tyrone Guthrie in this connection – was already a flourishing, if minority, interest.[10]

It is important to note, however, that until the late 1950s much of the more imaginative work came from the Features Department, not the Drama Department, which until that time, not long before the demise of Features, saw its principal function as broadcasting conventional drama. The complicated and messy history of radio drama in the BBC, compared with that of the *Hörspiel* in Germany, has not exactly helped its cause since it has led to critical uncertainty and confusion.

Yet can anything justify the extremely condescending attitude towards radio drama so frequently encountered that it almost becomes unexceptional? Searching through the arts columns of the nearest newspaper to hand for evidence, I find the following among the theatre reviews: 'Arthur Kopit's *Wings* started out as a radio play, which means that it is somewhat slight but also rather trim.'[11] Here there is a hardly qualified equation of the radio play with slightness. But are radio plays necessarily slighter than stage plays? After all, there is no shortage of slight stage plays. Most radio plays are, of course, shorter than stage plays for several reasons. It is obviously harder to hold a listener's attention in his own home for a long time than the attention of an audience in a theatre, especially as the listener does not have to pay through the nose for the privilege; but technically the radio play is extremely economical of time because it can compress things so easily and take all sorts of short cuts not possible on stage. But shortness is not slightness. A Hopkins sonnet is not slight, but highly concentrated and intense. So the general accusation of slightness inherent in the critic's words is deprecatory. And even the contrasting 'trim', though a word of approval, is less than wholehearted and again rather condescending as a term of even mild praise. The suggestion is that radio plays are neat and tidy rather than deep or exciting.

If this serendipitously discovered sentence from *The Observer* did not seem to epitomise a critical attitude, it would be rather cruel to subject it to the rack of verbal analysis. Similar condescension unfortunately abounds in writing about radio drama. No other work for radio has received a fraction of the commendation bestowed on *Under Milk Wood*, but even among the tributes there are signs of a grudging, patronising attitude towards the medium as a whole. Thomas's friend and co-writer of *The Death of the King's Canary*, John Davenport, wrote this: 'As a radio play it is marvellously successful; it is gay, it is tender; it sparkles. But it remains a radio play, no more.'[12] In other words, *Under Milk Wood* is an excellent example of its kind, but the kind itself is an inherently inferior art form. Two hundred years ago, or even one hundred, it was the novel that was the victim of exactly the same condescension; 'as a novel it is marvellously successful . . . but it remains a novel, no more'. Davenport's comment brings to mind neoclassical critical theory with its rigid hierarchy of genres, but in his modern version it is radio drama, not pastoral or satire, that occupies the humblest place at the bottom of the list.

Davenport was a poet and a lover of the arts, not a distinguished scholar and critic, so it would be unfair to make so much of his comment if it wasn't echoed by distinguished scholars and critics. Walford Davies, one of the leading experts on Thomas, says of *Under Milk Wood* in a book on the poet that 'it is, quite simply, the best radio play ever written',[13] but from his other remarks it is easy to deduce that this is very far from being unstinted praise. Davies stresses 'its essentially low-key ambitions' and 'its literary modesty',[14] describes it as 'unashamedly a trivialising work in that it reduces a view of life to immediately entertaining details',[15] and argues that 'the radio medium enabled Thomas to soft-pedal the difficulties he might have found in providing a stiffer, more challenging dramatic structure and to live . . . in a world of words'.[16] So even 'the best radio play ever written' is a lowly creature, outstanding only among even more lowly creatures, all the other plays for radio. Davies, like Davenport, would put the radio play near or at the bottom of a literary hierarchy.

Neither Davies nor Davenport are actually contemptuous of radio as an artistic medium, although they do not take its aspirations very seriously, but G.L. Roberts, in his remarks about *Under Milk Wood*, comes clean at once, and is forthright in his contempt where most literary critics engaging with radio tend to be more guarded and hypocritical:

> There is no intention here to consider *Under Milk Wood* as a work for radio, which is, in any case, a transitory art-form; anything which is good on the radio alone cannot be of much value.[17]

With its almost routine dismissal of radio drama as ephemeral, this is plainly an example of what oft is thought but ne'er so honestly and aggressively expressed. The place for radio drama is not the bottom of the literary hierarchy, but the scrapheap.

Some of the unfavourable, even downright hostile, comment that radio drama elicits has its origins in a conservative, even reactionary, critical orthodoxy deeply suspicious of and resistant to the 'media'. But is there something about radio drama, especially about original writing for the medium, that causes particular problems for the literary critic schooled in handling traditional forms? The terms 'radio drama' and 'radio play' are inescapable and convenient, but it is perhaps a pity that some other term has not established itself to describe original creative writing for the medium, without the connotations surrounding words like 'drama', 'play' and 'fiction'. Val Gielgud discusses the unsatisfactory nature of this borrowed terminology in his account of the problems that writers experienced in the early days of broadcasting when trying to think in terms of the microphone, not the stage:

> I believe that it is the use of the word 'play' which is the cause of so much misunderstanding, if not of definite error. To begin with, we are all accustomed, in everyday phraseology, to going 'to see' plays, as opposed to going 'to hear' them. In consequence the mere juxtaposition of the words 'radio' and 'play' must imply for many people a contradiction in terms. To go on with, the word 'play' implies a number of conventions – of length, of construction, of unities, and so forth – which, if accepted by the radio dramatist, serve only to hamper his freedom and cramp his style.[18]

Much of the really outstanding creative writing for radio, including *Under Milk Wood* and some of MacNeice's, Beckett's, Cooper's and Adrian's work, do indeed sit very uneasily under the label 'play' ('feature' is much more unsatisfactory because it suggests documentary, even though the Features Department was responsible for fictional as well as nonfictional programmes, including such classics of radio drama as *The Dark Tower* and *Under Milk Wood* itself). Their radio plays may involve characters in action, contain dialogue, and require actors, but they don't conform to our expectations of plays – expectations acquired from the theatre and from the long tradition of Western drama – even at a time when there are few norms governing stage plays and when the meaning of 'play' has been stretched by such stage works as Beckett's *Play* and *Not I*. Although Dylan Thomas wrote a number of film scripts, it is difficult to believe that he could have written a *play* to save his life, yet his *play for voices* (his own description), written for a medium he knew intimately and employing the structure of a feature complete with extended narration, is a triumph. There is plenty of evidence to support Alrene Sykes's claim that 'many of the best radio plays are in structure much closer to narrative form, to the tale told and the ballad sung round the camp fire, than to what has been regarded as conventional stage form'.[19] In a paper delivered at the annual national conference of the English Speaking Union in 1977, Emyr Edwards also stressed the way in which good radio writers disregard 'the rules of the conventional theatre play', and suggested that music provides a more appropriate analogue:

Acts are not characteristic of the genre; short scenes, following each other in good numbers, are. One might even tend to call them not short scenes, but movements in dialogue, patterns of dialogue, akin to the structure of musical compositions, where themes, tunes, melodies, occur, recur, and flow in a pattern of words, sounds and silences.[20]

It is therefore regrettable that 'theatre' and 'play' should have become so prominent, both in BBC nomenclature and in some of the little reviewing and criticism radio drama receives. In speaking of 'radio drama' and 'radio plays' the emphasis needs to be put very emphatically on *radio*. An overemphasis on 'drama' is one of the reasons for the elimination of that frequently abused but exceedingly useful and perfectly natural radio device, narration. The demise of the standard old-style BBC Narrator need not be lamented even by nostalgics, but other forms of narration, of direct, intimate speaker-to-listener contact, are possible and indeed abound in nondramatic broadcasting, and there is no reason to condemn and dispose of the baby because the bathwater is stagnant. What makes this development particularly ironic is that narration has been making inroads on the stage, partly under the influence of radio. Narration can, in fact, be incorporated in radio plays so unobrusively that it hardly seems like narration at all, as in the case of Giles Cooper's *The Disagreeable Oyster* and of several plays by one of the best living radio dramatists, Don Haworth. But direct narration, when used properly as an integral device (as in *Under Milk Wood* or, a very different example, *The Hitch-Hiker's Guide to the Galaxy*) and not improperly as an easy way around problems of exposition and continuity, needs no apologies.

Not surprisingly, those who have understood the distinctive qualities of radio most fully and have attempted a critical analysis of it as a medium for creative writing have been longtime and very distinguished practitioners in the medium, Louis MacNeice, Val Gielgud, Donald McWhinnie and Martin Esslin. Twenty years after its publication, McWhinnie's *The Art of Radio* is still the standard work on this subject, although Esslin's more recent scattered essays have updated the discussion by referring to developments in the 1960s and

1970s.[21] Yet some years before McWhinnie, MacNeice isolated most of the vital questions about the nature of radio drama in the critically pioneering prefaces he wrote for the published editions of his own radio scripts, *Christopher Columbus* (1944) and *The Dark Tower and Other Radio Scripts* (1947). In the first of these, he argued that since 'sound-broadcasting gets its effects through sound and sound alone' there is an inevitable 'subordination in radio of words to words-as-they-are-spoken' with the result that a good script for a radio play 'is not necessarily a piece of "good writing"'.[22] In making this distinction between 'good writing for radio' and 'good writing', MacNeice is not saying, as wilfully perverse critics have alleged, that anything is good enough for radio and that mediocre or poor writing will pass muster, but that literary criteria based on the notion of literature as words-on-the-page are not the appropriate ones for radio writing, intended for the listener not the reader. According to MacNeice, 'the first thing he [the radio writer] must do is to forget about "literature" and to concentrate upon sound', but what he has in mind here is what we would now call McLuhan's 'Gutenberg Galaxy' conception of literature as he goes on to explain:

This is not to deny literature, for this is how literature began – the Homeric or Icelandic bard shouting over the clamour of the banquet, the 'tale told in a chimney corner' while tankards clatter and infants squawl and somebody makes up the fire and old men snore and cough.[23]

MacNeice's point is that our current notion of literature, tied so much to print, is in fact more restricted than we realise, and the essential spokenness of radio drama ('the radio writer has to think of *words in the mouths of actors*'[24]) conflicts with this notion, just as the absence of a visual dimension conflicts with our conventional notion of drama. Since creative writing for radio forces us to reconsider and expand our conception of 'literature', a literary criticism devoted to words on the page has not welcomed this unintended challenge to its assumptions, and prefers to pretend that it doesn't exist or is of no importance. Recently, however, the study of communication, especially of the major shift from oracy to literacy in sixteenth- and seventeenth-century Europe, has stressed the limitations of our dominant post-Ramist outlook, with its separation of the written from the spoken language. Of major importance in this development is Walter J. Ong's study of the very influential sixteenth-century French thinker, Peter Ramus: *Ramus, Method, and the Decay of Dialogue* (1958). Whether we realise it or not, 'we are', as Terence Hawkes puts it, 'the children of Ramus'.[25]

Some remarks MacNeice made at the end of his life in yet another Introduction to published radio scripts clarify the uniqueness of radio as a medium and the consequent difficulties it presents to literary criticism. Referring to his own *The Mad Islands* and *The Administrator*, MacNeice writes:

First and most important, they are both essentially 'radio', i.e. with all their jumping about, whether in time or place and between the actual and the fantasy, they could not be anything else.[26]

If 'they could not be anything else', orthodox critical criteria cannot be applied without some rethinking and readjustment. He also made a valid point about the problems of reading radio plays:

Compared with plays written for the stage, works such as these may appear very bitty until you get used to them. I find myself that one of the attractions of radio is that you can move so fast, almost as fast as dreams do: this is why the medium is a good one for dealing with dreams and why, the other way round, a dream technique suits the medium.[27]

Yet it is only on the page, not on the air, that they appear bitty, and they appear bitty because we are not used to reading them – there isn't much opportunity considering the number published – and unconsciously approach them with nonradio, probably theatrical, expectations. MacNeice's contention in the Introduction to *Christopher Columbus* that 'radio plays . . ., when laid on the printed page, tend to lose even more than do plays written for the theatre'[28] may be true in an absolute sense – it certainly seems true 'until you get used to them' – but this could well be a response to a situation in which the reading of radio plays is much more unusual and unfamiliar than the reading of stage plays. If 'good radio plays are not easy to read on the printed page', as Donald McWhinnie argues,[29] it is not only because there is always a gulf between the text of a radio play and its realisation in performance, but also because we are not trained to read radio plays in an appropriately imaginative way.

Radio drama certainly presents literary criticism with unprecedented problems, but perhaps these are an extreme and peculiarly elusive form of the problems that drama as a whole poses. If the relations between drama and literary criticism often seem strained and contentious enough to suggest nothing less than a cold war, the blame assuredly rests with a critical orthodoxy determined to turn drama into literature without the necessary qualification, *dramatic*. To say that drama is drama, not literature, would seem as pointless as saying that water is water, not wine, were it not for the sustained attempt to effect this transformation, perhaps more obvious in the English-speaking world than elsewhere. In his Introduction to the recent Cambridge *Festschrift* for Muriel Bradbrook, Raymond Williams made the point that a prevalent approach to drama was pioneered and carried on by those who

assimilate dramatic texts to the status of all other printed texts, and indeed to printed texts which were intended from the beginning to be silently read. Everything of real importance, they argue, can be read where it is, on the page.[30]

Cambridge, with its early devotion to Practical Criticism, close verbal analysis, at least seven types of ambiguity, and the spirit of *Scrutiny*, certainly bears some of the responsibility for this unfortunate state of affairs, although the syndrome can be traced back through the Romantics to Dr Johnson and beyond.

Two of the most renowned and influential essays by one of the leading Cambridge Scrutineers, L. C. Knights, illustrate the tendency very well. In 'How many children had Lady Macbeth?' (1933), he states confidently and categorically, 'We start with so many lines of verse on a printed page which we read as we should read any other poem.'[31] Yet he is writing about *Macbeth*, a play, and his whole 'improved' approach to Shakespeare is seriously marred by his neglect of this elementary fact and his consequent overliterary approach to a work of drama. Then again in his famous demolition of Restoration comedy, 'Restoration comedy: the reality and the myth' (1937), Knights's argument is very badly flawed because he insists on treating the plays as works of literary prose intended for reading, not as drama consisting of dialogue intended for the stage. After citing a novelist, Henry James, as a standard for social comedy, he goes on to compare passages of Restoration prose with passages from the plays, to the detriment of the latter:

The observation to start from is that the prose in which Restoration comedy is written – select which dramatist you like – is poor and inexpressive in comparison with the staple non-dramatic prose.[32] . . . the prose is artificial and non-representative of the current non-dramatic medium.[33]

Yet 'non-dramatic prose' is an altogether perverse criterion to set up for judging dramatic writing. Would anyone seriously use Lawrence's prose in *The Rainbow* as a standard for judging Shaw's *Heartbreak House*, or Durrell's prose in the *Alexandria Quartet* as a standard for judging Beckett's *Waiting for Godot*? I would hope not, but things being what they are, I wouldn't be surprised. Given a training in the mechanics of practical criticism and the pursuit of polysemy, any critic with a certain amount of ingenuity and inventiveness can 'find' lines in Shakespeare, for example, containing quadruple puns and multiple ambiguities, but this is not a sign of extreme sensitivity to literary language, as it is often thought to be, but of crass insensitivity to the *dramatic* medium Shakespeare was using. And even if there is some truth in the argument that Elizabethans, inhabiting 'a culture dominated by the human voice and ear, an oral-aural world',[34] were more sensitive to language and verbal nuance than we are, despite their lack of exposure to I.A. Richards, William Empson, F.R. Leavis, and the American 'new' critics, it is far-fetched, to say the least, to suggest that during a theatrical performance they were conscious of the complex subtleties that highly-trained modern critics 'discover' after painstaking analysis of the text in the study or the library.

What all this amounts to is obvious enough. The preoccupation of much modern criticism since the 1920s with words, the very medium of literature, often at the expense of genre, theme, plot, narrative, character and a host of other abstractions, has been extremely salutary in the case of poetry and prose written for the page, a necessary corrective to nineteenth-century emphases but one that, by the process of the dialectic, is now itself in need of a corrective. In the hands of some genuinely sensitive critics, it has also, admittedly, been valuable in illuminating plays, but when applied in an unadapted form to a performance art like drama, which can be a form of literature but not in the purely literary sense that the poem or the novel is, the result is Procrustean distortion and mutilation. And if this has been the experience of orthodox stage drama, the unfamiliar form of radio drama, another performance art, can hardly expect to be treated any differently or any better. In the first and most famous of the very few substantial treatments of *Under Milk Wood*, one of the best-known sons of Cambridge English, David Holbrook, based part of his hostile criticism of the radio play, in *Llareggub Revisited* (1962), on a comparison between it and a novel, Joyce's *Ulysses*, a procedure recalling Knights's handling of Restoration comedy.

So far, of course, literary criticism has taken little notice of radio drama, but one final point emerges from this. Radio drama has been with us for over fifty years, since about the time of *Ulysses, The Waste Land, Kangaroo, A Passage to India, Juno and the Paycock, Saint Joan,* and *Mrs Dalloway*, and clearly has serious claims on the attention of scholars and critics, yet it remains largely disregarded. This fact forces us to ask fundamental questions about the bases of our received literary criticism and literary history. Generally speaking, we tend to assume that the literary history we are taught is an immutable truth and we do not challenge it in any radical way. There may be changes of emphasis so that reputations go up and down: Spenser, Milton and Shelley took a bit of a tumble at the hands of Cambridge English and New Criticism from the 1920s onwards, being relegated to Division Two, while Donne and the Metaphysicals United were rapidly promoted from Division Three to the top of Division One, but these revaluations, which are now in turn being revalued so that the League Tables are looking more like they used to, do not amount to a radical rewriting of literary history. When they occur, such changes of taste may appear to be major upheavals of the established order, but in perspective they can be seen to leave the underlying fabric and ideological basis of literary history intact: they are skirmishes and rebellions, not the revolutions they sometimes purport to be. This is obvious when one encounters a genuine attempt to rewrite literary history, such as Raymond Williams's recent *The Country and the City* (1973), which exposes and undermines the unconscious assumptions and ideology – a liberal, bourgeois one – on which the superstructure of received literary history is built.

The sheer quantity of radio drama now makes its neglect by literary historians so conspicuous and inexcusable to anyone who has bothered to look that he ends up asking similar questions to Williams, even though he hasn't necessarily arrived at them from modern Marxist theory. Who are the literary historians? From what position do they define literary history? What are their presuppositions, conscious and, even more important, unconscious? What are the built-in biases of their ideology? Why should criticism of film, a mass-media art form that cannot be subsumed under Literature, have reached such a degree of sophistication that literary critics are learning from it, while criticism of radio drama, a mass-media art form that for the most part can be subsumed under Literature, has hardly got off the ground? In asking questions like these, the student of radio finds himself being drawn into the centre of a debate about literary theory, criticism and history that is likely to shape the future of literary studies. The dominance of New Criticism and the concomitant methodology of Practical Criticism, with their stress on the aesthetic autonomy of the literary artefact and the consequent decontextualising of literature by abstracting it from its environment, are under fire from several fronts at the moment and this is no bad thing. Like most innovations, they have eventually shrunk into orthodoxy, so that what was fresh, invigorating and liberating in the 1920s and 1930s has now become stale, deadening and restricting. Is it too much to hope that radio drama will receive at least some of the recognition it deserves as postmodernist literary theories and critical ideas circulate more widely, perhaps expanding our literary consciousness to take more account of the media and of words not on the page but in the air?

Notes

1. 'Foreword', in MacNeice, *Persons from Porlock and Other Plays for Radio*. London 1969, p. 9.
2. *The Biggest Aspidistra in the World*. London 1972, p. 7.
3. *The Mad Islands and The Administrator: Two Radio Plays*. London 1964, p. 7.
4. 'Radio writing: Giles Cooper, talking to Michael Billington', *Plays and Players*, **13**(3) (Dec. 1965), p. 10.
5. 'General introduction', *The Dark Tower and Other Radio Scripts*. London 1947, p. 9.
6. *Christopher Columbus*. London 1944, p. 7.
7. *Ibid*, p. 9.
8. 'The mind as a stage'. *Theatre Quarterly*. **1**(3) (July-Sept, 1971), p. 6.
9. *Matrimonial News* (1928), *Squirrel's Cage* (1929), and *The Flowers Are Not for You to Pick* (1930), published in *Squirrel's Cage and Two Other Microphone Plays*. London 1931.
10. 'The early days: Val Gielgud, talking to Peter Roberts', *Plays and Players*, **13**(3) (Dec. 1965), p. 11.
11. Steve Grant, 'Brecht's youthful gem', *The Observer*, 19 Aug. 1979, p. 12.
12. E.W. Tedlock (ed.), *Dylan Thomas: The Legend and the Poet*. London 1960, p. 80.

184   *Radio Drama*

13. *Dylan Thomas*. Cardiff 1972, p. 68.
14. *Ibid*.
15. *Ibid*, pp. 68-9.
16. *Ibid*, p. 75.
17. Review of *Under Milk Wood, Dawn*, **30**(1) (1955), p. 27.
18. *British Radio Drama 1922-1956*. London 1957, p. 85.
19. 'Introduction', in Sykes (ed.), *Five Plays for Radio: Nightmares of the Old Obscenity Master and Other Plays*. Sydney and London 1975. p. xx.
20. 'The nature of radio as a medium of artistic communication', *Madog*, **1**(2) (Summer 1978), p. 8.
21. These are cited in Horst Priessnitz's contribution to this volume and the Select Bibliography.
22. *Christopher Columbus*, p. 8.
23. *Ibid*, p. 10.
24. *Ibid*, p. 8.
25. Hawkes, *Shakespeare's Talking Animals*. London 1973, p. 53.
26. *The Mad Islands and The Administrator*, p. 7.
27. *Ibid*, p. 8.
28. *Christopher Columbus*, p. 7.
29. 'Introduction', in Giles Cooper, *Six Plays for Radio*. London 1966, p. 12.
30. Marie Axton and Raymond Williams (eds), *English Drama: Forms and Development*. Cambridge 1977, pp. viii-ix.
31. *Explorations*. Harmondsworth 1964, p. 28.
32. *Ibid*, p. 142.
33. *Ibid*, p. 145.
34. Hawkes, op. cit., p. 49.

Chapter 11

The sponsor's v. the nation's choice: North American radio drama

Howard Fink

I like writing for sound radio, because of the freedom . . . I was able to experiment in form – a mobile, flexible structure, more flexible and mobile than in any other medium. And from the point of view of content I was able to go the whole hog and enjoy myself by exploring to a degree which wouldn't be acceptable in any other medium.

(Harold Pinter, 'Introduction', *Plays: Two*)

US background: the sponsor's choice

Radio drama in the US and in Canada, like the countries themselves, shows some striking similarities but some clear distinctions. Since the Golden Age of American radio arose and subsided before that of Canada, and the influences flowed mainly north, this chapter deals first with the US, then with Canada and finally with comparisons between the two.

Having steered a course through the history and the artefacts of American radio drama, I can say with some confidence that the primary and the background materials exist. But they have had very little in the way of description or organisation, though critical anthologies do exist. The relative lack of published work on the subject, together with the difficulty of access to the scripts and sound documents, has meant a job of reconstruction in the first place, and now necessitates the creation of a context for the phenomenon of American radio drama, before any description or analysis of the artefacts and their creators can become meaningful or useful. First, then, some necessary details of the beginnings of American radio and its commercial structures; then, an overview of the contexts of radio drama in American popular culture and theatre; finally, a broad history and description of American radio drama, in its popular genres as well as its 'prestige', serious forms.

American broadcasting: birth, structures and growth

Commercial radio in North America began with the opening of a station in Montreal by the Canadian Marconi Company in 1919. Known as XWA (now CFCF, with sixty years of continuous service), the station began regular broadcasts in December 1919. In the US the first station to go on the air was Westinghouse Electric's KDKA, Pittsburgh, in November 1921. It was the beginning of the 'broadcasting era', as Erik Barnouw calls it.[1] Barnouw, the major historian of American radio,[2] leaves no doubt in *The Sponsor* (1978) that he means by this a new commercial age, like the Age of Steam, rather than a new communications age *per se*, like the Age of Print. The beginnings of the Broadcasting Age were marked by a rapid scramble by purchasers for radio sets – one of the major peacetime technological benefits of the First World War – and an equally rapid scramble by entrepreneurs for commercial broadcasting licences. By the middle of 1922 there were some 400 American stations licenced[3]; ten months later there were over 550.[4] During this period the structures of American radio broadcasting developed rapidly in the direction of freedom from federal legislation and towards commercial monopoly.

Whatever the 'democratic' early history of American broadcasting, its most permanent shape was defined by the creation of the major networks and by their organisation of sponsored programming. The Radio Corporation of America (RCA) took over the AT&T (American Telephone and Telegraph) stations and facilities in 1924 and proceeded to formalise network arrangements. By September 1926 the National Broadcasting Company (NBC) and its two networks were created by RCA, the first of the two major American broadcasting corporations destined to dominate American radio until the 1950s. The form of that domination was, from the first, commercial. On the one hand, NBC made commercial arrangements with individual stations to give it coverage across the country (and into Canada) paralleling that of newspapers and magazines. On the other hand, it made commercial arrangements with 'sponsors' to buy time and programmes on the networks thus created, including the advertising of a sponsor's product on its programme. The latter arrangements paralleled those made between newspaper and magazine advertising sponsors and their advertising agencies. As a result, networks slipped easily into the commercial advertising world. The network that was to become the Columbia Broadcasting System (CBS) within the year began operations in competition with NBC in 1927, and the overall structure of commercial broadcasting in the US was complete, to be confirmed the same year by federal regulatory hands-off legislation.[5]

The commercial competition between NBC and CBS was pointed by new methods of analysing audience response to programmes, most precisely by more and more refined methods of discovering the size and nature of audiences for particular programmes and how these audiences changed in time as other programmes competed for them. It was mainly on the basis of these statistics that sponsors 'bought' programmes and programmes were developed, produced, maintained or dropped. The price of a programme's failure to be competitive was, simply, the loss of sponsorship; and without a sponsor, frequently a programme just disappeared, no matter what its positive qualities. In *The Sponsor* Barnouw is eloquent on the effects this had on the quality of programming: in the main, programmes were safe, 'wholesome', offended no one, especially not the sponsor or his product, and were created according to a formula proven by audience response. Thus by 1932, according to *Variety Radio Directory*, musical programmes were being replaced in the highest ratings by mystery programmes; and by the next year, radio drama of a more serious kind was beginning to rise in popularity. By 1932-3 variety programmes influenced by vaudeville were also on the rise.[6] *Variety Radio Directory* is quoting from the annual Cooperative Analysis of Broadcasting (CAB) reports, which were organised by American broadcasters, sponsors and advertising agencies from 1930 on. The CAB analysis had a major influence on the programmes sponsored and the kinds of programmes produced.

Yet another factor influenced commercial control over American programmes: the fact that, soon after the establishment of the major networks, the creation and production of most programmes was taken over from the networks by the advertising agencies representing the sponsors. Production went on in the agencies' own facilities and under their own – and the sponsors' – direct control. Decisions concerning the nature of individual programmes as well as their production and direction were thus related mainly to the needs of the sponsors. The only major exception was the creation of 'sustaining' programmes: unsponsored programmes provided by the networks to complete the schedules of their affiliates. Sustaining programmes occupied unsold time, usually outside of prime time, and constituted as small a proportion of the broadcasting day as could be contrived. The contents of sustaining programmes were often of a cultural or educational nature; and it was here, among the serious music and the talks, that serious 'prestige' radio drama could be heard – a very small proportion indeed of the schedule.

One important qualification must be made concerning the general effects of commercial control on radio-programme contents. If most programmes were safe and inoffensive, nevertheless public response did in a measure dictate the *forms* of programmes being sponsored. The much greater audience preference for dialogue and other dramatic forms of programme contents over 'talks' and even over musical programmes in the 1930s was a recognition of the essentially dramatic character of radio as a medium. Moreover, as we shall see, while democratic taste dictated that the most frequently broadcast dramatic forms would be popular radio, such as mystery, adventure, comedy, and soap opera, the necessity for radio dramatists to express themselves in these popular forms sometimes produced drama able to communicate serious themes in a meaningful fashion. The high absurdity of the best variety comedy is the most significant example of this phenomenon. The mention of popular influence on the forms and contents of radio programmes, especially in the formative stages, opens the question of American popular culture generally and of how it was newly channelled into radio in the early 1930s.

Popular culture: forms and relation to radio

The early history of American radio is marked by the taking over of a number of traditional forms of popular culture by the new medium. What is significant is the persistence of these forms or genres through the various primary media: theatre and print, then cinema and radio. Popular culture at the turn of this century was expressed, first, in popular-theatre forms, mainly vaudeville and burlesque. The motion picture, which first appeared at the beginning of the century, engendered a revolution in popular entertainment, prefiguring the growth of television in the 1950s. By 1919 a weekly movie had become a habit for an estimated ten million Americans. The cinema challenged the theatre as a popular medium because of the similarity in their conditions of delivery. Indeed, for many years after vaudeville had lost its primacy, it continued on (even into the 1960s) by pairing a live show with a movie. The limits of this new visual medium, including the conditions of delivery and its limited subgenres (the feature, the cartoon, the serial adventure and the news), were such that the silent movies of the first two decades of this century were not serious contenders with print as the dominant medium of popular culture. Another new popular medium early in the century, the comic strip, was even more limited in its form and specialised in its appeal, either in print or on film.

Pulp fiction was the most traditional of the popular genres. At the same time, it provided a full range of popular forms and, from the 1890s to 1920, was the dominant and most comprehensive of genres, in the print medium or any other.[7] Since the pulps have by now disappeared and since their subgenres were influential on radio, some essential details of their history would be useful. The pulps were anthologies of short stories, the succeeding issues of each magazine being dedicated to a single theme related to the interests of a group of readers, which loosely connected the magazine's individual stories. The themes ranged from childrens' stories, through detective and mystery fiction, horror and the supernatural, science, aviation, sports, western and adventure fiction, to love stories. In their day the pulps were the principal financial reward and audience for the early work of many writers, such as Edgar Rice Burroughs, Max Brand, Dashiell Hammett, H.P. Lovecraft and a myriad of lesser-known writers who shone and faded in the pulps. Moreover, many serious writers were published in this form, including H.G. Wells, Arnold Bennett, Rudyard Kipling, Stephen Crane, Mark Twain, Tennessee Williams and 'O. Henry'.

The pulp magazines burgeoned during the 1890s by the convergence of several causes: first, the rapid development of printing technology, which made the publishing of magazines much less expensive; then, the development of national distribution companies. Finally, with the recession of 1893, some 'slick' or 'glossy' magazines, reacting to a new audience, turned to the pulp format, either creating new pulps or reformatting their 'slicks', and aiming at not only the existing low-income dime-novel market but also a new middle-class audience. By the first years of this century, the pulps were firmly established as the major popular American entertainment. Like the American electronic media afterwards, the popularity of the pulps was the basis not only for a commercial production and distribution system but for an advertising system.

The end of the pulps' dominance began early in this century with the appearance of a number of alternative means of popular entertainment, including the movies and musical records. However, the pulps didn't finally disappear until the 1950s, though the end of their domination came in the early 1920s with the arrival of radio. Radio was the first of the new media to be able to provide comprehensive and inexpensive popular entertainment matching that of the pulps. With the coming of network programming late in the 1920s and with the Depression beginning in 1929, radio took over audiences from the pulps as well as from its rivals, the legitimate theatre and vaudeville, as well as providing a musical alternative to records and a live alternative to the movies, whose production budgets were seriously affected by depressed economic conditions. By the 1930s, radio provided a cheap, continuous form of popular entertainment, able to appeal at different times to very different audiences, by region, sex, age and class; audiences flocked to the new medium.[8]

Significantly, American radio was quite uniquely suitable for advertising, which could make use of not only its vast captive network audiences but also the great immediacy and effectiveness of radio's techniques: the spoken voice, music, sound effects, and the convincing methods of dramatic dialogue. It was therefore inevitable that, as soon as its commercial organisation was properly developed, radio should have firmly established itself by the early 1930s as not only the predominant medium of popular culture (replacing the pulps) but also the primary medium for advertising. It then attracted much American creative talent. Radio's effective talent, audience and financial monopolies in the 1930s enabled it to rapidly develop the techniques appropriate to the medium and to improve in quality. Soon it almost put vaudeville, the pulps and the record industry out of business. (CBS soon bought out Columbia Records, and NBC controlled the RCA phonograph industry.) The movies, also threatened, took on radio's audio technology for the talking picture. The success of radio in replacing the earlier media was itself a prefiguration of the takeover in the 1950s of radio's techniques, audiences and sponsors by the succeeding technology, television.

What is fascinating about the transformation from the earlier media to radio is the way in which radio literally took them over. It absorbed them and changed their forms into its own format (which I will argue is essentially dramatic) to capture their popular audiences. It is not by accident that the major categories of radio programming reflect the genres of previous pop culture. The forms of the short story and novel were easily transformed by dramatic adaptation into short plays and serial dramas respectively. Similarly, many classical and modern plays were presented in radio adaptations. Adaptations of films were extremely popular on radio, gaining incomparably larger audiences in such series as *Lux Radio Theatre* than in their original form. From pulp fiction especially, radio imported many of its subgenres; mystery, adventure, horror and western drama series were mainstays of radio from very early days, while the omnipresent radio soap operas were a direct extrapolation from pulp love-serials. Vaudeville's stars made new careers in radio: that is, those did who succeeded in transforming their acts from the visual to the aural; a dramatic context of contrasting voices and of situations and conflicts was necessary to replace the visual scene and humour. The story lines of comic strips were often (as with *Little Orphan Annie*) lifted unchanged, turned into dramatic dialogue, and broadcast as serial adventures; in this way nearly all the popular comic strips actually found their way on to radio. Newspaper reporting and commentary were also adapted to the radio medium, not only as straight talks but also in dramatised form, as in the *March of Time* series, which dramatised major stories from *Time* magazine. The straight essay in print became, in turn, the documentary drama on radio, such as the series *You Are There*.

In all these cases, radio took over the subgenres of the old media and transformed them into its own genre, a dramatic form. Those grey eminences, radio writers, were, in the main, creators of continuity dialogue: radio dramatists. The transformations involved suggest that radio is essentially a dramatic medium. The reasons for this are illuminating about the nature of radio drama as a form of artistic theatre.

Radio and the dramatic form

One of the most striking aspects of American radio is that the great majority of programmes shared in the form of drama: not simply dialogue, but dramatic situation, distinct characters, dramatic tension and resolution. A heterogenous group of programmes was thus closely related by technique and artistry, from straight drama, through popular dramatic adaptations, soap operas and variety shows, to (sometimes) information programmes, even (on occasion) current news and (best illustration of all) the ubiquitous dramatic commercial. The only strict exceptions in the schedules were straight talks, sports, classical-music programmes, and audience-participation shows. The commercial organisation of the American networks, which made American programme producers so sensitive to ephemeral public opinion, was one cause of this phenomenon. It became clear in the early 1930s that drama was what audiences wanted. By the mid-1930s, 65 per cent of listeners preferred dramatic programmes. The responses built into the system were swift and inevitable. The form of most programmes had become dramatic.

Public taste itself was not simply arbitrary. It is a fact that, in a medium communicating through the ear alone, dramatic form delivers complex information more efficiently and more entertainingly. It calls on the listener's mind to paint in a comprehensive context, supplying what is missing visually. It creates complex situations, and it calls on the listener to bring to bear most subtle apprehensions, not only of words, but of tones and accents, atmosphere and emotions. Radio, especially in its dramatic form, returns us to a preprint complexity of communication.

In analysing the nature of drama, Martin Esslin uses an illustration from his experience as a BBC documentary script writer tackling an assignment on the working of an employment office, and in doing so he helps to explain why radio falls so naturally into dramatic form.[9] He shows how much more immediate, effective and *efficient* it is to communicate by means of a dramatic sketch than to describe something in so many words, essay-fashion. Esslin is referring here to what linguists call communication codes.[10] These codes are the symbols or shorthand by means of which people communicate; language is only the most traditional and familiar form of these codes, the one used in the medium of print. These codes may take many different forms, from 'primitive' smoke or drum signals to the complex visual codes developed in film and even more in television. It is only necessary for the import of a code to be agreed upon in order for it to take on a significance broader than its simple denotation.

This concept is applicable to the multiple codes of drama, in which language is only one of the agreed means of communication. The point as regards radio is that its limitation to the aural demands complex aural codes to communicate, while its faithful and sensitive reproduction of a vast range of sounds (from that of the human voice in all its expressiveness, to the myriad sounds of the environment, and the wide variety of instruments of musical expression) provides the opportunity to develop such aural codes. And the search for these codes begins (though it does not, by any means, end) in the established traditions of drama. It became increasingly evident in the early 1930s that the dramatic form and dramatic codes applicable to radio concentrated and rendered much more meaningful the codes being communicated. For example, voices on the air became significant in their own right: their timbres, their emotions, their accents, and so on. Sound effects add other dimensions of information. The dramatic situation and conflicts create both a human context and a scene in which the action unrolls. We are no longer dealing with information in a script but with a whole dramatic subtext, with particular human personalities in a particular dramatic scene, many details of which are, in radio, being supplied by the listener.

Out of this concept grows a more complex definition. Perhaps ironically, drama in radio is an escape from the monotony of the voice alone. In the genre of radio drama, the complexity of sets and actors in a stage play is replaced by the complexity of *sounds* and the complexity of *situations* they provoke in the auditor's imagination. In this technique, radio borrows from the novel, which escapes from a similar monotony of the sequence of words – say, in the essay – by complexity of situation and personality. The secret in both radio and the novel is the generation of 'point of view'. It is therefore not surprising that, in one main stream of serious radio drama, poetic narration in a form paralleling that of fiction is used as a bridge between scenes as well as an instrument of information, summary or conclusion. And radio developed other similar techniques into a complex and efficient language of dramatic communication. If radio falls naturally into the dramatic form, it is because radio found the first and most powerful of its communicative codes in drama.

The two streams: serious drama and popular drama

It should be clarified at the outset that there were two streams of American radio drama. On the one hand, there was prestige sustaining drama: serious drama written especially for radio, and serious adaptations from classical and modern literature. This element was an extremely small proportion of the network schedules. Among the thousands of series broadcast (*Variety Radio Directory* lists some 6,000 network series to date), there were perhaps twelve series at most that fell into this category over the two-decade span of radio's rise and demise. On the other hand, the largest number of sponsored popular programmes took on a dramatic form of some kind, such as mystery and adventure dramas, variety-comedy programmes, soap operas, dramatised documentaries and news. Of the twenty-six leading evening programmes in the 1938-9 season, twenty were dramatic.[11] In the 1939-40 season the ratio remained very much the same: nineteen out of twenty-five. That proportion had risen steadily from 1930-1, in which only two of the top ten evening programmes had been dramatic. In the daytime there had been a similar rise from 1930; by 1938-9 the top ten included two musical shows, the dramatic serial *The Goldbergs* and seven soaps.

In serious radio-drama series there was a conscious attempt at contemporaneity and aesthetic experiment, an effort to create radio drama as an art form specifically for the medium. The governing concerns in popular drama were on the surface quite different: first, what would sell – both the programme and the sponsor's product; then, what would communicate most directly, most amuse; finally, what methods would translate ideas most directly into dialogue, and dialogue most directly into clear situation. Quantitatively, the varied series in this category provided, by 1940, almost three-quarters of all programmes and (as seen above) 80 per cent of the top twenty programmes. Much of the activity in radio, then, went into the creation of this massive and, for the most part, artistically unselfconscious stream of popular drama.

The 'two worlds', as Barnouw calls these two areas of sponsored and sustaining programmes, in which drama was the major element, 'used the same studios and were served by the same studio engineers. But . . . there was little interaction between the two worlds.'[12] Barnouw's point is correct in terms of the contrasts in budgets, origination of programme concepts, and their general formats, as seen above. It is not accurate, crucially, as regards production and writing staff. The organisation of programme and production activities at the networks and agencies responded to the prolific demands of daily radio, which necessitated the hiring of staff production-directors. These took on the responsibilities of a number of different programmes at the hierarchy's bidding. It was the same for staff writers, who were assigned everything from the most commercial to the most esoteric of programmes at the same time. Even the writers and directors best known for their serious experimental dramas, in so far as they were frequently on staff at a network, often worked on popular radio shows. Simply put, the two streams shared the same writers and directors, as well as technical staff. It is hardly surprising, therefore, to discover that there was a fruitful cross-fertilisation between the two streams. The artistic techniques of serious drama owed a real debt to the techniques developed in popular drama series.

The nature and causes of this cross-fertilisation will be even clearer if we recall that in the period under discussion – the Golden Age of American radio drama in the decade and a half beginning in 1929 – radio itself and its now-familiar techniques and formats were in the process of being newly created and rapidly developed. There was a general impetus in *all* the branches of this new medium towards innovation. There was a camaraderie among its young practitioners, a common feeling of adventure, an impulse to invent or borrow new techniques, even for the most mundane commercial programmes. On the one hand, it was a commercial detective series, *Gang Busters*, that gained a general reputation as 'a pioneer program in the use of new and startling sound technique, and many of the devices and effects that are now commonplace were developed by this series'.[13] And on the other hand, Norman Corwin's 'sustaining' aesthetic experiments in dramatic verse and music, which earned him the reputation of America's best radio dramatist, were paid the supreme compliment of being soon applied – effectively – to musical commercials, using the choir Corwin himself had trained.

Creative writers and directors brought their expertise to bear wherever they worked; moreover, their experiments proceeded sometimes with greater flexibility in simpler vehicles. Another advantage to experiments within sponsored programmes should also be remembered: they had substantial audiences on which new ideas were tested in the 'real' world of commercial competition. If the ideas were effective or otherwise, there was an immediate feedback in terms of audiences and sales. Finally, certain kinds of technical, artistic and philosophical experiments were specifically suggested by particular kinds of new popular programmes, which might not have occurred in a more traditional dramatic genre. One significant example of this is the kind of experiment in the manipulation of language, logic and, ultimately, reality that went on in the variety-comedy shows developed by the vaudeville comedians.

Beyond the efforts of individual artists there was a general cultural impetus behind American radio and radio drama. In all its sustaining and commercial forms, American radio drama was an instrument expressing a rapidly changing American culture from the 1920s to the 1940s. Like all such cultural vehicles, it had the function of reflecting new cultural phenomena back to the people, as a confirmation and a corrective. Beyond individual efforts, therefore, it was a principal instrument of the rapid changes going on in society. And the commercial nature of American radio meant that audience response fine-tuned which programmes were heard and which programme contents survived. This was a complex activity, which hardly respected the distinctions between serious and popular drama series. Finally, even within established categories, individual series progressed and matured, and new, more sophisticated series were being created. The styles and world-views of American radio drama reflected the rapid maturation of radio's audiences. Thus by 1940 both popular and serious drama series were more like *one another* than like series of both kinds from the early 1930s.

As we look at the series that made up popular radio drama, these parallels and distinctions between the two streams should be kept in mind, in particular the influence of popular on serious radio drama.

Popular radio drama

Mystery and detective series

One of the most ubiquitous of forms, mystery and detective radio-drama series are in a direct line of descent from the print medium, both nineteenth-century mystery fiction and its later version in pulp fiction. It is perhaps in mystery radio drama that one sees most clearly the transfer of popular culture from pulp fiction to the radio medium. It is this familiarity that seems the first explanation for the pervasiveness and popularity of this form of radio drama. Evidently, mystery series are formulas in several ways. First, at the centre of each series is a single protagonist with some extraordinary qualities; and it is this character who ties together the various distinct episodes in the series, stamping them with his own familiar pattern. Second, more generally, mystery radio dramas follow a fairly routine formula of introduction, complication and resolution, a kind of popularisation of the plot of traditional tragedy. *Oedipus Rex*, for example, is on one level a mystery with a similar plot and resolution; the deterministic universe invoked is not essentially different. The line of inheritance runs through the Victorian novel, such as Dickens's *Edwin Drood* or *Bleak House*, Wilkie Collins's *The Moonstone* and, of course, Dostoevsky's *Crime and Punishment*. In mystery radio drama the formula involves the inevitable solution of the mystery by the protagonist, bringing the antagonist to justice and recreating, in effect, universal order – until the next week's assault.

While this double formulation and patterning – of the central character and of the subgenre's structure – clearly imposed some restraints on the author's creative freedom, the resultant simplicity of plot and characterisation left greater freedom for pure experiments in radio-drama techniques: in the oral communication of information that would in the theatre be visual; in the expression of movement; in rapid change of scene, and so on. Finally, the ritual nature of the action and the idealisation of the protagonist gave many opportunities for didacticism: that is, mystery drama often played the role of an instrument of acculturation in general, and supplied clues concerning socially acceptable attitudes. The weekly frequency and fifteen- to thirty-minute length of these series gave ample scope for these goals.

One of the earliest of the mystery series, and one of the very best, was *The Shadow*. An example of the transfer of subgenres from the pulps to radio, it began in August 1930 as a development in the radio medium of the pulp-fiction *Shadow* novels written by Walter Gibson, published by Street and Smith.[14] *The Shadow* continued to be broadcast right through the radio era, until 1954. The familiar version was gradually developed over several years. The figure of the Shadow himself was slowly transformed from that of a narrator to the active central character with extraordinary hypnotic powers. The shift, characteristically, is away from the techniques of fictional narrative towards those of drama. It is not in its hero or its rather simple contents but in its techniques that the original contributions of *The Shadow* reside.[15]

The content of the plays is mainly at an adolescent level. The plots are like murder mysteries in the familiar format, with a touch of the supernatural only partly explained by the Shadow's 'hypnotic' powers. The episodes are full of familiar gothic touches, foggy mansions, mad scientists, sickly rich people with ominous butlers, and the mandatory villains threatening young damsels – Victorian melodrama clearly revealing its pulp-fiction antecedents. Even the Shadow's hypnotic 'power to cloud men's minds' is from an earlier, prescientific period, harking back to nineteenth-century mesmerism. The scene, on the other hand, is clearly New York between the world wars, and apart from the Shadow himself the characters, if simple in delineation, are appropriate to their scene. Clichés of good and evil are provided instead of character delineation or development. The major function of the Shadow is to solve the mysteries, and his powers are used only at the end, an almost irrelevant tool in bringing the criminals to justice though a useful instrument of dramatic climax. The representative plays in the recent Diana Cohen – I.B. Hoeflinger collection, *The Shadow Knows*, are virtually apolitical and asocial in theme; dates are not supplied, and it is almost impossible to date them by internal evidence (with the exception of an anti-communist play obviously from the McCarthy era). However, typical American social prejudices from between the wars are revealed in the depiction of relations between characters from various classes: from criminals, cab drivers and workers to the idle rich and film stars. The retailing of typical antifeminine prejudices can also be recognised.

The sound records of *Shadow* productions show how they surmount the simplicity of plot and characterisation by their technical excellence; the radio medium is expertly utilised in both text and production. The direction is fast-paced, the acting is sure and familiar, there are imaginative bridges between scenes, and the dramatic tensions, progressions and resolutions are very effective; information of a typically visual character is communicated aurally in an efficient, imaginative and natural fashion. It is clear that *The Shadow* was not only innovative in the techniques and codes of the radio medium, but also influential on succeeding radio drama, perhaps all the more influential because its innovations were quite clear in their context, uncomplicated by mature themes or characterisations. It is not surprising to discover that the actor who played the Shadow for over a year from 1937 (when its familiar form was first perfected) was none other than Orson Welles, who worked concurrently on the *Columbia Workshop* series and, while still in the role, created *Mercury Theatre on the Air*, perhaps the most innovative of the American serious radio-drama series. Moreover, Welles played the Shadow against the Margo Lane of none other than Agnes Moorehead, one of the female leads in the Mercury Players in both its radio and cinema forms.

Another of the early mystery series – it also began on radio in 1930 – was *The Adventures of Sherlock Holmes*, adapted from, and later written on the pattern of, the Conan Doyle stories and novels; the adaptations were by Edith Meiser until well into the 1940s, then by a variety of continuity writers almost until the end of network radio drama in 1962. Dunning says that the Holmes stories were well suited to radio drama,[16] and it seems clear what he means. The real emphasis in the stories is on the interaction between two intelligent and scientifically trained men to deduct the explanations for crimes from scant clues – an interaction both dramatic *and* verbal. This is another example of the popular subgenre of mystery fiction moving to the radio-dramatic mode.

Two other fiction-inspired mystery series began on radio within months of each other in 1932. The first was *Fu Manchu*, the mad Oriental scientist-criminal, a programme based on the stories of Sax Rohmer; the radio career of this pulp villain was short. The other was *Charlie Chan*, the inscrutable Oriental detective, written by E.D. Biggers; this had a longer radio career. They were both overshadowed in popularity by two original radio creations, both by the same Mutual Network (a regional network) team: *The Lone Ranger* (1933) and *The Green Hornet* (1936). Both of these series belong to the second generation of radio mystery-adventure, and the influence of the first generation, especially that of *The Shadow*, is evident in the general structure of the episodes, the powerful, unrealistic hero of mysterious identity, and the production techniques.

The next ten years saw the growing popularity and elaboration of the detective version of mystery drama. Perhaps the best known of these is *Gang Busters* (1936), which has the reputation (as noted above) of developing new sound techniques for the whole radio-drama industry. *Mr Keen, Tracer of Lost Persons* began in 1937 and *Mr District Attorney* in 1939. *The Thin Man* and *Bulldog Drummond* appeared in 1941. *Nick Carter, Master Detective*, the earliest and most famous hero of the Street and Smith pulps, didn't arrive on radio until 1943 and had a very short run, never quite making the transition successfully. Rex Stout's print-fiction hero, Nero Wolfe, also came to radio that year. By this late stage in American radio drama, there was a clearly defensive hewing to tried patterns in the creation of series, and anxious glances over the shoulder at the rival, television. The relatively few series that made the actual transition to television were mainly late radio creations tailored specifically for a quick jump to the new medium. Jack Webb, the star and creator of *Dragnet* (1949), ran through a set of earlier detective series, including *Pat Novak, For Hire* (1946), *Johnny Madero, Pier 23* (1947) and *Jeff Regan, Investigator* (1948), before hitting on the *Dragnet* formula, which was to take him to television.

Variety series

Variety simply was one of the most popular of all radio-drama entertainment genres. There were two major versions of this genre. One, growing out of a more traditional stage form, was situation comedy, a series of episodes in the life of a fictional group of people, each short episode being complete in itself but conforming to the general pattern of the series as a whole. We are familiar with it from television series such as *I Love Lucy* or *All in the Family*. The dramatic form was, in the main, traditionally realistic and as important an element as the comedy. The other version, far more flexible, was an importation into radio of the true stage-variety tradition: vaudeville and burlesque comedy. It showed its antecedents in both form and content, and the experiments in both were more outrageous and more significant than in the average situation comedy; its usual full-hour format provided the scope for these experiments.

One of the earliest variety series on the network was an original situation comedy called *The Goldbergs*, created by, written by and starring Gertrude Berg as Molly Goldberg, which began in 1929 and ran to 1934 and then from 1937 until 1945. It became a Broadway play in 1948 and was in the public eye on radio again, on film and on television for years afterwards. In self-contained fifteen-minute episodes it portrayed the lives of an immigrant Jewish family in New York. The major theme was the struggle of American immigrants for survival, acceptance and improvement. The series was strongly influenced by the realistic social drama of the 1930s, but with the radical impact blunted by its comic surface, which, however, offered a double-edged irony towards both the dominant culture and the immigrant strategies against it. Relative to most other variety series, it was unusually mature in its conception, characters and situations. While its popularity and influence on later series are clear, it is also plainly rooted in the form of traditional realistic stage drama, especially compared with the variety-comedy format.

Another of the very earliest of network situation comedies was *Vic and Sade*, which began in 1932: an influential original radio series written by Paul Rhymer, the scene of which was small-town middle America, the complete contrast to *The Goldbergs*. Because it was broadcast daily on weekday afternoons, it is sometimes confused with soap opera; and indeed it was one of the first daytime radio-drama series broadcast by NBC. Unlike the soap-opera format, however, the episodes of *Vic and Sade* were discrete, each with a self-contained situation, though all connected by the fictional family of the title and their friends. The comedy is understated, like that of *The Goldbergs*, but noticeably more sentimental. On the other hand, Ray Bradbury and Ross Firestone agree on the extraordinary imaginativeness and effectiveness of the writing and the production: *Vic and Sade* is considered in a class with Sherwood Anderson's *Winesburg, Ohio*, Thornton Wilder's *Our Town* and Arthur Miller's *Death of a Salesman* in its authenticity and the way it captures the essence of small-town mid-American life.[17] This assessment confirms that *Vic and Sade* is in the central tradition of American realistic theatre; moreover, the plays Firestone mentions (*Our Town* and *Death of a Salesman*) date from

1938 and 1949 respectively, and the influence would go from *Vic and Sade* to them. Arthur Miller, of course, began his career in the late 1930s with radio drama, so this theory is reasonable. If, finally, *Vic and Sade* is gentler and so more artificial than *The Goldbergs*, it is this very quality that makes it the stronger influence on variety comedy.

Certainly the most popular of the earliest variety series, and one that provides a revealing bridge between its two subforms, is *Amos 'n' Andy*. This series, started on local radio under the name of *Sam 'n' Henry* by its writer-stars, Freeman Gosden and Charles Correll, in 1920, was a radio version of traditional blackface vaudeville routine. It began to develop its dramatic qualities with the creation of consistent characters, a persistent scene, and situations developed not for comedy alone, but along the lines of dramatic progression and conclusion. This is a good example of the way in which radio, given materials imported from another genre, in time imposes its own dramatic forms. By the time the programme had become *Amos 'n' Andy* in 1928, it was recognisably a situation comedy, and the process continued when it went network in 1929. The characterisations became more complex, the situations more dramatically conceived; other actors took the minor roles Gosden and Correll had been doubling. One revealing development was the gradual disappearance of the Amos character, ascribed by Dunning to the fact that Amos was too straight to provide dramatic conflict with Andy.[18] By the early 1940s, Amos's role was completely usurped by the Kingfish, an antagonist who obviously provided the necessary dramatic opposition to Andy. It is a case of the transformation of a standard vaudeville team, of comic and straight man, to the structure of a typical radio situation comedy. Furthermore, the fact that the protagonist-antagonist confrontation and the comic absurdity of the situation assumed greater importance than the realistic details characteristic of situation comedy moved *Amos 'n' Andy* closer than the other early sitcoms to vaudeville comedy, in which variety made its most impressive achievement.

The vaudeville artists who created variety comedy on radio had to deal with the challenge of a transition from a medium whose visual element was central to a medium essentially verbal; they had to transform their comedy from visual to verbal. The transition is often marked, not surprisingly, by a movement from monologue to dialogue – that is, from a narrative to a dramatic form; and this helps to explain the proliferation of radio-comedy teams and of fictional dramatic situations. Some stand-up vaudeville comedians, like Eddie Cantor, Ed Wynn, Jack Pearl and Milton Berle, never quite made the transition from monologue. Others, like many of the singing stars who adopted the standard variety-skit format, were simply making use of a convenient form without inspiration or development. Some variety comics, though, brought original genius to bear on this form; they stretched it to accommodate their wider ironic visions.

The most important quality of the network variety-comedy programmes coming out of vaudeville is ironic iconoclasm. Nothing is sacred, from the social traditions to the very traditions of drama itself, especially the realistic social drama current in the 1930s; the usual expectations of ordinary reality are ignored. Variety of this stand-up comic form is, at its best in the 1930s, simply an absurd commentary on life and on social mores. The development of this theatre of the absurd is traceable in its major practitioners.

Among the earliest of the variety-comedy series were those making use of a husband-wife team. *Easy Aces*, which began in 1930, featured Goodman and Jane Ace, and was written by Goodman Ace. Firestone calls it 'probably the most literate, urbane comedy series of its time'[19]; the surviving texts bear this out. The comedy in this series comes out in dramatic dialogues centring on Jane Ace's supposedly peculiar qualities; these go beyond comic dumbness to an inspired absurdity of observation on the world which is surprisingly acute. Goodman meanwhile plays an ironic straight role. The work of George Burns and Gracie Allen, who began their own regular programme in 1932, is quite similar in structure as well as in humour; the difference is that while the *Burns and Allen* dialogue is even more absurdly inspired, the situations protrayed are more conventional and less insightful. In both cases, the acrid smoke of satire seeps in behind the benign good humour of the comedy routines. At their best, *Easy Aces* and *Burns and Allen*, like a number of the other variety-comedy shows, make use of the flexibility of the format: individual skits, loosely connected by the general format of the programme, skits with only an ironic or comic relation to ordinary life. Any idea, absurd, ironic, insightful, can be worked into this flexible form, the legacy of its stage-variety forebears.

The same husband-wife comedy-team format was used by the *Fibber McGee and Molly* show which, beginning in 1935, shows the influence of the two earlier programmes. It is Fibber himself who carries the absurd, self-denigrating comedy in this show, while his wife Molly is the straight person. The structure of this show, however, is usually a complete fictional dramatic situation within which the various encounters take place, with the 'regulars' providing the effect of individual skits; this places it within variety comedy rather than situation comedy. In the case of the ventriloquist Edgar Bergen and his dummy Charlie McCarthy in *The Charlie McCarthy Show* (1937), the comedy and irony issue from the alter-ego of the ventriloquist – in fact, two alter egos, for Bergen not only created Charlie, who was too clever by half, but also Mortimer Snerd, who erred on the other side. Bud Abbott and Lou Costello, who launched their own show in 1940, were a classic team of the second generation, straight man and dumb comic on the *Burns and Allen* pattern. Jimmy Durante, a variety star of long standing, only teamed up with Garry Moore in 1943 to form a team. While these teams all shared a similar variety dramatic-dialogue technique, they are distinguished by the forms of comedy used and by the objects of their irony. The great flexibility of the form and the ironic fantasy of scenes and situations were clearly new possibilities of the medium and most suggestive for practitioners of serious drama.

A related variety form, even more flexible, was created by vaudeville comics who made the move to radio without the use of an alter ego. In general, each of these comics was the single centre of his show, surrounding himself with a number of fictional characters to perform the dramatic interactions. The first and best of these was Fred Allen, who began in radio in 1932 and whose shows changed and developed in original ways throughout the 1930s and 1940s. The innovative Allen, who was the principle creator of his own shows, was the most self-conscious producer-director of a repertory comic-drama group. They were first known as *The Mighty Allen Art Players*, and they did popular burlesques of serious drama. Later the group metamorphosed into a more sophisticated format, comprising the fictional characters in 'Allen's Alley', the form in which they survived to the end of network radio drama. Allen would stroll down the Alley each week on the flimsy excuse of taking a survey of opinions on some ironic or comic topic. The secondary characters Allen met in the Alley were distinguished from one another not only by striking differences in voice quality but also by the characteristic quirks in their personalities, communicated both through their voices and in repeated set phrases and other orally communicated clichés. They were precisely established 'characters': that is, the audience was given precise aural clues on which to base their conceptions of the characters' visual and personality qualities. All these techniques were of great interest as communication codes to the writers of radio drama.

Another distinction of Fred Allen's shows was his persistence in satirising aspects of contemporary American life in a manner more explicit than most of the other radio variety artists – not even the networks and agencies that gave him a living escaped. His frankness and even the bitterness that sometimes appeared are evidence of the serious purpose behind the humour, a purpose that, like all great satire, created a screen of irony before the unacceptable truth. Allen's methods, then, were not simply techniques of radio communication, but literary-dramatic methods of expression in the satiric mode, significant generally in radio drama.

Another well-known comic who is alone at the centre of his show is Bob Hope, who began in 1935 but only went network in 1938. Bob Hope is better known than Allen because of Hope's popular movies (including the *Road* series) and his famous shows for servicemen (who doesn't know 'Thanks for the Memory'?). Hope, like Allen, progressed on the radio from a stand-up vaudeville routine, creating a repertory group for his comic dialogues, including such distinct characters as Jerry Colonna, and he used numerous invited guests for the same function. All the same, an important element in Hope's radio shows continued to be the comic monologue, an honourable but extremely restricted form of drama. Where Hope is not using the traditional monologue form, his dialogues seem derivative, lacking the critical bite of Allen's. Hope's major eccentricity, the sexual wisecracking for which he is best known, is not the least radical; rather it is an acceptable form of relief from the social mores regarding sex. Where Allen (and others) are on the ironic edge of society, Hope is establishment.

The third of these best-known vaudeville-comic singles is Jack Benny. He, too, remained at the centre of his show, though he also created a satellite group, including Mary Livingstone (his wife) and the 'Rochester' character, played by Eddie Anderson. Unlike Fred Allen's group, the members of which were all eccentric satiric characters, Benny's people were more normative; the roles were mainly straight – with the exception of Rochester. Nevertheless, they performed the necessary function for Benny of providing the basis of dramaic interaction as well as a varied aural texture and complications. Jack Benny's comedy was innovative in several ways. As Firestone points out, Benny pioneered such frequently copied ideas as the comic commercial and the parody movie. Benny was very much aware of the sound medium, and some of his comedy depended principally on the radio medium: for example, the comic use of sound effects. Timing is one important instrument of any comic and is a sound-oriented rather than a visual technique. Benny developed this technique, together with his development of the readers' expectations of his own and his characters' personalities, and this gave him a great range of complex aural communication codes for his comedy. The best example of this is a comic skit frequently told to show Benny's extreme stinginess, a cliché he cultivated. The skit consists of a confrontation between Benny and a mugger on the street. Says the mugger: 'Your money or your life.' Prolonged pause: growing laughter; then applause, as the audience gradually realises what Benny *must* be thinking, and eventually responds to the information communicated by the silence and to its comic implications. This is an example of the dramatic technique Harold Pinter (himself a radio dramatist) describes when he says that what is important in a play is not so much what is said as what is not said, the whole complex of things the audience can discern between the words or in the pauses. To repeat, it takes timing, the precreation of distinct character, and command of the aural medium to communicate information by this dramatic technique. The mark of Benny's success is the audience response to the comic element in this 'silent' communication. It should be apparent how innovative the technique is when it is remembered that Benny was using it in the 1930s, while Pinter (for example) only began writing in the 1950s.

Like mystery series, variety series offered many innovative ideas in radio-dramatic technique to the creators of serious radio drama. Mystery drama, however, issuing from pulp fiction, is not only relatively formulaic in structure and traditional in character, but simplistic in the vision of reality it offers. The variety form is not only more mature in its depiction of reality (in situation comedy especially) but is much more iconoclastic, more critical of society and of the radio medium itself. Moreover, the greater flexibility and innovativeness in dramatic structures of the best variety comedy is matched by the daring absurdity of vision revealed, an absurdity too close to the tradition of the Theatre of the Absurd for coincidence. Irving Wardle is right when, in the Penguin volume of British radio drama, he speaks of the freedom of radio drama from the (mainly visual) limitations of the stage leading to a kind of drama paralleling the Theatre of the Absurd.[20] What he hesitates to suggest, but what must be considered, is the possibly direct influence of certain types of radio drama on the absurdist stage play. Several more obvious correlations can be made: first, that a number of American playwrights wrote early in their careers for radio, including Edward Albee (as Martin Esslin relevantly points out in *The Theatre of the Absurd*). This phenomenon is even more pronounced among European absurdist playwrights, like Pinter and Beckett, for whom the radio medium remains viable.[21] Significantly, the tradition of absurdist theatre, a modern response to nineteenth-century bourgeois realism in the theatre, developed on a parallel with similar flights from realism in twentieth-century fiction, poetry and the plastic arts. But this phenomenon began years earlier in those other arts (*symbolisme*, Dadaism, Expressionism and so on), well before the First World War, while in the theatre it can be said to have flowered only in the late 1930s and the 1940s, after radio was well established. The 'absurdity' of the American radio variety comics of the 1930s was a specifically satiric instrument of criticism about life in the Depression. It was a specific and popular alternative to the committed Marxist critique of capitalist society, which issued forth in superrealist dramatic and other literary sermons during that period. Surely the complex and even absurd creations of radio comedy drama were a more stimulating model for dramatists seeking an alternative form to bourgeois realism, especially dramatists who cut their teeth on radio. Radio was certainly *pervasive* enough to have had this influence.

Soap operas

Soap opera is the third significant variant form of radio drama. Because of its simplicity of conception and style and its domestic themes and audience, this genre offers some of the most significant insights into both American society and the commercial radio industry, which dictated the forms of radio drama. The general form of the soap is serial drama: that is, a continuous story line slowly developing through short daily episodes, usually no more than ten minutes in length. Like the other genres of radio drama, soap opera developed out of earlier and more traditional cultural modes – in this case, from the sentimental novel and its popular form, serial fiction. The significant predecessors of serial radio dramas are found in the popular periodical format in which many nineteenth-century novels were first published. Raymond William Stedman refers specifically to Victorian domestic novels as in the direct line of influence on radio serials in content and audience.[22] The lineage descends through pulp romances and, as Stedman argues,[23] through the dramatic form of the serial film, which had a vogue between 1912 and 1922 and was originally an offshoot of pulp serial romances, with as sentimental a focus. It is significant that radio serials first appeared in 1930, only a few years after the serial film fell from popularity. While the earliest and most famous of serial films, *What Happened to Mary* (1912) and *The Perils of Pauline* (1914), were Victorian romantic melodramas much like the early radio soaps, later serial films copied other forms of pulp adventure fiction.

The themes of the soaps centred narrowly on the family and domestic complications. Broadcast in the daytime to a mainly female audience of millions, their usual basic concept was a story line with which housewives could identify, and in the 1930s that meant a patina of sentimental realism with a strong undercurrent of wish-fulfilment. Their protagonists were most often matriarchs and their ideals generally domestic as well; while many of the *adventures* were not domestic – such as abduction and adultery – this was more on the fantasy level than on the level of values.[24] In the 1940s, on the other hand, the new soaps were more realistic on the level of plot, reflecting the changes the war brought to women and the family. Apart from the audience they were aimed at, the contents of soap operas were dictated by their commercial sponsorship: the domestic soap products, the frequent publicity for which took up a large proportion of the short time the soap was on the air and interrupted the structure and continuity of the story line, necessitating an extremely slow plot development and frequent repetition. On the whole they were a dull and inferior kind of drama, but as with mystery drama, also appearing early in radio's history, they made a contribution to the techniques and codes of radio drama. Their example was widely dispersed among the American population, and many people's earliest experience of drama came from the soaps.

While many continuity writers were involved in the writing of soaps, their creation and production was monopolised from the first by two agencies: one run by the team of Frank and Anne Hummert, the other headed by Irna Phillips. Frank Hummert was an advertising executive: Anne, a continuity writer for radio. The Hummerts created soap operas to fill the commercial daytime schedules of the major networks, and they achieved almost a monopoly in the form. They were very prolific because they ran the operation like a business: Frank ran the financial and administrative end, while Anne created ideas for new serials and story lines for their soaps' continuity, employing a large staff of writers to execute her ideas. Irna Phillips was a teacher who decided to get into radio writing. She did most of the writing of her serials, at least for the first part of her career; later she gave writers specific and detailed instructions on what and how to write in continuity. Unlike the Hummerts, Phillips wrote from personal experience and her work has a more authentic ring. This is, though, a relative evaluation. During the 1930s and early 1940s the Hummerts' soap-opera factory-machine and the work of Irna Phillips found great favour with sponsors and the general listening public, and their products dominated the daytime airwaves.

The first national network soaps were broadcast on NBC. *Clara, Lu 'n' Em* was first heard in 1931. It was the continuing story of three domestic gossips living in the same building, written by the three young women who played the roles; they had adapted the series from their live skits. The first efforts of the Hummerts, rising to meet this challenge, were *Judy and Jane* and *Betty and Bob* (the latter starring Don Ameche), which started (ominously) on the same day in October 1932. Judy was a beautiful housewife, while Betty was a beautiful secretary who marries the boss. *Clara, Lu 'n' Em* and *Judy and Jane* were each a series of self-contained episodes, more like *Vic and Sade* in structure, if more like soaps in themes and the level of the writing. *Betty and Bob*, on the other hand, was the first American soap opera in continuing-plot episodic form. The pattern was set for succeeding soaps, not least because the Hummerts' first efforts were trial balloons, and the widespread positive response to *Betty and Bob* led the Hummerts to clone a large number of similar soaps.

Irna Phillips weighed in over the NBC network in 1933 with a serial called *Today's Children*, a version of a successful serial she had created in 1930 for local radio (WGN, Chicago). This soap concerned a set of neighbours, centring on one family and its matriarch, Mother Moran, who was played by Miss Phillips herself. Her hand in the writing, her voice in the principal part, made the serial a much more personal vehicle, and the effect was more realistic and less clichéd than the Hummerts' efforts. Moreover, Phillips had invented, in Mother Moran, a figure and a dramatic situation that became very influential in succeeding soaps: that of the wise older figure whose counsel and support counterpoint the misadventures of less mature characters. This, in a word, was a didactic dramatic device essential to one of the soaps' major social functions: to offer advice and consolation to the 1930s housewife, a purpose that ranked highest in audience evaluations. What must be underlined is that this kind of function, which could very well have taken another form (and indeed did so in a small number of letter-answering advice programmes), leaped into most popularity in dramatic form and proliferated. It is yet another example of the natural movement of materials on radio into dramatic structures.

In 1933 came the first rapid expansion of soap-opera serials, mainly the efforts of the Hummerts. The new soaps included the first Hummert production for rival CBS: *Marie, the Little French Princess*, which concerned a princess, formerly wealthy, who must come to terms with life as an ordinary American woman. Contradicting the soaps' formula of a patina of ordinary middle-class reality, *Marie, the Little French Princess* lasted only two seasons. Two of the Hummerts' other 1933 productions, however, became perhaps the best-known and certainly the longest-running of the soaps: *The Romance of Helen Trent* and *Ma Perkins*. *Helen Trent* was more of a fantasy, the continuing story of a single woman of a certain age who has numerous romantic entanglements. *Ma Perkins* used the Phillips matriarch formula; the heroine of the title was the owner of a small-town sawmill and the confessor and support of her family and neighbours. It was the same formula as the Hummert night-time serial, *Just Plain Bill*, which had a male protagonist. It was a format ideally suited to the relatively unsophisticated 1930s, and when *Just Plain Bill* was moved to its proper daytime position late in 1933, it became the most successful of the Hummerts' soap-opera productions.

While the Hummerts continued to regularly create new soaps, none seem to have been quite so successful as the above three. It was, perhaps, that these serials came to fill a social vacuum, and once it was filled nothing could take their places. In 1935 their *Mary Noble* and *David Harum* appeared; in 1936 *John's Other Wife*; in 1937 *Our Gal Sunday* and *Lorenzo Jones*. 1938 brought the Hummerts' *Valiant Lady, Young Widder Brown* and *Stella Dallas*. The best-known and best-written of Irna Phillips' soaps, on the other hand, came in the latter half of the decade: *The Guiding Light* in 1937, her most mature and influential serial drama; *Woman in White* in 1938; and in 1939 *The Right to Happiness*. These all reflected the authentic pattern Phillips established in her first years of writing; she carefully wrote or planned them all herself, and she wrote them from life. Even so, they never achieved quite the level of literature.

Two other soap writers achieved more success of an artistic nature than the Hummerts or Phillips: Elaine Carrington and Sandra Michael. Elaine Carrington was an established fiction writer in the 1920s, whose short stories were published in the prestige magazines. She also wrote screenplays and had a play accepted on Broadway. Her background in drama and literature was obviously more extensive than those of her rivals. Her first contact with radio was a commission to do a radio script for NBC, and she produced an outline for a family drama. Called *Red Adams*, this was accepted as a sustaining series on night-time radio and first broadcast in October 1932. It took several years for the programme and its protagonist to change from light comedy to serious serial drama. By 1936 it had assumed its final form as the well-known *Pepper Young's Family*. In recognition of its family themes and serial format, it was moved to a daytime location.

Dunning speaks of the high quality of the writing, especially in its complex and well-developed characterisations.[25] *Pepper Young's Family* survived well past the end of American radio's Golden Age, until 1959. Of course, Carrington's creative energies were much more specifically directed than either of her major rivals, which helps explain the consistent quality of this serial. Carrington did attempt two other serials. In 1936 she wrote *Trouble House*, a three-times-a-week insert in *Heinz Magazine of the Air*. But the mixed format of *Heinz Magazine* doomed this serial within a year. In 1939 she attempted a new serial called *When a Girl Marries*, which became one of the most popular soaps, lasting until 1958. Carrington's third successful soap, *Rosemary*, premiered very late in the Golden Age, in 1944; it maintained the same high literary quality as her other soaps, lasting until 1955.

Perhaps the most interesting and creative work in the field of the soap serial was done by Sandra Michael, though, inevitably, it enjoyed the least commercial success. Michael's first series, *Against the Storm*, began in October 1939; its audience was quite different from the one addressed at the beginning of the decade by the first soaps. It was the moment when several years of preliminary political skirmishes had developed into outright war, though it was not to be America's own war in literal terms for two years. The major theme of *Against the Storm* was inevitably the war, a radical departure from the minor domestic themes and the fantasies of previous soaps. The title suggests Michael's position: the war, too, will pass, like a violent storm. Erik Barnouw dignifies *Against the Storm* as the only soap opera included in his anthology of the best serious radio drama, revealing that Michael was quite conscious of making use of the serial-soap form to create a radically innovative work, a 'radio novel', and of employing an uncharacteristically serious theme.[26] Michael herself explains: 'I wanted to write a story set in a contemporary world, related to the forces that were at work in the social, economic, and political phases of our lives.'[27] This heresy in the field of daytime soaps, a serious drama drawn from her own experience, was rendered even more unusual by her attempt to develop her characters in a novelistic way. The literary qualities of this series were rewarded by a Peabody Award in 1942, one of radio's highest awards, granted for the first time to a daytime soap. It was cancelled by the sponsor only two months later. It is useful to speculate why audience ratings and sponsor appreciation for this quality serial were so low. Of course it didn't follow the soaps' formula. Perhaps, also, it moved too far from its dramatic base, as a 'radio *novel*'. But more than anything else, *Against the Storm* was a casualty of the commercial control of American radio. Michael resuscitated the academic-philosopher protagonist of her serial for another soap, *The Open Door*, which began in 1943; she proceeded with the same methods and the same lovingly built characterisations as in her previous serial. *The Open Door* lasted just one year. Michael's only other soap-opera effort of the 1940s, *Lone Journey*, was drawn from real events in the Montana ranch country, which she knew well. The distinction of her writing was clear in this work. It ran for three years in the early 1940s and was twice revived, in 1946 and in 1951-2. Her achievements in this form stand quite alone.

When transmuted to radio in the soap opera, the novel form, with its amplitude, creates some impressive *literary* possibilities, but is not perhaps the most fruitful form of *dramatic structure* in the radio medium. Nevertheless, the radio soaps were quantitatively the most pervasive form of radio drama in the 1930s and early 1940s. By the 1940s there were over thirty soap serials on the air daily, from mid-morning to late afternoon.[28] If not in structure, then in individual techniques and codes, the soaps were an important instrument of experiment and education in radio-drama communication.

Some minor forms

Several minor subgenres of radio drama should be mentioned for their own intrinsic interest and as a further illustration of how radio, importing materials from other media, changed them inevitably into dramatic form. These minor forms – in popularity and quantity – were the comic-strip serial, the film adaptation, and the dramatic documentary. Comic-strip serials show the movement, moreover, from the eighteenth-century medium of the cartoon to radio. Modern comic strips, a visual offshoot of pulp adventure stories, became popular in the US in the 1920s. At one time or another almost all of the well-known comic-strip heroes made their way into radio serials. The earliest and one of the most popular of the comic-strip protagonists to make the move was *Little Orphan Annie*, in 1931. The first of the comic-strip *heroes* in radio was *Buck Rogers* (1932). *Popeye* and *Dick Tracy* made it in 1935, while *Superman* became audible very soon after his creation, in 1938. It is significant that the comics making the transition to radio for junior audiences were those most closely fitting the radio-drama categories evolving in the 1930s. *Little Orphan Annie* has the closest affinities to soap opera, while *Buck Rogers*, *Dick Tracy* and *Popeye* are juvenile mystery-adventure series. *Superman*, of course, epitomises the last category: he is the superhero of mysterious birth and identity. *The Lone Ranger* had his roots specifically in the typical American folk hero of pulp fiction, the cowboy. The sociological and educative influence of the comic-strip serials is a study in itself; it is necessary at least to underline the effects of their popularity among young people in the area of radio drama. As seen above, the comic-strip serials were introductions to mature radio drama, means by which children and adolescents could learn the styles, structures and communication codes most useful to grasping adult forms of radio drama. Finally, as with mystery-adventure series, comic-strip series were convenient testing grounds of a pure and simple form for experiments in the medium.

Dramatic adaptations from film and fiction were a continuing activity in radio drama. In the case of fiction, the transfer to the dramatic medium involved major reconstructions from the narrative form. The transitions were by no means so extreme in the transfer of film features to radio, mainly because films were already cast in dramatic form; and film was an artificial, manipulated medium, like radio. Radio has, if anything, even more flexibility than film and can easily accommodate such film techniques as *montage*, panning and instant movement from scene to scene. Nevertheless, though *Lux Radio Theatre* was one of the most popular of radio shows, it had few imitators, and the film-to-radio dramatic form was a minor one in radio drama. *Lux Radio Theatre* premiered in October 1934 with a series of adaptations from Broadway plays. After a year, *Lux* adopted the format in which it would continue for twenty years: the Hollywood film adaptation. As Cecil B. DeMille ran it, *Lux Radio Theatre* often became an oral version of the kind of expensive extravaganza for which his films have become famous. At their best, the productions were sensitive translations from film to the radio medium, inventing new radio codes and techniques, especially, in DeMille's hands, the techniques of communicating action that had been visually conceived in its original form.

The third of the minor forms, drama-documentary, had very little vogue in American radio under that title until the war. Max Wylie calls it the 'nursling' of American radio, until the documentary series *Ecce Homo* produced in 1938 – for the BBC![29] However, there were several programmes dating from the early 1930s, notably *The March of Time*, that were in effect documentary in content. This form illustrates how radio, importing news materials from other media, transforms them into drama. *The March of Time*, which began in 1931, was an extremely popular series created weekly by the reporting staff of the Time-Life magazine organisation with the help of radio-continuity writers to cast the stories in dramatic form. Theoretically the whole venture was highly unlikely; actors were employed who could reproduce the voices of Hitler and Stalin, Chamberlain and King George V and VI, and other famous people in the news. Nevertheless, the plays made a strong impression on the listening audience, because the immediacy of the dramatic form was both appropriate and compelling. *The March of Time* is the major example of how even the news story or essay (like the comic strip) on radio was most naturally cast as drama.

There is no doubt that *The March of Time* was innovative in radio-drama codes and techniques. William Spier, who was a director of this series in the 1930s, later became famous for his work in the mystery-adventure-series format. His work on *Suspense* between 1942 and 1948, on the Dashiell Hammett *Sam Spade* series in 1946, and on

The Philip Morris Playhouse in 1948-9 (among others) shows how much he learned on *The March of Time* – and he is only one of the directors and actors, like Orson Welles, to have gone to school in the early 1930s on this series. It is an example of the varied efforts made on American radio in the 1930s to develop the dramatic instruments of the medium in formats of many different kinds.

Serious radio drama

The context and conditions

Some essentials of the comparison between popular and serious American radio drama have already been mentioned. To summarise: the primary goal of serious radio drama was to create artefacts in a new art form, while the prime concerns of those involved in popular drama were commercial. Nevertheless, there were many mutual influences resulting from the newness of the medium, which meant in effect that pop and serious drama shared the new techniques being developed. Moreover, most of the writers, actors and directors worked of necessity in both streams, the art stream being so extremely limited in its work opportunities in the US.

It was argued that the structures, methods and communication codes developed in popular radio drama were a major influence on serious radio drama. It must also be underlined that the influence was mutual. The very few prestige drama series had an influence out of proportion to their numbers or those of their audiences, because they were primarily dedicated to aesthetic innovation and because the series they issued from were in the nature of anthologies. The individual serious dramas in such series were thus free of the restraints of the strict formulations of structure, characterisation and themes marking most popular drama series. Variety-comedy shows were not excluded, in a general way, from these restraints; while they were more flexible than mystery series or soap operas, each was free only within the broad definition of its format and characters. Indeed, both the NBC and CBS networks recognised the valuable innovative functions of serious radio drama and, almost from the beginning, encouraged the small bank of its practitioners by the creation of a few sustaining drama series free from commercial interference. The rewards were more than simply sustaining filler for their programme schedules and the public service and culture images they undoubtedly won. Since there was a clear consciousness that drama was what radio was all about, the advances in radio-drama techniques and codes engendered by these experimental programmes were immediately applicable (sometimes by the same people!) in commercial prog-rammes.

These contributions were necessary because of the great technical limitations hampering radio production in the early days. It is clear that American networks were behind both the British and the Canadians in this area in the 1930s. To be specific, the technical development of studios, microphones, broadcasting and reception equipment was still in a relatively primitive state even as late as the mid-1930s. Radio had not yet gone far beyond the 1920s conditions of studios made of drapery, uncontrolled direction in microphones, and reception by earphones. These problems were accentuated by the early lack of radio-trained actors; for, as directors soon discovered, stage or film actors were particularly unsuited to the intimate, sensitive and nuanced acting style necessary for subtle communication in radio drama. The technical development of equipment, studios, the mixing of sound, and improvements in receivers went hand-in-hand with developments in acting styles, writing for an aural medium, the creation of communication codes, and the techniques of musical backgrounds, bridges and sound effects. The speed with which these techniques were advanced in the 1930s, creating masterfully profes-sional technical and creative drama productions, is astounding. The contributions of popular radio drama to these developments were crucial, as we have seen. The contributions of serious radio drama, while fewer, were more pointed and selfconscious. Ultimately, moreover, these techniques in serious radio drama were in the service of more serious goals: more mature, more complex and more critical definitions of life in general and of American society, mainly lacking in pop radio drama.

One other technical point should be underlined regarding the creation of radio drama in general and serious radio drama especially: the methods of live production. While it is true that many radio productions in the later 1930s were recorded for later broadcast in western time zones, replacing repeated live broadcasts, it is necessary to remember that the recording was mainly done on discs, a method with almost no flexibility for editing. The form of production of radio broadcasts, radio drama included, was essentially live: that is, as with early television, the production was created on live mike at the time and in the time of the broadcast; there was no way to eradicate mistakes. The effect of this knowledge on all those creating a broadcast was very akin to that of a live stage performance: the same immediacy, the same tension, which in an artist is the stimulus to give his very best. And if the stimulus of a live audience was often missing, it was adequately replaced by the feeling engendered by the knowledge that millions of people listening on radio sets across the country were experiencing the performance. Taped recording, with its possibilities for editing and indeed for the scheduling of actors out of sequence (on the film model), became available only by the mid-1940s, too late to have any influence on the formative techniques of American radio drama.

It is already clear that, generally, the same people created popular radio drama as created serious drama in this medium. This is certainly true of the actors involved and mainly true of the directors and the writers. The exceptions in this group include a small band of director-producers, like Arch Oboler, Norman Corwin, Orson Welles, Vernon Radcliffe, Irving Reis and so on, who were dedicated to serious radio drama and who spent a relatively large part of their time working in this field. It will be seen how most of these, however, also paid their dues in commercial popular radio drama. As for the writers, many of the producers mentioned above, especially Reis, Oboler, Corwin and Welles, also wrote much of their own material, thus giving them an unusually comprehensive control over their productions by contrast with popular radio drama, with its on-staff directors and continuity writers and its commercial control. There was another group of writers, independent of the networks, who also made a contribution to serious radio drama: the novelists, poets and stage dramatists who were attracted to the new medium and who experimented with it. Among these, Archibald MacLeish's poetic dramas such as *Air Raid* and *The Fall of the City* stand out, but Edna St. Vincent Millay, Stephen Vincent Benét, William Saroyan, Dorothy Parker, Ambrose Bierce and Arthur Miller (among others) also created serious radio dramas of high quality and great originality. Miller, indeed, like some other dramatists of the 1940s and 1950s, began his career in radio as one of the continuity writers in the early historical-drama series, *Cavalcade of America*, in 1935. Also in this group were those, among the myriad freelance writers making their living from radio who were attracted at times by the aesthetic possibilities of radio drama, such as Milton Geiger. Free of the constraints of network employment and of predefined series formulas, a freelance writer could, on occasion, create an original radio play of serious theme and innovative technique. And these were the source of many radio dramas of significant artistic achievement.

If one asks what serious radio-drama series appeared on the radio schedules, the list is short. Foremost were the anthology series like the NBC *Radio Guild* and *Columbia Workshop*, the experimental showcases to which a number of writers and directors made original contributions. Then there were the series under the control of a single director, like Welles, Corwin, Oboler and Elliott Lewis, who often wrote his own material or at least had strict control over it: series like *Mercury Theatre, Arch Oboler's Plays* or *Columbia Presents Corwin*. There were also the series of dramatic adaptations from serious literature, fictional or dramatic, the translation from which into drama involved much original creation. The term 'serious radio drama' is nevertheless blurred in this case. Finally, there was the show that included as a regular feature a dramatic sketch of about ten minutes, the sketch frequently being an original creation by a freelance writer. More than thirty important weekly radio series were using such sketches by the end of the 1930s, and they were an important market for original dramatic material.[30] Unfortunately, because of their nature and their position on programmes whose major focus was not dramatic, very little remains either of the scripts or of commentary on them.

Early radio drama and the major series

The first known serious dramatic work on radio was an adaptation of a full-length stage melodrama, *The Wolf*. It was broadcast in August 1922 over WGY, Schenectady, and gave rise the next month to a regular (but nameless) weekly drama series, frequently making use of adaptations from Broadway plays. The next year a similar series of adaptations called *Eveready Hour* began on WEAF.[31] By that time, however, WGY, on a new tack, was offering prizes for original radio scripts.[32] To understand why neither serious nor popular radio drama really burgeoned until the end of the 1920s, however, one must remember that radio as a commercial medium did not mature until the commercial structures of network broadcasting, sponsorship, advertising and production agencies, as well as radio manufacturing and audience-rating assessments, were smoothly interacting. These developments did not take place until the beginning of the 1930s. The 1920s were marked by isolated experiments in radio drama and the very occasional episodic drama series, such as *The House of Firestone* and *Real Folks* (1928).

NBC's first attempt at serious radio drama was the famous *Radio Guild* which began on the air in 1929 and was directed by Vernon Radcliffe throughout its ten-year run. It was a sustaining series, genuinely experimental and of ambitious full-hour length. Radcliffe quickly abandoned the Broadway actors he had first used in favour of fresh new acting talent which could be trained in the radio medium. The experiments were mainly in the area of technique and presentation, for *Radio Guild* usually presented adaptations of modern and classical stage plays from Galsworthy through Shakespeare to Greek tragedy. Radcliffe was very much aware of the limitations and flexibilities of the radio medium and of its aural modes of communication. While the *Radio Guild* series seemed old-fashioned even five years after its inception, it was the first serious radio-drama series in America, and its technical developments were seminal for succeeding series. It lasted until 1940. An extension of the *Radio Guild* series (educational, in effect) called *Great Plays*, using the same format and many of the same plays, was based on the idea of preparing study guides in advance of the actual broadcasts. *Great Plays* premiered in October 1937 and was directed by Charles Warburton. It survived for several seasons.

In 1932 CBS weighed into the serious drama stakes with a drama series based on American history called *Roses and Drums*, directed by Herschel Williams. All the scripts were original and historically accurate to boot. The major interest in the series as experimental drama lies in these scripts, for the actors used were all from Broadway or Hollywood. By 1934 *Roses and Drums* had earned a sponsor, and its scripts began to concentrate on the Civil War. It closed in 1936, only a few months before CBS inaugurated its famous sustaining radio-drama series, *Columbia Workshop*.

Columbia Workshop, beginning in July 1936, was perhaps the most influential of the serious radio-drama series of the 1930s. It was strictly an anthology series, with not only original scripts written especially for the radio medium, but radio actors and experimental production methods, in a full-hour format. It pioneered the latest of technical advances, especially under its founding director, Irving Reis, an engineer as well as a playwright. Reis, says Dunning, 'was given a free hand, lots of cheap talent, and a "laboratory" for use in developing new sound techniques'.[33] In the first year, Reis invited Val Gielgud, the best-known BBC drama producer, to direct a play and to demonstrate the use of the directional parabolic microphone. The characteristic style and sound of *Columbia Workshop* productions was quite unique, replacing traditional dramatic values by aural radio ones. Reis opened the series with a play he himself wrote for radio, *Meridian 7-1212*. In this suspense drama the radio techniques went behind the mechanical illusions of realistic sound to show a real understanding of the *space* of the medium, especially the necessity of creating verbal and intellectual complications to replace the visual complexities of the theatre.

The *Columbia Workshop* series achieved broad popularity the next year with the broadcast in April 1937 of Archibald MacLeish's *The Fall of the City*. This poetic drama lacked much of the dramatic tension of Reis's own radio play. It developed more as a long narrative poem with voices, and its interest was mainly in its beautiful poetry, in its mature and timely subject (the approaching war), and in the excellent production. MacLeish's similar drama, *Air Raid*, followed the next year. It was between the poles of Reis's dramatic and MacLeish's poetic work that the major experiments in radio drama were to take place in the next decade. In MacLeish's footsteps followed a number of well-known writers: William Saroyan, Dorothy Parker, Lord Dunsany and especially Stephen Vincent Benét. In Reis's path (by 1937 his protégé William N. Robson had taken over the productions) came a number of original radio writers, including Corwin, Oboler and Welles. The plays produced were a mix of original plays in both the literary and radio-dramatic styles mentioned above, adaptations from the modern theatre and from classical and modern fiction, and of course Shakespeare and the classics of the theatre.

The Second World War closed down *Columbia Workshop* in 1941, as it shut down many another radio show. The series was revived in 1946, but the age of television triumphed quite early in this case; it survived for only one season. A revival in 1956, under the title *CBS*

Radio Workshop, was a nostalgic attempt for a season at prestige radio drama in the very last days of network radio. The co-operation of the best of the early radio professionals ensured that high quality and exciting drama were produced in this revival. The sound records from this period confirm these qualities, for example in the adaptation of Aldous Huxley's *Brave New World*, the original radio musical drama *Jimmy Blue Eyes*, and the thriller *Nightmare*, written and directed by, as well as starring, Elliott Lewis. But the new *Radio Workshop*, was really out of its time in the second decade of the television era, and it closed after twenty months.

Another CBS prestige drama series appeared first in October 1937 as *Sunday Afternoon Theatre* but, soon gaining the sponsorship of International Silver, it became better known as *Silver Theatre*. Produced in Hollywood, the weekly programmes were half-an-hour in length, but the series accommodated longer dramas (almost half of all programmes) by producing them as episodes on succeeding weekly broadcasts for as many as four weeks. The host and director until 1942 was Conrad Nagel, a film star with silent movie experience, and many movie actors played roles. The scripts, including heavy drama and comedy, are described by Max Wylie as all 'original material specifically written for the program. Story ideas are purchased from both motion picture and radio writers and then adapted for the show.'[34] All the script 'adaptations' were done by the staff writer, True Boardman, who also wrote original scripts of his own for the series. It was Boardman who elevated *Silver Theatre* from the level of the usual sponsored popular drama series to the achievement of serious radio drama. One of the radio-drama devices he perfected on the series was that of *montage*, a kind of overlay or rapid movement from scene to scene only possible in the flexible radio medium. It is a technique very useful to radio dramatists and became typical of the experimental productions of American and Canadian serious radio drama. Between 1942 and 1945 Nagel was replaced by John Loder, but Nagel was directing the series again as a summer replacement by the time it folded in 1946.

The major directors: Corwin, Oboler, Welles

The second generation of serious radio drama is dominated by the figures of three directors: Norman Corwin, Arch Oboler and Orson Welles. Each of them in his own way made an original contribution to radio drama, and each demonstrated the major effects achievable by control over the various script and production aspects of a series. Finally, each left an indelible stamp on American radio drama.

Norman Corwin came to radio from newspaper work. His first radio assignment was as a newscaster and news commentator. Signed up by CBS as a staff writer in 1938, he first began directing some existing drama series, such as *Living History, Americans at Work* and *County*

Seat, a daily serial written by the innovative freelance, Milton Geiger. Before the year was out, Corwin had been given his own series, *Words Without Music*, combining some of his own original scripts with his adaptations of modern American classics, mainly poetry; these included Whitman's *Leaves of Grass*, Edgar Lee Masters's *Spoon River Anthology* and Carl Sandburg's *The People, Yes*. Erik Barnouw is speaking of this series when he describes Corwin's 'radio arrangements of poems':

The method varied according to the poem. It made use of any devices that would heighten the effect of a poem: sound effects, music, dramatization, choral speech, and even silence. The choral speech . . . was so successful with listeners that before long producers of dramatized commercials began to use Corwin's choral speech group for spot announcements.[35]

Words Without Music lasted for a year. Its directions were picked up by Corwin a few months afterwards in his new series, *Pursuit of Happiness*, which continued through the 1939-40 season. Corwin added a new concept to the *Pursuit of Happiness* series, a radio musical-documentary-drama form or 'radio opera'. One of these operas, *Ballad for Americans*, was an influential model for other such pieces, for example the Maxwell Anderson–Kurt Weill ballad opera *Magna Charta*, which Corwin directed on this series.

Corwin's characteristic writing style was in general fast-paced with punchy narration and extravagant, sometimes poetic language. His instinctive grasp of the radio medium made him a master of the production techniques of radio drama.[36] Joseph Julian, an experienced and well-known radio actor-writer who worked with him, says that 'no one stretched radio's horizons as did Norman Corwin'; and Julian goes on to describe not only Corwin's experiments with the medium, but his poetic love of words, his ability to create an amazing variety of exciting scripts, and his genius at extracting the perfomances he wanted from his actors and his equipment.[37] The success of Corwin's *Pursuit of Happiness* led CBS to give him free rein to follow his creative and technical experiments. He was one of only two people offered the chance at his own subseries on *Columbia Workshop* (the other was Orson Welles); called *Twenty-Six by Corwin*, it played in the 1941 season. These experiments were extended in the occasional pieces he did during the war, especially *We Hold These Truths* (1941), a musical documentary on the Bill of Rights in the series *The Free Company*; *On a Note of Triumph* (V-E Day 1945); *14 August*, for the Japanese surrender in August 1945; and the famous fantasy *The Undecided Molecule* (July 1945).

As seen above, during the war Corwin often took on the necessary task of documentary and propaganda, which was the fate generally of the radio industry during these years. The first war series Corwin produced was *This Is War*, in the summer of 1942. In that same summer Corwin flew to London to script and direct a series at the

BBC, *American in England*, the purpose of which was to inform Americans at first hand about the war. The next year he produced *Passport for Adams*, an episodic serial starring Robert Young as a newspaper editor visiting various countries in wartime. By March 1944 Corwin was taking a breather from his war work with a new series of experimental sustaining dramas; called *Columbia Presents Corwin*, it was perhaps the most imaginative and impressive work he had ever done. Corwin wrote most of the plays himself and directed them all. The series displayed an amazing variety of original ideas. The opener, *Movie Primer*, was a satire on the cinema. The famous fantasy, *The Odyssey of Runyon Jones*, tells the story of a child's visit to Heaven and other archetypal locations in search of his pet dog; it is a masterpiece of naturalistic dialogue in a fantasy setting, for which Corwin's imaginative grasp of the techniques of the radio medium is stretched to the limit. His treatment of the journey of the dead body of the assassinated Lincoln, *The Lonesome Train*, is also deservedly renowned.

The experience Corwin gleaned doing occasional pieces and war dramas during the early 1940s was useful when in 1947 he created a documentary series, *One World Flight*, based on a voyage around the world he had made the previous year, taping impressions and interviews. And in 1950 Corwin wrote and directed a documentary plea for an international Bill of Rights, *Document A/777*, for the United Nations. This was almost a last extravaganza for Corwin, starring an international cast of cinema, stage and radio stars. Network radio, in the form it had previously taken, had by then all but disappeared in the face of television.

What Norman Corwin was to CBS in the late 1930s and the 1940s, Arch Oboler was to NBC. Like Corwin, Oboler eventually controlled the major creative aspects of his own series, writing, producing and directing. And Oboler's work was in its own fashion as innovative as Corwin's; some say that their declamatory styles, verbal fireworks, realistic sound effects, unusual formats and overall control of the medium were very similar. It is hard to decide which way the influence went between them, since their careers were almost contemporary in time: Corwin's use of poetry and music is distinctive, as is Oboler's stream-of-consciousness technique. Oboler communicates in his scripts the sense of excitement and the struggle that characterised the adventure of radio in the late 1930s. As he stated to me in an interview in Hollywood in May 1978, everything had to be invented in this new medium whose communicative codes were just then becoming sophisticated enough for experiments with serious meaning.

Arch Oboler was a precocious writer, selling his first script to NBC while he was still in school in Chicago. It is significant that Oboler's writing was well grounded in the popular drama forms described above. His first network employment was as a continuity writer for two popular shows: *Grand Hotel*, an adventure series, and the long-running variety programme, *The Rudy Vallee Show*, a showcase for new radio talents, many of whom later became well known, like Eddie Cantor, Frances Langford, Bea Lillie, Milton Berle and Edgar Bergen. Oboler's experiences with these series were significant influences on his developing radio-drama techniques. His obvious talents led NBC in 1936 to put him in charge of the writing and direction of a popular horror-adventure series called *Lights Out*, when its founder, Wyllis Cooper, went to Hollywood. For two years *Lights Out* provided a flexible medium for Oboler's first innovative experiments with radio drama. By 1938 the series had made his reputation. That year he had the opportunity to further refine his techniques in the popular drama form with the romantic drama series *Curtain Time*, for which he helped adapt plays from the legitimate stage.

Oboler got his first chance at serious radio drama in 1939, a series called *Arch Oboler's Plays*. It was a sustaining series in direct competition with *Columbia Workshop* and Orson Welles's *Mercury Theatre*. *Arch Oboler's Plays*, written, cast and directed by Oboler, was heard for a year on NBC, offering tragedy, romance, fantasy and horror dramas in the mature Oboler style. One of the best programmes was the dramatised story of Tchaikovsky's long-distance love affair with a Russian noblewoman, a play called *This Lonely Heart*. Oboler's characteristically sparse, tight dialogue, with a minimum of narration and with information given in stream-of-consciousness form, was complemented by the use of music (Tchaikovsky's of course) for bridging and mood, and diversified by rapid but realistic *montage* cuts both in time and in place, possible in the radio-drama medium but not in the theatre. The same technique was successfully realised in other plays in this series, especially *Ivory Tower*.[38]

The first series of *Arch Oboler's Plays* ended in March 1940, and that October Oboler turned to a sponsored series, more popular in form, called *Everyman's Theatre*. It was a familiar mixture of original Oboler dramas and adaptations, using some of the scripts from earlier series, including *This Lonely Heart*, and *Cat Wife* from *Lights Out*. The second play in the *Everyman's Theatre* series was, however, already pointing the direction Oboler, in company with the other radio talents, was travelling: to war and war writing. The play was called *This Precious Freedom* and was a fantasy of the future, making a sharp attack on Nazism. At that moment, still poised on the brink of war, Oboler's sponsor could afford to be upset by the content of the play. By the spring of 1941, however, when *Everyman's Theatre* closed, the gears of the American government were beginning to grind out a plethora of war series.

Oboler's contributions to this propaganda element of the 'defense effort' included *Plays for Americans* in early 1942, *To the President* at the end of that year, *Free World Theatre* early in 1943, and a play in

Four for the Fifth in 1944. The plays in these series hold no surprises; we are no longer in the realm of fantasy but rather in the realm of simple social and political realism. *Letter at Midnight*, from *Plays for Americans*, is a monologue in the form of a last letter from a dead soldier. *Hate*, from the same series, is a play about a Norwegian pastor whose response to an occupying German officer's betrayal of his confidence, leading to the deaths of some of his congregation, is to strangle the officer responsible – on the air. *The Special Day*, from *To the President*, is measurably superior, a play about the last 'ordinary' day in the life of a young family; the husband is about to leave for the Front. One sees the typical Oboler stream-of-consciousness technique and a solid development of complication and information; but there is a narrator doing the bridges and moralising, and the speeches of the characters are often simple, flat and didactic. Oboler describes his *Surrender*, for *Four for the Fifth*, as 'a play which would indicate, through an emotional drama, the terrible warping of the German military mind and the dangers of conditional surrender'.[39] The play is a slightly melodramatic story of the betrayal of an American soldier by a seemingly friendly German soldier, who, it turns out, is power-mad. Oboler was involved in a second series of *Lights Out* in 1942-3 and revived *Arch Oboler's Plays* in April 1945, but the play he most wishes to remember from that series, *The House I Live In*, is an editorial about war itself.

I describe these plays at some length partly in order to make a more general point about the fate of American radio drama. In fact, the majority of radio writers were engaged in this war writing, which was organised not only by the networks but by many different branches of government, the Armed Forces, the major unions, the entertainment industry, and committees such as the Council for Democracy. The products of these efforts blanketed American civilian and armed-forces networks across the world. While it went on, any real experimentation or even subtlety of technique, expression or theme seems to have dried up. Neither Oboler nor any other major radio writer ever really recovered from the war. By the time the war was over, television, whose further development had been awaiting the end of the war, was beginning to overtake its senior sister and was capturing its sponsors and its markets – the days of serious radio drama were numbered. As it turned out, almost none of the radio writers made a successful transition to television, because of the radically different structures and techniques of the visual medium.[40] The writing careers of such men as Oboler and Corwin were virtually halted in 1946; and halted with them was the development of the radio-drama medium after only two short decades. It is useless to speculate on what might have occurred if the war had not intervened. Most probably television, which had been broadcasting experimentally since the mid-1930s, would simply have come several years earlier.

Orson Welles, born in 1915, began his career in drama in his teens, unlike Corwin and Oboler, who had no legitimate stage experience. He was an *enfant terrible* of drama from the early 1930s while he was learning about radio drama in a number of shows. He rose to virtual stardom by 1939 with *Mercury Theatre*, both on the stage and in radio drama. And he went on to other things, notably films, at about the time (1941) Corwin and Oboler were beginning to write war series. His unique stage experience notwithstanding, Welles was not an original creator of radio scripts like Corwin and Oboler. On the other hand, Welles was the first to adapt the repertory system to serious radio drama. And he was the first (if only a few months ahead of Corwin in 1938) to control all aspects of script and production – to which he added the primary acting roles. He thus centralised the creative power of a dramatic production in a single innovative mind, in a way not seen in the theatre for centuries – though, as we have seen, there were prominent models in popular radio of the 1930s, notably Fred Allen and some of the other stars of variety comedy. Finally, Welles proved in a startling way the power of radio to move the mass of men.

Welles's first contact with professional drama was in Dublin in 1931, where at the age of sixteen he got himself a role in a Gate Theatre production. Back in New York in 1934, he was part of the Broadway production of *Romeo and Juliet* starring Katharine Cornell. Welles was then asked to play the lead in a new play by Archibald MacLeish, *Panic*. In 1935 Welles got his first radio experience, on the *March of Time* series. The documentary techniques of the news dramas featured on this series were to prove a useful experience when Welles produced *The War of the Worlds*. In 1936 Welles and a colleague, John Houseman, took over a Negro unit of the WPA Federal Theatre Project and produced a number of plays including *Macbeth*, *Dr Faustus* and modern dramas. The last of these, Marc Blitzstein's *The Cradle Will Rock*, banned by the WPA, was put on privately by the repertory company Welles first organised at that time. In 1937 Welles and Houseman (who took the administrative responsibilities) rented the Comedy Theatre in New York, renamed it the Mercury, and took the name for their repertory group, the Mercury Players. In November they began the series of stage productions that was to bring Welles rapid fame. The plays included *Julius Caesar*, Shaw's *Heartbreak House*, Dekker's *Shoemaker's Holiday*, and Büchner's *Danton's Death*.

Meanwhile, Welles continued his career as an actor in radio drama. Earlier in 1937 he had taken on the leading role in *The Shadow* (as mentioned above), the mystery series noted for its innovative techniques and its timing. Agnes Moorehead, one of the Mercury Players' female leads, played opposite Welles's Shadow as Margo Lane. Welles also took parts in the historical docudrama series, *Cavalcade of America*, and in the CBS *Shakespeare* series that summer. He also worked for *Columbia Workshop*, where he made a deep impression. And that summer as well, four months before the first Mercury stage production, Welles was invited to lead the Mercury Players in the production of a seven-part radio-serial version of Hugo's *Les Misérables* for the Mutual Broadcasting Company.

Welles's reputation and that of the Mercury Players led CBS to offer him an hour-long weekly sustaining series. *Mercury Theatre on the Air* began in July 1938, just a few months before CBS offered Norman Corwin *his* own vehicle, *Words Without Music*. The competition between CBS and NBC in prestige drama was heating up as executives realised that such programmes could attract audiences; CBS had first challenged NBC's traditional *Radio Guild* with *Columbia Workshop* in 1936. NBC countered in 1937 with a *Shakespeare* series, and CBS replied by creating one of its own – Welles himself worked on the CBS version of Shakespeare, as mentioned above. Seen from the point of view of the CBS administration, *Mercury Theatre* and *Words Without Music* were double-barrelled shots in the fight for audiences. For serious radio drama, the fates had provided an unexcelled opportunity for experiment and achievement. Though Welles and Agnes Moorehead were, significantly, to continue in their roles in *The Shadow* for some months, *Mercury Theatre on the Air* plunged into enthusiastic and imaginative productions that summer. These were always under Welles's comprehensive artistic control, from the casting of the repertory company, through the choices and editing of scripts, to the organisation and direction of the broadcasts. And Welles played host and the lead roles as well. Moreover, many of the broadcasts had a live production before an audience on the stage of the Mercury Theatre, challenging Welles's capacities in *both* dramatic media. The first season (that summer) included innovative radio adaptations of classical works, mainly fiction, from Shakespeare to Sherlock Holmes. And despite its mediocre ratings, *Mercury Theatre* went regular that autumn. Everything Welles touched was transformed by his imagination and instinct for the medium. The productions had fast pacing, a sense of intimacy, and a mastery of the radio medium which Welles could only have learned during his work in popular radio drama. *Mercury Theatre* went on until the Autumn of 1939, when the series attracted a sponsor, Campbell Soups, and became known as *Campbell Playhouse*. The format of adaptations of famous works was continued, though more modern classics began to appear: Hemingway, Sinclair Lewis, even Dashiell Hammett. *Campbell Playhouse* closed in September 1940.

Welles revived the format again in a half-hour series, *The Orson Welles Theatre*, between 1941 and 1943. In September 1944 Welles was invited to become the acting star of an anthology series, *This Is My Best*, along with Mercury regular Agnes Moorehead. By early 1945 Welles had taken over the direction and hosting of the show as well. The scripts were in the familiar Mercury pattern: adaptations from the classics and from contemporary literature. The series continued until

May of that year. The Mercury Players were last heard on the air in a summer season in 1946. Meanwhile, of course, Welles had led them into the cinema. It was the Mercury Theatre repertory company – Agnes Moorehead, Joseph Cotton, *et al* – that Welles used in his 1940s films, beginning with *Citizen Kane* in 1941. And the influences on Welles's film work of his radio-drama techniques have not gone unnoticed.[41] Welles's last work for radio was a return to popular drama: the *Third Man* series (1950) and the thriller series *The Black Museum* (1952).

The Welles formula of dramatic adaptations was considered as experimental as the original radio scripts of Corwin, Oboler and *Columbia Workshop*. The best illustration of the reason for this assessment is Welles's treatment of H.G. Wells's science-fiction classic, *The War of the Worlds*. It was produced on *Mercury Theatre* on Halloween Eve 1938 and became the most famous, or notorious, radio drama ever broadcast. The first script for the programme was prepared by Howard Koch in close consultation with Welles, and, typical of the exigencies of translating a fiction into the dramatic medium, it bore little relation to the original novel. Then Welles and the Mercury cast took over, filling in the dramatic values by clever changes in dialogue, and adding the radio values by the addition of sound effects and music, *montage* and so on.[42] The goal, in the American tradition of radio drama, was to create for the ear as convincingly as possible an effect of realistic scene, character and plot. The methods were a variation of documentary drama (made famous on *The March of Time*) blended with actuality news reporting, as recently experienced by the American radio audience in the eyewitness report of the Hindenburg zeppelin disaster in New Jersey (transcripts of which were used as the basis for parts of the *War of the Worlds* script).

The effects of this programme, as we know, far surpassed Welles's wildest expectations. The widespread panic caused by this broadcast has been widely discussed and analysed. The explanations have varied, but most centre on the political and social situation in the days of the 'phoney war', especially the Czechoslovak crisis only five weeks earlier, which saw Chamberlain flying to Germany to negotiate 'peace' with Hitler. But it seems to me that these explanations put the cart before the horse. The real question must be: what particularly could have stimulated the fears of millions of people, forcing them to identify the programme with their political and military concerns, to produce mass hysteria? The answer must reside in the nature of the radio-drama broadcast – not simply in its realistic reproduction of life but, more important, in the convincing excellence of its combination of psychological, literary, dramatic and radio techniques. It is significant that *in no other genre* – not electronic, print or film – could such a set of fictional events have had such an extreme effect. It is specific evidence of the power of radio drama by the end of the 1930s to communicate, convince and move; it is evidence of the maturity of the medium and its dramatic form. It is also evidence of Welles's mastery of this medium and of his originality, despite the fact that his scripts were based on adaptations; as with all drama, much of the creative input is in the final script and in the production. Welles's originality is in his control over all aspects of the radio production, creating in the broadcast a new and unique artefact.

Behind the activities of the prestige radio-drama series, especially *Radio Guild* and *Columbia Workshop*, behind the work of the major radio-drama producers, especially Corwin, Oboler and Welles, are the activities of hundreds of freelance writers of radio drama. We have no records of these, though they made a valuable contribution to serious radio drama. And even if the information were available, the challenge of summarising a mass of information of such quantity and complexity would be too great. The careers and achievements of the three dominant creators of serious radio drama epitomise and summarise the history of and work in this field, up to the coming of television, better than any other method I can devise.

Last generation: Elliott Lewis, and recent developments

Elliott Lewis's career did not begin in earnest until the twilight of the Golden Age of American radio drama. He began (with one exception) as a producer and actor for wartime Armed Services Radio. By the time his work in postwar radio drama commenced, television had already begun to eat away at the audiences and the budgets of American radio. His work is in three phases: first, the journeyman acting roles, mainly in popular radio drama; then, his work as a director and writer, until the mid-1950s, the ultimate edge of old-time radio; finally, a new career in the 1970s, once again creating original radio drama, though in an industry far different from radio in the American Golden Age.

As a radio actor, Lewis worked in pretty nearly every one of the subgenres of popular radio drama: a situation-comedy series, *This Is Judy Jones* (1941); a suspense series, *I Love a Mystery* (1944); a western, *Hawk Larabee* (1946); an adventure series, *The Voyage of the Scarlet Queen* (1947-8); a detective series, *The Casebook of Gregory Hood* (1948); and a typical variety-comedy series, *The Phil Harris–Alice Faye Show*, from 1946 to 1954. He also directed a number of series, again mainly popular radio drama: *Pursuit*, a mystery series (1949-50 and 1951-2); *Broadway Is My Beat*, a detective series (1949-53); a long sequence of the prestige anthology, *Suspense* (1950-4); *Crime Classics* (starting 1953); and finally his own serious radio series, *On Stage*, in 1953-4. Lewis's work directing the *Suspense* series was the first to really illuminate his unusual talents. Dunning speaks of it as the most distinctive work of the several well-known directors who did the programme, not excepting the excellent William Spier, who made his name in the show.[43] Lewis acted in many of his own *Suspense* productions. He also began to create his own scripts for the series, some originals, some classics like Shakespeare, some adaptations from moderns and contemporaries. The casts he gathered for the productions included many of those who had created the techniques for the radio-drama mode, like Jack Benny and Red Skelton; and he used them in serious roles, a concept that was extended to his production of *Othello*.

The series that gave Lewis the most scope for his creative talents was *On Stage*, a serious drama anthology. He exercised in this series the kinds of creative control used by Corwin, Oboler and Welles, and in some ways his influence on his productions, from scripting and casting through direction and acting, was the most extensive of all. *On Stage* was broadcast for two seasons; its plays included the adventure and romance forms with which Lewis had trained, adaptations from the classics, and original scripts on modern themes, many of these experimental, by well-known radio writers. It was the last serious radio-drama series in this phase of radio's history except for the *CBS Radio Workshop* revival.

Though Elliott Lewis's impressive work is in the great tradition of the major figures of American radio drama discussed above, it has had the least impact of any of them, certainly much less than it deserves, because it appeared at the end of radio's Golden Age, well into the age of television. His work serves as a valuable recapitulation of the sources of American serious radio drama in popular radio drama, and it is a further illustration of the possibilities of this form as a high art when practiced by a person of dominant will, imagination and talent, one who controls all the creative aspects of his productions and who has a sensitive awareness of the possibilities of the form and of the medium in general.

None of the above should be an invitation to count Lewis – or American radio drama – out. For, after the great creative surge of television drama (an activity in which few of the radio-drama practitioners joined); after the disappointing end to the group of impressive television-drama anthologies in the early 1960s, to be replaced by the dominance of television's version of popular drama, mainly mystery series strongly marked by gratuitous violence; after the disappearance of the commercial-network system itself in radio; after the decision in 1960 by CBS to cease producing drama on radio; after a silence, to say the least, Elliott Lewis's work appeared again on radio in 1973, in the form of the suspense series called *The Zero Hour*. It was, in fact, the first new series created to respond to the nostalgia now developing around old-time radio.

It is clear that in the intervening years radio has undergone some basic changes. First, the effective end of network organisation allowed for the proliferation of large numbers of local stations with quite particular audiences. The growth of music programming was aided by the move to high-fidelity frequency modulation, and many mainly-music stations became FM. For a time, then, the whole cultural-social-commercial nexus of radio broke down, and radio underwent a change not only in quantity and quality but in function and kind. But several factors have come into play on the other side: first, the growth in the 1970s of the American nostalgia-kick mentioned above, seen in the last few years in styles of clothing and décor and in television and films. Radio, as the instrument and record of so much of the American culture of the decades since the start of the 1930s, has shared largely in this impulse to nostalgia, with the return to the air in the 1970s of transcripts of some of the most popular radio programmes of the past, especially variety-comedy shows and mystery series. Available on records, they can be aired on individual stations at will. Unfortunately, records of vintage serious drama (with the exception of *The War of the Worlds*) are not equally available.

Meanwhile, the agencies who spend the sponsors' money have recently begun to take note of the fact that radio's audiences, while much shrunken, are still of a respectable size: enough to be able to sell time on individual stations and to begin to resuscitate the networks. Some of the exposure to the variety of vintage radio has made audiences restless with an unadulterated diet of music and news, and there is a new market for imaginative and entertaining programming, which, on radio, still means drama. Thus from two directions, audience interest and sponsor interest, there is an impetus for new radio drama.

As I have said, one of the first responses to this interest was Lewis's *The Zero Hour*. This is not to blow up the phenomenon out of proportion. The current activity in radio drama is minute by comparison with its heyday when radio was our primary cultural and entertainment medium; but some concrete activities are taking place that promise to revive radio drama as an art. Another example is that of Fletcher Markle, former CBC-Drama writing and acting whiz-kid, who has worked out of Los Angeles for many years in the entertainment industry (with the exception of his time in Toronto as Head of CBC TV Drama). In 1978 Markle was invited to create a series of radio dramas on American National (Public) Radio. Called *Earplay*, it uses some vintage scripts, popular and serious, and some of Markle's new adaptations. It is mainly light, technically excellent, and makes use of a number of the old-time radio-drama professionals who are still around Hollywood. When I visited him in 1978, Arch Oboler himself was considering a contribution. Again, Himan Brown, another vintage American radio producer, was invited by CBS in 1978 to do a commercial series called *CBS Mystery Theatre*, which has been gaining a good audience. Finally, Elliott Lewis himself has created a production agency and, with the help of Fletcher Markle and many others in the vintage radio colony, last year began producing another commercial series called *Sears Radio Theatre*. My information is that they are creating one hundred and thirty plays each year.

It is, of course, too early to say if this activity will develop into a full-blown renaissance of radio drama. Already the proportions of serious to popular radio drama are beginning to fall into the typical American pattern. But nevertheless vintage radio continues to resensitise an older generation to the possibilities of the form and to attract new listeners. And there is a small but healthy activity in the creation of new drama programmes in the old medium. History moves so fast in this century that many of those of American radio's first Golden Age are still active and able to pass on the necessary techniques; indeed, some of them are picking up their work where they left off some twenty years ago. Finally, there is a new and equally resourceful generation beginning to enter the picture. The signs are good. The Golden Age will never return, but radio drama as art and entertainment is returning in the US.

Canadian background : the nation's choice

If the materials of American radio drama are dispersed, difficult of access and relatively ignored critically, the situation as regards English-Canadian radio drama is even worse. There exist published critical anthologies of American radio-drama programmes of every kind, and commercial recordings of many plays; while, of the many thousands of English-Canadian radio plays produced, the latest count indicates that perhaps a hundred and fifty have been published.[44] The differences in the conception and practice of broadcast drama between the US and Canada have resulted, however, in the survival of a fairly large number of the scripts (and some tapes) of serious Canadian radio drama, which together with a bibliography of dramas broadcast on Canadian national networks are only now becoming available.[45] It is partly from these materials that the following descriptions, summaries and analyses of the artists, the artefacts and their series have been prepared. There does not yet exist a general survey of the field, and there is almost no published analysis; indeed, there is little awareness of Canadian radio drama as a distinct form, of major literary and cultural influence in its time. It is therefore necessary to provide a broad context, including a summary of the history of Canadian broadcasting as it affected Canadian radio-drama production; some indication of the influence of American drama broadcasts in Canada, together with a description of the distinctions between the two drama broadcasting systems; and an explanation of the influence of Canadian radio drama on Canadian theatre. The chapter now proceeds in roughly chronological order to suggest the progression of events. As above, only the major series and producer-directors are treated; and in this case, only the productions of the national broadcasting organisation.

Canadian broadcasting : growth and institutionalisation

The nature of broadcasting makes glaringly evident the artificiality of the border between Canada and the United States. Most of the Canadian population live in a line not more than a hundred miles wide, running north of the American border from coast to coast. From the beginning, influences in broadcasting have crossed the border as easily as the Hertzian waves that carried the broadcasts without hindrance in both directions – but mainly north. The Canadian broadcasting system is an artificial creation, ultimately political, like the border itself. Canadian broadcasting institutions were created to defend Canadians from the powerful cultural and commercial influences carried on American programmes which, even in the first few years of broadcasting and especially after the creation of the American networks, were providing broadcasts so numerous as to swamp the Canadian airwaves and so entertaining as to provide a large proportion of Canadians' radio listening.

As Frank Peers, the historian of Canadian broadcasting, points out, broadcasting in Canada progressed in the early days almost indistinguishably from that in the US. As mentioned above, the first commercial station on the continent was Canadian: Montreal's XWA. Private stations proliferated in the 1920s in Canada on a parallel with the US and in quantities proportional to their populations: by 1923 there were some forty Canadian stations to the Americans' five hundred and fifty-six.[46] When the American networks were created in 1926 and 1927, they considered the Canadian 'market' to be a natural extension of the American one, and proceeded to make affiliation arrangements with Canadian stations, especially in the cities of larger population, Montreal (CFCF and CKAC) and Toronto (CFRB). Their only real competition until 1930 was the first Canadian 'network', CNRB, a group of stations created by the newly nationalised Canadian National Railways (CN) to service its transcontinental trains with entertainment in the new medium and to publicise its railway, ship and hotel operations. The CN Radio Department, which ran CNRB, was in fact set up in 1924, several years before NBC began, and the network of CNRB-owned stations grew to cover the most populated regions of Canada by 1929. It was not commercial in the sense of American networks; there were no sales of time or programmes for sponsorship. All its programmes were in effect sustaining, and the cultural and service nature of the majority of them reflected this fact. While the CN Radio Department published monthly schedules announcing local programmes across the country from 1925 onwards, there was almost no network broadcasting until 1929, and then for only an hour each evening. Nevertheless, the programmes, both local and network, were distinctly Canadian, both in style and artists, and the CN Radio Department gave Canadians a preliminary taste of both Canadian and nationalised broadcasting.

Fierce debates raged in Canada between 1929 and 1932 concerning the nature of public control over broadcasting, made necessary by the chaos in the airwaves resulting from a lack of regulation of Canadian and American broadcasters, and by the threat to Canadian culture posed by the penetration of Canadian airspace by American stations. The private Canadian broadcasters, arguing for the American commercial system though for Canadian networks, were opposed by a group including not only Graham Spry and Alan Plaunt (the Canadian Radio League) but also Austin Weir, the Head of the CN Radio Department – all staunch defenders of a national monopoly broadcasting system patterned after the British model.[47] In the event, the Canadian government decided to create a national radio system at just the time the US was confirming its free-enterprise system in the regulation of radio. In 1932 the Canadian Radio Broadcasting Commission (CRBC) was created and was given the monopoly over Canadian network broadcasting, a monopoly the government reinforced by making the CRBC the national regulatory and licence-granting body for commercial radio as well. The CRBC was empowered to buy up the CN Radio Department's production and broadcasting facilities, and it took over their staff as well. CRBC operations were funded by a licence fee on radio sets and by capital funds from Parliament. It established the principle of no commercial sponsorship and extended the CNRB policy of sustaining cultural and entertainment programming.

When the awkward administrative system of the CRBC created problems, a succeeding government was forced in 1936 to replace it with the Canadian Broadcasting Corporation (CBC), separating the broadcasting and the regulative functions of the CBC by appointing an Operations Manager and Board of Governors. The actual facilities and personnel of the CRBC were taken over. Austin Weir, the former Head of the CN Radio Department, was appointed Commercial Manager of the CBC, with responsibilities to extend the CBC group of owned and affiliated stations so as to finally create a network of some fifty stations across the country in competition with the American networks. The success of Weir in this venture did, indeed, create a certain amount of commercial sponsorship of programmes, but the tradition of a decade of Canadian programming in which sustaining cultural programmes dominated was only dented by these changes. The Drama Department of the CRBC carried over to the CBC and was the most important programme department; and when the CBC at the end of 1943 created a second CBC network to accommodate the growing commercial traffic, the programming on the Trans-Canada Network included a number of serious cultural programmes, among them two prestige sustaining radio-drama anthologies, which became renowned in the US as in Canada: *CBC Stage* and *CBC Wednesday Night*.

It is not by accident that the popularity and achievements of Canadian radio outlasted those of the US networks. It was partly owing to the difference in timing of the arrival of television in the two countries. The rapid growth of the new visual medium in the US in the mid-1940s was, as we have seen, the final blow to the dominance of radio, already suffering from the dislocations of the war. Canadian television, on the other hand, did not commence until 1952 and was established by the CBC itself, naturally with care to create the least possible disturbance in the operations of radio, the 'senior' CBC service. As American radio gradually wound down after 1945, Canadian radio, whose monopoly over Canadian communications became even more monolithic during the war, was embarking on the ambitious network and cultural programming expansion just mentioned. The Golden Age of Canadian radio did not really commence until 1944 (as American radio was folding), and that Age would not decline until almost two decades later.

CBC drama: organisation, influence, relation to American radio drama

The CBC in the 1940s occupied a unique position in the Canadian cultural milieu. There was a lack of such cultural institutions as an indigenous national theatre or a national funding council for the arts. The US and Britain dominated not only Canadian theatre but magazine and book publishing and the film industry. It is crucial to underline that the CBC, with its finances, facilities, cultural programming, and monopoly of nationwide audiences, became the financial sustenance of and showcase for a majority of Canada's creative artists: not only a proto-Canada Council, but in the realm of drama the acknowledged Canadian National Theatre, the major employer for several decades of virtually all Canadian theatre professionals – writers, producer-directors, technical staff and composers.[48] Weir quotes Herbert Whittaker (1961):

For the past twenty-five years, the CBC has supplied most of the dramatic intake of Canada. No other country has had to rely so heavily on one single source for its theatrical knowledge, experience, and expression . . . In short, the CBC has subsidized a whole theatre for us for a quarter century.[49]

The CBC had it both ways. While the CBC Trans-Canada Network was partly functioning on the pattern (quite conscious) of the BBC Third Programme, the CBC Dominion Network was broadcasting light programmes, by which the CBC earned a good proportion of its commercial revenue: programmes including not only Canadian-produced popular drama series but many familiar American popular drama shows, which had never ceased to entertain Canadians since the beginning of radio in the 1920s. The fact is that the total experience by Canadians of radio programmes had not differed much from that of Americans during this whole period. Before radio was regulated, powerful American stations had blanketed Canadian reception. And even after Canada had carved out its own channels on the air by the early 1930s, Canadians heard American programmes: direct from the US; over private Canadian stations, which were freely broadcasting programmes of American origin over their own wavelengths; and very soon over the CRBC itself. The CRBC did not dare to broadcast a Canadian programme in competition with *Amos 'n' Andy*, but bought that programme, as popular with Canadians as it was with Americans, and broadcast it over the Canadian national network, as it did the majority of the most popular American programmes.[50] And the CBC simply extended that policy. In both Toronto and Montreal, CBC had an arrangement with NBC from the very first. One can assume, then, on the authority of the radio schedules and reviews, that Canadians were exposed to almost all the American radio series that I have discussed above as being influential in the creation and development of radio drama; so that Canadian radio drama would have benefited in similar ways to the American version.

One major difference between the two countries in this experience was the *context* of Canadian programming in which these American shows appeared, and especially the experience of those Canadian programmes central to the progress of indigenous Canadian radio drama. Several points need underlining here. First, that from the earliest CNRB schedules in 1925 there was a growing number of sustaining Canadian radio-drama series, many of them, like *The Romance of Canada* and *Radio Theatre Guild*, with ambitious goals in the realm of drama. Second, that these serious artistic efforts on radio resulted from the fact that Canadian Radio Drama Departments were almost the only professional outlet for Canadian dramatists and other people of the Canadian theatre until the 1950s. Last, that the proportion of serious to popular radio drama on the CBC was much greater than on the American networks at any time. Of the several thousands of American network programmes in dramatic form (as we have seen), one can count only five or six anthology series with pretensions to prestige drama, and only three major long-running sustaining series of serious radio drama. The combined CNRB-CRBC-CBC Drama Department production of network radio drama from the beginnings to the end of 1961 totals only some three hundred series; yet two major sustaining serious radio-drama series came out of Toronto alone, each spanning several decades. There were similar long-running series from each of the four major regions, and numerous shorter serious series from all locations, providing an outlet for local culture and a frequent source of talent for recruitment to the networks.

The effect of both the Drama Department organisation and the large number of Canadian sustaining drama series was to provide a context for audiences and indeed for writers quite different from the American experience, despite the fact that most American radio drama was also available in Canada. The current domination of American (and American-style) television in Canada is in strict contrast to the radio situation in the 1930-60 period. Another difference between Canadian and American radio should be mentioned: the CRBC and the CBC were created with the specific and declared purposes of serving as instruments of Canadian culture and as major tools to weld the widely dispersed Canadian population into a single nation. The effect on programming of these declared goals was not necessarily a high proportion of Canadian content, for that has always been difficult. There was, rather, a consciousness of these goals on the part of radio dramatists and producers, the results of which appeared quite clearly in the themes and styles of Canadian radio-drama series. To choose only one example: there has always been a didactic motivation in Canadian radio drama and a related superiority in the documentary.

To speak of serious Canadian radio drama in English is to speak of the national broadcasting institutions. Private broadcasters originated a number of commercial radio dramas in the 1930s, but most of these were below the level of imaginative American popular radio drama[51]; by the 1940s this continuity writing around commercials had all but disappeared. There were some interesting popular drama programmes, including serials and variety-comedy shows, and some sponsored serious radio-drama series, in which the major Canadian producers were involved. On the other hand, the quantities of these programmes in Canada were very small in proportion to the sustaining series and only a minor part of producers' responsibilities. A Canadian producer could genuinely make a career in serious drama, and perhaps several dozen did so in the Canadian Golden Age of radio.

Though it is impossible to discuss Canadian French-language radio-drama production in detail here, the general parallels to and contrasts with English-language radio drama are illuminating. The effect of the language barrier between French-speaking Canadians and American broadcasts, together with the separate Radio-Canada French network set up by the CBC in 1938, encouraged a very distinct tradition in French-Canadian radio drama, including a complete range of indigenous programmes of the types English Canadians were receiving from the US. The role of private stations was also different in French Canada. Because of the market for indigenous programmes, there was a significant production of popular and serious radio dramas on the private stations. The culture reflected and indeed influenced by these productions was more homogeneous than in the US or English Canada. Moreover, French-language radio drama reflected the local middle-class and working-class cultures more than did English-language productions.

As for serious drama, there were numerous prestige drama series which were a primary showcase and instrument for French-Canadian dramatists. However, the stage in French-speaking Quebec and Manitoba was much less dominated by imported American and British troupes and plays than was the English-Canadian theatre. As a result, an indigenous live theatre grew up far earlier in French Canada than in English Canada; and radio drama, while an important part of this scene (especially in terms of the large audiences radio could command), did not *dominate* the development of live theatre in French Canada as it did in English Canada. Happily, many of the scripts and sound versions of CBC and privately produced radio drama have been collected, a bibliography has been published, and both selections from the scripts and critical studies are being published as well, by the project called *Archives québecoises de la radio-télévision.*[52]

Canadian radio drama

Early radio drama: CNRB, CRBC, CBC to the war years

The Head of the CN Radio Department, Austin Weir, was directly involved in programme planning. Urbane and committed to public-service programming, he encouraged the kinds of cultural program-mes, including music, talks and drama, that came to characterise Canadian national broadcasting in succeeding years. The lack of network lines in the 1925-9 period meant that programmes (including dramas) broadcast over CNRB stations usually reached only a regional audience. On the other hand, the relatively few stations broadcasting meant that local stations' broadcasts reached a very wide regional audience. The first radio play in the CNRB schedules, *The Rosary*, broadcast over CNRA, Moncton, in May 1925, blanketed most of the Maritimes, penetrated far into New England, and reached across the Atlantic to Ireland. Moncton continued in the next few years to broadcast occasional dramas, the titles of which hint at their contents: *Nothing but the Truth, The Fortune Hunter, Out to Win, Paddy Turns the Trick, Fast Friends, The Awakening.* They were all popular stage plays of hardly post-Victorian vintage, transposed to radio without any attempt at adaptation for the new medium. The CN Radio Department schedules occasionally offered the printed 'prog-ramme' of a future play, including descriptions of scenes, characters and plot: information crucial to the understanding of a visually conceived drama in the aural medium.

Another of the earliest CNRB stations, CNRV, Vancouver, played a special role in radio drama. It had the only continuing drama series on the CNRB schedules in the 1920s, a weekly programme called by the name of the repertory company that created the productions: *CNRV Players*. Directed by the knowledgeable and energetic Jack

Gilmour, they were active from 1926 to the end of the CNRB schedules in 1932 (and, if Weir is correct, on into the CRBC as well); more than a hundred radio dramas were produced on *CNRV Players* between 1927 and 1932 alone, according to Weir. They included adaptations from Shakespeare and the classical theatre and fiction, as well as a number of original radio plays, some by local writers, which were certainly the first Canadian radio dramas. The extraordinary achievements of *CNRV Players* anticipated those of the NBC *Radio Guild* by fully three years, and from 1929 they were heard over the new CNRB network.

With the coming of the Depression to Canada in 1930, CN Railways was forced to curtail the activities of the Radio Department. It supported nationalisation of broadcasting in the debates of 1930-2 in the hope that the broadcasting activities it had successfully initiated would be perpetuated by the government buying up its facilities. The CN Radio Department, to illustrate just what nationalised sustaining radio could accomplish, decided to produce a major series of original Canadian radio plays, a decision that turned out to be of crucial importance to the future of Canadian radio drama. In the autumn of 1930, Merrill Denison, a young Canadian with radio experience, was asked to write a series of dramatisations of Canadian history. On Denison's advice, Austin Weir went to England to acquire the services of Tyrone Guthrie, then a promising young London director who had produced radio drama for the BBC; Guthrie had also written some startlingly good original plays showing a clear mastery of the new medium. Guthrie was to become a Director at the Old Vic in 1933 and was also, of course, to become the Manager of the English National Theatre and a foremost exponent of Shakespeare production within the decade.[53] The CN Radio Department acquired not only Guthrie but the latest plans of the BBC's studios, and they constructed in Montreal the most advanced radio-drama production facilities in North America. Between January and May of 1931 Tyrone Guthrie directed the first fourteen plays in the *Romance of Canada* series. For this purpose he trained a group of radio actors, led by the young traditional-theatre actor, Rupert Caplan. This was a repertory group, which formed the nucleus of talent for the CRBC and later the CBC Drama Departments. Broadcast over the CNRB network, the plays achieved widespread popularity. After Guthrie's departure, Caplan himself directed the last eight plays in the *Romance of Canada* series the following spring, again to the vast enthusiasm of Canadian audiences. It was only a few months later that Parliament passed the legislation nationalising Canadian radio and, as hoped, the CN Radio Department facilities and staff were acquired for the new CRBC network.

The plays in the *Romance of Canada* series, in the writing of which Denison had the support of Guthrie's experience, embody the basic concepts of drama for radio. Despite their relative lack of sophistication and their documentary concerns, each play achieves a clear progression of action, distinct characterisations, scenes and transitions, and the kind of sequential dramatic crisis necessary to radio. Through the team trained by Guthrie, especially Rupert Caplan, these lessons informed subsequent radio-drama production in Canada.

The nationalisation of radio in Canada at the end of 1932 brought about the consolidation and expansion of the Canadian radio network and an increase in the number and variety of drama series. From Montreal between 1933 and 1935 Rupert Caplan produced for the CRBC a series of serious radio plays, mainly Canadian originals, called *Radio Theatre Guild*. Only one script survives, Horace Brown's memorial to T.E. Lawrence, *Desert Warrior*. Title and programme schedules indicate that this ambitious series (rivalling its NBC namesake) included a broad variety of dramas, from Eugene O'Neill's *Ile*, through an English comedy of manners, *'Op-O' Me-Thumb*, and some historical dramas on Montreal, to an adaptation of Anatole France's *The Man Who Married a Dumb Wife*. Meanwhile, from Toronto in 1933 came a mystery series, *Eight Bells*, and Stanley Maxted's *Musical Comedy* series. In 1934 two short new series were begun, in Toronto and in Kamloops, and a long-running series from Vancouver called *Theatre of the Air*. In 1935 Rupert Caplan created a series of dramas from the Bible, *And It Came to Pass*, which won great popularity in its long run over CRBC and CBC. Halifax offered a drama series called *Nova Scotia on the Air*, while Winnipeg originated a series of mainly original radio plays called *Western Radio Players*.

Perhaps the most interesting productions in 1935 were a series of seven episodes in a serial format called *Mr Sage*, the most famous (or notorious) of several serials prepared by the Conservative Party's advertising agency for the forthcoming general elections. Clever dialogue and clear characterisation made the *Mr Sage* series effective publicity in a powerful dramatic form. This Conservative publicity over the Canadian National network (using the CRBC's own team of dramatic talent) while the Conservative Party was in power provoked unexpected repercussions. The Liberals were furious, and when they won the election they used the *Mr Sage* incident as a focus of criticism of the CRBC. It enabled them to more easily carry out the necessary administrative restructuring of the CRBC in 1936, which resulted in the appointment of a single General Manager (the first was a former BBC Publicity Director, Gladstone Murray) and in the change of title to the CBC. Meanwhile, Rupert Lucas had produced a drama series for CRBC from Toronto earlier in the year, offering a rich variety of original dramas and adaptations, while from Vancouver had come the popular *Theatre Guild*.

There was an infusion of new ideas in 1937 by Murray, and an infusion of government money for CBC facilities and programming as well. Not only was the CBC network extended to cover almost 90 per cent of the country, but a total of almost fifty new series had their inception in the first three years of the CBC. Rupert Caplan and Rupert Lucas continued their valuable contributions to serious radio drama, and their work was increasingly supplemented by new writing and directing talent. Andrew Allan, a young writer who was then working as a staff announcer, continuity writer and producer for a private Toronto station, wrote much of the 1937 series produced by Lucas called *Within These Walls*; Allan was soon to be invited to become a CBC producer. In 1939 Winnipeg undertook an extensive series of serious radio dramas, *Everyman's Theatre*, about half of them Canadian scripts; one of the producers was the young Esse W. Ljungh. From Halifax, meanwhile, *Atlantic Nocturne*, a poetry and music series similar to the work of Norman Corwin, was being created and spoken by another young producer, J. Frank Willis. The scene was set for a second stage of CBC radio-drama expansion.

This expansion was given a structure and direction by the appointment of Rupert Lucas to the new post of National Supervisor of Drama in Toronto, by the creation of regional supervisory positions in the major production centres across the country, and by the setting up of a National Script Department as a clearing-house and liaison for new writers. Finally, there was the development of a long-running series in each region as the showcase for serious radio-drama activities across the country. Each series received the creative stamp of the producers who were responsible in turn for its production. This national and regional support for Canadian drama activities was a prefiguration of the structure of regional theatres created quite recently by the Canada Council for the Arts; and the CBC's Drama Department functioned for exactly the same purposes, underlining its central role in Canadian theatre. The major regional series, *Winnipeg Drama*, began in February 1939 and, with a change in title to *Prairie Playhouse* in 1951, continued into the 1960s. Esse W. Ljungh, Drama Supervisor in Winnipeg, was one of the first producers, while Archie MacCorkindale, James Kent, Emrys Jones and Guy Kristjanson succeeded Ljungh in turn as producers. The Vancouver sustaining series was called *Theatre Time* at first and began in December 1939 with Andrew Allan, the new Regional Drama Supervisor, in charge. It became *Vancouver Playhouse* in 1944, *Pacific Playhouse* in early 1946, finally *Vancouver Playhouse* by September 1946, and continued into the 1960s. Allan was succeeded by Archie MacCorkindale, then Mavor Moore, Doug Nixon, Peter MacDonald, Raymond White-house, Neil Sutherland and, in the 1960s, Gerald Newman.

As for Montreal, Rupert Caplan took on an administrative position in programming at about the time the other regional series were commencing, and he did not return to full-time production until 1941 when the Montreal regional series, *Montreal Drama*, was established. Caplan retained responsibility for that series until his retirement in 1968. The Second World War intervened, and the Halifax regional series, *Maritime Workshop*, did not commence until 1947, under

Stephen K. Appleby's direction. In 1948 it changed title to *Maritime Theatre* and continued until the end of 1953. It reappeared at the start of 1954 as *Halifax Theatre*, directed at first by Robert Alban, then by Hector MacFayden, John Hobday and Anthony Ross. It ended in September 1961. Though in Halifax the creation of the major series was delayed, in general the nature of the structures within which CBC radio drama would be produced and the four major producers were established by the first year of the war. The intervention of the war delayed the pace of development of CBC radio drama in a way similar to that in the US. The energies of producers and production staff in general were much engaged in patriotic, information and propaganda series, sponsored by various government departments. There was a significant difference, however, in the Canadian experience, for CBC drama production was relatively less affected. Some thirty radio-drama series not directly related to the war were produced across the regions between 1940 and the end of the war. While only two of these appeared in the 1940-1 season, the pace quickened after that, partly because of the CBC's employment of a new National Script Editor in Toronto in 1941, Alice Frick. Energetic and well trained, with excellent dramatic instincts, she was to make a significant contribution in support of the new departures in radio drama initiated by the Department. This is especially true of activities in Toronto after 1943, following the departure of Rupert Lucas for a radio career in New York. Delayed by the start of the war, the Golden Age of Canadian radio drama would commence in January 1944.

The Golden Age of CBC drama

The Canadian radio-drama Golden Age was dominated by the work of the four major producers: Andrew Allan (the new National Drama Supervisor), Esse W. Ljungh, J. Frank Willis and Rupert Caplan. Its featured series included the major regional serious drama series mentioned above, but especially two national series created in Toronto under Allan's new mandate, *CBC Stage* and *CBC Wednesday Night*. The achievements in the National Drama Department were partly the effect of a decision to centralise talent in Toronto as much as possible. Allan was brought from Vancouver, Ljungh from Winnipeg, and Willis from Halifax; Rupert Caplan was the only one who did not join the group but remained in Montreal, though in close contact with Toronto developments and a contributor with the others to the *Wednesday Night* series. The Toronto producers were constantly in one another's Jarvis Street offices, enjoying an enormously fruitful artistic intercourse which rapidly advanced the techniques and communicative codes of radio drama. Each of the four producers took a clearly defined area of drama in which to specialise. Alice Frick supported them as the first liaison with new writers, and she directed each suitable script to the producer who in her experience would best appreciate it. For his part, each producer developed a repertory team of actors, a composer and technicians, and adopted a group of favourite writers, lending continuity to the experiments in radio-drama technique. There was a unique camaraderie, artistic ferment, and *esprit de corps* in the CBC Drama Department at this time; there does not seem to have been anything comparable in the American networks.

Andrew Allan had impressed the CBC ever since he had taken over responsibility for the Vancouver Drama Department in 1939 and especially with the productions of the experimental *Baker's Dozen* series, written by Fletcher Markle. When Allan arrived in Toronto at the end of 1943, he had already resolved to create on radio an indigenous Canadian national theatre, something Canada had never before had. By January 1944 the first play of the series that would carry out this mandate, *Stage 44* (as it was first known), was broadcast over the network.[54] Commencing in a half-hour format, *Stage* was expanded to full-hour plays by 1947. *CBC Stage* was a national showcase for the best Canadian dramatic talent in writing, acting and composing, an acknowledged National Theatre[55]; but it was more. In it Allan continued his experiments in the radio-drama genre. He had received a solid classical-theatre training in Toronto's Hart House Theatre; on this base he added a decade's training in the rough work of popular radio in its formative years, so that he was very much aware of the challenges and possibilities of a drama for the ear. He knew of the importance of the actor's voice in radio drama, but considered the writer and his script the crucially important element.[56] The excellence of his work was acknowledged on both sides of the border. *Stage* repeatedly won the Ohio State Radio Institute Award for radio drama. The mix of *Stage* is familiar; there were classics of fiction and of the theatre, especially Allan's *forte*, Shakespeare, but at least half of the plays were original Canadian dramas. The writers included Len Peterson, Fletcher Markle, Lister Sinclair, Harry Boyle, W.O. Mitchell, Alan King, Mavor Moore, Hugh Kemp, Joseph Schull, Allan himself and a host of other well-known Canadian playwrights of the time. A number of the plays were characterised by startlingly frank social comment as well as technical originality. Allan produced *Stage* for almost eleven years, until 1955, when he retired as Drama Supervisor. Esse Ljungh, who had been invited to Toronto in 1946, took over, both as Supervisor and as producer of *Stage*. Ljungh retired in 1969, but *Stage* continued its career under a variety of directors into the 1970s; the latest of these was John Reeves.

In 1947 CBC decided to create an omnibus cultural series stretching over the whole four hours of the evening schedule every Wednesday, on the pattern of the BBC Third Programme. *CBC Wednesday Night* was the second of the major national series to give the Golden Age its shape and glory. It was a mix of serious drama, music, documentaries and talks, the various elements in each evening's programmes blending harmoniously. The full evening format meant that the length of any play produced was open-ended, with a full-hour minimum. If *CBC Stage* was the flowering of the mature CBC Drama Department in Canadian drama, then the *CBC Wednesday Night* drama productions were the fruit, in a broader context. There were occasional Canadian dramas on this series, but not featured as on *Stage*. There were full-length productions of Shakespeare and the classics as well as of modern European dramatists; but also adaptations from modern European, American and Canadian novels, and ambitious drama-documentaries, many on Canadian subjects. Where *Stage* concentrated on 'the state of Canadian drama' (as Allan subtitled it), the *Wednesday Night* dramas encompassed a broader cultural context.

The production organisation for *Wednesday Night* was as innovative as its format and contents. A Program Committee was set up, which involved many of the senior Drama Department staff, including Allan, Robert Weaver and Alice Frick, under the Production Head, Harry Boyle. Direction of individual plays was shared among the senior producers, including Allan, Willis, Caplan and Ljungh. The work of these four on this series reflected the way they divided the field of drama among themselves. Allan, with his classical and modern training, preferred Canadian originals, Shakespeare and the Elizabethans, and Greek drama. Ljungh, who had attended the Royal Swedish Dramatic Academy, was immersed in modern European playwrights, especially the Scandinavians and Germans, as well as a more heterogeneous group of classical plays. Rupert Caplan, whose first professional experience was in the US with Eugene O'Neill and the Provincetown Players, concentrated on O'Neill and other modern American dramatists as well as other twentieth-century plays, especially French. Frank Willis was the perfect radio man among the four. He had come to drama production through his features and documentaries, such as the First World War *Flanders Fields* series (he was also National Supervisor of Features); his emphasis in drama reflected this particular expertise, documentary-drama and epic. This was complemented by his interest in poetry and music, from *Atlantic Nocturne*.

It was in the *Wednesday Night* series that the full potential of the creative co-operation between these major producer-directors in the Drama Department was realised. The history of *Wednesday Night* continued on into the 1970s, though the creative partnership described above came to an end with the retirement of all four producers by the end of the 1960s.

CBC radio drama in the television age

Unlike its American counterpart, Canadian radio-drama production hardly faltered quantitatively in the 1960s and maintained production levels in the 1970s. Nevertheless, the later history of Canadian radio drama follows somewhat the path of American radio's decline in popularity and cultural importance and for some of the same reasons, though much later in time. Canadian radio lost its near-monopoly of funds, audiences and talent in 1952-3, to television, to the Canada Council for the Arts, and to the live theatre, which it had itself spawned, especially in Toronto (New Play Society, Jupiter Theatre and Crest Theâtre) and in Stratford, Ontario. The Shakespeare Festival was produced by Tyrone Guthrie, the British director who had set up the first Canadian radio-drama studios and directed the first Canadian radio-drama series over CNRB in 1931. Guthrie, re-establishing his radio-drama and theatre contacts after twenty-odd years, obtained the services of many Canadian theatre professionals trained by the CBC Drama Department. It was an extraordinary continuity.

The effects of the above changes were inevitable. Canadian audiences for radio drama slowly shrank, and talent began to move elsewhere in Canadian theatre. But with the waning of the sense of national cultural responsibility mentioned above, with audiences small enough to be conceived in a more personal fashion, and with the retirement in the late 1960s of the great Golden Age producers, the nature of CBC radio drama began to change. There began more contemporary experiments in theme and technique, paralleling those in the rest of the increasingly accessible global village of American and European radio drama. New producer-directors of the third generation began to move in fresh directions. Sometimes they were inspired by the increasing use of tape, which made a significant difference in radio-drama production in Canada in the 1950s, whereas it had come too late to affect American radio plays.

Of the producers who began to make a reputation in the late 1950s, two stand out as exceptional: John Reeves and Gerald Newman. Reeves, who works to this day in the Toronto Drama Department (now Radio Arts), began directing drama for CBC on an occasional basis in the mid-1950s. From 1957 he contributed to *Wednesday Night* and *Focus*. In 1957-8 he produced a number of plays on a series of Canadian originals called *Première on the Air*. Another well-known series he directed, for four seasons, was *Four's Company*, all the plays being written by the Canadians Alan King, James Bannerman, John Drainie and Mavor Moore. Reeves also wrote a number of original plays for CBC radio, notably *A Beach of Strangers* and *Triptych*. *A Beach of Strangers* shows an original variation on the influential radio play by Dylan Thomas, *Under Milk Wood*. Both these plays show Reeves's interest in poetic experiment. Reeves was the last of the *Stage* producers.

The other pole of modern Canadian experiment in radio drama is illustrated by the impressive work of Gerald Newman out of that other creative centre of CBC drama activity, Vancouver. Newman began his radio-drama work in Vancouver at about the same time as Reeves in

Toronto; in 1957 Newman took over the Western Region's sustaining drama series, *Pacific Playhouse*, for two seasons. He soon became Regional Drama Supervisor. In the summer of 1958, he also began to make regular contributions to the national *Wednesday Night* series, meanwhile producing a regional variant on that series called *CBU Sunday Night*, the innovative history of which extended into the 1970s. Newman combined an appreciation of classical and modern stage drama with a love of contemporary Canadian drama. The particular nature of his experiments was in the area of production-direction. He insists on a pure style mainly devoid of music and sound effects, with the emphasis on the script, timing and the pregnant silence. Newman is an eloquent defender of the necessity for taping and editing a performance before broadcast, a position quite the opposite from the fondness for 'live performance' of the previous generation of producers. Still a theorist of radio drama, Newman retired from the CBC in 1965 to teach drama at Simon Fraser University.

Radio drama on CBC continues unbroken to the present, a continuity unmatched in the US. Moreover, the fact of the matter is that much of the output of contemporary Canadian dramatists continues to serve the CBC: Michael Cook, George Ryga, Sharon Pollock and a host of lesser-known writers.[57] On the other hand, the sense of a 'Canadian National Theatre on the Air' is gone past recall; contemporary radio-drama experiments have a much less well-defined context. The Golden Age of Canadian radio drama, surviving for much longer than the American version, has, nevertheless, also disappeared.

Final comparison: US and Canadian radio drama

The distinctions between (English) Canadian and American radio drama are much more than a matter of style or literary-dramatic tradition – though these are also involved. The major contrasts result from the differences between American commercial networks in competition with one another, and the state-monopoly Canadian networks (CNRB, CRBC, CBC). On the whole, prestige drama in the US was generated as exceptional sustaining filler in a mainly sponsored programme schedule. The techniques developed there were interesting to the networks in so far as they could be applied widely in popular shows and even (as we have seen) in commercials. Moreover, most of the American professionals involved in serious radio drama expended much of their creative energies in popular programmes, which sometimes, however, achieved the status of high drama on their own, from variety to soap opera. This harnessing of the most creative dramatic minds in radio to popular entertainment may be one of the secrets of the great attraction of American entertainment in other countries.

With no indigenous institution comparable to the American or British legitimate theatre, Canadian radio drama took on responsibilities to express a Canadian dramatic culture, which led it to develop in quite different directions from its American counterpart. When to this is added the expressed purpose of Canadian radio as an instrument for national unity, the differences become even greater. The public funding of the CBC state monopoly of broadcasting produced a much larger proportion of serious Canadian radio drama than in the US.

The above distinctions created major differences in the themes and aesthetic of radio-drama production in the two countries. There never was an American *Stage* or an American *Wednesday Night*: that is, no American series so narrowly focused on the national dramatic literature as *Stage*, and no series so broadly representing the dramatic literatures of the world as *Wednesday Night*. Finally, the commercial orientation of the American networks dictated the virtual demise of American radio drama of the Golden Age by the late 1940s with the coming of television; while in Canada, the combined effects of television, the Canada Council and the new live theatres were not enough to quite break the continuity of radio-drama production, though its nature changed radically. It is now on a level with other more private Canadian literary forms, such as fiction and poetry, in goals and audiences.

We have been speaking of a period in total of no more than a half century from the very beginnings of network radio to the present. Some of the people who have made the history discussed above are still active. The vagaries of cultural history in this century, which undercut radio in its young prime when its language was just being perfected, might well yet take a different turn, and perhaps, like drama in the Restoration, radio drama may have another flowering.

Notes

1. *The Sponsor: Notes on a Modern Potentate*. New York 1978, p. 9.
2. *A History of Broadcasting in the United States*, 3 vols: *A Tower in Babel*. New York 1966; *The Golden Web*. New York 1968; *The Image Empire*. New York 1970.
3. Barnouw, *The Sponsor*, p. 9.
4. Frank W. Peers, *The Politics of Canadian Broadcasting 1920-1951*. Toronto 1969, p. 6.
5. The American Radio Act of 1927 simply established governmental control over the available broadcasting channels, confirming the big networks' monopolies; it said nothing to prevent commercial competition or advertising on those channels (see Barnouw, *The Sponsor*, p. 22). Indeed the Communications Act of 1934 *confirmed* the *requirement* of sponsor-identification on programmes (*ibid*, p. 61).
6. Edgar A. Grunwald (ed.), *Variety Radio Directory 1939-1940*. New York 1939, pp. 42–57.

7. Tony Goodstone (ed.), *The Pulps*. New York 1970.
8. Barnouw, *The Sponsor*, p. 27.
9. Esslin, *An Anatomy of Drama*. London 1976, pp. 14–16.
10. John Fiske and John Hartley, *Reading Television*. London 1978, pp. 59–67.
11. Grunwald (ed.), op. cit., p. 91.
12. *The Sponsor*, p. 32.
13. Max Wylie (ed.), *Best Broadcasts of 1938-39*. New York 1939, p. 368.
14. John Dunning, *Tune in Yesterday*. Englewood Cliffs, N.J. 1976, p. 542.
15. For the texts of a number of *Shadow* episodes, see Diana Cohen and I.B. Hoeflinger (eds), *The Shadow Knows*. Glenview, Illinois, 1977.
16. Dunning, op. cit., p. 548.
17. Ross Firestone (ed.), *The Big Radio Comedy Program*. Chicago 1978, p. 27.
18. Dunning, op. cit., p. 32.
19. Firestone (ed.), op. cit., p. 226.
20. 'Introduction', *New English Dramatists 12: Radio Plays*. Harmondsworth 1968, pp. 14–15.
21. Esslin, op. cit., pp. 83–5.
22. Stedman, *The Serials*. Norman, Okla. 1971, pp. 284–9.
23. *Ibid*, pp. 3-49.
24. Robert LaGuardia, *From Ma Perkins to Mary Hartman: The Illustrated History of Soap Operas*. New York 1977, pp. 6–8.
25. Dunning, op. cit., p. 475.
26. *Radio Drama in Action*. New York and Toronto 1945, pp. 346–7.
27. Quoted in *ibid*, p. 346.
28. LaGuardia, op. cit., pp. 5-6.
29. Wylie (ed.), op. cit., pp. 448-9.
30. *Ibid*, p. 340.
31. Barnouw, *The Sponsor*, p. 20.
32. Stedman, op. cit., p. 145.
33. Dunning, op. cit., p. 144.
34. Wylie (ed.), op. cit., p. 391.
35. *Radio Drama in Action*, pp. 204-5.
36. Clifton Fadiman, 'Introduction', in Norman Corwin, *More by Corwin*. New York 1944, pp. ix-xi.
37. *This Was Radio*. New York 1975, pp. 72-5.
38. For the texts of these plays, see Arch Oboler, *Oboler Omnibus*. New York 1945 [North Hollywood 1971].
39. *Ibid*, p. 256 [212].
40. Richard Averson and David Manning White (eds), *Electronic Drama: Television Plays of the Sixties*. Boston 1971; hardly a single name among the well-known radio writers is found here.
41. Evan William Cameron, '*Citizen Kane*: the influence of radio drama on cinematic design', in Peter Lewis (ed.), *Papers of the Radio Literature Conference 1977*. Durham 1978, vol. 1, pp. 85-98.
42. Howard Koch, *The Panic Broadcast*. Boston 1970; Koch's account of the production precedes the script of the play.
43. Dunning, op. cit., p. 587.
44. 'Radio', in *The First Supplement to the Brock Bibliography of Published Canadian Plays in English*. St. Catharines, Ontario 1973, pp. 24-8.
45. The Concordia University CBC Radio Drama Archives, Montreal; Howard Fink, with Brian Morrison, *Canadian National Theatre on the Air:*

A Bibliography of CBC-CRBC-CNR Radio Drama in English (forthcoming); Public Archives of Canada, Sound Division.

46. Peers, op. cit., p. 6.
47. E. Austin Weir, *The Struggle for National Broadcasting in Canada*. Toronto 1965, especially 'National Broadcasting', pp. 107–204.
48. George Woodcock, 'Massey's harvest', *Canadian Literature*, 73 (Summer 1977), pp. 2–7; also 'Saving the radio plays', *ibid*, p. 128.
49. Weir, op. cit., pp. 394-5.
50. See the admission by the Chairman of the CRBC to the 1934 Parliamentary Committee on Broadcasting, quoted in Thomas James Allard, *Straight Up: Private Broadcasting in Canada: 1918-1958*. Ottawa 1979, p. 93.
51. Andrew Allan, *A Self-Portrait*. Toronto 1974, p. 73; Ron Hambleton, *How I earned $250,000 as a free lance writer . . . even if it did take 30 years!* Toronto 1977, pp. 71–2.
52. Pierre Pagé, *Répertoire des oeuvres de la littérature québecoise 1930-1970*. Montreal 1973; and, for example, Renée Legris, *Robert Choquette: romancier et dramaturge de la radio-télévision*. Montreal 1977.
53. James Forsyth, *Tyrone Guthrie*. London 1976.
54. Allan, op. cit., pp. 105-7.
55. Vincent Tovell, 'Letters in Canada: 1947 – Drama', *University of Toronto Quarterly*, **17**(3) (Apr. 1948), p. 279 (see whole 'Drama' section, pp. 278-85).
56. Allan, op. cit., pp. 3-4.
57. For further information, see Malcolm Page, 'Canadian radio drama', in Lewis (ed.), op. cit., vol. 1, pp. 99-120.

Chapter 12

Radio drama : the Australian experience

Rodney Pybus

Context and background

Radio broadcasting in Australia is now more than fifty years old. Drama of all kinds, ranging from productions of Shakespeare and modern plays written for the medium to fifteen-minute thrillers in serial form and adaptations of lightweight stage comedies, played an important part in the development of Australian radio from the 1930s to the late 1950s, when the novelty of television intruded and swiftly altered the existing pattern. In the last decade or so there have been encouraging signs that serious radio drama (which is not only serious as dramatic entertainment but which also seriously explores for the benefit of the listener the possibilities of a still-developing medium) has begun to find a new lease of life and a new, if necessarily rather limited, audience on the channels of the Australian Broadcasting Commission.

The geography and recent history of the Australian continent have posed specific problems for, and imposed special conditions on, such a relatively new medium of communication as radio. In a country whose three million square miles make it about the same size as the United States, the population has only recently exceeded fourteen million; the majority live in or near the state-capital cities of Sydney and Brisbane in the east, Melbourne and Adelaide in the south, and Perth in the west. On the other hand, the Northern Territory's capital, Darwin, is nearer to Djakarta than to Sydney, and 'the tyranny of distance' (to use the title of Geoffrey Blainey's 1966 book) can make life exceedingly hard for the broadcaster and the mass-communication entrepreneur, not to mention the audience. The powerful cultural influences of the United States and Britain are discernible in Australian commercial and public-service broadcasting respectively, from the early years to the present day. Indeed, such influence in its more exaggerated forms has long been felt to be suffocatingly oppressive by many Australians, though that by no means implies that Australian radio is or ever has been only an imitative amalgam of American and British radio. It simply indicates that Australian radio has quite naturally, given the linguistic bond of a common language and a particular combination of economic and political factors, borrowed much from the two most influential English-speaking countries; I do not believe that, among developed countries at least, 'cultural imperialism' is entirely dependent on one-way traffic. And it is fair to say that Australia now has an adequate (and in some areas of broadcasting much more than that) radio system for the needs of its various audiences, given the variety of physical, economic, political and linguistic constraints under which it has to operate. While the British listener might find much of it excessively 'commercial' and the American listener might be surprised that it is not more so, this, I think, merely underlines the point that Australian radio does have an identity of its own.

An important factor in the development of Australian radio – and one that is most relevant to radio drama, compared, say, with the British experience – is that, from the time the first licences were granted in Sydney in 1923, the commercial sector has always had a stronger base than the non-commercial. A national broadcasting system was introduced in 1928 when the government took over those stations funded by licence fees and a minimum of advertising (as opposed to those entirely funded by advertising revenue), although programmes were provided by independent organisations. The system, *mutatis mutandis*, was not unlike that administered by the Independent Broadcasting Authority in Britain today.[1] By 1930 there were twenty-five commercial and nine national stations. Two years later the Australian Broadcasting Commission was established, largely on the model of the BBC and financed by licence fees, to provide a public broadcasting service. The ABC incorporated twelve national stations (as against forty-three commercial stations); throughout the remainder of the 1930s and the 1940s there were more than three times as many commercial stations as ABC stations. In other words, listening habits and preferences were established mainly by the commercial stations, and even now, when the ABC with about one hundred stations has very largely caught up with the number of commercial stations, it can maintain only a small share of the national audience. The ABC has thus never enjoyed the kind of long monopoly the BBC used to hold, despite the many points of similarity between the two organisations, and indeed at the start is was very much the 'gatecrasher' into the Australian broadcasting system. As Ellis Blain, who was an ABC broadcaster for forty years, has suggested, the already established audience did not take very kindly to the early ABC's sense of 'cultural mission' derived from the BBC, and on the whole found it 'infinitely boring'.[2] At the same time the audience that the ABC did gain received an almost exclusively BBC-style diet, and ingested the BBC's cultural attitudes to a degree that might be considered quite extraordinary were it not for the then very close relationship between Australia and what was still considered by many as 'the mother country'. (The relationship now, of course, grows weaker year by year except for the older generations of Anglo-Saxon descent.)

An important additional factor here is that the ABC's first General Manager was, at least in terms of views about the role and responsibilities of the national public broadcasting service if not of personality, not unlike Lord Reith. Charles Moses, the son of a Cumberland farmer, had a long and formative 'reign' during 1935-65, and it was under his aegis that Frank Clewlow, who had been a friend of John Drinkwater's at Birmingham University, became the ABC's first Federal Director of Radio Drama and Leslie Rees the first Federal Play Editor.[3] These two established a pattern, which still continues, of maintaining a close working relationship between the ABC Drama Department and both new and experienced writers. (Such a relationship may be considered a prerequisite for anything more than at best sporadically successful production of radio drama by any organisation.)

1930s and 1940s

Australian radio drama, then, did not begin with the ABC. Haphazard and ill-organised though the first decade of commercial radio in the country may have been, drama (if the term is interpreted broadly) was there from the start. According to R.R. Walker, the first broadcast of a play, a melodrama of the Sweeney Todd type entitled *The Barbarous Barber*, was on 21 March 1925 on the Melbourne station 3LO.[4] In the early days of the commercial stations, drama amounted to little more than readings of popular plays, comedies and melodramas. Radio adaptations of popular English and American stage plays were soon introduced, and also drama in serial form. The 1940s and early 1950s are considered to be 'the golden years' of the popularity of Australian radio drama, but the 1930s saw the start of the boom. The commercial stations' bill of fare was, of course, almost exclusively 'light' at that time. Much of it was imported from the United States, a representative serial being *Flash Gordon*, but local production began to establish itself, for instance with the formation of *George Edwards and his Radio Players* and the groups of actors run by such Sydney stations as 2CH and 2UE. Recording and dramatic techniques were primitive but certainly cost-effective: actors were expected to record anything up to fifteen episodes of a fifteen-minute serial in a single day with only a quick perusal of the scripts beforehand – and sometimes not even that.[5] Mystery stories, soap operas, comedy serials, adaptations of popular classics, all poured from the assembly line, leading to the entertainment of a mass audience, to profits for broadcasting companies and advertisers, to increasing technical expertise among actors and writers, and, importantly, to the formation of habits and expectations among listeners.

By 1939 the drama industry for commercial radio could support a dozen companies to supply serials to the stations on a mass-production basis. The titles alone indicate sufficient of their genre, content and quality (*qua* drama): *Portia Faces Life*, *Pinto Pete and his Ranch Boys*, *Chandu the Magician*,, *Fred and Maggie Everybody*, *East Lynne*, *Dad and Dave* ('George Edwards would record five episodes of *Dad and Dave* in a morning, without a rehearsal'[6]), and so on. Such serials ran to thousands of episodes over the years, broadcast at the rate of three or four episodes a week. More prestige-bearing productions were known by the names of their sponsors – *General Motors Hour* or *Caltex Theatre*. *Lux Radio Theatre*, for instance, was launched in 1939 by Cecil B. DeMille on relay from the United States, and *Macquarie Radio Theatre* instituted annual production awards for commercial radio drama.

It was in this context, against this kind of background and 'opposition', that Clewlow and Rees of the ABC tried to establish the public broadcasting system's concept of radio drama. During 1936-8, for example, they broadcast thirty-seven Shakespeare plays on alternate Sunday afternoons in winter; in 1939 one of their highlights was a series called *From Shakespeare to Shaw*. What was lacking was Australian material: twenty years later Ian K. Mackay argued that 'possibly 95 per cent of all broadcasting drama, excepting serials, depends on overseas scripts'.[7] This has been a continuing problem for the ABC despite its determined efforts to encourage Australian talent. In fact the ABC's sense of cultural mission was given more practical and financial expression in the field of classical music than in drama; in 1940 only 3.5 per cent of programme expenditure was devoted to drama and features.[8] This is not to underplay the work of such writers as Max Afford and Edmund Barclay who were engaged as adapters by the ABC and also provided original material for the medium. Afford specialised in thrillers and mysteries, and Barclay in Australian historical drama, thus helping the ABC to provide a range of lighter popular drama in addition to the classics and more serious material. Afford, in fact, was one of the most prolific writers of the 1935-55 period, turning out well-crafted work for commercial stations as well as the ABC, and also stage plays and novels, some of which were performed and published in New York and London. He was in every sense of the term a professional writer, and was extremely successful in writing comedies and thrillers for specific markets. He would, no doubt, have adapted his techniques with equal success to television had he not died at the age of forty-eight in 1954, only two years before the medium was introduced in Australia.

Barclay wrote the first historical drama serial for radio in Australia, *As Ye Sow*. It ran for nine months in weekly half-hour episodes, exploring the country's history through six generations of a family.[9] It became immensely popular and built up a large coast-to-coast audience. It was the first of many such programmes, because historical drama has proved to be perhaps the most popular of the more serious genres for an audience that may in some ways still feel the lack of a secure national identity. (Many successful Australian films and television dramas of the 1970s have similarly been set in the past for perhaps the same reason:*Picnic at Hanging Rock*, *Ned Kelly*, *The Chant of Jimmy Blacksmith*, *My Brilliant Career*, *Rush*, *Ben Hall*, *Luke's Kingdom* are among some of the better known.) The professional expertise and flexibility of such radio dramatists of the 1930s may be indicated by Barclay's ability to produce both an original light thriller like *Murder in the Silo* and an adaptation of *The Book of Job* suitable for the new medium. It indicates, too, that the ABC was not catering for an up-market, cultured audience to the exclusion of all else – the duty to entertain the audience at the lighter end of the spectrum was also recognised. At the same time, under the guidance of people like Leslie Rees, the ABC was laying the foundations of its policy for the encouragement of more serious writers for the medium. (By 'serious' I do not mean to imply that entertainment is something that need not be taken seriously; I mean only to distinguish those programmes not likely, because of their content and style, to appeal to a large audience from those that are.) Among these, for instance, were Alexander Turner and Catherine Shepherd, who began writing plays for radio in the late 1930s and were to make a substantial contribution to the medium over the following thirty years.

Turner was English-born but became a West Australian and set many of his plays in that state. His strength in plays like *Hester Siding*, *Neighbours* and their successors (*Hester Siding and Other Plays* (1937) was the first collection by an Australian author to include work for both stage and radio[10]) is an unforced naturalism and a sense of controlled passion; there is also a more adventurous side to his work, characterised by his verse play of the Second World War, *Australian Stages*. Turner was one of the first to experiment with verse in Australian radio drama, and in this play he combines his interest in the aural and symbolic value of trains with a montage of male voices in the setting of a troop-train journey. The various rhythms of the train, the Aboriginal place names recited by the chorus ('Through Narngaloo Through Narngaloo Through Narngaloo . . . Utakarra-Bookara, Utakarra-Bookara, Utakarra-Bookara . . .'), and reflective monologue are interwoven in a successfully inventive and atmospheric piece of radio.

Catherine Shepherd, who was born in Southern Rhodesia, educated in Britain, and later lived mainly in Tasmania, was one of the most intelligent and introspectively sensitive playwrights of this period. Many of her plays use historical figures, such as Hans Andersen, Pushkin, Bunyan, Balzac and Goldsmith, to focus on the problems and values of the artistic life in relation to the moral life, and on points of existential tension. Comparatively little of her radio work, unlike her stage plays, is overtly concerned with Australia.

Other prominent though not necessarily prolific radio dramatists of the late 1930s and early 1940s include Richard Lane, Charles Porter, George Farwell, Musette Morell, Betty Roland, Dorothy Blewett and Gwen Meredith (who later earned a legendary reputation as the sole author of the longest-running popular radio serial in the world). Many writers, of course, did not restrict their activities to radio: some were better known for their stage plays, others were writing fiction. Indeed, Dymphna Cusack, Ruth Park and her husband D'Arcy Niland, and Sumner Locke-Elliott later earned international reputations for their novels and short stories, though they all made worthwhile contributions to the medium, with either original plays or adaptations of stage plays. It was certainly a period when Australian radio and its audiences took drama seriously, however lightweight the content may have been much of the time, and when a generation of actors increased their technical expertise through both the variety of parts they were offered in every genre and the highly competitive and pressurised recording schedules. Peter Finch, Ray Barrett, Rod Taylor and Keith Michell, for example, gained much of their early experience and skills in Australian radio (though Hollywood and British cinema and television later claimed their somewhat variable talents) and, importantly, such actors learned how to deliver Australian dialogue naturally rather than to continue to ape standard middle-class or BBC English. The same point is applicable to writers: the opportunities and demands of the new medium meant that playwrights did have the chance to explore, however tentatively, the possibilities of *Australian* drama rather than preserving unquestioningly the pattern of stage plays that copied the fashions of successful Broadway and West End productions. Leslie Rees makes the point that Max Afford and Sumner Locke-Elliott, for example, wrote stage plays actually set in England, partly because Australian audiences were largely convinced that this was a guarantee of credibility and quality, partly in the hope of attracting London theatre productions – an instance of what is known in Australia as 'the cultural cringe'.[11] The time of Ray Lawler's *Summer of the Seventeenth Doll* was still a long way off.

Verse drama: Douglas Stewart

In the 1930s the dominant mode of Australian radio drama was naturalistic prose, with a strong though not exclusive bent towards historical themes. This is in no way surprising, given that most twentieth-century stage playwrights in English have found the problems posed by verse drama to be almost insuperable. Not even T.S. Eliot and Christopher Fry may be considered to have been more than partly successful (though of course they have their defenders in this respect), never mind the more mannered, not to say debilitated, attempts of such predecessors as James Elroy Flecker, Gordon

Bottomley and John Masefield. There were Australian playwrights in the earlier part of the century, including Jack Lindsay, Helen Simpson and John le Gay Brereton, who wrote plays of some merit in blank verse, but these are vitiated by excessive literariness and, typically, both an inability to escape from the clutch of Elizabethan verse and a reluctance to deal with Australian themes rather than a Renaissance Italy or an ancient Greece infused by Victorian sensibility.

In the United States and Britain, however, Archibald MacLeish and Louis MacNeice, respectively, showed some of the great possibilities of modern verse drama for radio, and in Australia Douglas Stewart wrote two verse plays for the medium and two for the stage in the early 1940s. Nearly forty years later, the first of these still has a strong claim to be considered the best Australian radio verse drama, and perhaps one of the best anywhere in English. Stewart's work merits rather more detailed consideration, even within the confines of a brief conspectus such as this. During the 'golden years' of Australian radio, Stewart was an outstanding figure in terms of his artistic imagination and the quality of his writing, even if this reputation rests largely on his first radio play, *The Fire on the Snow*, rather than the second, *The Golden Lover*.

Stewart is a New Zealander by birth but settled in Australia as a young man in the 1930s, working as a literary journalist and publishing poetry. He is now known mostly as a poet, but his dramatic work in the 1940s played an important part in encouraging other writers to use verse for radio drama, and there can be few Australians with any interest in radio drama who have not heard one of the many ABC productions of *The Fire on the Snow*, first produced by Frank Clewlow in 1941. (That *The Fire on the Snow* was actually produced on radio seems to have been due to the determination and persuasiveness of Leslie Rees: Stewart at that time did not want it produced.[12]) When Stewart came to write the play, he had no experience of writing for either the stage or radio; but he chose a theme – Scott's last Antarctic expedition – that clearly had great dramatic potential. Stewart takes up the story at the point when Scott and his four companions (Wilson, Oates, Bowers and Evans) set off in 1912 on the last stage of their journey to the Pole. These are the five characters in the play, with the addition of The Announcer. This sixth voice is used as a narrator of the action, as a commentator on the men's sufferings and states of mind, and also as a linking device, fulfilling a function to some extent comparable to that of the Chorus in Greek tragedy. The use of The Announcer permits Stewart to vary the language and the verse as well as the pacing of the story. The Announcer's lines are sometimes in formal rhymed verse, frequently trimeters or tetrameters, and sometimes in free verse, but overall they are characterised by a more stately, dignified tone and movement than the contrasting and colloquially idiomatic free verse used by the explorers. Stewart movingly conveys the decline of initial confidence in Scott's party as they near the Pole, only to find that Amundsen has been there before them. The fluctuating hope and despair as they embark on their return trek of eight hundred miles, the subsequent suicide of Oates and death of Evans en route, and the overwhelming power of the climate and terrain make for convincingly powerful poetic drama in Stewart's version. And the drama is not so much one of relationships between the members of Scott's party, though that is present, as one of Man against Nature. The predominant feature of the play is the heroic courage and strength of will displayed by the explorers – will to reach the Pole, will to survive, will to return home – but remorselessly sapped and at last overcome by the implacable elements. The intensity of both the extreme cold and the men's will to survive is focused throughout the play by Stewart's imagery, centred on extremes of cold and heat: 'the fire on the snow'. The natural imagery of cold, ice, snow and avalanches steadily permeates other orders and areas of experience, as in these lines spoken by The Announcer:

. . . and combers of violent ice
Crash at the back of the brain where the still white spindrift lies.
. . . . . .
Time is an avalanche, time and action are hurtling down,
The glacier seems like a cataract beating their heads with its din.[13]

and in another speech by The Announcer:

Above the chasms of to-morrow and yesterday
The hour towers from the peaks of storm to brightness.[14]

In a reflective speech towards the end of the play, when Scott and Wilson, the last two left alive, know that they will not see home again, Scott's language brings this oppositional imagery (it is difficult in this context to say 'polarised') to a pitch of visionary intensity:

One night I walked to the cliffs alone, and the moon
Was pure and burning on those frozen spires and crags,
So that they leapt like flames. The ice was blazing.[15]

This note is sustained to the end of the play and Scott's last speech:

. . . and a dying man remembering
The burning snow, the crags towering like flame.[16]

The whole play is quite unabashed in its praise for the heroic life of the Romantic dreamer who, at least in Stewart's view of Scott, seems to yearn for some kind of purification through extreme suffering, which is offered by Stewart with what seems to me dangerous conviction as almost an end in itself. The notion is adumbrated in a speech of Wilson's:

. . . Endurance may have a meaning
For men in the snow as for saints and martyrs in flames.[17]

But the point is brought out more strongly nearer the end when Scott is made to reflect, in the most questionable passage in the play, that the 'delight' to be derived from a life of hard, heroic endurance cannot be known by bird or beast:

It's reserved for the saint, the martyr; perhaps for the soldier
On the peak of death: and women tortured by cancer.
I am glad we have lived so bitterly and die so hard.[18]

As a martyr's rationalisation this does not carry a great deal of conviction. If it is to be taken at face value, then I must say that the use of 'delight' in the context of cancer (which of course is not something assumed voluntarily) is utterly indefensible. It has also been pointed out that the real Scott was not motivated solely by a desire to pit himself against the elements and the limits of physical endurance in a race to be first at the South Pole.[19] While *The Fire on the Snow* is obviously not intended as a dramatised documentary, the presentation of the historical figure of Scott without giving any indication of the man's scientific passion does seem to be a flaw. Such objections make the play less satisfying and convincing than it might have been. Nevertheless, it remains a most powerful and evocative piece of radio drama, in which Stewart's language leads to some memorable moments of poetic intensity for the listener. Tyrone Guthrie praised it in 1951 at the time of his BBC production as 'one of the few important works which radio has so far produced'.[20] The passage of nearly thirty years does not seem to me to have altered the value of that judgement very significantly.

Stewart's other verse play written expressly for radio, *The Golden Lover*, was first produced in 1943. By way of complete contrast with the rest of his drama, this is a light romantic comedy based on a Maori folk tale about a young wife who falls in love with a handsome man from a fairy people ('the golden lover'), but finally returns to her husband. It has, certainly, moments of genuine dramatic humour and perhaps rather better-defined characterisation than *The Fire on the Snow*. But it remains a very slight piece, much of it written in a too-poeticised free verse, rather as if a latter-day James Elroy Flecker had found a Golden Road to the South Seas. Only the natural imagery carries much conviction or effectiveness, even allowing for the fact that the play is set in the context of an exotically primitive folk culture.

In considering a third play by Stewart, *Ned Kelly*, I want to make an exception to the rule I have followed so far, of discussing only plays written with radio in mind. While *Ned Kelly* was written for the stage, it received its first production on ABC radio in 1942,[21] and more than thirty years later it was, in an excellent production by Robert Peach, the first ABC drama in stereo to be entered for the Prix Italia. Now one of the mythicised folk heroes of Australia, Kelly had perhaps not acquired his present status at the time Stewart wrote his play, though, as Leslie Rees has indicated,[22] the bushranger's death was speedily followed by celebratory melodramas in the 1880s, and one of the world's first full-length feature films was an Australian silent film about the Kellys. Stewart's version is an ambitiously large-scale drama, an epic combination of verse and prose, moving through a year-and-a-half and various locations. There is something of a thoughtful antipodean Western in the story, with the gangsters as 'heroes', understandably anti-social but bound to come to a violent end. As a play it seems to me not to cohere properly, but it has some magnificent writing that says much about a past (and still lingering) anti-establishment ethos among the people of a physically lonely and awe-inspiring continent. Ned Kelly himself is another version of Stewart's Romantic Hero, but the characterisation of Joe Byrne, the 'brains' of the Kelly gang, is often more interesting. Here, one feels, Stewart's eloquence was most fully engaged:

What was the land of your childhood, Curnow? The frogs,
Cicadas and crickets shrilling like a million bells
One mad white night of moonlight? The magpies rolling
The light of morning like fire around their throats
And turning it into song? The green grass, Curnow,
Or the washing in the yard next door?[23]

Stewart manages to give impressive credibility to the belief that, much more than might be the case in Europe, the hard physical facts of the land and climate have had a strongly determinant effect on the character of Australians; here, for example, is the Reverend Gribble:

Australia's the violent country, the earth itself
Suffers, cries out in anger against the sunlight
From the cracked lips of the plains; and with the land,
With the snake that strikes from the dust,
The people suffer and cry their anger and kill.
I have come to understand it in love and pity;
Not horror now; I understand the Kellys.[24]

Stewart was not the only radio dramatist to use verse in the 1940s. There was, on a small scale, a fashion for it. Stewart himself admitted that a reading of Archibald MacLeish's *The Fall of the City* had prompted him to attempt the form.[25] Catherine Duncan (*The Path of the Eagle, Sons of the Morning*), Alexander Turner (*Neighbours*), T. Inglis Moore (*We're Going Through*) and Colin Thiele (*Burke and Wills*) all wrote verse drama for radio. The last of these shows signs of having been influenced by Stewart's techniques in *The Fire on the Snow*; the narrator's lines, for instance, are written in verse, while the explorers use prose.[26] Apart from Stewart's work, Thiele's *Burke and Wills* (1949) seems to have survived best from the verse dramas of the 1940s.

1950s to 1970s

During the Second World War and for the next decade, radio drama on the commercial stations continued and developed the production patterns established in the 1930s: mass production of mass-appeal serials, series, and single plays, mostly of mind-numbing banality. Soap operas (or 'drip dramas') and fifteen-minute serials were poured into the avid ears of the listening population: the familiar titles (*Delia of the Four Winds*, *Prodigal Father*, *Here Comes O'Malley*, etc.) and largely predictable content appealed enormously to an audience who could not view their equivalent on television until after 1956. In this 'golden age' of popularity, as many as ten full-length plays a week might be produced in Sydney or Melbourne. Serials alone kept a score of commercial recording studios busy in the production of between four hundred and five hundred quarter-hour episodes every week.[27] The commercial stations retained their Sunday evening *Radio Theatre* sessions for more serious offerings. These 'slots' of fifty-two minutes (one hour minus the time devoted to commercials) continued to be sponsored by such business concerns as Caltex, Lux, and General Motors. There seems little doubt that on Sunday evenings the majority of the population could be found at home listening to a play on either an ABC or a commercial station.

The plays, however, were immutably radio *theatre* when produced by a commercial organisation. The audience had to imagine, while sitting at home, that they were actually in the theatre, a subterfuge assisted by, for instance, the station announcer introducing the producer to give a brief preamble to the play, on the lines of 'As the curtain rises and the lights go down in the house . . .'. The plays were adaptations for radio, not plays written *for* radio. The offerings ranged from the competent thriller (a British equivalent of the time would be something like *Paul Temple*) to a middlebrow theatre play (e.g. James Bridie's *A Sleeping Clergyman*) or an adaptation of a proven success in another medium (e.g. Paul Gallico's *The Snow Goose*). What was lacking was the encouragement of Australian writers to tackle intelligent Australian themes in radio drama and to venture much beyond the hackwork of endless serials and adaptations of overseas material. Even the occasional bow in the direction of potentially more demanding material (e.g. the serialisation of *Madame Bovary*) was limited by these constraints. Even the attempt to give a production extra 'gloss' by importing overseas talent (e.g. Ralph Richardson, Sybil Thorndike, Margaret Rutherford and Margaret Rawlings), as well as the undoubted skill of local actors like Peter Finch or writers like Morris West, could not make up for the commercial stations' lack of interest in specifically Australian material in all but their most trivial (though very popular) offerings. The different attitude of the ABC in this respect, as I have noted, has always been one of its strengths. The bulk of the commercial presentations continued to be horse-racing sagas like *The Golden Colt*, war stories of the 'Now It Can Be Told' variety, Westerns like *Gunsmoke* and *The Fastest Gun*, situation comedies like *Fred and Maggie Everybody*, *Dagwood and Blondie* and *Mrs 'Obbs*, and even a bastardised form based on Ripley's *Believe-It-Or-Not* newspaper strip. For children they offered *Biggles* stories, *Tarzan*, *King of the Apes* and *Superman*. The American influence here is obvious, and the reason of course is that such programmes had already proved their popularity, and therefore their commercial success, with unsophisticated mass audiences elsewhere. By the time television had really begun to grip the attention of Australian audiences in the 1960s, the commercial stations had already realised that they would have to rethink their schedules radically: radio drama in any form steadily declined as television soap operas, situation comedies and thrillers took over. In 1960 there were still six play series a week on Australian radio and a variety of serials (three of the former were from the ABC).[28] This soon changed to a concentration on music, news and talk-back programmes, all with more mass appeal and less cost in the new television age. By the early 1970s, radio drama of any kind on the metropolitan commercial channels was 1.7 per cent of their total output, and even that category included 'the arts and variety'.[29] Today it has, to all intents and purposes, completely vanished. Under the system in which commercial radio drama was produced, it could not possibly have had any purpose other than anodyne, profitable light entertainment, reassuring and in every way mentally undemanding. All popular drama scripts had to be approved by the sponsors and consequently no mention could be made of sex, religion, politics or liquor.[30]

The ABC, on the other hand, has continued to encourage interest in all kinds of radio drama among both writers and listeners. D'Arcy Niland paid tribute to the Commission's philosophy twenty years ago when he wrote: 'It is not just a machine for finding plays, it is an institution for finding writers.'[31] In the 1950s and 1960s the ABC managed to sustain a consistent volume and variety of radio drama. Playwrights from the 1940s who continued to produce work that at the very least helped to interpret Australian life and history for an Australian audience (and often did much more than that) included Ruth Park and D'Arcy Niland, Coral Lansbury, Colin Thiele, Catherine Shepherd, Catherine Duncan and Alexander Turner. New names appeared, of whom some of the most prominent were Peter Kenna, Patricia Hooker, Hal Porter, Shan Benson and Colin Free; these have all made significant contributions to Australian writing in one form or another. A representative example of some of the good work from this period is Shan Benson's *Voyage on a Dinner Table* (1954), an interesting portrait of Captain Cook, which used verse for the narrator's part and was perhaps influenced by Kenneth Slessor's well-known poem, 'Five Visions of Captain Cook'. Many of the more successful plays, however, had a rural setting: a typical outback town, or the Queensland banana country, or the fishing coast of South Australia. The bush and rural life in general have always attracted Australian artists of every kind in the two centuries of European occupation, and still do, perhaps because of the influence of imported nineteenth-century Romanticism, or perhaps because to North European immigrants the landscape seems so utterly non-European in all its physical qualities; and also perhaps because in the nineteenth and early twentieth centuries there was less emphasis than now on life and work in the urban and suburban sprawl of the coastal cities. This interest in rural affairs was no doubt partly responsible for the popularity of one of the most appreciated productions the ABC has ever done: a serial written by Gwen Meredith about family life in the country. It started as *The Lawsons* in 1944, and after 1,299 episodes became *Blue Hills* in 1949. It was the world's longest-running radio serial and only came to a full stop on 30 September 1976 after 5,795 further episodes. Its legendary status as a national institution suggests immediately a British parallel in the BBC's *The Archers*, though the Australian writer's ability to create and sustain a lively interest in her characters and stories through more than 7,000 episodes surely makes it a more prominent landmark in popular radio drama.

Despite the ABC's concern for radio drama after the advent of television had weakened its appeal to general audiences, it was nevertheless still true that the great majority of plays broadcast on the national stations came from overseas, mostly from the BBC. And it is arguable that, after the interest in radio drama in the 1940s and 1950s, the Australian plays of the 1960s tended to mark time in terms of creative use of the medium and, with exceptions such as Mungo MacCallum's quartet, *The Stonehams of Stonehenge*, not very memorably. Mention should be made, however, of two verse plays for radio by one of Australia's finest poets, Francis Webb (1925–73): *Birthday* and *The Ghost of the Cock*, both included in his *Collected Poems* (1969). Neither play is very successful in terms of radio drama, but they are interesting in the light of the earlier achievement of Douglas Stewart, whose own poetry is neither so dramatic nor so tragic as Webb's. *Birthday* (1953) is a strange and somewhat strained retrospective attempt to endow Hitler with a degree of humanity usually denied him. In no sense an apologia for Hitler, the play does try to recall him from the pigeonhole of history and remind the audience that, because Hitler was a human being, he must have had qualities in common with other, less monstrous human beings. Sadly, and perhaps revealingly, Webb's verse and his gift for a vibrant rhetoric let him down here; even the scene between Eva and Hitler in the bunker on his birthday during their last few days fails to convey the genuine tenderness Webb was clearly striving for. *The Ghost of the Cock* (1964) is a verse parable, a dramatised morality debate between Tobias, Michael and various animals and birds about the last Man and Woman's fitness to enter Heaven after a final nuclear disaster. In this case, I don't think the lack of success is because the language is 'too thickly textured' for radio, as John Thompson has proposed,[32] but because there is a failure in conception and execution: it seems to me quite simply a very weak piece of writing in no way comparable to the achievement of Webb's best poetry.

During the 1970s there have been promising signs that Australian radio drama is once more finding new audiences, good new writers, and a revival of creativity, even in the face of the savage budgetary and staffing constraints imposed in the last two or three years by Malcolm Fraser's right-wing government. In 1975, for example, the *Soundstage* series was introduced on Sunday afternoons specifically to generate interest in the radio play. It was then the avowed intention of the ABC's Radio Drama and Features Department that at least three-quarters of the plays in this series should be Australian-scripted as well as Australian-produced. There were in fact fewer Australian plays than hoped for, and in 1978 *Soundstage* was replaced by the less adventurous and less costly *The Sunday Play*, but the basic aim of trying to expand the quality and quantity of Australian plays still remains. Indeed, in the 1970s the amount of radio drama produced by the ABC as a proportion of their overall radio broadcasting has actually increased to a small degree. The ABC no longer feels obliged to restrict plays to a set length of, say, sixty or seventy-five minutes: modern plays as well as the classics are given the running-time they are considered to merit. FM radio has been in operation since early in 1976: one of the earliest productions was Douglas Stewart's *Ned Kelly*, produced by Robert Peach with the author. For more than ten years the Australian Writers' Guild has made awards to outstanding drama scripts. And there have certainly been some imaginative and exciting plays in the 1970s, some of them conveniently collected by Alrene Sykes in *Five Plays for Radio: Nightmares of the Old Obscenity Master and Other Plays* (1975).

Of the newer writers of the past ten years or so, Colin Free is widely recognised as one of the most outstanding. He had a background in television scriptwriting before coming into prominence in the radio medium, though one of his early plays, *A Walk Among the Wheeneys* (1966), which Sykes includes in her anthology, was produced on the stage a few days after its first radio production. It is a short amusing comedy about two brothers on a lonely fruit farm (a Wheeney is a type of grapefruit), one of whom invites a woman friend up for the day from the city to lay plans for marriage. The theme is not particularly original – the two bickering brothers, Mort and Jack, are in effect 'married' to each other – but the writing is wittily idiomatic and pointed, and the characterisation strong in an economical, traditional fashion. It is a play that could work well in any medium, but still deserves its status, I think, as a minor classic of modern Australian radio drama.

A much more interesting work by Free, also included in Sykes's collection, is *Nightmares of the Old Obscenity Master*, first produced in

1973 by Richard Connolly, which won an Australian Writers' Guild Award. This is a complex and imaginative piece of writing, owing a limited but clear debt to *Under Milk Wood*. Free's imagination has more room to manoeuvre here – it is perhaps more suited to the invisible medium of radio than the often limiting 'reality' of television – and its blend of fantasy and naturalism is something that Free handles extremely successfully. Alrene Sykes's comment on its affinity with Strindberg's dream plays is suggestive,[33] allowing for Free's natural gift for comedy, which in *Nightmares of the Old Obscenity Master*, by contrast with *A Walk Among the Wheeneys*, gains much of its force from inventive wordplay and vividly grotesque imagery; the notion of an *Under Milk Wood* set in Sydney and rewritten by Tom Stoppard may suggest something of its style. The black, often rather surrealistic humour works well precisely because it is rooted in selectively detailed naturalistic references to the city, as Cello, the old pornographer overtaken by the permissive society, passes through a succession of nightmare experiences, his footsteps dogged by Septimus Mortimus's horse-drawn hearse, which (contrary to the pattern of such stories) he manages to evade in the last scene.

Australian radio dramatists of the last ten years seem increasingly to have acquired a confidence in the possibilities of the medium, or perhaps reacquired the confidence of those writing in the 1940s, and a new maturity in their best work which is realised in their avoidance of both the parochial insularity typical of an isolated community and the dependence of such a community on outworn conventions and subjects from overseas. Playwrights have had the encouragement and the freedom to experiment, to find as it were their national bearings; and writers such as those included in Alrene Sykes's collection continue to repay that encouragement. The fact that the ABC, despite its financial and other problems, still manages to present more than two dozen plays by Australian authors each year (in addition to the presentation of good overseas material), in a country with one-quarter of the population of Britain and where drama is ignored by the relatively wealthy commercial stations, is a precious achievement.

Notes

1.   R.R. Walker, *The Magic Spark*. Melbourne 1973, p. 29.
2.   Blain, *Life with Aunty: Forty Years with the ABC*. Sydney 1977, p. 13.
3.   *Ibid*, pp. 48-51.
4.   Walker, op. cit., p. 28.
5.   *Ibid*, pp. 51-2.
6.   Blain, op. cit., p. 53.
7.   *Broadcasting in Australia*. Melbourne 1957, p. 70.
8.   *Ibid*, p. 69.
9.   Leslie Rees, *The Making of Australian Drama*. Sydney 1973, p. 157. I am

glad here to acknowledge my very considerable debt to Leslie Rees's excellent survey of the growth of drama in Australia. The thoroughness of this work, which includes radio and television drama, and its successor, *Australian Drama in the Seventies* (1978), makes them invaluable. While his emphasis is primarily historical and descriptive, the sound common-sense of his critical judgements is grounded in long practical experience of production and writing. He is, of course, the same Leslie Rees who was the ABC's first Federal Play Editor.

10. *Ibid*, p. 182.
11. *Ibid*, p. 177.
12. *Ibid*, p. 235.
13. *The Fire on the Snow and The Golden Lover: Two Plays for Radio*. Sydney 1944, p. 19.
14. *Ibid*, p. 30.
15. *Ibid*, p. 41.
16. *Ibid*, p. 42.
17. *Ibid*, p. 29.
18. *Ibid*, p. 40.
19. Rees, op. cit., p. 219, cites Flexmore Hudson in *Poetry*, 15 (June 1945).
20. Quoted in Rees, op. cit., p. 218.
21. *Ibid*, pp. 225-6.
22. *Ibid*, p. 220.
23. *Ned Kelly*. Sydney 1946, p. 137.
24. *Ibid*, p. 46.
25. Rees, op. cit., p. 234.
26. *Ibid*.
27. Robert Peach, 'Die Hörspielarbeit der ABC', a talk broadcast on 31 May 1977 by Westdeutscher Rundfunk, Cologne.
28. Rees, op. cit., p. 308.
29. Walker, op. cit., p. 128.
30. *Ibid*, p. 58.
31. Quoted in Rees, op. cit., p. 330.
32. 'Broadcasting and Australian literature', in Clement Semmler and Derek Whitelock (eds), *Literary Australia*. Melbourne 1966, p. 105.
33. 'Introduction', in Sykes (ed.), *Five Plays for Radio: Nightmares of the Old Obscenity Master and Other Plays*. Sydney and London 1975, p. xix.

Select bibliography

Bibliographies relating to radio drama are conspicuous by their rarity. For a list of British radio plays that have been published, consult Manfred Erdmenger, 'Bibliographie des englischen Hörspiels', *Anglia*, **95** (3/4) (1977), pp. 454-69; and the Bibliography in John Drakakis (ed.), *British Radio Dramatists* (Cambridge 1981). For information about the broadcasts of radio plays and features since 1923, see the absolutely indispensable Chadwyck-Healey *BBC Radio, Drama Catalogue*, a microfiche of the Catalogue of the Play Library in the BBC Radio Drama Department, Broadcasting House, London.

The annual reports published by the BBC since 1928, except for 1952-4, always contain material about radio drama: usually *BBC Handbook*, but *BBC Yearbook* (1930–4 and 1943–52), and *BBC Annual* (1935-7). The eight volumes of *BBC Quarterly*, published between April 1946 and August 1954, contain a number of important essays on the subject, and three issues of the monthly magazine *Plays and Players* (**13**(3-5) (Dec. 1965-Feb. 1966)) are also valuable in this respect. At one time, *Plays and Players* carried a regular column about radio drama, but the most valuable sources of historical information among periodical publications are, inevitably, the weeklies *Radio Times* and *The Listener*. David Wade's weekly 'Radio' column in *The Times* every Saturday is outstanding among contemporary journalistic writing, although it is concerned with the whole range of radio, not just drama; but see also Anne Karpf's recent article listed below.

Adorno, Theodor W., *Prisms*, London 1967.
Allan, Andrew, *A Self-Portrait*. Toronto 1974.
Arnheim, Rudolf, *Radio*. London 1936.
Barnouw, Erik, *Radio Drama in Action*. New York and Toronto 1945.
— *Handbook of Radio Writing*. Boston 1945.
— *A History of Broadcasting in the United States*, 3 vols. New York 1966-70.
— *The Sponsor: Notes on a Modern Potentate*. New York 1978.
Baseley, Godfrey, *The Archers: A Slice of my Life*. London 1971.
Bigsby, C.W.E. (ed.), *Approaches to Popular Culture*. London 1976.
Black, Peter, *The Biggest Aspidistra in the World*. London 1972.

Blain, Ellis, *Life with Aunty: Forty Years with the ABC*. Sydney 1977.

Brandt, George, 'Radio, film and television', in John Russell Brown (ed.), *Drama and Theatre with Radio, Film and Television*. London 1971.

Bridson, D.G., *Prospero and Ariel: The Rise and Fall of Radio*. London 1971.

Briggs, Asa, *The History of Broadcasting in the United Kingdom*, 4 vols. London 1961-79.

BBC, *British Broadcasting 1922-1972: A Select Bibliography*. London 1972.

— *Writing for the BBC*. 5th ed., London 1977.

Burns, Elizabeth and Tom (eds), *Sociology of Literature and Drama*. Harmondsworth 1973.

Burns, Tom, *The BBC: Public Institution and Private World*. London 1977.

Chaney, David, *Processes of Mass Communication*. London 1972.

Curran, James; Gurevitch, Michael; Woollacott, Janet (eds), *Mass Communication and Society*. London 1977.

Drakakis, John (ed.), *British Radio Dramatists*. Cambridge 1981.

Dunning, John, *Tune in Yesterday*. Englewood Cliffs, N.J. 1976.

Edwards, Emyr, 'The nature of radio as a medium of artistic communication', *Madog*, **1** (2) (Summer 1978), pp. 5-15.

Edwards, Rex, *The Dales*. London 1969.

Esslin, Martin, *The National Theatre of the Air* (BBC Lunch-time Lectures, Second Series, 4). London 1964.

— 'Radio drama today', in BBC, *New Radio Drama*. London 1966.

— 'The mind as a stage', *Theatre Quarterly*, **1** (3) (July-Sept. 1971), pp. 5-11.

— *The Theatre of the Absurd*. 3rd ed., London 1974.

— *An Anatomy of Drama*. London 1976.

Evans, Elwyn, *Radio: A Guide to Broadcasting Techniques*. London 1977.

Felton, Felix, *The Radio-Play: Its Technique and Possibilities*. London 1949.

Firestone, Ross (ed.), *The Big Radio Comedy Program*. Chicago 1978.

Fiske, John, and Hartley, John, *Reading Television*. London 1978.

Frank, Armin P., *Das Hörspiel*. Heidelberg 1963.

Gielgud, Val, *How to Write Broadcast Plays*. London 1932.

— 'Foreword to authors', *Radio Theatre*. London 1946.

— *The Right Way to Radio Playwriting*. Kingswood, Surrey 1948.

— *British Radio Drama 1922-1956*. London 1957.

— *Years in a Mirror*. London 1965.

Gillard, Frank, *Sound Radio in the Television Age* (BBC Lunch-time Lectures, Second Series, 6). London 1964.

Gilliam, Laurence (ed.), *BBC Features*. London 1950.

Goodlad, J.S.R., *A Sociology of Popular Drama*. London 1971.

Heppenstall, Rayner (ed.), 'Introduction', *Imaginary Conversations*.

London 1948.

— *Portrait of the Artist as a Professional Man*. London 1969.

Horkheimer, Max, and Adorno, Theodor W., *Dialectic of Enlightenment*. London 1973.

Julian, Joseph, *This Was Radio*. New York 1975.

Karpf, Anne, 'A theatre in transmission', *Time Out*, 495 (12-18 Oct. 1979), pp. 10-13.

Koch, Howard, *The Panic Broadcast*. Boston 1970.

LaGuardia, Robert, *From Ma Perkins to Mary Hartman: The Illustrated History of Soap Operas*. New York 1977.

Lazarsfeld, P.F. and Stanton, F.N. (eds), *Radio Research 1942-1943*. New York 1944.

Lea, Gordon, *Radio Drama and How to Write It*. London 1926.

Lewis, Peter (ed.), *Papers of the Radio Literature Conference 1977*, 2 vols. Durham 1978. Reissued as 1 volume, 1979.

Mackay, Ian K., *Broadcasting in Australia*. Melbourne 1957.

McLuhan, Marshall, *Understanding Media*. London 1964.

MacNeice, Louis, 'Introduction', *Christopher Columbus*. London 1944.

— 'General introduction', *The Dark Tower and Other Radio Scripts*. London 1947.

McQuail, Denis (ed.), *Sociology of Mass Communications*. Harmondsworth 1972.

McWhinnie, Donald, *The Art of Radio*. London 1959.

Painting, Norman, *Forever Ambridge: Twenty-five Years of The Archers*. London 1975.

Paulu, Burton, *British Broadcasting: Radio and Television in the United Kingdom*. Minneapolis 1956.

— *British Broadcasting in Transition*. London 1961.

Peers, Frank W., *The Politics of Canadian Broadcasting 1920-1951*. Toronto 1969.

Priessnitz, Horst, *Das englische 'radio play' seit 1945: Typen, Themen und Formen*. Berlin 1977.

— *Das englische Hörspiel: Interpretationen*. Düsseldorf 1977.

Rees, Leslie, *The Making of Australian Drama*. Sydney 1973.

— *Australian Drama in the Seventies*. Sydney 1978.

Reith, J.C.W., *Broadcast over Britain*. London 1924.

— *Into the Wind*. London 1949.

Sieveking, Lance, *The Stuff of Radio*. London 1934.

Smith, Anthony, *The Shadow in the Cave*. London 1973.

Snagge, John, and Barsley, Michael, *Those Vintage Years of Radio*. London 1972.

Stedman, Raymond William, *The Serials*. Norman, Okla. 1971.

Sykes, Alrene (ed.), 'Introduction', *Five Plays for Radio: Nightmares of the Old Obscenity Master and Other Plays*. Sydney and London 1975.

Thompson, Denys (ed.), *Discrimination and Popular Culture*. 2nd ed., Harmondsworth and London 1973.

Thompson, John, 'Broadcasting and Australian literature', in Clement Semmler and Derek Whitelock (eds), *Literary Australia*. Melbourne 1966.

Trethowan, Ian, *Radio in the Seventies* (BBC Lunch-time Lectures, Eighth Series, 4). London 1970.

Wade, David, 'Radio writers', in James Vinson (ed.), *Contemporary Dramatists*. 2nd ed., London and New York 1977.

Walker, R.R., *The Magic Spark*. Melbourne 1973.

Wardle, Irving, 'Introduction', *New English Dramatists 12: Radio Plays*. Harmondsworth 1968.

Weir, E. Austin, *The Struggle for National Broadcasting in Canada*. Toronto 1965.

Williams, Raymond, *Communications*. Revised ed., Harmondsworth 1968.

— *Drama in a Dramatised Society*. Cambridge 1975.

Notes on contributors

JOHN DRAKAKIS is a Lecturer in the Department of English Studies at the University of Stirling, where he teaches Shakespeare and Elizabethan and Jacobean drama. He has published studies of *Othello* and *Much Ado About Nothing* in the York Notes series, and has written on drama of the Shakespearean period as well as on radio drama. He gave a paper at the Radio Literature Conference 1977, and is the editor of *British Radio Dramatists*.

HOWARD FINK is an Associate Professor in the English Department of Concordia University, Montreal, concentrating on modern literature and drama. In recent years, as Director of the Concordia Radio Drama Project, he has been collecting and indexing Canadian radio drama for the Concordia-CBC Archives, and a Bibliography of these materials will appear soon, to be followed by several critical anthologies. He is also founding President of the Association for the Study of Canadian Radio-Television.

FRANCES GRAY has worked for BBC Radio as a studio manager but is now a Lecturer in the Department of English Literature at the University of Sheffield, where she teaches drama. She has written on modern dramatists such as Joe Orton and, above all, Giles Cooper, who is the subject of her M.A. thesis, her paper delivered to the Radio Literature Conference 1977, and her contribution to *British Radio Dramatists*.

PETER LEWIS is a Lecturer in the Department of English Studies at the University of Durham and a member of The Welsh Academy. Many of his publications are in the field of Restoration and eighteenth-century drama, including a critical edition of *The Beggar's Opera* and a book about Gay's play, but he has edited an anthology of modern Anglo-Welsh poetry as well as the *Papers of the Radio Literature Conference 1977*, an event he helped to organise. He writes regularly for *TLS*, *Stand* and *Poetry Wales*, and is a contributor to *British Radio Dramatists*.

DONALD A. LOW is a Senior Lecturer in the Department of English Studies at the University of Stirling and has recently been elected a Fellow of the Scottish Society of Antiquaries. In addition to writing *That Sunny Dome: A Portrait of Regency England*, he has edited two collections of essays on Burns and is the author of articles on Scottish and eighteenth-century literature. He gave a paper at the Radio Literature Conference 1977 and is a contributor to *British Radio Dramatists*.

GRAHAM MURDOCK is a Research Associate at the Centre for Mass Communication Research of the University of Leicester. He has written numerous articles on communications and popular culture, and is the co-author of *Demonstrations and Communication* and of a forthcoming book on the political economy of the mass media, *Cultural Capitalism*. He is currently working on a study of contemporary writers.

HORST P. PRIESSNITZ is Professor of English Literature at the Bergische Universität Wuppertal in West Germany and a leading German scholar of British radio drama. He has written on English, American and Australian literature and is interested in Commonwealth literature, but his major contribution to literary scholarship has been in the field of radio drama: *Das englische 'radio play' seit 1945* and the large collection of essays he edited, *Das englische Hörspiel*. He gave a paper at the Radio Literature Conference 1977.

RODNEY PYBUS spent fifteen years as a journalist and a writer/producer in British television before taking an academic post in Australia during the 1970s. As a Lecturer in the School of English and Linguistics at Macquarie University, Sydney, he specialised in mass communications and media studies. Immediately after completing his contribution to this volume, he returned to England to work for Northern Arts in Cumbria. During the 1970s he published three collections of poetry in England.

JONATHAN RABAN, who is a Fellow of the Royal Society for Literature, spent several years as a university lecturer in English during the 1960s before becoming a full-time writer over ten years ago. He has written plays for the stage and television, but it is as a radio dramatist that he has excelled and is best known. During the 1970s BBC Radio produced seven radio plays by him, including *Will You Accept the Call?*, *The English Department*, *Falling* and *Possibilities*. His books include *The Society of the Poem*, *Soft City* and *Arabia Through the Looking Glass*.

JOHN TYDEMAN joined the BBC in 1959 and has worked in both its TV Drama and Radio Drama Departments. He has, however, concentrated on radio production and is now one of the senior producers in the Radio Drama Department, specialising on plays by new authors and on Shakespeare and other stage classics. He also works in the theatre, and has directed plays in America and on the Continent.

DAVID WADE began his working life in industry before turning to writing, although he is also a partner in a small company making educational audio-visual programmes. He was a radio critic for *The Listener* from 1965 until 1967, since when he has been the radio critic of *The Times*, although he has written on radio for other publications such as *Plays and Players*. He is himself the author of a number of radio plays.

Index